The CAR Book

2020

by

Jack Gillis

and

Richard Eckman

Foreword by

Jason Levine
Center for Auto Safety

A Center for Auto Safety Publication

ACKNOWLEDGMENTS

Forty years is a long time for anything, but there are two reasons why *The Car Book* has endured: the strong desire for unbiased car buying assistance and the hard work of many who ensured that consumers had access to this life, and pocketbook, saving information. During its 40 years *The Car Book* has been accompanied by a variety of consumer guides including *The Used Car Book* 1998-02; *The Truck Van and 4x4 Book* 1991-99; *The Value and Luxury Car Books*; *How to Make Your Car Last Forever*; *The Armchair Mechanic*; and, *The Car Repair Book*. 40 years and 70 books is a monumental undertaking made possible by the co-authors and contributors below who compiled hundreds of thousands of data points. The list below recognizes those who helped make these books possible and the number of books on which they worked.

Co-authors: *Ailis Aaron 14, Deirdre Aaron 2, Ivy Baer 1, Scott Beatty 12, Ashley Cheng 11, Amy Curran 52, Richard Eckman 4, Dabney Edwards 2, Jay Einhorn 6, Alisa Feingold 16, Karen Fierst 34, Brennan Gillis 1, Brian Gillis 1, John Gillis Jr. 1, Katie Gillis 2, Eric Glen 1, Eli Greenspan 1, Daniel Gustafson 4, Ben Hardaway 3, David Iberkleid 3, Tom Kelly 2, Peter Kitchen 3, Nicole Klein 3, Seth Krevat 1, Michael McQiller 1, Julia Redmon 5, Virginia Redmon 1, Jerilyn Saxon 7, Evan Shurak 2, Andrew Siegel 1, Julie Beth Wright 4.*

Contributors: *Stephanie Ackerman 7, Jim Armstrong 1, Stu Armstrong 1, Anu Ashutosh 2, Chris Atkinson 1, Judith Bailey 3, Jessica Baldwin 1, Debra Barclay 11, Jennifer Barrett 3, Ben Becker 2, Carol Berger 1, Nancy Berk 2, Kristin Beyard 1, Debbie Bindeman 15, David Biss 4, Michael Brooks 6, Elizabeth Brown 2, Joe Bruha 1, Kevin Busen 1, Martha Casey 9, Andrew Chap 1, Jeff Clark 1, David Cokely 1, Susan Cole 24, Jennifer Cook Mirabito 1, Alan Coombs 1, Ben Crenshaw 1, Caroline Cruz 1, Jim Cullum 5, Brad Daniels 1, Jennifer Davidson 2, John DeCicco 2, Joe DeGrande 1, Cheryl Denenberg 7, Clarence Ditlow 66, Pat Donlon 6, Rosemary Dunlap 3, Bill Earp 1, Marshall Einhorn 2, Morshed El Hag 6, Mari Beth Emigh 1, Jerret Engle 3, Meaghan Farrell 1, Barry Fierst 9, Eyal Fierst 4, Matthew Figueroa 1, Anne Fleming 1, Nicole Freydberg 1, Edna Friedberg 3, Grant Gasson 1, Sherrie Good 4, Christy Goodrich 1, Carolyn Gorman 12, Nancy Green 7, Sharon Guttman 2, John Guyton 1, Kim Hazelbaker 11, Karen Heckler 5, Vico Henriques 6, Maggie Herman 3, Kaz Hickok 4, Ann Himmelberg 1, Neene Hirata 2, Susan Hoffmann 1, Bill Hogan 1, Bryan Hoopman 1, Dan Howell 1, Mizuho Ikeuchi 1, Mark Jacobson 1, Richard Jester 1, Alisa Joaquin 3, Evan Johnson 7, Steve Julius 3, Irvine Kaplan 2, George Kaveney 1, Al Kettler 1, Mike Kido 4, Lisa Kitei 3, Michael Kott 3, Stuart Krichevsky 45, Bill Kumbar 3, Sonia Kundert 1, Christopher Lank 1, Ann Lavie 10, Elaine Lawless 1, Jason Levine 2, Ed Lewis 3, David Lewkowict 3, Shelley Liebman 3, Mary Kay Linge 1, Faith Little 5, Lou Lombardo 3, Ann Lyons 1, Roger MacBride Allen 2, Joel Makower 3, James Marshall 4, Patricia McCullen-Noettl 1, Kathy Melborn 2, Cristina Mendoza 6, John Michel 9, Cynthia Miller 1, Trina Mohrbacher 1, Rick Morgan 2, Stephanie Narva 6, Carl Nash 2, Debra Anne Naylor 1, David Noettl 3, John Noettl 24, Karen Noettl 5, Steven Noettl 7, Bill North-Rudin 6, Phil Nowicki 15, Ted Orme 1, Stephanie Ortbals 3, George Ottoson 1, Pete Packer 15, Katie Pedersen 1, Wendy Pellow 2, Mary Penrose 1, Roy Perkins 1, Elisa Petrini 1, Fran Pflieger 1,Torryn Phelps 2, Sarah Phillips 3, Laura Polachek 3, Carol Pollack 1, Wayne Powell 3, Bryan Pratt 2, Stephen Quine 1, Toufic Rahman 6, Tammy Rhodes 1, Jennifer Rieder 2, Sara Roberts 2, Sara Roschwalb 3, Jill Rosensweig 2, Harriet Rubin 4, Beth Schelske 1, Susan Schneider 3, Roger Scholl 1, Lois Sharon 1, Jerry Sheehan 1, Anne Marie Shelness 1, Russell Shew 16, Amy Shock 4, David Smith 1, Malcolm Smith 2, Steve Smith 4, Sherri Soderberg Pittman 4, Beverly Southerland 1, Tanny Southerland 1, Erika Sova 3, Karen Steinke 2, Martin Thomas 2, Susan Tiffany 1, Stephanie Tombrello 2, Barbara Tracey 2, Keren Trost 1, Buddy Vagoni 1, Jon Vernick 1, Darlene Watson 1, Elaine Weinstein 2, Ray Weiss 11, Clay White 1, Donna Whitlow 1, Teresa Wooten-Talley 8, Ken Wright 2, Susan Beth Wright 1, Peter Zetlin 1.*

While each person above played an important role in our publications, certain people stood out: Joan Claybrook, whose vision initially created *The Car Book*; the great Clarence Ditlow, long-time head of the Center for Auto Safety, who was at my side for 38 years; Amy Curran, graphics maven who, for 52 books, was responsible for the graphics that distinguished our publications from any other on the market; Stuart Krichevsky, my long-time agent and Jerret Engle my first editor who made *The Car Book* into a national commercial success.

However, for 40 years the most important factor in being able to bring this information to the American car buyer is the encouragement and love from my brilliant and beautiful wife, Marilyn Mohrman-Gillis. For her and our four terrific children (and former *Car Book* co-authors!)–Katie, John, Brian, and Brennan–and daughter-in-laws, Jessie and Marine, I am eternally grateful. —J.G.

JASON LEVINE, CENTER FOR AUTO SAFETY

Forty years ago, when the Center for Auto Safety began to publish *The Car Book* by Jack Gillis consumers were in the desert: thirsty for information about the safety of the vehicles they were looking to buy. There was a new President (Reagan) who didn't want to provide easy to understand data about crash tests and fuel efficiency to consumers because the car companies did not like the idea. *The Car Book* became an oasis where consumers were able to educate themselves before making one of the most significant purchases of their lives. This publication, now in its 40th and final print edition, truly changed the world of car safety by making safety information as important and as easy to find as paint color options.

Today, car companies think they can co-opt terms and ideas around "safety," and bombard consumers with so much information that it makes it impossible to tell the difference between one car and another, aside from the price tag. You know better – or you wouldn't be holding *The Car Book* in your hands.

Yet, the Center for Auto Safety knows that not everyone is as well-informed as *The Car Book* readers, making our work more critical than ever. In 1970, coming out of the Corvair crisis, it was vital that an independent organization serve as a watchdog over both the industry and the federal government when it came to car safety issues. The Center has been that watchdog for the last five decades.

As the Center embarks upon our Golden Anniversary year, we are excited overall fatality rates in the United States from motor vehicle crashes have decreased slightly; hopefully this is a trend and not a statistical anomaly. However, death rates for pedestrians, bicyclists, and truck related crashes have all increased. This is a worrying pattern. Despite much progress, over 36,500 people were killed in motor vehicle crashes in 2018: More than 100 every single day.

The National Highway Traffic Safety Administration (NHTSA) is tasked with writing safety regulations for cars and enforcing motor vehicle laws. However, the current leadership of NHTSA, perhaps taking its cues from the current President, has chosen a path of deregulation and has brought enforcement efforts to a crawl. What NHTSA has apparently misunderstood is that traffic-related crashes and death rates didn't decrease by 78% over the last 5 decades because of the kindness and charity of the car manufacturers. The safety features now standard in modern vehicles, from seatbelts to airbags, and from rollover-preventing electronic stability control to backup cameras, are standard because of government mandates passed after the urging of public safety advocates and over the objections of the auto companies.

The Center for Auto Safety remains at the forefront of the fight for car safety not only for our members, but for all drivers, passengers, and pedestrians. In the past year, we have successfully petitioned the government to open defect investigations, used the courts to force progress on rulemaking and transparency by the Department of Transportation, and walked the halls of Congress educating members on what is needed to remove cars from their position as the number one killer of Americans ages 5-24.

The truth is, recall rates are too high, which is why the Center created www.FixAutoRecalls.com to help close the recall completion gap. In 2020, the Center will work to make it illegal to sell a used car with an open recall; will advocate for policy changes by companies like Uber and taxis across the country so that the car that picks you up isn't under recall; and we'll continue to pressure NHTSA to force manufacturers to use electronic communication in addition to letters when notifying you about a recall.

There's no reason to wait for the information to come to you when it comes to vehicle safety. The Center's unique Safety Tune-Up Reports provide recalls, complaints, the latest service alerts, and investigations about your car. You can even get regular safety updates delivered to your email in-box monthly, arming you with safety information the manufacturers often try to hide!

Car crashes take an unimaginable toll on people just going about their everyday lives. The almost 40,000 deaths, 2.7 million injuries, and 6 million collisions create an estimated societal cost approaching $1 trillion every single year. There's no doubt that cars are safer today than they once were, and with the proper oversight it is possible that autonomous vehicle technology will help make self-driving cars a safe reality in the future. However, recent increases in road deaths and pedestrian fatalities point to a system that is far from perfect and needs an independent watchdog like the Center to keep a look out for you! Please visit www.autosafety.org to learn how you can support the fight for safety.

JACK GILLIS

40 years ago in 1981, we set out on a unique path to change the safety and performance of America's automobiles. The concept, conceived by Joan Claybrook, Administrator of the National Highway Safety Transportation Administration under President Jimmy Carter, was to provide the American public with access to millions of dollars of auto safety and maintenance information collected at the taxpayers' expense. We believed we could use the marketplace, informed by data, to improve vehicle safety and performance.

The result was *The Car Book*, one of the most unique and popular books in the history of the federal government. It permanently changed the way consumers buy cars, the way automakers build them, and how dealers sell them.

40 years ago, as a young staffer at the National Highway Traffic Safety Administration, I was asked by Claybrook to compile the first edition of *The Car Book*. The challenge was great—translate thousands of bits of complicated safety and performance data into a simple index. The first edition of *The Car Book* was a colorful, 68-page guide using clear and easy-to-understand tables and charts on crash tests, maintenance costs and other performance factors. Consumers devoured this new information with 2 million people requesting the free guide. It still holds the record for their most requested government publication with 200,000 requests received in one day.

Notwithstanding its popularity, President Regan, under intense pressure from the car companies, banned further publication of book when he assumed office from Jimmy Carter. Ironically, the book was a non-regulatory, free market approach to consumer protection, which was consistent with Republican policies. Manufacturers were not required to comply with any new laws or regulations. Rather, the transparent publication of data and information gave the consumers the ability to vote for better performers with their dollars.

> **The Car Book has changed the way consumers buy cars and how the car companies build them.**

In 1982, unable to save *The Car Book* as a government publication, I left NHTSA and joined with Clarence Ditlow, Executive Director of the Center for Auto Safety, to save the book from extinction and ensure continued consumer access to the vital information.

At first, the carmakers attempted to discredit *The Car Book*, saying that consumers didn't care about safety and that the ratings were "unfair." Ironically, U.S. carmakers were trying to deny consumers access to information about the one area in which they had a clear competitive advantage over the Japanese carmakers—safety. The Japanese reacted very differently. They went back to the drawing boards, built safety into their cars, and introduced America to some of the safest small cars on the market. They likely spent less money building safety into their cars than Detroit spent fighting safety regulations. The Japanese carmakers had a better sense of what American consumers wanted than Detroit's big three.

The continued publication of *The Car Book* eventually forced the auto industry to respond. Cars today are safer and better performing, warranties have improved, and even the government changed its rating system to be more consumer friendly. In fact, *The Car Book* spawned new ratings programs, including a series of crash tests sponsored by the insurance industry.

Over the years *The Car Book* introduced a number of innovations into the car marketplace. In 1984, we developed the original Gillis Crash Test Index, in which we reduced the thousands of bits of complex crash test data into a single number that allowed for consistent and clear car-to-car comparisons.

The Car Book was the first publication to provide car buyers with comparative, objective maintenance cost information. Knowing the difference in maintenance costs can save consumers hundreds of dollars in operating costs. Because insurance is one of the most overlooked expenses of car ownership, we included whether the vehicle got a discount or surcharge on premiums.

In 1985, we developed a way for consumers to compare complex warranties using a simple index number. After years of struggling with buried, fine print warranty details, consumers could now easily compare their coverage. As a result, most car companies improved their warranties. Today, carmakers are eager to promote their better warranties.

In 1989, through Center for Auto Safety Freedom of Information Act requests, we provided consumers with their first look at the hundreds of thousands of car complaints on file with the U.S. Department of Transportation. We developed *The Car Book* complaint index using complaint data normalized for sales.

In 1990, as Americans began buying SUVs, trucks, and minivans in record numbers, we provided consumers with their first insight into the comparative safety, or lack thereof, of this fast growing class of vehicles.

In 1992, we developed a parking index to enable consumers to quickly compare a vehicle's ease of parking.

In 2000, we were the first to publish a rollover rating index, which allowed *Car Book* readers to compare the rollover potential of the growing number of SUVs and minivans. While some car companies threatened us with lawsuits, the government later began to use the same formula to explain the risk of rollovers.

There is no question that initially publishing the government's crash test scores did more to improve performance than any other single initiative. However, by the mid-2000s nearly every vehicle (98% of the 2009 models) received a four or five star rating from the government, making it impossible for car buyers to separate the truly good performers from those at the bottom of the list. The government rating program was essentially burying important differences in how the vehicles compared in crash test performances thereby cutting competition on this most critical safety factor. In response, we developed a new Gillis Crash Test Rating Index for the 2009 edition of *The Car Book*, which compared the results of all the vehicles on a relative basis, and created a new rating that combined the front and side crash tests. This new rating system continued *The Car Book*'s tradition of "consumer empowerment" by giving car buyers the ability to identify the truly best performers on the market.

The 2009 *Car Book* also separated the car side crash test ratings of SUVs. Cars and trucks perform very differently in the government side crash test due to their different body structures and the nature of the test. *The Car Book* takes this into consideration by rating these two types of vehicles separately.

Most recently, *The Car Book* was the first publication to include ratings on safety features in its overall ratings, such as automatic braking, lane warnings and rear cameras. As the industry moves toward autonomous vehicles, these innovative safety features are dramatically improving the ability of vehicles to avoid crashes. By rating these features, *The Car Book* allows consumers to make life-saving choices when buying a new car.

But we didn't just rate cars, *The Car Book* helped consumers cope with dealer sales tactics and pressures that make the car buying experience a huge challenge. We provided car buyers what they needed to know to survive the showroom and get the best possible price, including guidance on financing and whether to lease or buy. Dealer efforts to intimidate buyers often leads to poor choices. Our advice on getting the best deal levels the playing field between buyer and seller.

Each year *The Car Book* enables market forces to generate tremendous improvements in auto safety. It has been a powerful example of what I call "regulation by information." By allowing consumers to make informed purchase decisions, *The Car Book* has forced the market to make improvements in safety and performance to stay competitive. It has given consumers the power to bring about profound changes in automobiles. After years of fighting our efforts to promote safety, carmakers have finally come around. Today, nearly every single carmaker uses safety as a key selling factor. Why? Because they realize what we and our readers have been telling them for years—safety sells! Carmakers who once attempted to kill *The Car Book* are now making sure that consumers know how their products perform.

What began as an innovative government program 40 years ago has changed not only the way consumers buy their cars, but most importantly, the way manufacturers make them. As *The Car Book* transitions to an entirely digital publication, this final 40th print edition is a testament to the hundreds of staffers who have contributed to its development and success over the years and to the unwavering support of the Center for Auto Safety.

As always, buy safety and drive safely!　　　*—Jack Gillis*

Every year, car manufacturers spend tens of millions of dollars to influence government decision making. General Motors, Ford, and all the other major automakers have large staffs in Washington to represent their interests. But who looks out for the consumer? Who works on behalf of safety and not shareholders? For 49 years, the independent, member supported, non-profit Center for Auto Safety has been the voice for consumers before government agencies, Congress, and the courts. The Center was co-founded in 1970 by Ralph Nader and Consumers Union, publisher of Consumer Reports. As consumer concerns about auto safety issues have expanded, so has the work of the Center. Center accomplishments include:

Advocating for Safety Recalls: Annually, the Center analyzes thousands of consumer complaints. Based on these complaints and other reports, the Center requests government investigations and pursues recalls by manufacturers of defective vehicles. Center advocacy has resulted in the recall of millions of vehicles, including the deadly GM faulty ignition switches, Jeep fuel tank fires, and exploding Takata airbags.

Representing the Consumer in Washington: The Center monitors the activities of our government to ensure it carries out its responsibilities to the American taxpayer. The Center's fulltime job is to see the consumer's point of view represented in vehicle safety policies and rules. Over the course of our history, the Center has submitted hundreds of comments on government safety standards, and testified repeatedly before Congress on auto safety, consumer protection, and fuel economy. One major Center success was the fight to get airbags in every car. Another was working to change the practice of manufacturers using weak roofs that crush vehicle occupants in rollovers. Since 2013, vehicle roofs are more than twice as strong as before, and rollover deaths and injuries have dramatically declined.

Exposing Secret Warranties and Making Repair Bulletins Public: The Center played a prominent role in the exposure of secret warranties — or "policy adjustments," as manufacturers call them. These occur when an automaker agrees to pay for certain repairs beyond the warranty period but refuses to notify consumers. More recently, the Center went to court to make Technical Service Bulletins sent by manufacturers to their dealers publicly available — and we won!

Lemon Laws: The Center's work on Lemon Laws has aided in the enactment of laws in all 50 states, making it easier to return a defective new car and get your money back. Before Lemon Laws, auto- makers would refuse to buy back vehicles. Today, it is your legal right in every state to have a bad car bought back by the manufacturer.

Tire Ratings: Thanks to a Center lawsuit overturning the Department of Transportation's revocation of a valuable tire information program, consumers have reliable treadwear ratings to help them get the most miles for their dollar.

Legal Action: When the Center has exhausted other means of obtaining relief for consumers, we go to court. Currently, we are suing the Federal Trade Commission as we work to overturn its dangerous policy allowing used cars with unrepaired recalls to be sold as "safe," and we are in court in Arizona trying to force Goodyear to release information about dangerous tires it prefers to keep under seal after secret settlements.

CENTER FOR AUTO SAFETY ONLINE

The Center is your representative fighting for auto safety, quality, and fuel economy every day. We depend on public support to keep us running. Learn more about at our advocacy efforts at our website: www.autosafety.org. Once there you can sign up for our member-only CAS Safety Tune-Up Reports, including customized email updates about your car. To become a member, or make a tax-deductible contribution to auto safety, visit: www.autosafety.org/make-donation/. To contribute by mail, send a check to: Center for Auto Safety, 1825 Connecticut Ave., NW #330, Washington, DC 20009-5708.

WWW.AUTOSAFETY.ORG

THE CAR OF TODAY—40 YEARS AGO—STILL A DREAM

Since the very first edition of *The Car Book* in 1980, we've highlighted how introducing advanced technology into new vehicles can improve safety. In 1980, *The Car Book* profiled airbags and automatic safety belts, which were revolutionary safety technology at the time. In the twenty years since airbags became a standard safety feature on all vehicles (1999), there's been amazing progress in improving vehicle safety and reducing car crash fatalities. However, there is so much more that could have been done, and our 1980 profile of "The Car for Today" serves as a poignant reminder.

"The Car for Today" was the Research Safety Vehicle (RSV) developed by Minicars, Inc., and the U.S. Department of Transportation. This 1980s-era vehicle protected occupants in crashes at up to 50 mph, weighed only 2500 pounds (the average then was 3,228 pounds), and got 30 mpg in city driving. The U.S. DOT estimated that the RSV could be mass-produced and sold for less than $7,000 (under $22,000 in today's dollars). The idea behind the RSV was to prove that style, safety and fuel efficiency were not incompatible.

The RSV included safety features such as airbags and three-point seat belts, and items that, sadly, still have not been incorporated in today's vehicles. The exterior sheet metal was filled with lightweight, inexpensive polyurethane foam which reduced the force of a crash and kept other cars from penetrating the interior. The good news—the auto industry is finally consider-ing using this feature to reduce weight without compromising safety. The bad news—they've waited nearly 40 years to do so.

The RSV was equipped with "gull-wing" doors, which are much less likely to be crushed inward in a crash than standard doors. While some manufacturers (Tesla and DeLorean) have incorporated this technology, the feature remains highly unusual. The RSV also had roof supports decades before they were required. The 1980 Car Book noted that if all new cars had the characteristics of the RSV, Americans would reduce their gas consumption by 50% and the number of crash fatalities by 12,000 each year. Tragically, actual progress on car safety and fuel efficiency has been much, much slower.

This trip through history is a poignant, and tragic, example of lost opportunity. For 40 years, car makers have had the technology to create vehicles that could have saved money at the pump, protected the environment and saved lives. And while there are great new safety features avail-able today, unfortunately they are frequently sold as an expensive luxury add-ons, instead of standard features.

With the RSV, the government was leading the conversation on vehicle safety. It proved what was possible 40 years ago. Tragically, with autonomous vehicles on the horizon, the U.S. DOT is no longer taking the lead in improving vehicle safety. Instead it waits for the car companies to decide when to prioritize people over profits. Because of this, fifty years after being founded to fight for the implementation of life saving vehicle technology, the Center for Auto Safety is needed more than ever. Today, the Center for Auto Safety is leading the fight for safer vehicles on behalf of the over 325 million Americans whose lives are impacted everyday by the 275 million vehicles on U.S. roads. And *The Car Book* is helping the nearly 70 million new and used car buyers in separating the "lemons" from the "peaches."

–Katie Pedersen
Center for Auto Safety

The 1980 RSV as profiled in the 1980 edition of *The Car Book*.

USING THE BUYING GUIDE

The "Buying Guide" provides a quick comparison of the 2020 cars in terms of their safety, warranty, fuel economy, complaint rating, and price range—arranged by size class. To fully understand the information in the charts, it is important to read the related section in the book.

Overall Rating: This shows how well this car stacks up on a scale of 1 to 10 when compared to all others on the market. We have adopted the Olympic rating system with "10" being the best. Because safety is the most important component of our ratings, cars with no crash test results at the time of printing are not given an overall rating.

Combined Crash Test Rating: This indicates how well the car performed in the government's frontal and side crash test programs compared to this year's vehicles tested to date. See pages 16-23 for details. Note: In order to qualify for a *Best Bet*, the vehicle may not have any Poor or Very Poor crash test or safety feature ratings.

Safety Feature Rating: This is an evaluation of how many extra safety features are available in comparison to all the vehicles. See pages 58-60.

Warranty Rating: This is an overall comparative assessment of the car's warranty. See pages 31-33.

Fuel Economy: This is the EPA city/highway mpg for, what is expected to be, the most popular version of each model. See pages 25-26.

Complaint Rating: This is based on complaints received by the U.S. Department of Transportation. If not rated, the vehicle is too new to have a complaint rating. See page 41.

Price Range: This will give you a general idea of the "sticker," or manufacturer's suggested retail price (MSRP).

 Indicates a *Car Book* Best Bet.

☼CAR☼ ABOUT THE CAR BOOK BEST BETS ☼CAR☼

It is important to consult the specific chapters to learn more about how *The Car Book* ratings are developed and to look on the car pages, beginning on page 61, for more details on these vehicles. In order to be considered as a "Best Bet" the vehicle must have a crash test rating as safety is a critical factor in gaining that recognition. _Vehicles with "Poor" (3 or 4) or "Very Poor" (1 or 2) in Combined Crash Tests, or Front or Side Crash Test Ratings, or an additional injury warning will not qualify as a "Best Bet." In addition, vehicles with a poor or Very Poor safety feature rating will not qualify as a "Best Bet."_ Because most people are considering vehicles in the same size category, the "Best Bets" beginning on page 10 are by size—indicating how these vehicles compared against others in the same size class. You will note that some of our "Best Bets" have some "not so good" ratings on the next pages. Nevertheless, these vehicles still rise to the top in their size class. This points to the trade offs we often make when buying a new vehicle.

Vehicle	Pg #	Overall Rating	Combined Crash Test Rating	Safety Features Rating	Warranty Rating	Fuel Economy Rating	Complaint Rating	Price Range
Subcompact								
BMW i3	77			Average	Very Good	137/111	Poor	$42-$47,000
Chevrolet Sonic	101	9	Good	Good	Average	25/34	Average	$15-$21,000
Chevrolet Spark	102	5	Very Poor	Good	Average	29/38	Poor	$13-$17,000
Honda Fit	135	9	Very Good	Very Poor	Very Poor	33/41	Good	$16-$21,000
Hyundai Accent	139			Very Poor	Very Good	28/38	Good	$14-$17,000
Hyundai Veloster	146	6	Poor	Poor	Very Good	28/36	Good	$18-$23,000
Kia Rio	158			Poor	Very Good	28/37	Very Good	$14-$20,000
Mazda MX-5	184			Very Poor	Very Poor	27/36	Average	$24-$34,000
Mini Hardtop	192	6	Poor	Poor	Very Good	27/35	Good	$20-$30,000
Mitsubishi Mirage	193	3	Very Poor	Very Poor	Very Good	37/43	Poor	$13-$16,000
Nissan Versa	206			Very Poor	Very Poor	31/40		$11-$15,000
Compact								
Acura ILX	61			Good	Average	25/35	Very Good	$27-$34,000
Audi A3	65	5	Average	Good	Good	24/33	Poor	$31-$49,000
Audi A4	66	2	Very Poor	Average	Good	25/33	Poor	$36-$50,000
BMW 2 Series	72			Average	Very Good	23/35	Average	$34-$47,000
BMW 3 Series	73			Good	Very Good	23/36	Very Good	$34-$48,000
BMW 4 Series	74			Good	Very Good	23/35	Good	$42-$59,000
Chevrolet Bolt	93			Very Good	Average	128/110	Very Poor	$36-$40,000
Honda Civic	133	10	Average	Average	Very Poor	31/41	Good	$19-$26,000
Hyundai Elantra	140			Good	Very Good	28/37	Average	$16-$22,000
Kia Forte	156			Very Poor	Very Good	29/37	Poor	$16-$22,000
Kia Soul	161		Good	Poor	Very Good	25/30		$16-$35,000
Lexus IS	170	8	Average	Very Good	Good	21/30	Very Good	$37-$43,000
Lexus RC	172			Good	Good	22/32	Very Good	$40-$45,000
Mazda 3	179	6	Poor	Average	Very Good	28/37	Very Good	$18-$24,000
Mercedes-Benz C	185	1	Poor	Very Good	Poor	22/30	Average	$39-$67,000
Nissan Leaf	199			Very Poor	Very Poor	126/101	Very Good	$30-$36,000
Nissan Sentra	204	5	Very Poor	Very Poor	Very Poor	30/39	Very Good	$16-$21,000
Subaru Impreza	212	5	Average	Good	Poor	20/27	Average	$18-$24,000
Toyota 86	219			Very Poor	Very Poor	25/34	Very Good	$26-$29,000
Toyota Corolla	222	7	Poor	Good	Very Good	27/36	Very Good	$18-$22,000

Vehicle	Pg #	Overall Rating	Combined Crash Test Rating	Safety Features Rating	Warranty Rating	Fuel Economy Rating	Complaint Rating	Price Range
Compact (cont.)								
Toyota Corolla HB	223			Poor	Very Poor	28/36	Poor	$18-$19,000
Toyota Prius	225	7	Average	Good	Very Poor	54/50	Poor	$23-$30,000
Toyota Prius Prime	226			Very Good	Very Poor	55/53	Average	$27-$33,000
Toyota Yaris	232	6	Average	Very Poor	Very Poor	32/40	Poor	$15-$17,000
Volkswagen Jetta	234			Very Poor	Very Good	28/39	Very Poor	$17-$28,000
Intermediate								
Acura TLX	64	9	Very Good	Good	Average	23/33	Poor	$33-$45,000
Audi A5	67			Very Good	Good	24/34	Very Good	$42-$52,000
Audi A6	68			Good	Good	20/29	Very Good	$47-$61,000
BMW 5 Series	75	6	Poor	Good	Very Good	23/34	Good	$52-$73,000
Buick Regal	85			Very Good	Good	22/32	Very Good	$27-$36,000
Chevrolet Camaro	94	4	Good	Poor	Average	19/28	Good	$26-$42,000
Chevrolet Corvette	96			Very Poor	Average	15/25		$55-$83,000
Chevrolet Malibu	99	9	Average	Very Good	Average	27/36	Very Good	$21-$27,000
Ford Fusion	121	4	Poor	Good	Poor	21/32	Poor	$22-$36,000
Ford Fusion Energi	122	8	Good	Good	Poor	40/36	Very Poor	$33-$41,000
Ford Mustang	123	6	Good	Very Poor	Poor	19/28	Average	$24-$54,000
Honda Accord	132			Very Good	Very Poor	23/34	Poor	$22-$34,000
Hyundai Sonata	144			Average	Very Good	25/35		$22-$32,000
Infiniti Q50	147	3	Poor	Average	Very Good	20/29	Good	$34-$52,000
Kia Optima	157			Good	Very Good	24/34	Average	$22-$30,000
Lexus ES	167			Very Good	Good	21/31	Very Good	$38-$41,000
Lexus GS	168			Very Good	Good	19/29	Poor	$46-$56,000
Lincoln MKZ	176	4	Poor	Average	Very Good	18/27	Average	$35-$47,000
Mazda 6	180	6	Good	Average	Very Poor	26/38	Good	$21-$30,000
Nissan Altima	196			Poor	Very Poor	27/38	Average	$22-$32,000
Nissan Maxima	200	4	Good	Poor	Very Poor	22/30	Good	$32-$40,000
Subaru Legacy	213			Good	Poor	26/36		$22-$31,000
Tesla Model 3	215			Good	Very Good	131/120	Very Poor	$35-$45,000
Toyota Avalon	220	8	Good	Very Good	Very Poor	21/31	Good	$33-$42,000
Toyota Camry	221	8	Very Good	Very Good	Very Poor	28/39	Good	$24-$34,000
Volkswagen Passat	235	4	Average	Very Poor	Very Good	25/36	Poor	$22-$33,000

Vehicle	Pg #	Overall Rating	Combine Crash Test Rating	Safety Feature Rating	Warranty Rating	Fuel Economy Rating	Complaint Rating	Price Range
Intermediate (cont.)								
Volvo S60	237			Average	Good	25/36	Very Good	$33-$47,000
Volvo V60	238			Average	Good	25/36	Very Good	$38-$49,000
Large								
BMW 7 Series	76			Very Good	Very Good	21/29	Average	$83-$96,000
Cadillac CT6	86			Very Good	Very Good	18/27	Good	$54-$88,000
Chevrolet Impala	98	4	Average	Average	Average	18/28	Good	$27-$36,000
Chrysler 300	107	1	Very Poor	Average	Poor	19/30	Poor	$28-$40,000
Dodge Challenger	109	4	Good	Very Poor	Poor	19/30	Very Good	$26-$63,000
Dodge Charger	110	2	Poor	Average	Poor	19/31	Poor	$28-$66,000
Genesis G80	125			Very Good	Very Good	19/27	Very Good	$41-$59,000
Lincoln Continental	174	6	Very Good	Good	Very Good	17/26	Very Poor	$44-$64,000
Mercedes-Benz E	186	3	Average	Very Good	Poor	22/30	Average	$52-$69,000
Mercedes-Benz S	191			Very Good	Poor	19/28	Good	$89-$147,000
Tesla Model S	216	10	Very Good	Very Good	Very Good	88/90	Very Poor	$69-$135,000
Minivan								
Chrysler Pacifica	108	8	Good	Good	Poor	18/28	Very Poor	$26-$43,000
Honda Odyssey	137	9	Good	Very Good	Very Poor	19/28	Very Poor	$29-$44,000
Kia Sedona	159			Poor	Very Good	18/25	Good	$26-$41,000
Toyota Sienna	229	2	Average	Good	Very Poor	18/25	Poor	$29-$47,000
Small SUV								
Acura RDX	63	9	Very Good	Very Good	Average	19/27	Good	$35-$40,000
Audi Q3	69			Very Poor	Good	20/28		$32-$37,000
BMW X1	78			Average	Very Good	22/32	Poor	$33-$35,000
Buick Encore	83	10	Good	Good	Good	23/30	Very Good	$24-$32,000
Cadillac XT4	89			Good	Very Good	22/29	Very Good	$35-$42,000
Chevrolet Equinox	97	3	Average	Average	Average	26/32	Very Poor	$23-$37,000
Chevrolet Trax	106	10	Good	Good	Average	24/30	Very Good	$21-$28,000
Fiat 500X	113			Poor	Average	22/31	Poor	$19-$27,000
Ford EcoSport	114			Poor	Poor	27/29	Good	$19-$26,000
Ford Escape	116			Average	Poor	22/31		$23-$33,000
GMC Terrain	129	5	Average	Poor	Average	26/30	Good	$24-$39,000
Honda CR-V	134	10	Very Good	Good	Very Poor	26/32	Good	$24-$33,000
Honda HR-V	136	5	Poor	Very Poor	Very Poor	28/34	Average	$19-$26,000

Vehicle	Pg #	Overall Rating	Combined Crash Test Rating	Safety Features Rating	Warranty Rating	Fuel Economy Rating	Complaint Rating	Price Range
Small SUV (cont.)								
Hyundai Kona	141			Good	Very Good	28/32	Very Good	$20-$29,000
Hyundai Tucson	145	8	Poor	Good	Very Good	24/28	Very Poor	$22-$31,000
Infiniti QX50	148			Poor	Very Good	17/24	Average	$34-$36,000
Jeep Compass	152	4	Very Poor	Very Poor	Poor	22/30	Poor	$20-$29,000
Jeep Renegade	154	1	Very Poor	Poor	Poor	22/31	Very Poor	$17-$27,000
Jeep Wrangler	155			Very Poor	Poor	17/21	Very Poor	$23-$37,000
Kia Sportage	162	9	Good	Average	Very Good	22/29	Good	$23-$34,000
Land Rvr Rng Rvr Evoque	165			Average	Good	21/30		$41-$54,000
Lexus NX	171	5	Good	Good	Good	22/28	Good	$35-$39,000
Lincoln Corsair	175			Very Good	Very Good	22/29		$36-$44,000
Mazda CX-3	181	10	Very Good	Average	Very Poor	29/34	Very Good	$19-$26,000
Mazda CX-5	182	4	Average	Poor	Very Poor	26/32	Very Good	$24-$30,000
Mercedes-Benz GLA	187			Good	Poor	23/31	Average	$32-$49,000
Mercedes-Benz GLC	188			Very Good	Poor	21/28	Very Poor	$39-$54,000
Mitsu. Outlander Sport	195	3	Poor	Very Poor	Very Good	23/29	Good	$19-$27,000
Subaru Crosstrek	210	5	Average	Good	Poor	27/33	Poor	$21-$26,000
Subaru Forester	211			Good	Poor	24/32	Very Poor	$22-$36,000
Toyota RAV4	227			Good	Very Poor	22/29	Very Good	$24-$32,000
Volkswagen Tiguan	236			Poor	Very Good	22/27	Poor	$25-$37,000
Mid-Size SUV								
Acura MDX	62	7	Good	Very Good	Average	18/27	Poor	$44-$58,000
Audi Q5	70			Poor	Good	23/27	Average	$41-$50,000
Audi Q7	71	3	Average	Good	Good	19/25	Poor	$49-$65,000
BMW X3	79			Good	Very Good	22/29	Very Poor	$39-$47,000
BMW X5	80			Good	Very Good	18/27	Very Good	$55-$72,000
BMW X6	81			Average	Very Good	18/24		$60-$104,000
Buick Envision	84			Very Good	Good	21/27	Poor	$36-$45,000
Cadillac XT5	90	3	Poor	Good	Very Good	19/25	Very Poor	$40-$63,000
Cadillac XT6	91			Good	Very Good	17/24		$53-$57,000
Chevrolet Blazer	92			Good	Average	21/27	Very Good	$30-$45,000
Dodge Durango	111	2	Poor	Good	Poor	18/25	Very Good	$29-$62,000
Dodge Journey	112	1	Very Poor	Poor	Poor	19/25	Very Poor	$22-$34,000
Ford Edge	115	9	Very Good	Good	Poor	20/30	Poor	$29-$40,000

Vehicle	Pg #	Overall Rating	Combined Crash Test Rating	Safety Features Rating	Warranty Rating	Fuel Economy Rating	Complaint Rating	Price Range
Mid-Size SUV (cont.)								
Ford Explorer	118			Average	Poor	17/23		$31-$53,000
GMC Acadia	126	2	Poor	Good	Average	18/25	Very Poor	$32-$47,000
Honda Pilot	138	8	Good	Average	Very Poor	19/27	Poor	$30-$43,000
Hyundai Palisade	142			Very Good	Very Good	19/24		$32-$47,000
Hyundai Santa Fe	143			Average	Very Good	21/27	Poor	$24-$37,000
Infiniti QX60	149	5	Average	Average	Very Good	19/26	Average	$43-$44,000
Jeep Cherokee	151	5	Average	Good	Poor	21/28	Very Poor	$24-$37,000
Jeep Grand Cherokee	153	4	Average	Very Poor	Poor	14/22	Very Poor	$30-$47,000
Kia Sorento	160	6	Good	Poor	Very Good	21/28	Poor	$25-$45,000
Kia Telluride	163			Very Good	Good	19/24		$32-$42,000
Land Rvr Rng Rvr Sport	166			Average	Good	14/19	Very Good	$65-$94,000
Lexus RX	173	4	Poor	Good	Good	20/28	Very Good	$43-$53,000
Lincoln Nautilis	177	5	Very Poor	Average	Very Good	17/25	Poor	$39-$56,000
Mazda CX-9	183			Average	Very Poor	20/26	Good	$31-$44,000
Mercedes-Benz GLE	189			Very Good	Poor	18/23		$53-$101,000
Mitsubishi Outlander	194	4	Average	Average	Very Good	24/29	Poor	$23-$31,000
Nissan Murano	201			Poor	Very Poor	21/28	Good	$29-$40,000
Nissan Pathfinder	202			Poor	Very Poor	19/26	Poor	$29-$43,000
Nissan Rogue	203	3	Very Poor	Average	Very Poor	25/32	Very Good	$23-$31,000
Porsche Macan	207			Average	Good	17/23	Very Good	$47-$77,000
Subaru Outback	214			Good	Poor	25/33		$25-$35,000
Tesla Model X	217	10	Very Good	Very Good	Very Good	89/90	Very Poor	$79-$140,000
Toyota 4Runner	218	2	Very Poor	Poor	Very Poor	17/21	Very Good	$34-$44,000
Toyota Highlander	224			Very Good	Very Poor	18/24		$30-$47,000
Volkswagen Atlas	233	6	Very Good	Good	Very Good	18/25	Poor	$30-$48,000
Volvo XC60	239			Very Good	Good	22/28	Very Good	$40-$51,000
Large SUV								
Buick Enclave	82	4	Average	Average	Good	18/26	Average	$39-$55,000
Cadillac Escalade	87	3	Good	Average	Very Good	14/21	Good	$76-$97,000
Cadillac Escalade ESV	88	4	Average	Average	Very Good	14/20	Very Good	$80-$99,000

Vehicle	Pg #	Overall Rating	Combined Crash Test Rating	Safety Features Rating	Warranty Rating	Fuel Economy Rating	Complaint Rating	Price Range
Large SUV (cont.)								
Chevrolet Suburban	103	2	Average	Poor	Average	15/22	Poor	$50-$67,000
Chevrolet Tahoe	104	4	Good	Poor	Average	16/22	Average	$47-$65,000
Chevrolet Traverse	105	4	Average	Average	Average	18/27	Average	$32-$52,000
Ford Expedition	117			Good	Poor	17/22	Good	$48-$75,000
Ford Flex	120			Very Poor	Poor	16/23	Poor	$30-$40,000
GMC Yukon	130	5	Very Good	Average	Poor	16/22	Very Poor	$49-$69,000
GMC Yukon XL	131	4	Average	Average	Poor	15/22	Very Poor	$52-$72,000
Infiniti QX80	150			Good	Very Good	14/20	Good	$63-$89,000
Land Rover Range Rover	164			Average	Good	14/19	Good	$85-$140,000
Lexus GX	169			Very Good	Good	15/20	Very Good	$51-$63,000
Lincoln Navigator	178			Average	Very Good	16/21	Very Good	$72-$93,000
Mercedes-Benz GLS	190			Very Good	Poor	17/22		$67-$124,000
Nissan Armada	197			Good	Very Poor	14/19	Good	$44-$60,000
Subaru Ascent	209			Very Good	Poor	21/27	Poor	$32-$45,000
Toyota Sequoia	228			Poor	Very Poor	13/17	Very Good	$48-$67,000
Volvo XC90	240	8	Very Good	Very Good	Good	22/28	Very Poor	$45-$104,000
Compact Pickup								
Chevrolet Colorado	95	2	Poor	Very Poor	Average	20/27	Average	$20-$33,000
Ford Ranger	124			Very Good	Poor	21/26	Poor	$25-$36,000
GMC Canyon	127			Very Poor	Poor	20/26	Poor	$20-$43,000
Nissan Frontier	198	1	Poor	Very Poor	Very Poor	15/21	Average	$18-$35,000
Toyota Tacoma	230	1	Very Poor	Poor	Very Poor	19/23	Poor	$24-$39,000
Standard Pickup								
Chevrolet Silverado	100			Poor	Average	16/22	Poor	$28-$55,000
Ford F-150	119	9	Very Good	Poor	Poor	17/23	Very Good	$27-$57,000
GMC Sierra	128			Poor	Average	16/22	Poor	$29-$56,000
Nissan Titan	205	1	Good	Very Poor	Very Poor	15/21	Very Poor	$35-$55,000
Ram 1500	208			Very Poor	Very Poor	13/19	Average	$27-$53,000
Toyota Tundra	231			Average	Very Poor	13/18	Very Good	$32-$50,000

CRASH TESTS

Safety is likely the most important factor that most of us consider when choosing a new car. In the past, evaluating safety was difficult. Now, thanks to the information in *The Car Book*, it's much easier to pick a safe vehicle. The bottom line: For the greatest protection, you'll want the maximum number of safety features (see Safety Checklist, pages 64-66) and good crash test results (the following tables).

A key factor in occupant protection is how well the car protects you in a crash. This depends on its ability to absorb the force of the impact rather than transfer it to the occupant. In the frontal test, the vehicle impacts a solid barrier at 35 mph. In the side test, a moving barrier is crashed into the side of the vehicle at 38.5 mph. A second side test simulates hitting a tree or roadside pole by smashing a vehicle onto a vertical pole at the driver's door at 20 mph. The only occupant in this side pole test is a small female dummy in the driver seat.

The dummies measure the impact on the head, chest, neck and thighs.

Not all 2020 vehicles have undergone a crash test. The good news is that by carrying forward previous tests from cars that haven't changed, we have results for 115 2020 models. The bad news is that there are 82 models for which we don't have crash test results.

How the Cars are Rated: The combined crash test ratings are based on the *relative* performance of the 2020 vehicles tested to date. *This is a big difference from the government's "star" program.* Rather than large groups of undifferentiated vehicles in the government's star ratings, *The Car Book* rates them from best to worst. This means that those manufacturers really working on safety each year will rise to the top.

The first column provides *The Car Book's* Combined Crash Test Rating. The cars are rated from 10 (best) to 1 (worst). The front is weighted 60%, the side 36%, and the pole test 4% with results compared among all new 2020 crash tests to date.

Next are the individual front and side tests. Again, relative to all other 2020 vehicles with crash test results, we indicate if the vehicle was Very Good, Good, Average, Poor or Very Poor. For side tests, the cars are rated separately from the trucks. Because of their construction, the dynamics of a side test are different in cars and light trucks.

The next five columns indicate the likelihood of the occupant sustaining a life-threatening injury. The percent likelihood is listed for the driver and front passenger in the front test, the driver and rear passenger in the side test, and the driver in the side pole test. Lower percentages mean a lower likelihood of being seriously injured if there is a crash test of this type. This information is taken directly from the government's analysis of the crash test results.

USING CRASH TEST DATA

TIP

One of the most important results of our being the first to publish crash test data, and later develop our relative comparative ratings, is that it has put enormous pressure on the manufacturers to improve. Today's manufacturers are feverishly competing on safety features thanks to *The Car Book*, whereas years ago competition was based on style and horsepower. While the most important factors in evaluating the safety of today's vehicles are crash test performance and advanced safety features, size and weight do play a role. It is important to compare vehicles in the size classes that follow. For example, in a frontal collision between a subcompact and SUV rated 'Very Good," you'll be better off in the SUV. Nevertheless, selecting the best performers in whatever size class you are buying, is fundamental to protecting yourself. And remember, these tests are conducted with fully belted dummies, if you are not wearing your safety belt, then test results do not really apply.

CRASH TESTS

Crash Test Performance (10=Best, 1=Worst)	Combined Car Book Crash Test Rating	Test Type	Car Book Crash Test Rating-Index (Lower numbers are better)	Likelihood of Life Threatening Injury				
				Front Fixed Barrier		Side Moving Barrier		Side Pole
				Front Driver	Front Pass.	Side Driver	Side Pass.	Pole Driver
Subcompact								
Chevrolet Sonic	7	Front	Very Good-165	8.3%	8.1%			
		Side	Very Poor-153			9.5%	7.6%	3.8%
Chevrolet Spark	2	Front	Very Poor-228	13.6%	10.7%			
		Side	Poor-147			9.2%	6.8%	5.6%
Fiat 500	1	Front	Very Poor-256	11.4%	16.0%			
		Side	Poor-148			5.3%	8.0%	15.8%
Ford Fiesta	3	Front	Average-199	8.2%	12.8%			
		Side	Very Poor-154			8.9%	8.2%	3.6%
Honda Fit	9	Front	Good-175	9.2%	9.1%			
		Side	Good-85			6.8%	2.5%	3.5%
Mini Hardtop	4	Front	Average-194	10.7%	9.7%			
		Side	Very Poor-250			7.5%	18.7%	8.6%
Mitsubishi Mirage	2	Front	Poor-218	12.6%	10.5%			
		Side	Very Poor-210			7.5%	11.8%	22.1%
Toyota Prius C	2	Front	Poor-206	11.7%	10.1%			
		Side	Very Poor-196			17.7%	5.2%	5.1%
Toyota Yaris	2	Front	Poor-217	9.9%	13.1%			
		Side	Average-111			7.7%	4.6%	2.9%
Compact								
Audi A3	6	Front	Average-197	11.2%	9.6%			
		Side	Average-113			7.0%	5.1%	4.2%
Audi A4	2	Front	Very Poor-276	12.9%	16.9%			
		Side	Average-119			4.3%	8.2%	2.6%
Cadillac ATS	2	Front	Very Poor-237	10.3%	14.9%			
		Side	Poor-138			7.5%	7.4%	4.8%
Chevrolet Cruze	5	Front	Good-176	9.0%	9.5%			
		Side	Very Poor-192			8.7%	12.7%	2.6%
Chevrolet Volt	4	Front	Poor-216	8.4%	14.5%			
		Side	Good-95			6.0%	4.7%	1.4%
Honda Civic	5	Front	Average-197	9.3%	11.5%			
		Side	Poor-153			4.9%	10.0%	9.6%

CRASH TESTS

Crash Test Performance (10=Best, 1=Worst)	Combined Car Book Crash Test Rating	Test Type	Car Book Crash Test Rating-Index (Lower numbers are better)	Likelihood of Life Threatening Injury				
				Front Fixed Barrier		Side Moving Barrier		Side Pole
				Front Driver	Front Pass.	Side Driver	Side Pass.	Pole Driver
Compact (cont.)								
Lexus IS	5	Front	Poor-219	12.4%	10.9%			
		Side	Good-85			5.6%	2.8%	7.1%
Mazda 3	4	Front	Poor-209	10.3%	11.7%			
		Side	Poor-119			11.5%	2.4%	2.8%
Mercedes-Benz C-Class	3	Front	Average-203	7.8%	13.6%			
		Side	Very Poor-170			5.7%	12.2%	4.8%
Nissan Sentra	2	Front	Very Poor-242	11.8%	14.%			
		Side	Average-118			6.6%	6.5%	1.7%
Subaru Impreza	6	Front	Good-172	9.5%	9.0%			
		Side	Poor-127			8.5%	5.2%	5.6%
Toyota Corolla	4	Front	Poor-217	9.6%	13.4%			
		Side	Average-105			3.6%	6.7%	5.6%
Toyota Prius	5	Front	Average-203	10.3%	11.1%			
		Side	Average-116			6.5%	2.0%	23.2%
Toyota Yaris iA	5	Front	Poor-205	9.9%	11.7%			
		Side	Average-111			7.7%	4.6%	2.9%
Volkswagen Golf	5	Front	Average-198	9.8%	11.1%			
		Side	Average-116			9.1%	3.9%	3.6%
Intermediate								
Acura TLX	10	Front	Very Good-156	7.3%	8.9%			
		Side	Very Good-58			4.4%	1.7%	3.4%
BMW 5 Series	4	Front	Very Poor-233	13.1%	11.7%			
		Side	Good-85			8.4%	0.8%	5.5%
Chevrolet Camaro	7	Front	Average-201	10.7%	10.5%			
		Side	Very Good-78			5.9%	2.3%	4.7%
Chevrolet Malibu	5	Front	Poor-223	10.4%	13.3%			
		Side	Very Good-73			6.0%	1.2%	6.4%
Ford Fusion	3	Front	Very Poor-226	8.7%	15.2%			
		Side	Average-117			6.3%	6.2%	4.1%
Ford Fusion Energi	7	Front	Very Good-154	7.3%	8.7%			
		Side	Very Poor-158			14.6%	3.6%	4.7%
Ford Mustang	8	Front	Very Good-162	7.0%	9.9%			
		Side	Poor-140			3.3%	10.4%	7.0%
Infiniti Q50	4	Front	Very Poor-246	10.7%	15.6%			
		Side	Very Good-68			6.5%	1.2%	2.6%

CRASH TESTS

Crash Test Performance (10=Best, 1=Worst)	Combined Car Book Crash Test Rating	Test Type	Car Book Crash Test Rating-Index (Lower numbers are better)	Likelihood of Life Threatening Injury				
				Front Fixed Barrier		Side Moving Barrier		Side Pole
				Front Driver	Front Pass.	Side Driver	Side Pass.	Pole Driver
Intermediate (cont.)								
Kia Optima	7	Front	Good-175	7.3%	11.0%			
		Side	Poor-128			4.2%	9.3%	2.2%
Lincoln MKZ	3	Front	Very Poor-226	8.7%	15.2%			
		Side	Average-117			6.3%	6.2%	4.1%
Mazda 6	7	Front	Good-185	7.6%	11.7%			
		Side	Good-96			8.2%	2.5%	3.5%
Nissan Maxima	7	Front	Good-185	8.7%	10.8%			
		Side	Average-111			6.0%	4.3%	11.4%
Toyota Avalon	8	Front	Average-194	10.1%	10.4%			
		Side	Very Good-63			4.1%	1.2%	9.1%
Toyota Camry	9	Front	Very Good-170	8.4%	9.3%			
		Side	Good-80			3.5%	4.8%	2.5%
Toyota Prius V	6	Front	Poor-211	10.3%	12.0%			
		Side	Very Good-70			4.3%	1.5%	10.5%
Volkswagen Passat	5	Front	Very Poor-238	12.6%	12.8%			
		Side	Very Good-76			4.4%	3.1%	5.3%
Large								
Buick LaCrosse	5	Front	Good-188	8.1%	11.6%			
		Side	Very Poor-168			11.6%	7.7%	2.9%
Cadillac XTS	9	Front	Very Good-160	7.6%	9.1%			
		Side	Good-88			4.2%	4.3%	6.7%
Chevrolet Impala	6	Front	Good-173	7.5%	10.6%			
		Side	Poor-142			10.1%	6.1%	2.9%
Chrysler 300	2	Front	Very Poor-236	12.7%	12.5%			
		Side	Poor-120			12.9%	0.8%	5.1%
Dodge Challenger	7	Front	Average-204	11.7%	9.8%			
		Side	Very Good-56			4.7%	1.4%	2.6%
Dodge Charger	3	Front	Very Poor-232	14.3%	10.4%			
		Side	Average-110			12.2%	0.6%	3.8%
Ford Taurus	6	Front	Very Good-164	8.4%	8.7%			
		Side	Very Poor-154			8.3%	8.3%	5.8%
Lincoln Continental	10	Front	Very Good-158	7.6%	8.9%			
		Side	Very Good-67			3.9%	3.0%	3.4%
Mercedes-Benz E-Class	5	Front	Poor-206	9.6%	12.1%			
		Side	Good-87			6.4%	2.4%	6.8%

CRASH TESTS

Crash Test Performance (10=Best, 1=Worst)	Combined Car Book Crash Test Rating	Test Type	Car Book Crash Test Rating-Index (Lower numbers are better)	Likelihood of Life Threatening Injury				
				Front Fixed Barrier		Side Moving Barrier		Side Pole
				Front Driver	Front Pass.	Side Driver	Side Pass.	Pole Driver
Large (cont.)								
Tesla Model S	9	Front	Good-180	9.4%	9.5%			
		Side	Very Good-58			3.5%	1.5%	7.9%
Minivan								
Chrysler Pacifica	8	Front	Very Good-159	8.7%	7.9%			
		Side	Poor-93			5.8%	4.3%	3.2%
Honda Odyssey	7	Front	Good-180	9.5%	9.4%			
		Side	Good-58			2.3%	3.4%	3.1%
Toyota Sienna	6	Front	Average-197	8.6%	12.1%			
		Side	Average-71			2.9%	4.0%	4.5%
Small SUV								
Acura RDX	9	Front	Average-202	11.1%	10.4%			
		Side	Very Good-50			2.8%	1.3%	0.8%
Buick Encore	8	Front	Very Good-165	8.3%	9.0%			
		Side	Average-66			3.3%	3.0%	5.4%
Chevrolet Equinox	6	Front	Very Good-166	7.6%	9.8%			
		Side	Very Poor-230			6.2%	18.0%	5.6%
Chevrolet Trax	8	Front	Very Good-165	8.3%	9.0%			
		Side	Average-66			3.3%	3.0%	5.4%
GMC Terrain	6	Front	Very Good-166	7.6%	9.8%			
		Side	Very Poor-230			6.2%	18.%	5.6%
Honda CR-V	9	Front	Very Good-155	7.5%	8.6%			
		Side	Good-58			2.9%	2.3%	6.1%
Honda HR-V	3	Front	Poor-214	11.9%	10.8%			
		Side	Average-70			4.4%	2.6%	5.1%
Hyundai Tucson	4	Front	Poor-210	11.2%	11.1%			
		Side	Average-72			3.7%	1.7%	12.8%
Jeep Compass	2	Front	Poor-211	11.3%	11.1%			
		Side	Very Poor-120			4.1%	8.1%	4.4%
Jeep Renegade	2	Front	Poor-207	10.4%	11.6%			
		Side	Very Poor-187			3.8%	15.8%	2.4%
Kia Sportage	7	Front	Average-195	10.9%	9.6%			
		Side	Good-59			3.5%	1.6%	7.4%
Lexus NX	7	Front	Very Good-153	7.7%	8.3%			
		Side	Very Poor-108			10.9%	0.9%	6.5%

CRASH TESTS

Crash Test Performance (10=Best, 1=Worst)	Combined Car Book Crash Test Rating	Test Type	Car Book Crash Test Rating-Index (Lower numbers are better)	Likelihood of Life Threatening Injury				
				Front Fixed Barrier		Side Moving Barrier		Side Pole
				Front Driver	Front Pass.	Side Driver	Side Pass.	Pole Driver
Small SUV (cont.)								
Lincoln MKC	3	Front	Poor-213	8.9%	13.7%			
		Side	Poor-84			2.5%	5.8%	3.4%
Mazda CX-3	9	Front	Very Good-169	8.5%	9.2%			
		Side	Good-62			4.8%	1.8%	3.2%
Mazda CX-5	6	Front	Good-173	8.6%	9.5%			
		Side	Very Poor-128			2.7%	10.1%	4.5%
Mitsubishi Outlander Sport	4	Front	Average-203	10.0%	11.3%			
		Side	Poor-97			2.8%	6.3%	6.8%
Subaru Crosstrek	5	Front	Average-201	10.0%	11.2%			
		Side	Average-65			4.3%	2.0%	5.6%
Mid-Size SUV								
Acura MDX	7	Front	Very Good-168	8.3%	9.2%			
		Side	Average-68			2.5%	4.2%	3.6%
Audi Q7	6	Front	Average-195	10.0%	10.6%			
		Side	Average-67			3.7%	3.5%	2.0%
Cadillac XT5	3	Front	Average-199	8.2%	12.7%			
		Side	Very Poor-104			4.7%	5.6%	7.2%
Dodge Durango	3	Front	Very Poor-226	14.1%	9.9%			
		Side	Average-63			6.4%	.6%	2.9%
Dodge Journey	2	Front	Poor-222	9.6%	14.0%			
		Side	Very Poor-154			5.7%	9.7%	9.1%
Ford Edge	10	Front	Very Good-161	8.3%	8.5%			
		Side	Good-53			2.6%	2.7%	2.9%
GMC Acadia	3	Front	Poor-204	9.1%	12.4%			
		Side	Very Poor-121			5.0%	7.7%	4.0%
Honda Pilot	8	Front	Good-189	9.9%	10.0%			
		Side	Very Good-46			2.5%	1.0%	8.1%
Infiniti QX60	6	Front	Average-196	11.2%	9.5%			
		Side	Average-64			4.9%	1.8%	4.2%
Jeep Cherokee	5	Front	Very Poor-228	11.2%	13.1%			
		Side	Very Good-45			3.2%	1.7%	1.6%
Jeep Grand Cherokee	6	Front	Good-178	9.4%	9.3%			
		Side	Poor-93			8.3%	2.3%	2.4%

Crash Test Performance (10=Best, 1=Worst)	Combined Car Book Crash Test Rating	Test Type	Car Book Crash Test Rating-Index (Lower numbers are better)	Likelihood of Life Threatening Injury				
				Front Fixed Barrier		Side Moving Barrier		Side Pole
				Front Driver	Front Pass.	Side Driver	Side Pass.	Pole Driver
Mid-Size SUV (cont.)								
Kia Sorento	7	Front	Good-177	8.8%	9.7%			
		Side	Poor-84			3.2%	5.3%	3.7%
Lexus RX	3	Front	Very Poor-251	13.7%	13.2%			
		Side	Good-54			3.1%	2.2%	3.7%
Lincoln MKX	2	Front	Very Poor-313	16.1%	18.1%			
		Side	Poor-81			5.3%	2.3%	8.3%
Mitsubishi Outlander	5	Front	Average-195	12.4%	8.0%			
		Side	Poor-91			3.8%	4.7%	7.8%
Nissan Rogue	1	Front	Very Poor-240	10.5%	15.0%			
		Side	Very Poor-116			6.5%	4.6%	10.4%
Tesla Model X	10	Front	Very Good-152	8.3%	7.5%			
		Side	Very Good-43			3.3%	1.1%	3.1%
Toyota 4Runner	1	Front	Very Poor-255	11.9%	15.5%			
		Side	Poor-88			7.1%	0.9%	11.7%
Volkswagen Atlas	9	Front	Good-182	10.1%	9.0%			
		Side	Very Good-43			2.0%	1.7%	5.6%
Large SUV								
Buick Enclave	5	Front	Average-191	7.1%	12.9%			
		Side	Poor-74			4.4%	3.5%	2.3%
Cadillac Escalade	7	Front	Poor-209	10.1%	12.0%			
		Side	Very Good-45			3.0%	0.4%	8.6%
Cadillac Escalade ESV	5	Front	Average-199	9.5%	11.5%			
		Side	Average-69			4.5%	1.0%	12.2%
Chevrolet Suburban	6	Front	Average-195	10.4%	10.2%			
		Side	Average-69			4.5%	1.0%	12.2%
Chevrolet Tahoe	8	Front	Good-185	9.7%	9.7%			
		Side	Very Good-45			3.0%	0.4%	8.6%
Chevrolet Traverse	5	Front	Average-191	7.1%	12.9%			
		Side	Poor-74			4.4%	3.5%	2.3%
GMC Yukon	9	Front	Good-185	9.7%	9.7%			
		Side	Very Good-45			3.0%	0.4%	8.6%
GMC Yukon XL	6	Front	Average-195	10.4%	10.2%			
		Side	Average-69			4.5%	1.0%	12.2%

Crash Test Performance (10=Best, 1=Worst)	Combined Car Book Crash Test Rating	Test Type	Car Book Crash Test Rating-Index (Lower numbers are better)	Likelihood of Life Threatening Injury				
				Front Fixed Barrier		Side Moving Barrier		Side Pole
				Front Driver	Front Pass.	Side Driver	Side Pass.	Pole Driver
Large SUV (cont.)								
Subaru Ascent	10	Front	Very Good-158	7.6%	8.9%			
		Side	Very Good-39			8.9%	0.7%	2.6%
Volvo XC90	9	Front	Very Good-170	9.3%	8.5%			
		Side	Good-54			3.7%	2.3%	1.1%
Compact Pickup								
Chevrolet Colorado	3	Front	Poor-223	10.4%	13.3%			
		Side	Poor-73			6.0%	1.2%	6.4%
GMC Canyon	3	Front	Poor-223	10.4%	13.3%			
		Side	Average-73			6.0%	1.2%	6.4%
Nissan Frontier	4	Front	Very Poor-357	18.5%	21.1%			
		Side	Very Good-37			3.0%	0.5%	4.1%
Toyota Tacoma	1	Front	Very Poor-258	14.2%	13.5%			
		Side	Very Poor-115			10.1%	1.0%	12.7%
Standard Pickup								
Ford F-150	10	Front	Very Good-167	8.1%	9.4%			
		Side	Very Good-43			3.6%	0.7%	3.9%
Nissan Titan	7	Front	Average-200	11.5%	9.7%			
		Side	Very Good-46			4.1%	0.9%	2.0%
Ram 1500	5	Front	Poor-214	10.8%	11.9%			
		Side	Good-59			5.2%	0.3%	7.3%
Toyota Tundra		Front	Very Poor-236	12.0%	13.2%			
		Side	No Index-			2.7%		7.5%

2020 CRASH TESTS AND THE GOVERNMENT SHUTDOWN

Unfortunately, *The Car Book* 2020 contains about 15% fewer crash tests this year. This is due to the 2018-2019 federal government shutdown. Due to the absence of staff at the National Highway Traffic Safety Administration during this period, on-going and planned crash tests on 2020 model year vehicles were halted. Because *The Car Book* prioritizes safety, and does not give Overall Ratings to vehicles without crash tests, there are fewer vehicles in vehicles with Overall Ratings in this year's edition. As new results become available, you can find them at TheCarBook.com.

BUYING FOR SAFETY

TIP

So how do you buy for safety? Many consumers mistakenly believe that handling and performance are the key elements in the safety of a car. While an extremely unresponsive car could cause an accident, most new cars have adequately safe handling. In fact, many people actually feel uncomfortable driving high performance cars because the highly responsive steering, acceleration, and suspension systems can be difficult to get used to. However, the main reason handling is overrated as a safety measure is that automobile collisions are, by nature, accidents. Once they've begun, they are beyond human capacity to prevent, no matter how well your car handles. So the key to protecting yourself is to purchase a car that offers a high degree of crash protection and automatic crash avoidance features. When it comes to crash protection and crash avoidance, here's a general list of what you should look for:

Dynamic Head Restraints: They adjust automatically to give better protection in an accident.

Air Belts: Belts that blow up like long, soft balloons in a crash. Just being introduced in rear seats on some Ford vehicles.

Lane Keeping Assist: Keeps you within the white lines.

Automatic Braking: Applies the brakes faster than you can, or if you are not paying attention.

Blind Spot Detection: Keeps you from hitting another vehicle that you may not see.

Rear View Camera: Keeps children behind your car safe and helps with parking.

Adaptive Cruise Control: Adjusts your speed based on surrounding highway traffic.

Roll Sensing Airbags: Offer extra protection in a rollover–standard in many new cars.

Bicycle Detection: Alerts you when a bicycle has been detected.

Left Turn Crash Avoidance: Prevents a crash if turning left into the path of another car.

Adaptive Headlights: Increases vision by turning headlights when steering wheel turns.

FUEL ECONOMY

As gas prices bounce up and down, regular driving still takes a big bite out of our pocketbooks. Even at today's lower gas prices, the average household spends $1,500 a year on gas. The good news is that higher fuel efficiency standards are forcing car companies to provide more fuel efficient vehicles. Listed below are the best and worst of this year's ratings according to annual fuel cost. The complete EPA fuel economy guide is available at www.fueleconomy.gov.

FUEL ECONOMY MISERS AND GUZZLERS

Vehicle	Specifications	MPG (city/hwy)	Annual Fuel Cost
THE BEST	**Electric Vehicles (EV)***		
BMW I3 BEV	Automatic, RWD	137/111	$550
Chevrolet Bolt EV	Automatic, FWD	128/110	$550
Hyundai Ioniq Electric	Automatic, FWD	150/122	$500
Nissan LEAF	Automatic, FWD	124/101	$600
Kia Soul Electric	Automatic, FWD	124/93	$600
Plug In Hybrid Electric Vehicles (PHEVs)*			
Ford Fusion Energi Plug-in Hybrid	2.0L, 4 cyl., Continuously Variable, FWD	43/41	$750
Chrysler Pacifica Hybrid	3.6L, 6 cyl., Continuously Variable, FWD	32/33	$900
Audi A3 e-tron ultra	1.4L, 4 cyl., 6-sp. Automated Manual-Selectable, FWD	34/39	$1,000
Gas			
Hyundai Ioniq Blue	1.6L, 4 cyl., 6-sp. Automated Manual, FWD	57/59	$635
Honda Insight	1.5L, 4 cyl., 1-sp. Continuously Variable, FWD	55/49	$703
Hyundai Ioniq	1.6L, 4 cyl., 6-sp. Automated Manual, FWD	55/54	$674
Kia Niro FE	1.6L, 4 cyl., 6-sp. Automated Manual, FWD	52/49	$726
Honda Insight Touring	1.5L, 4 cyl., 1-sp. Continuously Variable, FWD	51/45	$761
Toyota Camry Hybrid LE	2.5L, 4 cyl., 6-sp. Selectable Cont. Variable, FWD	51/53	$708
Kia Niro	1.6L, 4 cyl., 6-sp. Automated Manual, FWD	51/46	$754
Chevrolet Malibu	1.8L, 4 cyl., 1-sp. Continuously Variable, FWD	49/43	$794
Toyota PRIUS c	1.5L, 4 cyl., 1-sp. Continuously Variable, FWD	48/43	$803
Honda Accord	2.0L, 4 cyl., 1-sp. Continuously Variable, FWD	48/48	$766
Kia Niro Touring	1.6L, 4 cyl., 6-sp. Automated Manual, FWD	46/40	$849
Toyota Camry Hybrid XLE/SE	2.5L, 4 cyl., 6-sp. Selectable Cont. Variable, FWD	44/47	$810
Ford Fusion Hybrid FWD	2.0L, 4 cyl., 1-sp. Continuously Variable, FWD	43/41	$873
Lexus ES 300h	2.5L, 4 cyl., 6-sp. Selectable Cont. Variable, FWD	43/45	$837
Toyota Avalon Hybrid	2.5L, 4 cyl., 6-sp. Selectable Cont. Variable, FWD	43/43	$855
Lincoln MKZ Hybrid FWD	2.0L, 4 cyl., 1-sp. Continuously Variable, FWD	42/39	$904
Hyundai Sonata Hybrid	2.0L, 4 cyl., 6-sp. Automated Manual, FWD	40/46	$861
Kia Optima Hybrid	2.0L, 4 cyl., 6-sp. Automated Manual, FWD	39/45	$881
Mitsubishi Mirage	1.2L, 3 cyl., 1-sp. Continuously Variable, FWD	36/43	$939
Mitsubishi Mirage	1.2L, 3 cyl., 5-sp. Manual, FWD	33/41	$1,004
THE WORST**			
Jeep Grand Cherokee Trackhawk 4x4	6.2L, 8 cyl., 8-sp. Automatic, AWD	11/17	$3,252
Mercedes-Benz AMG GLE 63	5.5L, 8 cyl., 7-sp. Automatic, 4WD	12/18	$3,031
Toyota Tundra 4WD	5.7L, 8 cyl., 6-sp. Semi-Automatic, 4WD	13/17	$2,483
Toyota Sequoia 2WD	5.7L, 8 cyl., 6-sp. Semi-Automatic, RWD	13/17	$2,483
Toyota Tundra 2WD	5.7L, 8 cyl., 6-sp. Semi-Automatic, RWD	13/18	$2,410
Lexus LX 570	5.7L, 8 cyl., 8-sp. Semi-Automatic, 4WD	13/18	$2,410
Mercedes-Benz AMG GLS 63	5.5L, 8 cyl., 7-sp. Automatic, 4WD	13/18	$2,410
Chevrolet Corvette	6.2L, 8 cyl., 8-sp. Semi-Automatic, RWD	12/20	$2,856
Chevrolet Corvette	6.2L, 8 cyl., 7-sp. Manual, RWD	13/19	$2,838
Dodge Durango SRT AWD	6.4L, 8 cyl., 8-sp. Automatic, AWD	13/19	$2,341
Infiniti QX80 4WD	5.6L, 8 cyl., 7-sp. Semi-Automatic, 4WD	13/19	$2,341
Jeep Grand Cherokee SRT 4x4	6.4L, 8 cyl., 8-sp. Automatic, AWD	13/19	$2,341
Land Rover Range Rover LWB SVA	5.0L, 8 cyl., 8-sp. Semi-Automatic, 4WD	13/19	$2,341
BMW M760i xDrive	6.6L, 12 cyl., 8-sp. Semi-Automatic, AWD	13/20	$2,759
Chevrolet Camaro	6.2L, 8 cyl., 10-sp. Semi-Automatic, RWD	13/21	$2,684
Mercedes-Benz AMG S 65 (coupe)	6L, 12 cyl., 7-sp. Automatic, RWD	13/21	$2,684
Dodge Challenger SRT	6.2L, 8 cyl., 6-sp. Manual, RWD	13/21	$2,684
Dodge Challenger SRT	6.2L, 8 cyl., 8-sp. Automatic, RWD	13/22	$2,613
Dodge Charger SRT	6.2L, 8 cyl., 8-sp. Automatic, RWD	13/22	$2,613
Mercedes-Benz AMG S 65	6.0L, 12 cyl., 7-sp. Automatic, RWD	13/22	$2,613

Note: 2020 annual fuel cost based on driving 15,000 miles and a projected regular gas price of $2.45; #=Premium Required; *=Annual cost based on epa estimate for electric use; **=Fuel Economy rating based on Hybrid function only; annual cost based on epa estimate for gas and electric use; ***=Low volume exotic vehicles (over $120,000) and cargo vans were excluded.

TWELVE WAYS TO SAVE MONEY AT THE PUMP

Here are a few simple things you can do that will save you a lot of money. Specific savings are based on gas at $2.45.

1. Pump 'Em Up: 27% of vehicles have tires that are underinflated. Properly inflated tires can improve mileage by 3%, which is like getting 7 cents off a gallon of gas. Check the label on your door or glove box to find out what the pressure range should be for your tires. Don't use the "max pressure" written on your tire. Electronic gauges are fast, easy to use and accurate. Don't rely on the numbers on the air pump. The good news–all new cars must have a low tire pressure warning on the dash.

2. Check Your Air Filter: A dirty air filter by itself can rob a car by as much as 10% of its mileage. If an engine doesn't get enough air, it will burn too much gasoline. Replacing a dirty filter can in effect knock up to 25 cents off a gallon of gas.

3. Straighten Out: Not only does poor wheel alignment cause your tires to wear out faster and cause poor handling, but it can cause your engine to work harder and reduce your fuel efficiency by 10%.

4. Be A Regular: Check your owner's manual. Very few cars actually need high-octane gas. Using 87-octane (regular) gas can save you over 28 cents per gallon over mid-grade and 52 cents over premium.

5. Tune Up: A properly tuned engine is a fuel saver. Have a trusted mechanic tune your engine to factory specifications and you could save up to 8 cents a gallon.

6. Check Your Cap: It is estimated that nearly 15% of the cars on the road have broken or missing gasoline caps. This hurts your mileage and can harm the environment by allowing your gasoline to evaporate. Many Ford products have a capless gas filler, which is a great convenience.

7. Don't Speed: A car moving at 55 mph gets better fuel economy than the same car at 65 mph. For every 5 mph you reduce your highway speed, you can reduce fuel consumption by 7%, which is like getting 17 cents off a gallon of gas.

8. Don't Idle: An idling car gets 0 mpg. Cars with larger engines typically waste more gas at idle than cars with smaller engines. If you're stopped for more than a minute, consider turning your engine off. Some new cars do that automatically.

9. Drive Smoother: The smoother your accelerations and decelerations, the better your mileage. A smooth foot can save 38 cents a gallon.

10. Combo Trips: Short trips can be expensive because they usually involve a "cold" vehicle. For the first mile or two before the engine gets warmed up, a cold vehicle only gets 30 to 40% of the mileage it gets at full efficiency. Combine your trips.

11. Lose Weight: For every 100 pounds you carry around, you lose 1 to 2% in fuel efficiency. Remove extra items from your trunk or the rear of your SUV. Empty your roof rack—50% of engine power, traveling at highway speed, is used in overcoming aerodynamic drag or wind resistance.

12. Choose Your Gas Miser: If you own more than one vehicle, choosing to drive the one with better gas mileage will save you money. If you drive 15,000 miles per year, half in a vehicle with 20 mpg and half with a 30 mpg vehicle and switch to driving 75% of your trips in the 30 mpg vehicle, you will save $153 annually with gas at $2.45.

FUEL ECONOMY

TIP

Get up-to-date information about fuel economy at www.fueleconomy.gov, a website created by the Department of Energy and the EPA. There you'll find the EPA's Fuel Economy Guide, allowing you to compare fuel economy estimates for today's models and back to 1985. You'll also find out about the latest technological advances pertaining to fuel efficiency. The site is extremely useful and easy to navigate. Also, see the Fuel Factor section on our car rating pages.

COMPARING WARRANTIES

After buying your car, maintenance will be a significant portion of your operating costs. The strength of your warranty and the cost of repairs after the warranty expires will determine these costs. Comparing warranties and repair costs before you buy can save you thousands of dollars down the road.

Along with your new car comes a warranty which is a promise from the manufacturer that the car will perform as it should. Most of us never read the warranty until it is too late. In fact, because warranties are often difficult to read and understand, most of us don't really know what our warranty covers.

To keep your warranty in effect, you must operate and maintain your car according to the instructions in your owner's manual. It is important to keep a record of all maintenance performed on your car.

Do not confuse a warranty with a service contract. A service contract must be purchased separately while a warranty is yours at no extra cost when you buy the car.

Warranties are difficult to compare because they contain fine print and confusing language. The following table will help you compare this year's warranties. Because the table does not contain all the details about each warranty, review the actual warranty to understand its fine points. You have the right to inspect a warranty before you buy—it's the law.

The table provides information on five critical items in a warranty:

The **Basic Warranty** covers most parts against a manufacturer's defects. Tires, batteries, and items added to the car at the time of sale are covered under separate warranties. The table describes coverage in terms of months and miles. For example, 48/50 means the warranty is good for 48 months or 50,000 miles, whichever comes first. This is the most important part of your warranty because it covers the items most likely to fail. We give the basic warranty the most weight.

The **Power Train Warranty** often lasts longer than the basic warranty. Because each manufacturer's definition of the power train is different, it is important to find out exactly what your warranty will cover. Power train coverage should include the engine, transmission, and drive train. Some luxury cars will cover additional systems such as steering, suspension, and electrical systems. We give the powertrain warranty less weight than the basic because it doesn't cover as much as the basic warranty. Even with less weight in our rating, it can have a lot of influence in the overall index if it is very long.

The **Corrosion Warranty** usually applies only to actual holes due to rust. Read this section carefully because many corrosion warranties do not apply to what the manufacturer may describe as cosmetic rust or bad paint.

The **Roadside Assistance** column indicates whether or not the manufacturer offers a program for helping with breakdowns, lockouts, jump starts, flat tires, running out of gas, and towing. Some have special limitations or added features. Because each one is different, check yours carefully.

The **Scheduled Maint. (Free)** column indicates whether or not free scheduled maintenance is included and for how long. These programs cover parts scheduled to be replaced such as filters. If there is an asterisk next to the coverage, that means the manufacturer also covers the cost of any parts that need to be replaced because of wear. Covering the cost of "wear" parts is a terrific feature and offered by very few manufacturers.

The last column, the **Warranty Rating Index**, provides an overall assessment of this year's warranties. **The higher the Index number, the better the warranty.** We give the most weight to the basic and power train components of the warranties. Roadside assistance was weighted somewhat less, and the corrosion warranty received the least weight.

Finally, we also considered special features such as extra coverage on batteries or wheel alignment. These benefits added to the overall ratings, whereas certain limitations (shortened transferability) took away from the rating.

The best ratings a **BOLD**.

BEST AND WORST WARRANTIES

Manufacturer Warranty	Basic Warranty	Power Train Warranty	Corrosion Assistance	Roadside Maint. (Free)	Scheduled Index	Warranty	Rating
Acura[1]	48/50	72/70	60/75	48/50		1106	Average
Audi	48/50	48/50	144/180	48/Unlimited	12/5	1203	Good
BMW[2]	**48/50**	**48/50**	**144/180**	**48/Unlimited**	**48/50**	**1288**	**Vry. Gd.**
Buick	48/50	72/70	72/90	72/90	24/24	1259	Good
Cadillac[3]	**48/50**	**72/70**	**72/90[4]**	**72/70**	**48/50**	**1320**	**Vry. Gd.**
Chevrolet	36/36	60/60[5]	72/90	60/60	24/24	1062	Average
Chrysler[6]	36/36	60/60[7]	60/75	60/60		1010	Poor
Dodge[8]	36/36	60/60[9]	60/75	60/60		1010	Poor
Fiat[10]	48/50	48/50	60/75[11]	48/50		1014	Average
Ford[12]	36/36	60/60	60/Unlimited	60/60		989	Poor
Genesis[13]	**60/60**	**120/100**	**72/Unlimited**	**60/60**	**36/36**	**1578**	**Vry. Gd.**
GMC	36/36	60/60	72/90	60/60	24/24	1026	Average
Honda[14]	36/36	60/60	60/Unlimited	36/36		912	Vry. Pr.
Hyundai[15]	**60/60**	**120/100[16]**	**84/Unlimited**	**60/Unlimited**		**1469**	**Vry. Gd.**
Infiniti[17]	**48/60**	**72/70**	**84/Unlimited**	**60/Unlimited**		**1299**	**Vry. Gd.**
Jeep[18]	36/36	60/60[19]	36/Unlimited	60/60		964	Poor
Kia[20]	**60/60**	**120/100[21]**	**60/10**	**60/60**		**1276**	**Vry. Gd.**
Land Rover	60/60	60/60	72/Unlimited	36/50	12/15	1169	Good
Lexus[22]	48/50	72/70	72/Unlimited	48/Unlimited	12/10	1200	Good
Lincoln[23]	**48/50**	**72/70**	**60/Unlimited**	**72/70[24]**	**24/24**	**1271**	**Vry. Gd.**
Mazda	36/36	60/60	36/Unlimited	36/36		846	Vry. Pr.
Mercedes-Benz[25]	48/50	48/50	48/50	48/50		937	Poor
Mini	**48/50**	**48/50**	**144/Unlimited**	**48/Unlimited**	**36/36**	**1280**	**Vry. Gd.**
Mitsubishi	**60/60**	**120/100**	**84/100[26]**	**60/Unlimited**		**1429**	**Vry. Gd.**
Nissan	36/36	60/60	60/Unlimited			798	Vry. Pr.
Porsche	48/50	48/50	144/180	48/50		1157	Good
Ram	60/60	60/60	36/Unlimited			930	Vry. Pr.
Subaru[27]	36/36	60/60	60/Unlimited	48/50		972	Poor
Tesla	**48/50**	**96/Unlimited**	**48/50**	**48/50**		**1357**	**Vry. Gd.**
Toyota	36/36	60/60	60/Unlimited	24/Unlimited	25/25	926	Vry. Pr.
Volkswagen	**72/72**	**72/72**	**120/120**	**36/36**	**12/12**	**1374**	**Vry. Gd.**
Volvo	48/50	48/50	120/Unlimited	48/Unlimited	36/36	1220	Good

[1] Wheel Alignment and Balancing 12/12
[2] Free Scheduled Maintenance includes wear parts but is not transferable
[3] Wheel Alignment and Balancing 12/7.5
[4] All Corrosion 48/50
[5] All Corrosion 36/36
[6] Wheel Alignment and Balancing 12/12
[7] All Corrosion 36/Unlimited
[8] Wheel Alignment and Balancing 12/12
[9] All Corrosion 36/Unlimited
[10] Wheel Alignment and Balancing 12/12
[11] All Corrosion 36/Unlimited

[12] Wheel Alignment and Balancing 12/12; Brake Pads 12/18
[13] Free Scheduled Maintenance includes wear parts but is not transferable
[14] Wheel Alignment and Balancing 12/12
[15] Wheel Alignment and Balancing 12/12; Wear Items 12/12
[16] Only transferable up to 60/60
[17] Wheel Alignment and Balancing 12/12
[18] Wheel Alignment and Balancing 12/12
[19] All Corrosion 36/Unlimited
[20] Wheel Alignment and Balancing 12/12

[21] Transferable only to 60/60
[22] Wheel Alignment and Balancing 12/12
[23] Wheel Alignment and Balancing 12/12; Brake Pads 12/18
[24] Lifetime for original owner
[25] Wheel Alignment and Balancing 12/12
[26] Transferable only up to 60/60
[27] Wear Items 36/36

SECRET WARRANTIES AND TECHNICAL SERVICE BULLETINS

If dealers report a lot of complaints about a certain part or system and the manufacturer determines that the problem is due to faulty design or assembly, the manufacturer may permit dealers to repair the problem at no charge to the customer, even though the warranty is expired. In the past, this practice was often reserved for customers who made a big fuss. The availability of the free repair was never publicized, which is why we call these "secret warranties."

Manufacturers deny the existence of secret warranties. They call these free repairs "policy adjustments" or "goodwill service." Whatever they are called, most consumers never hear about them. Many secret warranties are disclosed in technical service bulletins that the manufacturers send to dealers. These bulletins outline free repair or reimbursement programs, as well as other problems and their possible causes and solutions.

Technical service bulletins from manufacturers must, by law, be sent to, and be on file at, the National Highway Traffic Safety Administration (NHTSA). In 2012, Congress required NHTSA to make all of these bulletins, and an accompanying index, publicly available through NHTSA's website. However, the agency did not take sufficient steps to fulfill this obligation. In 2016, the Center for Auto Safety sued the Department of Transportation to force it to comply with the congressional mandate to begin publishing all service bulletins and related manufacturer communications. The court ruled for the Center, on behalf of consumers and forced NHTSA to publish all service bulletins online. The Center for

Auto Safety continues to monitor the agency's progress to ensure the up-to-date service bulletins are posted in a timely fashion.

To view service bulletins on your vehicle, visit www.nhtsa.gov/recall to look up your vehicle by VIN, or make and model, and then click on "Manufacturer Communications" to view a list of all available communications between the automaker and dealers, the great majority of which are service bulletins.

Additionally, you can look up all service bulletins relating to your car at the Center's website at www.autosafety.org/vehicle-safety-check. While there, take advantage of a members-only feature which enables you to get a customized monthly email Safety Tune-Up Report, listing all new service bulletins on your car!

Secret Warranty Disclosure Laws: Spurred by the proliferation of secret warranties and the failure of the FTC to take action, California, Connecticut, Virginia, Wisconsin, and Maryland have passed legislation that requires

consumers to be notified of secret warranties on their cars. Several other states have introduced similar warranty bills. You can find out more online through your state attorney general or consumer protection division website.

Typically, disclosure laws require the following: direct notice to consumers within a specified time after the adoption of a warranty adjustment policy; notice of the disclosure law to new car buyers; reimbursement within a number of years after payment to owners who paid for covered repairs before they learned of the extended warranty service; and dealers must inform consumers who complain about a covered defect that it is eligible for repair under warranty.

If you live in a state with a secret warranty law already in effect, write your state attorney general's office (in care of your state capitol) for information. To encourage passage of such a bill, contact your state representatives (in care of your state capitol).

LITTLE SECRETS OF THE AUTO INDUSTRY

Some state lemon laws require dealers and manufacturers to give you copies of technical service bulletins on problems affecting your vehicle. These bulletins may alert you to a secret warranty on your vehicle or help you make the case for a free repair if there isn't a secret warranty. See page 42 for an overview of your state's lemon law. If you would like to see the complete law, go to www.autosafety.org/lemon-laws-state to view your state's lemon laws. To see technical service bulletins on your vehicle you can also use the Center for Auto Safety's "Vehicle Safety Check" features at www.autosafety.org.

KEEPING IT GOING

Comparing maintenance costs before you buy can help decide which car to purchase. These costs include preventive maintenance servicing—such as changing the oil and filters—as well as the cost of repairs after your warranty expires. The following tables enable you to compare the costs of preventive maintenance and nine likely repairs.

Preventive Maintenance: The first column in the table is the periodic servicing, specified by the manufacturer, that keeps your car running properly. For example, regularly changing the oil and oil filter. Every owner's manual specifies a schedule of recommended servicing for at least the first 60,000 miles and many now go to 100,000 miles. The tables on the following pages estimate the labor cost of following this preventive maintenance schedule for 60,000 miles, the length of a typical warranty. Service parts are not included in this total.

Repair Costs: The tables also list the costs for nine repairs that typically occur during the first 100,000 miles. There is no precise way to predict exactly when a repair will be needed. But if you keep a car for 75,000 to 100,000 miles, it is likely that you will experience many of these repairs at least once. The last column provides a relative indication of how expensive these nine repairs are for many cars. Repair cost is rated as Very Good if the total for nine repairs is in the lowest fifth of all the cars rated, and Very Poor if the total is in the highest fifth. Most repair shops use "flat-rate manuals" to estimate repair costs. These manuals list the approximate time required for repairing many items. Each automobile manufacturer publishes its own manual and there are several independent manuals as well. For many repairs, the time varies from one manual to another. Some repair shops even use different manuals for different repairs. To determine a repair bill, a shop multiplies the time listed in its manual by its hourly labor rate and then adds the cost of parts. Some dealers and repair shops create their own maintenance schedules which call for more frequent (and thus more expensive) servicing than the manufacturer's recommendations. If the service recommended by your dealer or repair shop doesn't match what the manufacturer recommends, make sure you understand and agree to the extra items. Our cost estimates are based on published repair times multiplied by a nationwide average labor rate of $90 per hour and include the cost of replaced parts and related adjustments. Prices in the following tables may not predict the exact costs of these repairs. For example, labor rates for your area may be more or less than the national average. However, the prices will provide you with a relative comparison of costs for various automobiles. Finally, for many of the electric vehicles, you'll see a $0. That's because the EV doesn't have that part. This is one reason why EVs can be less expensive to maintain.

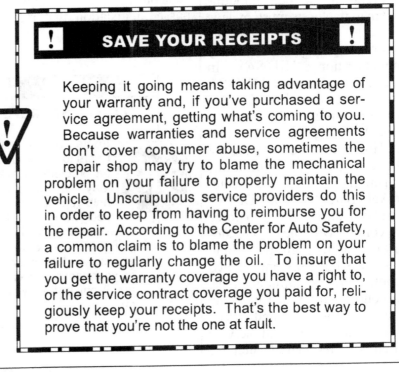

! SAVE YOUR RECEIPTS !

Keeping it going means taking advantage of your warranty and, if you've purchased a service agreement, getting what's coming to you. Because warranties and service agreements don't cover consumer abuse, sometimes the repair shop may try to blame the mechanical problem on your failure to properly maintain the vehicle. Unscrupulous service providers do this in order to keep from having to reimburse you for the repair. According to the Center for Auto Safety, a common claim is to blame the problem on your failure to regularly change the oil. To insure that you get the warranty coverage you have a right to, or the service contract coverage you paid for, religiously keep your receipts. That's the best way to prove that you're not the one at fault.

	PM Costs to 60,000 Miles	REPAIR COSTS									Relative Repair Cost*
		Front Brake Pads	Starter	Fuel Injector	Fuel Pump	Struts/ Shocks	Timing Belt/ Chain	Water Pump	Muffler	Headlamps	
Subcompact											
BMW i3	1009	177	0	0	0	232	0	896	0	1504	Vry. Gd.
Chevrolet Sonic	545	253	346	129	427	159	417	410	722	801	Vry. Gd.
Chevrolet Spark	545	235	286	173	449	181	877	448	478	884	Good
Ford Escape	764	213	438	203	400	219	1093	321	1680	941	Poor
Honda Fit	482	173	415	286	468	398	523	300	268	683	Vry. Gd.
Hyundai Accent	873	171	383	362	447	121	463	248	387	340	Vry. Gd.
Hyundai Veloster	891	181	377	180	460	289	375	311	433	776	Vry. Gd.
Kia Rio	782	190	398	242	357	197	464	288	452	641	Vry. Gd.
Mazda MX-5	873	220	380	253	504	349	490	279	658	1508	Average
Mini Cooper	927	236	582	221	613	358	828	491	530	1373	Poor
Mitsubishi Mirage	618	209	539	296	142	226	469	482	444	1352	Good
Nissan Versa	600	220	430	300	535	196	447	225	392	707	Vry. Gd.
Toyota Yaris	491	202	437	276	486	149	636	259	289	342	Vry. Gd.
Compact											
Acura ILX	582	195	638	516	568	349	454	375	376	943	Good
Audi A3	1391	220	595	387	388	468	520	582	635	1080	Average
Audi A4	982	255	870	380	625	821	740	742	704	609	Vry. Pr.
BMW 2 Series	1009	284	659	516	305	311	1227	787	853	757	Poor
BMW 3 Series	954	284	659	516	299	588	1232	787	940	934	Vry. Pr.
BMW 4 Series	954	284	659	516	299	588	1232	787	940	934	Vry. Pr.
Chevrolet Bolt	836	212	0	0	0	130	0	394	0	1040	Vry. Gd.
Honda Civic	427	173	654	203	556	200	583	318	337	702	Good
Hyundai Elantra	991	150	365	240	324	190	504	259	390	833	Vry. Gd.
Kia Forte	591	190	228	215	335	174	511	325	339	596	Vry. Gd.
Kia Soul	964	190	417	281	315	170	603	346	458	1015	Good
Lexus IS	764	179	1031	678	482	351	1358	574	472	1523	Vry. Pr.
Lexus RC	809	179	847	602	539	297	1385	668	462	1721	Vry. Pr.
Mazda 3	800	203	363	298	612	208	471	307	453	732	Vry. Gd.
Mercedes-Benz C-Class	1300	221	571	365	892	423	413	698	983	1080	Poor
Nissan Leaf	673	188	0	0	0	232	0	690	0	1409	Vry. Gd.
Nissan Sentra	709	201	368	376	537	168	606	334	444	658	Vry. Gd.
Subaru Impreza	1018	201	580	243	458	382	581	387	413	469	Good
Toyota 86	982	218	690	616	741	355	706	409	653	999	Poor
Toyota Corolla	554	176	452	342	488	188	1136	299	434	660	Good
Toyota Corolla iM	518	179	511	326	455	333	656	273	407	539	Vry.Gd.
Toyota Prius	564	210	0	683	524	164	1231	376	495	1285	Average
Toyota Prius Prime	564	185	0	308	471	351	1332	726	299	709	Good
Volkswagen Golf	1100	209	738	226	394	421	566	489	492	614	Good
Volkswagen Jetta	927	195	720	455	578	410	615	712	760	753	Poor
Intermediate											
Acura TLX	945	175	860	671	520	335	427	328	748	1483	Poor
Audi A5	982	255	726	370	548	471	736	748	834	671	Poor
Audi A6	982	285	946	1706	609	426	666	693	717	622	Vry. Pr.
BMW 5 Series	573	287	649	447	578	492	1366	740	1120	1065	Vry. Pr.
Buick Regal	1264	352	663	350	428	279	526	826	1172	1075	Poor
Chevrolet Camaro	1264	346	359	401	658	282	719	457	921	715	Average
Chevrolet Corvette	1291	385	391	545	683	232	1335	319	1445	1409	Vry. Pr.
Chevrolet Malibu	718	288	396	356	444	247	545	516	692	500	Good
AVERAGE OF ALL VEHICLES	**$920**	**$241**	**$494**	**$376**	**$516**	**$316**	**$832**	**$497**	**$682**	**$972**	

	PM Costs to 60,000 Miles	REPAIR COSTS									Relative Repair Cost*
		Front Brake Pads	Starter	Fuel Injector	Fuel Pump	Struts/ Shocks	Timing Belt/ Chain	Water Pump	Muffler	Headlamps	
Intermediate (cont.)											
Ford Fusion	691	298	279	329	279	113	654	195	599	946	Vry. Gd.
Ford Fusion Energi	854	187	0	133	326	132	592	225	422	1043	Vry. Gd.
Ford Mustang	609	240	204	219	247	166	845	274	968	1472	Average
Honda Accord	509	183	557	501	606	263	432	339	479	1106	Average
Hyundai Sonata	900	181	315	255	359	154	729	329	680	833	Good
Infiniti Q50	891	193	523	427	526	547	762	277	646	1467	Poor
Kia Optima	873	190	247	281	345	165	612	269	339	633	Vry. Gd.
Lexus ES	873	217	568	450	498	458	1543	423	542	1446	Vry. Pr.
Lexus GS	664	178	889	760	496	243	1851	622	581	1707	Vry. Pr.
Lincoln MKZ	691	224	297	398	504	300	1210	364	1113	1448	Vry. Pr.
Mazda 6	807	212	257	578	562	239	562	238	379	709	Good
Nissan Altima	964	215	354	354	430	237	664	282	432	710	Vry. Gd.
Nissan Maxima	836	199	429	440	487	234	908	432	696	925	Average
Subaru Legacy	1200	195	472	233	454	330	636	387	281	504	Vry. Gd.
Tesla Model 3	709	216	0	0	0	278	0	922	0	1337	Vry. Gd.
Toyota Avalon	873	229	568	450	498	359	1571	423	409	619	Poor
Toyota Camry	873	217	587	479	507	323	1534	480	413	1127	Poor
Volkswagen Passat	927	197	773	267	512	384	969	485	754	680	Average
Volvo S60	918	263	544	420	887	226	509	511	705	573	Average
Volvo V60	1127	254	486	420	887	234	608	511	580	610	Average
Large											
BMW 7 Series	1264	349	773	629	617	2104	1408	869	1110	2016	Vry. Pr.
Cadillac CT6	1191	352	691	597	600	367	674	685	834	1061	Vry. Pr.
Chevrolet Impala	1264	283	403	459	532	205	780	518	656	713	Average
Chrysler 300	636	239	253	238	455	879	765	379	1826	1257	Vry. Pr.
Dodge Challenger	636	478	309	218	778	263	687	284	1012	1471	Poor
Dodge Charger	636	307	254	218	624	155	650	314	1144	669	Good
Genesis G80	1054	268	484	227	450	341	1264	391	617	1109	Poor
Lincoln Continental	909	240	278	322	445	490	1164	514	1143	1469	Vry. Pr.
Mercedes-Benz E-Class	1027	215	887	538	520	311	1169	794	1183	1244	Vry. Pr.
Mercedes-Benz S-Class	1027	250	727	466	552	763	408	990	1548	1662	Vry. Pr.
Tesla Model S	709	244	0	0	0	306	0	1065	0	1447	Vry. Gd.
Minivan											
Chrysler Pacifica	509	313	481	203	517	318	909	356	1003	621	Average
Honda Odyssey	545	192	584	211	519	153	359	491	683	727	Good
Kia Sedona	1000	190	266	339	420	226	761	332	577	404	Vry. Gd.
Toyota Sienna	1127	176	569	441	709	184	1404	564	581	707	Poor
Small SUV											
Acura RDX	918	446	573	277	566	277	339	435	549	1406	Average
Audi Q3	982	220	757	418	343	673	777	672	404	1288	Poor
BMW X1	791	281	750	568	659	435	1325	807	1101	1373	Vry. Pr.
Buick Encore	727	369	287	118	461	206	741	378	640	673	Good
Cadillac XT4	1264	237	434	448	391	176	1071	541	987	990	Poor
Chevrolet Equinox	1291	352	478	484	773	169	832	492	1073	822	Poor
Chevrolet Trax	782	207	331	122	588	230	1057	520	841	1021	Average
Fiat 500X	636	195	330	425	606	105	373	476	341	713	Vry. Gd.
Ford EcoSport	764	210	356	225	472	287	1000	213	514	1067	Good
GMC Terrain	1291	352	478	484	773	169	832	492	1073	935	Poor
Honda CR-V	509	173	644	364	517	242	425	271	428	780	Good
AVERAGE OF ALL VEHICLES	**$920**	**$241**	**$494**	**$376**	**$516**	**$316**	**$832**	**$497**	**$682**	**$972**	

	PM Costs to 60,000 Miles	Front Brake Pads	Starter	Fuel Injector	Fuel Pump	Struts/ Shocks	Timing Belt/ Chain	Water Pump	Muffler	Headlamps	Relative Repair Cost*
Small SUV (Cont.)											
Honda HR-V	754	183	678	158	491	219	453	333	416	799	Good
Hyundai Kona	809	155	410	157	333	228	475	448	661	715	Vry. Gd.
Hyundai Tucson	982	185	374	322	349	197	312	348	611	652	Vry. Gd.
Infiniti QX50	600	201	591	328	531	307	819	782	724	1529	Vry. Pr.
Jeep Compass	455	207	394	135	469	366	513	354	490	389	Vry. Gd.
Jeep Renegade	954	350	781	144	412	495	559	396	570	464	Good
Jeep Wrangler	409	258	254	307	599	146	761	400	406	268	Vry. Gd.
Kia Sportage	936	190	247	250	344	249	538	367	658	1498	Good
Land Rover Range Rover Evoque	864	322	617	539	732	616	629	314	754	538	Average
Lexus NX	1445	165	607	607	526	249	1340	550	871	673	Poor
Lincoln Corsair	1254	288	443	406	614	288	983	528	745	1398	Poor
Mazda CX-3	782	210	391	378	343	234	426	260	423	743	Vry. Gd.
Mazda CX-5	718	190	411	369	352	232	405	253	498	634	Vry. Gd.
Mercedes-Benz GLA-Class	491	372	778	581	582	445	405	924	876	1396	Vry. Pr.
Mercedes-Benz GLC-Class	1073	382	718	570	554	495	391	877	876	1419	Vry. Pr.
Mitsubishi Outlander Sport	800	200	541	370	727	283	531	549	483	1185	Average
Subaru Crosstrek1018	195	580	243	458	383	581	387	415	473	Good	Subaru
Forester	1036	201	628	557	480	348	636	478	425	510	Good
Toyota RAV4	973	223	549	304	612	132	1100	338	315	611	Good
Volkswagen Tiguan	1064	195	720	432	578	430	624	711	779	744	Poor
Medium SUV											
Acura MDX	945	355	604	1398	725	293	386	533	768	1247	Vry. Pr.
Audi Q5	982	297	780	484	630	441	800	729	943	670	Vry. Pr.
Audi Q7	1091	309	1081	793	497	741	1448	401	1039	763	Vry. Pr.
BMW X3	1254	284	773	563	624	526	1097	897	1229	1728	Vry. Pr.
BMW X5	1064	355	735	559	664	580	1857	786	2176	2305	Vry. Pr.
BMW X6	1118	386	686	464	831	502	838	1211	1720	2507	Vry. Pr.
Buick Envision	1182	320	469	218	518	780	814	462	644	1129	Poor
Cadillac XT5	1264	237	434	448	391	176	1071	541	987	990	Poor
Cadillac XT6	1264	237	434	448	391	176	1071	541	987	990	Poor
Chevrolet Blazer	1218	317	410	321	542	187	1181	489	650	1323	Poor
Dodge Durango	927	258	510	246	553	436	955	322	568	880	Average
Dodge Journey	591	258	434	250	775	339	946	436	1490	333	Poor
Ford Edge	864	253	190	246	415	263	1025	314	868	1085	Average
Ford Explorer	918	187	241	219	495	149	864	509	870	1226	Average
GMC Acadia	1218	317	410	321	542	187	1181	489	650	1323	Poor
Honda Pilot	527	194	531	297	661	226	433	557	681	870	Good
Hyundai Palisade	1254	288	443	406	614	288	983	528	745	1398	Poor
Hyundai Santa Fe	982	200	315	298	471	253	551	318	622	1265	Good
Infiniti QX60	1100	199	517	429	510	360	1086	268	745	1518	Poor
Jeep Cherokee	436	258	552	198	708	313	983	440	943	548	Average
Jeep Grand Cherokee	636	258	510	246	489	252	955	307	877	622	Average
Kia Sorento	945	199	246	282	514	223	566	305	604	1034	Good
Kia Telluride	1254	288	443	406	614	288	983	528	745	1398	Poor
Land Rover Range Rover Sport	1291	279	709	677	672	423	1325	400	501	296	Poor
Lexus RX	909	259	772	327	496	140	2043	1172	730	2333	Vry. Pr.
Lincoln MKX	764	232	190	219	396	259	1016	514	737	1190	Average
Mazda CX-9	800	214	330	240	605	322	1125	1110	642	911	Poor
Mercedes-Benz GLE-Class	1064	371	715	603	592	476	378	896	910	1396	Vry. Pr.
Mitsubishi Outlander	991	199	431	314	660	250	522	465	426	785	Good
Nissan Murano	709	222	527	442	640	313	910	513	663	1216	Poor
AVERAGE OF ALL VEHICLES	**$920**	**$241**	**$494**	**$376**	**$516**	**$316**	**$832**	**$497**	**$682**	**$972**	

	PM Costs to 60,000 Miles	REPAIR COSTS								
		Front Brake Pads	Starter	Fuel Injector	Fuel Pump	Struts/ Shocks	Timing Belt/ Chain	Water Pump	Muffler	Head-lamps	Relative Repair Cost*
Medium SUV (cont.)											
Nissan Pathfinder	1454	222	653	442	626	221	972	529	713	835	Poor
Nissan Rogue	1064	199	462	440	532	170	949	354	619	1400	Poor
Porsche Macan	1091	438	580	447	557	588	1170	526	1279	1047	Vry. Pr.
Subaru Outback	1200	201	472	234	468	348	627	387	300	504	Vry. Gd.
Tesla Model X	709	244	0	0	0	315	0	1065	0	1447	Vry. Gd.
Toyota 4Runner	564	173	617	389	639	139	1691	634	579	509	Poor
Toyota Highlander	727	176	536	469	601	114	1793	282	272	553	Average
Volkswagen Atlas	1091	266	768	541	492	491	1420	787	962	1351	Vry. Pr.
Volvo XC60	918	321	641	476	902	283	357	511	525	657	Average
Volvo XC90	1054	279	661	439	745	333	549	1012	606	1290	Vry.Pr.
Large SUV											
Buick Enclave	1218	327	434	438	621	164	802	711	668	1418	Poor
Cadillac Escalade	1291	251	339	382	630	823	1006	424	1255	1653	Vry. Pr.
Cadillac Escalade ESV	1291	251	339	382	655	823	1006	424	1299	1653	Vry. Pr.
Chevrolet Suburban	1291	251	349	388	658	219	1252	390	741	647	Average
Chevrolet Tahoe	1291	235	349	388	683	213	1252	537	1150	638	Poor
Chevrolet Traverse	1218	313	424	457	618	161	1247	588	556	741	Average
Ford Flex	809	177	222	219	275	195	1051	547	1015	823	Average
Ford Expedition	1109	191	243	161	396	199	734	210	495	991	Vry. Gd.
GMC Yukon	1291	235	349	388	683	213	1252	537	1150	768	Poor
Infiniti QX80	1091	223	508	344	487	230	1302	320	540	1393	Poor
Land Rover Range Rover	882	279	709	677	672	502	1232	400	501	295	Poor
Lexus GX	827	173	819	446	629	127	1264	495	791	1369	Vry. Pr.
Lincoln Navigator	1136	191	214	246	415	299	947	298	524	1396	Average
Mercedes-Benz GLS-Class	1073	351	737	596	592	495	387	842	832	1430	Vry. Pr.
Nissan Armada	1091	199	529	318	538	386	1124	311	660	952	Average
Subaru Ascent	1073	214	600	240	484	558	295	482	347	476	Vry. Gd.
Toyota Sequoia	827	217	989	323	724	389	1367	478	368	394	Poor
Compact Pickup											
Chevrolet Colorado	1291	258	508	398	435	187	503	440	365	699	Good
Ford Ranger	1185	221	563	477	593	133	581	517	493	730	Average
GMC Canyon	1291	258	508	398	435	187	503	440	365	736	Good
Nissan Frontier	1091	222	563	395	712	171	901	378	468	451	Good
Toyota Tacoma	564	201	654	554	617	108	1469	525	533	574	Poor
Standard Pickup											
Chevrolet Silverado	1291	285	459	407	643	176	1265	390	755	652	Average
Ford F-150	618	191	224	531	419	121	838	537	388	630	Good
GMC Sierra	1291	285	459	407	643	176	1265	390	793	792	Average
Nissan Titan	1127	194	596	317	578	207	1305	323	624	772	Average
Ram 1500	673	175	310	151	433	185	530	429	421	475	Vry. Gd.
Toyota Tundra	827	175	1041	323	559	128	1265	440	654	429	Average
AVERAGE OF ALL VEHICLES	$920	$241	$494	$376	$516	$316	$832	$497	$682	$972	

SERVICE CONTRACTS

Service contracts are one of the most expensive options you can buy. In fact, service contracts are a major profit source for many dealers.

A service contract is not a warranty. It is more like an insurance plan that, in theory, covers repairs that are not covered by your warranty or that occur after the warranty runs out. They are often inaccurately referred to as "extended warranties."

Service contracts are generally a poor value. The companies who sell contracts are very sure that, on average, your repairs will cost considerably less than what you pay for the contract—if not, they wouldn't be in business.

Here are some important questions to ask before buying a service contract:

How reputable is the company responsible for the contract? If the company offering the contract goes out of business, you will be out of luck. The company may be required to be insured, but find out if they actually are and by whom. Check with your Better Business Bureau or office of consumer affairs if you are not sure of a company's reputation. Service contracts from car and insurance companies are more likely to remain in effect than those from independent companies.

Exactly what does the contract cover and for how long? Service contracts vary considerably—different items are covered and different time limits are offered. This is true even among service contracts offered by the same company. For example, one company has plans that range from 4 years/36,000 miles maximum coverage to 6 years/100,000 miles maximum coverage, with other options for only power train coverage. Make sure you know what components are covered because if a breakdown occurs on a part that is not covered, you are responsible for the repairs.

If you plan to resell your car in a few years, you won't want to purchase a long-running service contract. Some service contracts automatically cancel when you resell the car, while others require a hefty transfer fee before extending privileges to the new owner. Check out the transferability of the service contract.

Some automakers offer a "menu" format, which lets you pick the items you want covered in your service contract. Find out if the contract pays for preventive maintenance, towing, and rental car expenses. If not written into the contract, assume they are not covered.

Make sure the contract clearly specifies how you can reach the company. Knowing this before you purchase a service contract can save you time and aggravation in the future.

How will the repair bills be paid? It is best to have the service contractor pay bills directly. Some contracts require you to pay the repair bill, and reimburse you later. This can be a major hassle.

Where can the car be serviced? Can you take the car to any mechanic if you have trouble on the road? What if you move?

What other costs can be expected? Most service contracts will have a deductible expense, which means you will have to pay part of the repair cost. Compare deductibles on various plans. Also, some companies charge the deductible for each individual repair while other companies pay per visit, regardless of the number of repairs being made.

What are your responsibilities? Make sure you know what you have to do to uphold the contract. For example if you have to follow the manufacturer's recommended maintenance, keep detailed records or the contract could be voided. You will find your specific responsibilities in the contact. Be sure to have the seller point them out.

SERVICE CONTRACTS VS. SAVINGS ACCOUNT

TIP

One alternative to buying a service contract is to deposit the cost of the contract into a savings account. If the car needs a major repair not covered by your warranty, the money in your account is likely to cover the cost. Most likely, you'll be building up a down payment for your next car!

Insurance is a big part of ownership expenses, yet it's often forgotten in the show-room. As you shop, remember that the car's design and accident history may affect your insurance rates. Some cars cost less to insure because experience has shown that they are damaged less, less expensive to fix after a collision, or stolen less.

Auto insurance covers different aspects of damage and injury. The term "first party" refers to you and "third party" means someone else who was involved in a crash with your vehicle. The critical parts of your insurance are:

Liability (third party): This pays for damage or injury you or your vehicle may inflict on others. It is generally limited (in some cases to only $10,000 but may be several hundred thousand dollars) so that if you severely or fatally injure someone, the liability insurance will not be adequate to pay the costs. For minor or moderate damage or injury, insurance companies generally negotiate payments, but for major ones, there may be lawsuits.

Collision Damage (first party): This pays for crash damage to your own car when no other party is found to be at fault for the accident. If you lease your vehicle or have an outstanding loan on it, you will be required to have collision damage insurance.

Uninsured or Underinsured drivers: This pays your expenses when someone else is at fault, but lacks sufficient insurance or personal resources to pay for the damage or injury. The amount typically covers property damage, but may not cover serious injuries.

Comprehensive (first party): This covers the cost of some types of damage not related to crashes including theft.

Supplementary Insurance: Additional forms of insurance that may apply when auto insurance doesn't cover loss are health insurance, which may pay the cost of more serious injuries, life insurance which pays if you are killed in a crash and umbrella policy insurance which may pay liability costs beyond what is covered by your auto policy. An umbrella policy may be important if you want to protect assets such as savings, your house or business, or other major assets.

Shop Around: You can save hundreds of dollars by shopping around for insurance.

There are a number of factors that determine what coverage will cost you. A car's design can affect both the chances and severity of an accident. For example, a well-designed bumper, which few cars have, may escape damage in a low-speed crash. Some cars are easier to repair than others or may have less expensive parts. Cars with four doors tend to be damaged less than cars with two doors.

Other factors that affect your insurance costs include:

Your Annual Mileage: The more you drive, the more your vehicle will be "exposed" to a potential accident. Driving less than 5,000 to 7,500 miles per year often gets a discount. Ask your insurer if they offer this option.

Where You Drive and Park: If you regularly drive and park in the city, you will most likely pay more than if you drive in rural areas. You may get a discount if you garage your car.

Youthful Drivers: Usually the highest premiums are paid by male drivers under the age of 25. Whether or not the under-25-year-old male is married also affects insurance rates. (Married males pay less.) As the driver gets older, and if he or she has good driving record, rates are lowered.

Insurance discounts and surcharges depend upon the way a vehicle is traditionally driven. Sports cars, for example, are usually surcharged due, in part, to the typical driving habits of their owners. Four-door sedans and station wagons generally merit discounts. Not all companies offer discounts or surcharges, and many cars receive neither. Some companies offer a discount or impose a surcharge on collision premiums only. Others apply discounts and surcharges on both

REDUCING INSURANCE COSTS

collision and comprehensive coverage. Discounts and surcharges usually range from 10 to 30 percent. Remember that one company may offer a discount on a particular car while another may not.

Major crashes are rare events for individuals, but more than 37,000 people are killed and double that number suffer serious injuries in crashes each year. In a very severe crash with major injury or death, the limits on first and third party auto insurance will be inadequate to cover the costs. NHTSA estimates that the economic cost of a fatality may range from several million to more than ten million dollars, and injuries such as quadriplegia and serious brain damage could easily have a lifetime cost of ten million dollars for each individual. If a crash is not deemed to be the fault of another motorist (such as with a single vehicle crash), your health insurance may cover the cost of your injuries, but is unlikely to cover such things as long-term rehabilitation and loss of income.

Get Your Discounts: After you have shopped around and found the best deal by comparing the costs of different coverages, be sure you get all the discounts you are entitled to.

Most insurance companies offer discounts of 5 to 30 percent on various parts of your insurance bill. Ask your insurance company for a complete list of the discounts that it offers. These can vary by company and from state to state.

Here are some of the most common insurance discounts:

Driver Education/Defensive Driving Courses: Discounts for completing a state-approved driver education course can mean a $40 reduction in the cost of coverage. Discounts of 5 to 15 percent are available in some states to those who complete a defensive driving course.

Good Student Discounts of up to 25 percent for full-time high school or college students who are in the upper 20 percent of their class, on the dean's list, or have a B or better grade point average.

Good Driver Discounts are available to drivers with an accident and violation-free record, (or no incidents in the past 3 years).

Mature Driver Credit: Drivers ages 50 and older may qualify for up to a 10 percent discount or a lower price bracket.

Sole Female Driver: Some companies offer discounts of 10 percent for females, ages 30 to 64, who are the only driver in a household.

Non-Drinkers and Non-Smokers: A few companies offer incentives ranging from 10–25 percent to those who abstain.

Farmer Discounts: Many companies offer farmers either a 10 to 30 percent discount or a lower price bracket.

Car Pooling: Commuters sharing driving may qualify for discounts of 5 to 25 percent or a lower price bracket.

Children Away at School: Students enrolled in school away from their family don't

! DON'T SPEED !

Besides endangering the lives of your passengers and other drivers, speeding tickets will increase your insurance premium. It only takes one speeding ticket to lose your "preferred" or "good driver" discount, which requires a clean driving record. Two or more speeding tickets or accidents can increase your premium by 40% to 200%. Some insurers may simply drop your coverage. According to the Insurance Institute for Highway Safety (IIHS), you are 17% more likely to be in an accident if you have just one speeding ticket. Insurance companies know this and will charge you for it.

drive the family car very often, so if they're on your policy, let your company know. If you insure them separately, discounts of 10–40 percent or a lower price bracket are available.

Desirable Cars: Premiums are usually much higher for cars that are the favorite target of thieves.

Anti-Theft Device Credits: Discounts of 5-15 percent are offered in some states for cars equipped with a hood lock and an alarm or a disabling device (active or passive) that prevents the car from being started without a key.

Multi-policy and Multicar Policy Discount: Some companies offer discounts of up to 10–20 percent for insuring your home and auto with the same company, or more than one car.

First Accident Allowance: Some insurers offer a "first accident allowance," which guarantees that if a customer achieves a certain number of accident-free years, his or her rates won't go up after the first at-fault accident.

Deductibles: Opting for the largest deductible you're comfortable with will reduce your premiums. Increasing your deductible to $500 from $200 could cut your collision premium about 20 percent. Raising the deductible to $1,000 from $200 could lower your premium

about 45 percent. The discounts may vary by company.

Collision Coverage: The older the car, the less the need for collision insurance. Consider dropping collision insurance entirely on an older car. Regardless of how much coverage you carry, the insurance company will only pay up to the car's "book value." For example, if your car requires $1,000 in

repairs, but its "book value" is only $500, the insurance company is required to pay only $500.

Organizations: If you are a member of AARP, AAA, the military, a union, a professional group, an alumni association, or similar organization, you may be able to get lower cost insurance or a discount.

YOUNG DRIVERS

Each year, teenagers account for about 15 percent of highway deaths. According to the Insurance Institute for Highway Safety (IIHS), the highest driver death rate per 100,000 people is among 18-year-olds. Parents need to make sure their children are fully prepared to be competent, safe drivers before letting them out on the road. All states issue learner's permits. However, only 35 states and the District of Columbia require permits before getting a driver's license. It isn't difficult for teenagers to get a license and only 14 states prohibit teenagers from driving during night and early morning. Call your state's MVA for young driver laws.

Because of the challenges in learning how to drive safely, parents should not to let their teenagers drive an older SUV, very small car, or one without airbags.

Americans spend billions of dollars on vehicle repairs every year. While many of those repairs are satisfactory, there are times when getting your vehicle fixed can be a very difficult process. In fact, vehicle defects and repairs are the number one cause of consumer complaints, according to the Federal Trade Commission. This chapter is designed to help you if you have a complaint, whether it's for a new vehicle still under warranty, or for one you've had for years. In addition, we offer a guide to arbitration, the names and addresses of consumer groups, federal agencies, and the manufacturers themselves. Finally, we tell you how to take the important step of registering your complaint, particularly if it involves safety, with the U.S. Department of Transportation.

No matter what your complaint, keep accurate records. Copies of the following items are indispensable in helping to resolve your problems:
- ☑ your original purchase papers
- ☑ your service invoices
- ☑ bills you have paid
- ☑ letters or emails you have written to the manufacturer or the repair facility owner
- ☑ written repair estimates from your independent mechanic
- ☑ notes on discussion with company representatives including names and dates

RESOLVING COMPLAINTS

Here are some basic steps to help you resolve your problem:

1 First, return your vehicle to the repair facility that did the work. Bring a written list of the problems and make sure that you keep a copy of the list. Give the repair facility a reasonable opportunity to examine your vehicle and attempt to fix it. Speak directly to the service manager (not to the service writer who wrote up your repair order), and ask him or her to test drive the vehicle with you so that you can point out the problem.

2 If that doesn't resolve the problem, take the vehicle to a diagnostic center or another mechanic for an independent examination. This may cost $45 to $60. Get a written statement defining the problem and outlining how it may be fixed. Give your repair shop a copy. If your vehicle is under warranty, do not allow any warranty repair by an independent mechanic; you may not be reimbursed by the manufacturer.

3 If your repair shop does not respond to the independent assessment, present your problem to an arbitration panel. These panels hear both sides of the story and try to come to a resolution.

If the problem is with a new vehicle dealer, or if you feel that the manufacturer is responsible, you may be able to use one of the manufacturer's arbitration programs.

If the problem is solely with an independent dealer, a local Better Business Bureau (BBB) may be able to mediate your complaint. It may also offer an arbitration hearing. In any case, the BBB should enter your complaint into its files on that establishment.

When contacting any arbitration program, determine how long the process takes, who makes the final decision, whether you are bound by that decision, and whether the program handles all problems or only warranty complaints. Beware of "binding arbitration" because you give up your right to later pursue legal action.

4 If there are no arbitration programs in your area, contact private consumer groups, local government agencies, or your local "action line" newspaper columnist, newspaper editor, or radio/TV broadcaster. A phone call or letter from them may persuade a repair facility to take action. Send a copy of your letter to the repair shop.

5 One of your last resorts is to bring a lawsuit against the dealer, manufacturer, or repair facility in small claims court. The fee for filing such an action is usually small, and you generally act as your own attorney, saving attorney's fees. There is a monetary limit on the amount you can claim, which varies from state to state. Your local consumer affairs office, state attorney general's office, or the clerk of the court can tell you how to file such a suit.

6 Finally, talk with an attorney. It's best to select an attorney who is familiar with handling automotive problems and has no ties to the local business community. Lawyer referral services can provide names of attorneys who deal with automobile problems. If you can't afford an attorney, contact the Legal Aid Society.

WARRANTY COMPLAINTS

If your vehicle is under warranty or you are having problems with a factory-authorized dealership, here are some guidelines:

1 Have the warranty available to show the dealer. Make sure you call the problem to the dealer's attention before the end of the warranty period.

2 If you are still dissatisfied after giving the dealer a reasonable opportunity to fix your vehicle, contact the manufacturer's representative (also called the zone representative) in your area. This person can authorize the dealer to make repairs or take other steps to resolve the dispute. Your dealer will have your zone representative's name and telephone number. Explain the problem and ask for a meeting and a personal inspection of your vehicle.

3 If you can't get satisfaction from the zone representative, call or write the manufacturer's owner relations department. Your owner's manual contains this phone number and address. In each case, as you move up the chain, indicate the steps you have already taken and keep careful records of your efforts.

4 Your next option is to present your problem to a complaint handling arbitration program. Beware of "binding arbitration" because you give up your right to later pursue legal action and beware of arbitrators selected by a manufacturer, dealer or repair shop.

If you complain of a problem during the warranty period, you have a right to have the problem fixed even after the warranty runs out. If your warranty has not been honored, you may be able to "revoke acceptance," which means that you return the vehicle to the dealer. If you are successful, you may be entitled to a replacement vehicle or to a full refund of the purchase price and reimbursement of legal fees under the Magnuson-Moss Warranty Act. Or, if you are covered by one of the state lemon laws, you may be able to return the vehicle and receive a refund or replacement from the manufacturer.

NEED HELP?

If you need assistance with a vehicle safety issue or repair problem, the Center for Auto Safety is here to help! The Center collects consumer complaints in an effort to require automakers and the government to address safety defects and to prevent consumers from being ripped off on repairs. To file a complaint with the Center, visit www.autosafety.org/submit-complaint and provide as much detail as you can on your vehicle problem. To stay up to date on Center for Auto Safety vehicle safety activities, sign up by visiting www.autosafety.org and clicking on the "Join Our Mailing List" button.

AUTO SAFETY HOT LINE: 800-424-9393
TTY FOR HEARING IMPAIRED: 800-424-9153
WWW.SAFERCAR.GOV

The toll-free Auto Safety Hot Line can provide information on recalls, record information about safety problems, and refer you to the appropriate government experts on other vehicle related problems. You can even have recall information mailed to you within 24 hours of your call at no charge. Most importantly, you can call the hot line to report safety problems which will become part of the National Highway Traffic Safety Administration's complaint database. If you have access to the internet, www.safercar.gov is a more efficient way to register complaints and obtain recall and safety information. You can also look up the individual complaints about a particular vehicle.

Thanks to the efforts of the Center for Auto Safety, we are able to provide you with a car by car index of vehicle complaints on file with the National Highway Traffic Safety Administration (NHTSA). Each year, thousands of Americans file online, or call the government, to register complaints about their vehicles. *The Car Book* Complaint Index is the result of our analysis of these complaints. It is based on a ratio of the number of complaints for each vehicle to the sales of that vehicle. In order to predict the expected complaint performance of the 2020 models, we have examined the complaint history of that car's series. The term series refers to the fact that when a manufacturer introduces a new model, that vehicle remains essentially unchanged, on average, for four to six years. For example, the Chevrolet Impala was redesigned in 2014 and remains essentially the same car for 2020. As such, we have compiled the complaint experience for that series in order to give you some information to use in deciding which car to buy. For vehicles introduced or significantly changed in 2020, we do not yet have enough data to develop a complaint index.

The following table presents the projected best and worst complaint ratings for the 2020 models for which we can develop ratings. Higher index numbers mean the vehicle generated a greater number of complaints. Lower numbers indicate fewer complaints.

2020 PROJECTED COMPLAINT INDEX

THE BEST	INDEX*
Audi A5	415
Lexus RC	491
Toyota Corolla	499
Genesis G80	616
Cadillac Escalade ESV	668
BMW X3	726
Infiniti QX50	816
BMW 2 Series	872
Audi Q3	952
Chevrolet Cruze	1,049
Mazda 3	1,063
Porsche Macan	1,209
Lexus RX	1,269
Lexus IS	1,263
Buick Encore	1,281
Toyota Corolla	1,300
Chevrolet Trax	1,312
Chevrolet Malibu	1,369
Nissan Rogue	1,377
Cadillac XT4	1,489

THE WORST	INDEX*
Hyundai Santa Fe	>20,000
Chrysler Pacifica	>20,000
Tesla Model S	>20,000
Hyundai Tucson	14,401
Ford Fusion Energi	12,119
Jeep Cherokee	10,628
Dodge Journey	9,736
Mercedes-Benz GLC	9,574
Mercedes-Benz CLA	9,296
Dodge Durango	9,183
Jeep Grand Cherokee	8,638
Chevrolet Bolt	8,463
Jeep Renegade	7,496
Volvo XC90	7,435
Nissan Titan	6,958
Tesla Model X	6,723
Cadillac XT5	6,519
Chevrolet Equinox	6,328

*IMPORTANT NOTE: The numbers represent relative index scores, not the number of complaints received. The complaint index score considers sales volume and years on the road. Lower index numbers are better. We capped the complaint index at 20,000 for excessively high complaint indices.

LEMON LAWS

Sometimes, despite our being an educated shopper, we buy a new vehicle that just doesn't work right. There may be little problem after little problem, or perhaps one big problem that the dealer cannot seem to fix. Because of the "sour" taste that such vehicles leave in the mouths of consumers who buy them, these vehicles are known as "lemons."

In the past, it was difficult to obtain a refund or replacement if a vehicle was a lemon. The burden of proof was left to the consumer. Because it is hard to define exactly what constitutes a lemon, many lemon owners were unable to win a case against a manufacturer. When they won, consumers had to pay for their attorneys, giving them less than if they had traded in their lemon.

Thanks to the urging of the Center for Auto Safety, "Lemon Laws" have been passed by all states, making help available when consumers get stuck with a lemon. Although there are some important state-to-state variations, all of the laws have simi-larities: they establish a period of coverage, usually two years from delivery or the written warranty period (whichever is shorter). They may require some form of non-court arbitration and, most importantly, they define what qualifies as a lemon. In most states a new car, truck, or van is "presumed" to be a lemon when it has been taken back to the shop 3 to 4 times for the same problem or is out of service for a total of 30 days during the covered period. This time does not mean consecu-tive days and can be for different problems. Twenty states have safety lemon provisions which presume a vehicle is a lemon after only 1 to 2 repairs of a defect likely to cause death or serious injury. Be sure to keep careful records of your repairs since some states now require only one of the repairs to be within the specified time period. Thirty-three states provide for the award of attorney fees to consumers, with the other 17 relying on the federal Lemon Law (the Magnuson-Moss War-ranty Act) for fees. A vehicle may be covered by the federal Lemon Law even if or when it doesn't meet the specific state require-ments.

Specific information about your state's Lemon Law can be obtained at the Center for Auto Safety's Lemon Law Library, which has helpful links to state laws and information from your state attorney general or con-sumer protection office. The Center's Lemon Law Library may be found at www.autosafety.org/lemon-law-library.

The following table offers a general description of the Lemon Law in every state and what you need to do to set it in motion (Notification/Trigger). We indi-cate where state-run arbitration programs are available. State-run programs are the best type of arbitration. Be aware, a few state lemon laws are so bad con-sumers should also consider rely-ing on the federal Lemon Law and state contract law. We have marked these bad laws with a ☒ while the best laws have a ☑.

Alabama	Qualification: 3 unsuccessful repairs or 30 calendar days within shorter of 24 months or 24,000 miles, provided 1 repair attempt or 1 day out of service is within shorter of 1 year or 12,000 miles. Notice/Trigger: Certified mail to manufacturer + opportunity for final repair attempt within 14 calendar days.
Alaska	Qualification: 3 unsuccessful repairs or 30 business days out of service within shorter of 1 year or warranty. Notice/Trigger: Certified mail to manufacturer + dealer (or repair agent) that problem has not been corrected in reasonable number of attempts + refund or replacement demanded within 60 days. Manufacturer has 30 calendar days for final repair attempt.
Arizona	Qualification: 4 unsuccessful repairs or 30 calendar days out of service within warranty period or shorter of 2 years or 24,000 miles. Notice/Trigger: Written notice + opportunity to repair to manufacturer.
Arkansas	Qualification: 3 unsuccessful repairs, 5 total repairs of any nonconformity, or 1 unsuc-cessful repair of problem likely to cause death or serious bodily injury within longer of 24 months or 24,000 miles. Notice/Trigger: Certified or registered mail to manufacturer who has 10 days to notify consumer of repair facility. Facility has 10 days to repair

L—Law specifically applies to leased vehicles; S-C—State has certified guidelines for arbitration; S-R—State-run arbitration mechanism available

California

Qualification: 4 repair attempts or 30 calendar days out of service or 2 repair attempts for defect likely to cause death or serious bodily injury within shorter of 18 months or 18,000 miles, or "reasonable" number of attempts during entire express warranty period. Notice/Trigger: Direct written notice to manufacturer at address clearly specified in owner's manual. Covers small businesses with up to 5 vehicles under 10,000 pounds GVWR.

Colorado

☒ WORST

Qualification: 4 unsuccessful repairs or 30 business days out of service within shorter of 1 year or warranty. Notice/Trigger: Prior certified mail notice + opportunity to repair for manufacturer.

Connecticut

Qualification: 4 unsuccessful repairs or 30 calendar days out of service within shorter of 2 years or 24,000 miles, or 2 unsuccessful repairs of problem likely to cause death or serious bodily injury within warranty period or 1 year. Notice/Trigger: Report t o manufacturer, agent, or dealer. Written notice to manufacturer only if required in owner's manual or warranty. S-R

Delaware

Qualification: 4 unsuccessful repairs or 30 calendar days out of service within shorter of 1 year or warranty. Notice/Trigger: Written notice + opportunity to repair to manufacturer.

D.C.

Qualification: 4 unsuccessful repairs or 30 calendar days out of service or 1 unsuccessful repair of safety-related defect, within shorter of 2 years or 18,000 miles. Notice/Trigger: Report to manufacturer, agent, or dealer.

Florida

Qualification: 3 unsuccessful repairs or 15 calendar days within 24 months from delivery. Notice/Trigger: Certified or express mail notice to manufacturer who has 10 days to notify consumer of repair facility plus 10 more calendar day s for final repair attempt after delivery to designated dealer. S-R

Georgia

Qualification: 1 unsuccessful repair of serious safety defect or 3 unsuccessful repair attempts or 30 calendar days out of service within shorter of 24,000 miles or 24 months. Notification/Trigger: Overnight or certified mail notice return receipt requested. Manufacturer has 7 days to notify consumer of re pair facility & consumer has 14 days from manufacturer receipt of original notice to deliver vehicle to repair facility. Facility has 28 calendar days from manufacturer receipt of original notice to repair. State-run arbitration mechanism available.

Hawaii

☑ BEST

Qualification: 3 unsuccessful repair attempts, or 1 unsuccessful repair attempt of defect likely to cause death or serious bodily injury, or out of service for total of 30 days within shorter of 2 years or 24,000 miles. Notice/Trigger: Written notice + opportunity to repair to manufacturer. S-R

Idaho

Qualification: 4 repair attempts or 30 business days out of service within shorter of 2 years or 24,000 miles, or 1 repair of complete failure of braking or steering likely to cause death or serious bodily injury. Notice/ Trigger: Written notice to manufacturer or dealer + one opportunity to repair to manufacturer. S-R.

Illinois

☒ WORST

Qualification: 4 unsuccessful repairs or 30 business days out of service within shorter of 1 yea r or 12,000 miles. Notice/Trigger: Written notice + opportunity to repair to manufacturer.

Indiana

Qualification: 4 unsuccessful repairs or 30 business days out of service within shorter of 18 months or 18,000 miles. Notice/Trigger: Written notice to manufacturer only if required in the warranty.

Iowa

Qualification: 3 unsuccessful repairs, or 1 unsuccessful repair of nonconformity likely to cause death or serious bodily injury, or 30 calendar days out of service within shorter of 2 years or 24,000 miles. Notice/Trigger: Certified registered mail + final opportunity to repair within 10 calendar days of receipt of notice to manufacturer

Kansas	Qualification: 4 unsuccessful repairs or 30 calendar days out of service or 10 total repairs within shorter of 1 year or warranty. Notice/Trigger: Actual notice to manufacturer.
Kentucky	Qualification: 4 unsuccessful repairs or 30 calendar days out of service within shorter of 1 year or 12,000 miles. Notice/Trigger: Written notice to manufacturer.
Louisiana ☒ WORST	Qualification: 4 unsuccessful repairs or 90 calendar days out of service within shorter of 1 year or warranty. Notice/Trigger: Report to manufacturer or dealer.
Maine	Qualification: 3 unsuccessful repairs (or 1 unsuccessful repair of serious failure of brakes or steering) or 15 business days out of service within shorter of warranty or 3 years or 18,000 miles. Applies to vehicles within first 18,000 miles or 3 years regardless of whether claimant is original owner. Notice/Trigger: Written notice to manufacturer or dealer. Manufacturer has 7 business days after receipt for final repair attempt. S-R
Maryland	Qualification: 4 unsuccessful repairs, 30 calendar days out of service or 1 unsuccessful repair of braking or steering system within shorter of 15 months or 15,000 miles. Notice/Trigger: Certified mail return receipt requested + opportunity to repair within 30 calendar days of receipt of notice to manufacturer or factory branch.
Massachusetts	Qualification: 3 unsuccessful repairs or 10 business days out of service within shorter of 1 year or 15,000 miles. Notice/Trigger: Notice to manufacturer or dealer who has 7 business days to attempt final repair. S-R
Michigan	Qualification: 4 unsuccessful repairs within 2 years from date of first unsuccessful repair or 30 calendar days within shorter of 1 year or warranty. Notice/Trigger: Certified mail return receipt requested to manufacturer who has 5 business days to repair after delivery. Consumer may notify manufacturer after third repair attempt.
Minnesota	Qualification: 4 unsuccessful repairs or 30 business days or 1 unsuccessful repair of total braking or steering loss likely to cause death or serious bodily injury within shorter of 2 years or warranty. Notice/Trigger: Written notice + opportunity to repair to manufacturer, agent, or dealer.
Mississippi	Qualification: 3 unsuccessful repairs or 15 business days out of service within shorter of 1 year or warranty. Notice/Trigger: Written notice to manufacturer who has 10 business days to repair after delivery to designated dealer.
Missouri ☒ WORST	Qualification: 4 unsuccessful repairs or 30 business days out of service within shorter of 1 year or warranty. Notice/Trigger: Written notice to manufacturer who has 10 calendar days to repair after delivery to designated dealer.
Montana	Qualification: 4 unsuccessful repairs or 30 business days out of service after notice within shorter of 2 years or 18,000 miles. Notice/Trigger: Written notice + opportunity to repair to manufacturer. S-R
Nebraska	Qualification: 4 unsuccessful repairs or 40 calendar days out of service within shorter of 1 year or warranty. Notice/Trigger: Certified mail + opportunity to repair to manufacturer.
Nevada	Qualification: 4 unsuccessful repairs or 30 calendar days out of service within shorter of 1 year or warranty. Notice/Trigger: Written notice to manufacturer.
New Hampshire	Qualification: 3 unsuccessful repairs by same dealer or 30 business days out of service within warranty. Notice/Trigger: Report to manufacturer, distributor, agent, or dealer (on forms provided by manufacturer) + final opportunity to repair before arbitration. S-R

New Jersey
☑ BEST

Qualification: 3 Unsuccessful repairs or 20 calendar days out of service within shorter of 2 years or 24,000 miles; or 1 unsuccessful repair of a serious safety defect likely to cause death or serious bodily injury. Notice/Trigger: Certified mail notice, return receipt requested to manufacturer who has 10 days to repair. Consumer may notify manufacturer at any time after the second repair attempt, or after the first repair attempt in the case of a serious safety defect.

New Mexico

Qualification: 4 unsuccessful repairs or 30 business days out of service within shorter of 1 year or warranty. Notice/Trigger: Written notice + opportunity to repair to manufacturer, agent, or dealer.

New York
☑ BEST

Qualification: 4 unsuccessful repairs or 30 calendar days out of service within shorter of 2 years or 18,000 miles. Notice/Trigger: Notice to manufacturer, agent, or dealer.

North Carolina

Qualification: 4 unsuccessful repairs within shorter of 24 months, 24,000 miles or warranty or 20 business days out of service during any 12 month period of warranty. Notice/Trigger: Written notice to manufacturer + opportunity to repair within 15 calendar days of receipt only if required in warranty or owner's manual.

North Dakota
☒ WORST

Qualification: 3 unsuccessful repairs or 30 business days out of service within shorter of 1 year or warranty. Notice/Trigger: Direct written notice + opportunity to repair to manufacturer. (Manufacturer's informal arbitration process serves as prerequisite to consumer refund or replacement.)

Ohio
☑ BEST

Qualification: 3 unsuccessful repairs of same nonconformity, 30 calendar days out of service, 8 total repairs of any nonconformity, or 1 unsuccessful repair of problem likely to cause death or serious bodily injury within shorter of 1 year or 18,000 miles. Notice/Trigger: Report to manufacturer, its agent, or dealer.

Oklahoma

Qualification: 4 unsuccessful repairs or 30 calendar days out of service within shorter of 1 year or warranty. Notice/Trigger: Written notice + opportunity to repair to manufacturer.

Oregon

Qualification: 3 unsuccessful repairs or 30 business days within shorter of 2 years or 24,000 miles, or 1 unsuccessful repair of a serious safety defect likely to cause death or injury. Notice/Trigger: Direct written notice + opportunity to repair to manufacturer.

Pennsylvania

Qualification: 3 unsuccessful repairs or 30 calendar days within shorter of 1 year, 12,000 miles, or warranty. Notice/Trigger: Delivery to authorized service + repair facility. If delivery impossible, written notice to manufacturer or its repair facility obligates them to pay for delivery.

Rhode Island
☑ BEST

Qualification: 4 unsuccessful repairs or 30 calendar days out of service within shorter of 1 year or 15,000 miles. Notice/Trigger: Report to dealer or manufacturer who has 7 days for final repair opportunity.

South Carolina

Qualification: 3 unsuccessful repairs or 30 calendar days out of service within shorter of 1 year or 12,000 miles. Notice/Trigger: Certified mail + opportunity to repair (not more than 10 business days) to manufacturer only if manufacturer informed consumer of such at time of sale.

L—Law specifically applies to leased vehicles; S-C—State has certified guidelines for arbitration; S-R—State-run arbitration mechanism available

South Dakota	Qualification: 4 unsuccessful repairs, 1 of which occurred during shorter of 1 year or 12,000 miles, or 30 calendar days out of service during shorter of 24 months or 24,000 miles. Notice/Trigger: Certified mail to manufacturer + final opportunity to repair + 7 calendar days to notify consumer of repair facility.
Tennessee	Qualification: 4 unsuccessful repairs or 30 calendar days out of service within shorter of 1 year or warranty. Notice/Trigger: Certified mail notice to manufacturer + final opportunity to repair within 10 calendar days.
Texas	Qualification: 4 unsuccessful repair attempts, 30 days out of service, 2 unsuccessful repair attempts of a serious safety hazard within shorter of manufacturer warranty, 24 months or 24,000 miles. Notice/Trigger: Written notice to manufacturer. S-R
Utah	Qualification: 4 unsuccessful repairs or 30 business days out of service within shorter of 1 year or warranty. Notice/Trigger: Report to manufacturer, agent, or dealer. S-R
Vermont	Qualification: 3 unsuccessful repairs when at least first repair was within warranty, or 30 calendar days out of service within warranty. Notice/Trigger: Written notice to manufacturer (on provided forms) after third repair attempt, or 30 days. Arbitration must be held within 45 days after notice, during which time manufacturer has 1 final repair. S-R Note: Repairs must be done by same authorized agent or dealer, unless consumer shows good cause for taking vehicle to different agent or dealer.
Virginia	Qualification: 3 unsuccessful repairs, or 1 repair attempt of serious safety defect, or 30 calendar days out of service within 18 months. Notice/Trigger: Written notice to manufacturer. If 3 unsuccessful repairs or 30 days already exhausted before notice, manufacturer has 1 more repair attempt not to exceed 15 days.
Washington ☑ BEST	Qualification: 4 unsuccessful repairs, 30 calendar days out of service (15 during warranty period), or 2 repairs of serious safety defects, first reported within shorter of warranty or 24 months or 24,000 miles. One repair attempt + 15 of 30 days must fall within manufacturer's express warranty of at least 1 year of 12,000 miles. Notice/ Trigger: Written notice to manufacturer. S-R Note: Consumer should receive replacement or refund within 40 calendar days of request.
West Virginia	Qualification: 3 unsuccessful repairs or 30 calendar days out o f service or 1 unsuccessful repair of problem likely to cause death or serious bodily injury within shorter of 1 year or warranty. Notice/Trigger: Written notice + opportunity to repair to manufacturer.
Wisconsin	Qualification: 4 unsuccessful repairs or 30 calendar days out of service within shorter of 1 year or warranty. Notice/Trigger: Report to manufacturer or dealer. Note: Consumer should receive replacement or refund within 30 calendar days after offer to return title.
Wyoming	Qualification: 3 unsuccessful repairs or 30 business days out of service within 1 year. Notice/Trigger: Direct written notice + opportunity to repair to manufacturer. S-R

L—Law specifically applies to leased vehicles; S-C—State has certified guidelines for arbitration; S-R—State-run arbitration mechanism available

5 BASIC STEPS TO CAR BUYING

Buying a car means matching wits with a seasoned professional. But if you know what to expect, you'll have a much better chance of getting a fantastic deal!

There's no question that buying a car can be an intimidating experience. But it doesn't have to be. First of all, you have in your hands all of the information you need to make an informed choice. Secondly, if you approach the purchase logically, you'll always maintain control of the decision. Start with the following basic steps:

1 Consider your needs and how you will use a vehicle. Based on that, narrow your choice down to a particular class of car—sports, station wagon, minivan, sedan, large luxury, SUV, truck, or economy car. These are general classifications and some cars may fit into more than one category. In most cases, *The Car Book* presents the vehicles by size class.

2 Determine what features are really important to you. Most buyers consider safety on the top of their list, which is why the "Safety Chapter" is right up front in *The Car Book*. Specifically items such as blind spot detection, automatic braking, and lane keeping assist along with airbags, power options, the general size, fuel economy, number of passengers, as well as "hidden" elements such as maintenance and insurance costs, should be considered at this stage in your selection process.

3 Find three or four cars that meet your budget, and the needs you outlined above. It's important not to narrow your choice down to one car because then you lose all your bargaining power in the showroom. (Why? Because you might lose the psychological ability to walk away from a bad deal!) In fact, because cars today are more similar than dissimilar, it's not hard to keep three or four choices in mind. In the "Car Rating Pages" in the back of the book, we suggest some competitive choices for your consideration. For example, if you are interested in the Honda Accord, you should also consider the Toyota Camry, Ford Fusion, and Hyundai Sonata.

4 Make sure you take a good, long test drive. The biggest car buying mistake most of us make is to overlook those nagging problems that seem to surface only after we've brought the car home. Spend at least an hour driving the car and preferably without a salesperson. If a dealership won't allow you to test drive a car without a salesperson, go somewhere else. The test drive should include time on the highway, parking, taking the car in and out of your driveway or garage, sitting in the back seat, and using the trunk or storage area. Renting the car you're interested in for a day can be very insightful.

TIP: Whatever you do, don't talk price until you're ready to buy!

5 This is the stage most of us dread—negotiating the price. While price negotiation is a car buying tradition, a few dealers are trying to break tradition by offering so-called "no-haggle" or "posted" pricing. Since they're still in the minority and because it's very hard for an individual to establish true competition between dealers, we recommend avoiding negotiating altogether by using the non-profit CarBargains pricing service described on page 50.

THE U-TURN

When buying a car, you have the most important tool in the bargaining process: the U-turn. Be prepared to walk away from a deal, even at the risk of losing the "very best deal" your salesperson has ever offered, and you will be in the best position to get a real "best deal." Remember: dealerships need you, the buyer, to survive.

IN THE SHOWROOM

Being prepared in the showroom is the best way to turn a potentially intimidating showroom experience into a profitable one. Here's some advice on handling what you'll find in the showroom.

Beware of silence. Silence is often used to intimidate, so be prepared for long periods of time when the salesperson is "talking with the manager." This tactic is designed to make you want to "just get the negotiation over with." Instead of becoming a victim, do something that indicates you are serious about looking elsewhere. Bring the classified section of the newspaper and begin circling other cars or review brochures from other manufacturers. By sending the message that you have other options, you increase your bargaining power and speed up the process.

Don't fall in love with a car. Never look too interested in any particular car. Advise family members or friends who go with you against being too enthusiastic about any one car. Tip: Beat the dealers at their own game—bring along a friend who tells you that the price is "too much compared to the other deal," or "I liked that other car much better," or "wasn't that other car much cheaper?"

Keep your wallet in your pocket. Don't leave a deposit, even if it's refundable. You'll feel pressure to rush your shopping, and you'll have to return and face the salesperson again before you are ready.

Shop at the end of the month. Salespeople anxious to meet sales goals are more willing to negotiate a lower price at this time.

Buy last year's model. The majority of new cars are the same as the previous year, with minor cosmetic changes. You can save considerably by buying in early fall when dealers are clearing space for "new" models. The important trade-off you make using this technique is that the carmaker may have added a new safety feature to an otherwise unchanged vehicle.

Buying from stock. You can often get a better deal on a car that the dealer has on the lot. However, these cars often have expensive options you may not want or need. Do not hesitate to ask the dealer to remove an option (and its accompanying charge) or sell you the car without charging for the option. The longer the car sits there, the more interest the dealer pays on the car, which increases the dealer's incentive to sell.

Ordering a car. Cars can be ordered from the manufacturer with exactly the options you want. Simply offering a fixed amount over invoice may be attractive because it's a sure sale and the dealership has not invested in the car. All the salesperson has to do is take your order.

If you do order a car, make sure when it arrives that it includes only the options you requested. Don't fall for the trick where the dealer offers you unordered options at a "special price," because it was their mistake. If you didn't order an option, don't pay for it.

⚠ BEWARE OF MANDATORY ARBITRATION AGREEMENTS

More and more dealers are adding mandatory binding arbitration agreements, which they often call "dispute resolution mechanisms," to your purchase contract. What this means is that you waive the right to sue or appeal any problem you have with the vehicle. In addition, the dealer often gets to choose the arbitrator. Before you start negotiating the price, ask if the dealer requires Mandatory Binding Arbitration. If so, and they won't remove that requirement, you should buy elsewhere. Many dealers do not have this requirement.

GETTING THE BEST PRICE

One of the most difficult aspects of buying a new car is getting the best price. Most of us are at a disadvantage negotiating because we don't know how much the car actually cost the dealer. The difference between what the dealer paid and the sticker price represents the negotiable amount.

Beware, now that most savvy consumers know to check the so-called "dealer invoice," the industry has camouflaged this number. Special incentives, rebates, and kickbacks can account for $500 to $2,000 worth of extra profit to a dealer selling a car at "dealer invoice." The non-profit Center for the Study of Services recently discovered that in 37 percent of cases when dealers are forced to bid against each other, they offered the buyer a price below the "dealer invoice"—an unlikely event if the dealer was actually losing money. The bottom line is that "dealer invoice" doesn't really mean dealer cost.

You can't really negotiate with only one dealer, you need to get two or three bidding against each other. Introducing competition is the best way to get the lowest price on a new car. To do this you have to convince two or three dealers that you are, in fact, prepared to buy a car; that you have decided on the make, model, and features; and that your decision now rests solely on which dealer will give you the best price. You can try to do this by phone, but often dealers will not give you the best price, or will quote you a price over the phone that they will not honor later. Instead, you should try to do this in person. If you have ever ventured into an auto showroom simply to get the best price, you know the process can be lengthy and terribly arduous. Nevertheless, if you can convince the dealer that you are serious and are willing to take the time to go to a number of dealers, it will pay off. Be sure the dealer knows that you simply want the best price for the particular make, model and options. Otherwise, we suggest you use the CarBargains service described on page 50.

Here are some other showroom strategies:

Shop away from home. If you find a big savings at a dealership far from your home or on the Internet, call a local dealer with the price. They may match it. If not, pick up the car from the distant dealer, knowing your trip has saved you hundreds of dollars. You can still bring it to your local dealer for warranty work and repairs.

Beware of misleading advertising. New car ads are meant to get you into the showroom. They usually promise low prices, big rebates, high trade-in, and spotless integrity—don't be deceived. Advertised prices are rarely the true selling price. They usually exclude transportation charges, service fees, or document fees. Always look out for the asterisk, both in advertisements and on invoices. Asterisks can be a signal that the advertiser has something to hide.

Don't talk price until you're ready to buy. On your first few trips to the showroom, simply look over the cars, decide what options you want, and do your test-driving.

Shop the corporate twins. Page 55 contains a list of corporate twins—nearly identical cars that carry different name plates. Check the price and options of the twins of the car you like. A higher-priced twin may have more options, so it may be a better deal than the lower-priced car with the added options you want.

Watch out for dealer preparation overcharges. Before paying the dealer to clean your car, make sure that preparation is not included in the basic price. The price sticker will state: "Manu-facturer's suggested retail price of this model includes dealer preparation."

If you must negotiate . . . negotiate up from the "invoice" price rather than down from the sticker price. Simply make an offer close to or at the "invoice" price. If the salesperson says that your offer is too low to make a profit, ask to see the factory invoice.

Don't trade in. Although it is more work, you can usually do better by selling your old car yourself than by trading it in. To determine what you'll gain by selling the car yourself, check the NADA Official Used Car Guide at your credit union or library. On the web, the Kelly Blue Book website at kbb.com is a good source for determining the value of your used car. The difference between the trade-in price (what the dealer will give you) and the retail price (what you can typically sell it for) is your extra payment for selling the car yourself. Another option is to get a bid for your car from one of the national used car chains, such as CarMax. They do buy used cars with no obligation for you to buy from them.

If you do decide to trade your car in at the dealership, keep the buying and selling separate. First, negotiate the best price for your new car, then find out how much the dealer will give you for your old car. Keeping the two deals separate ensures that you know what you're paying for your new car and simplifies the entire transaction.

Question everything the dealer writes down. Nothing is etched in stone. Because things are written down, we tend not to question them. This is wrong—always assume that anything written down, or printed, is negotiable.

CARBARGAINS' BEST PRICE SERVICE

Even with the information that we provide you in this chapter of *The Car Book*, many of us still will not be comfortable negotiating for a fair price. In fact, as we indicated on the previous page, we believe it's really very difficult to negotiate the best price with a single dealer. The key to getting the best price is to get dealers to compete with each other.

CarBargains is a service of the non-profit Consumers' CHECKBOOK, a consumer group that provides comparative price and quality information for many products and services.

CarBargains will "shop" the dealerships in your area and obtain at least five price quotes for the make and model of the car that you want to buy. The dealers who submit quotes know that they are competing with other area dealerships and have agreed to honor the prices that they submit. It is important to note that CarBargains is not an auto broker or "car buying" service; they have no affiliation with dealers.

Here's how the service works:

1. You provide CarBargains with the specific make, model, and style of car you wish to buy (Toyota Camry XLE, for example).

2. Within two weeks, CarBar-gains will send you dealer quote sheets from at least five local dealers who have bid against one another to sell you that car. You get the name and phone number of the manager responsible for handling the quote.   When you receive your quotes, you will also get some suggestions on low-cost sources of financing and a valuation of your used car (trade-in).

The price for this service ($250, or $225 if you become a member) may seem expensive, but when you consider the savings that will result by having dealers bid against each other, as well as the time and effort of trying to get these bids yourself, we believe it's a great value. The dealers know they have a bona fide buyer; they know they are bidding against 5-7 of their competitors; and, you have CarBargains' experts on your side.

To obtain CarBargains' competitive price quotes, call them at 800-475-7283 or visit their website at www.carbargains.org, model, style, and year of the car you want to buy. You should receive your report within two weeks.

FINANCING

You've done your test-drive, researched prices, studied crash tests, determined the options you want, and haggled to get the best price. Now you have to decide how to pay for the car.

If you have the cash, pay for the car right away. You avoid finance charges, you won't have a large debt haunting you, and the full value of the car is yours. You can then make the monthly payments to yourself to save up for your next car.

However, most of us cannot afford to pay cash for a car, which leaves two options: financing or leasing. While leasing may seem more affordable, financing will actually cost you less and give you flexibility. When you finance a car, you own it after you finish your payments. At the end of a lease, you have nothing. We don't recommend leasing, but if you want more information, see page 55.

Shop around for interest rates. Most banks and credit unions will knock off at least a quarter of a percent for their customers. Have these quotes handy when you talk financing with the dealer.

The higher your down payment, the less you'll have to finance. This will not only reduce your overall interest charges, but often qualifies you for a lower interest rate.

Avoid long car loans. The monthly payments are lower, but you'll pay far more in overall interest charges. For example, a two-year, $25,000 loan at 4 percent will cost you $1,055 in interest; the same amount at five years will cost you $2,625— well over twice as much!

Beware of manufacturer promotional rates—the 0 to 1 percent rates you see advertised. These low rates are usually only valid on two or three-year loans and only for the most credit-worthy customers.

Read everything you are asked to sign and ask questions about anything you don't fully understand.

Make sure that an extended warranty has not been added to the purchase price. Dealers will sometimes do this without telling you. Extended warranties are generally a bad value. See the "Warranties" chapter for more information.

Credit Unions vs. Banks: Credit unions generally charge fewer and lower fees and offer better rates than banks. In addition, credit unions offer counseling services where consumers can find pricing information on cars or compare monthly payments for financing. You can join a credit union either through your employer, an organization or club, or if you have a relative who is part of a credit union.

DON'T BE TONGUE-TIED

Beware of high-pressure phrases like "I've talked to the manager and this is really the best we can do. As it is, we're losing money on this deal." Rarely is this true. Dealers are in the business to make money and most do very well. Don't tolerate a take-it-or-leave-it attitude. Simply repeat that you will only buy when you see the deal you want and that you don't appreciate the dealer pressuring you. Threaten to leave if the dealer continues to pressure you to buy today.

Don't let the dealer answer your questions with a question. If you ask, "Can I get this same car with leather seats?" and the salesperson answers, "If I get you leather seats in this car, will you buy today?" this response tries to force you to decide to buy before you are ready. Ask the dealer to just answer your question and say that you'll buy when you're ready. It's the dealer's job to answer questions, not yours.

If you are having a difficult time getting what you want, ask the dealer: "Why won't you let me buy a car today?" Most salespeople will be thrown off by this phrase as they are often too busy trying to use it on you. If they respond in frustration, "OK, what do you want?" you can simply say "straightforward answers to simple questions."

Get a price; don't settle for: "If you're shopping price, go to the other dealers first and then come back." This technique ensures that they don't have to truly negotiate. Your best response is: "I only plan to come back if your price is the lowest, so that's what I need today, your lowest price."

LEASING VS. BUYING

About 25% of new car transactions are actually leases. Unfortunately, most leasees don't realize that, in spite of the low monthly payments, leasing costs more than buying.

When you pay cash or finance a car, you own an asset; leasing leaves you with nothing except all the headaches and responsibilities of ownership with none of the benefits. When you lease you pay a monthly fee for a predetermined time in exchange for the use of a car. However, you also pay for maintenance, insurance, and repairs as if you owned the car. Finally, when it comes time to turn in the car, it has to be in top shape—otherwise, you'll have to pay for repairs, clean up, or body work. One of the most important things to remember about a lease is that it is very difficult and expensive to end it early. If you are considering a lease, here are some leasing terms you need to know and some tips to get you through the process:

Capitalized Cost is the price of the car on which the lease is based. Negotiate this as if you were buying the car. Capitalized Cost Reduction is your down payment.

Know the make and model of the vehicle you want. Tell the agent exactly how you want the car equipped. You don't have to pay for options you don't request. Decide in advance how long you will keep the car.

Find out the price of the options on which the lease is based. Typically, they will be full retail price. Their cost can be negotiated (albeit with some difficulty) before you settle on the monthly payment.

Find out how much you are required to pay at delivery. Most leases require at least the first month's payment. Others have a security deposit, registration fees, or other "hidden costs." When shopping around, make sure price quotes include security deposit and taxes—sales tax, monthly use tax, or gross receipt tax. Ask how the length of the lease affects your monthly cost.

Find out how the lease price was determined. Lease prices are generally based on the manufacturer's suggested retail price, less the predetermined residual value. (Residual value is how much the seller expects the vehicle to be worth at the end of the lease.) The best lease values are cars with a high expected residual value. To protect themselves, leasers tend to underestimate residual value, but there is little you can do about this estimate.

Find out the annual mileage limit. Don't accept a con-tract with a lower limit than you need. Most standard contracts allow 15,000 to 18,000 miles per year. If you go under the allowance one year, you can go over it the next. Watch out for excess mileage fees. If you go over, you'll get charged per mile.

Avoid "capitalized cost reduction" or "equity leases." Here the leaser offers to lower the monthly payment by asking you for more money up front—in other words, a down payment.

Ask about early termination. Between 30 and 40 percent of two-year leases are terminated early and 40–60 percent of four-year leases terminate early—this means expensive early termination fees. If you terminate the lease before it is up, what are the financial penalties? They are typically very high so watch out. Ask the dealer exactly what you would owe at the end of each year if you wanted out of the lease. Remember, if your car is stolen, the lease will typically be terminated. While your insur-

LEASEWISE

TIP

If you must lease, why haggle when you can let someone else do it for you? LeaseWise, a service from the non-profit Center for the Study of Services, makes dealers bid for your lease. First, they get leasing bids from dealers on the vehicles you're interested in. Next, you'll receive a detailed report with all the bids, the dealer and invoice cost of the vehicle, and a complete explanation of the various bids. Then, you can lease from the lowest bidder or use the report as leverage with another dealer. The service costs $350. For more information, call 800-475-7283, or visit www.checkbook.org/auto/leasew.cfm

ance should cover the value of the car, you still may owe additional amounts per your lease contract.

Avoid maintenance contracts. Getting work done privately is cheaper in the long run. Don't forget, this is a new car with a standard warranty.

Arrange for your own insurance. By shopping around, you can generally find less expensive insurance than what's offered by the lessor.

Ask how quickly you can expect delivery. If your agent can't deliver in a reasonable time, maybe he or she can't meet the price quoted.

Retain your option to buy the car at the end of the lease at a predetermined price. The price should equal the residual value; if it is more, then the leaser is trying to make an additional profit. Regardless of how the end-of-lease value is determined, if you want the car, make an offer based on the current "Blue Book" value of the car at the end of the lease. Again, residual value is the value of your car at the end of the lease. The Automotive Lease Guide is often used by leasing companies to determine the residual value. It is very difficult to determine residual value because it means predicting what the car is going to be worth some time in the future. As such, leasing companies often underestimate the residual value which means you'll absorb more of the cost of the vehicle in the lease. On the other hand, if the residual value at the end of the lease is very low, consider buying the vehicle for that amount.

LEASING VS. BUYING

The following table compares the costs of leasing vs. buying the same car over three and six years. Your actual costs may vary, but you can use this format to compare the cars you are considering. Our example assumes the residual value of the purchased vehicle to be 55 percent after three years and 40 percent after six years.

3 Years	Lease 36 Month	Finance 5 Yr Loan-3.6% Sell in 3 Yrs.
MSRP	$33,500	$33,500
Lease Value/Purchase Cost of Car[1]	$30,150	$30,150
Initial Payment/Down Payment[2]	$3,015	$3,015
Loan Amount		$27,135
Monthly Payments[3]	$320	$495
Total Payments (first 3 years of loan)[4]	$11,520	$17,662
Amount Left on Loan		$11,385
Excess Miles and Disposition Fees[5]	$480	
Total Cost[6]	$15,015	$32,062
Less Value of Vehicle .55 Residual[7]		$18,425
Overall Cost, First 3 years	**$15,015**	**$13,637**
Savings over Leasing 3 Years		**$1,378**

6 Years	Lease 2nd 36 Month	Finance 5 Yr Loan-3.6% Keep Car 6 Yrs.
MSRP-2nd Car 5% Increase in Cost[8]	$35,175	$33,500
Lease Value/Purchase Cost of Car	$31,658	$30,150
Initial Payment/Down Payment[2]	$3,166	$3,015
Loan Amount		$27,135
Monthly Payment[9]	$340	$495
Total Payments[10]	$12,240	$29,700
Amount Left on Loan		$0
Excess Miles and Disposition Fees[5]	$480	
Total Cost of Second Lease	$15,886	
Total Cost[11]	$30,901	$32,715
Less Value of Vehicle .40 Residual 6 yrs[12]		$13,400
Total Cost, 6 years	**$30,901**	**$19,315**
Savings Over Leasing 6 Years		**$11,586**

1. Purchase price reflects that most buyer's pay about 90% of the MSRP.
2. Initial lease payment based on leases with 10% due at signing and loans with 10% down payment.
3. Monthly lease payments based on typical leases as reported by US News and World Report. Monthly finance payments based on a 5 year, 3.59% loan.
4. Total payments (lease and finance) paid for 3 years.
5. Average excess mileage fee of $480 based on a 12000 mile limit and averages 3 typical situations: 25% going 1500 mile over the limit at $0.15/mile; 50% pre-paying for 1500 in mile overages at $0.10/mile, and 25% not exceeding the mileage limit–plus a typical disposition fee of $350.
6. Total amount paid; includes down payment, monthly payments, and end of lease fees.
7. Three-year residual value of 55 percent based on average actual 36-month residual value for the top 10 selling vehicles for model year 2020.
8. Represents the expected 5% increase in the cost of a similar leased vehicle 3 years later.
9. Estimated increase in lease payment.
10. Total payments for the second 3 year lease and total payments for the 5 year loan at 3.59%.
11. Total cost of 2 3-year leases and total cost for 5 year loan purchase.
12. Six-year residual value of 40 percent based on average actual 72-month residual value for the top 10 selling vehicles for model year 2020.

DEPRECIATION

Over the past 20 years, new vehicle depreciation costs have steadily increased. A study conducted by Runzheimer International shows that depreciation and interest now account for just over 50 percent of the costs of owning and operating a vehicle. Recently, however, the increasing cost of depreciation has slowed down. This is due to the increased prices of new vehicles and the stabilization in finance rates.

While there is no foolproof method for predicting retained vehicle value, your best bet is to purchase a popular vehicle model. Chances are, though not always, it will also be a popular used vehicle, meaning that it will retain more of its value when you go to sell it.

Most new cars are traded in within four years and are then available on the used car market. The priciest used cars may not be the highest quality. Supply and demand, as well as appearance, are important factors in determining used car prices.

The table indicates which of the top-selling 2015 cars held their value the best and which did not.

2016 VEHICLES WITH THE BEST AND WORST RESALE VALUE

THE BEST				THE WORST			
Model	2016 Price	2019 Price	Retain. Value	Model	2016 Price	2019 Price	Retain. Value
Toyota Tacoma	$27,785	$26,950	97.0%	Chrysler 200	$21,700	$11,560	53.3%
Jeep Wrangler	$30,995	$29,650	95.7%	Ford Focus	$18,515	$9,950	53.7%
Toyota 4Runner	$32,820	$28,600	87.1%	Chevrolet Malibu	$23,510	$12,650	53.8%
Chevrolet Equinox	$26,190	$21,820	83.3%	Chevrolet Impala	$29,135	$15,850	54.4%
Toyota Tundra	$31,825	$26,500	83.3%	Volkswagen Passat	$23,945	$13,250	55.3%
Jeep Patriot	$18,295	$14,550	79.5%	Chevrolet Cruze	$23,805	$13,250	55.7%
Jeep Grand Cherokee	$29,195	$23,150	79.3%	Ford Fusion	$23,855	$13,465	56.5%
Nissan Murano	$30,230	$23,785	78.7%	Toyota Sienna	$30,490	$17,350	56.9%
Chevrolet Silverado	$31,310	$23,875	76.3%	Kia Forte	$16,100	$9,250	57.5%
GMC Acadia	$34,335	$25,650	74.7%	Ford Taurus	$28,900	$16,625	57.5%
Cadillac SRX	$42,880	$31,650	73.8%	Nissan Maxima	$31,200	$17,975	57.6%
Subaru Forester	$22,995	$16,820	73.2%	Cadillac CTS	$41,495	$24,150	58.2%
BMW 3 Series	$43,200	$31,600	73.2%	Mini Cooper	$19,950	$11,970	60.0%
Chevrolet Camaro	$23,555	$17,100	72.6%	Nissan Altima	$22,110	$13,450	60.8%
Ford F-150	$31,555	$22,750	72.1%	Volkswagen Jetta	$17,820	$10,865	61.0%
Hyundai Santa Fe	$29,800	$21,400	71.8%	Subaru Legacy	$23,295	$14,275	61.3%
Honda Accord	$21,955	$15,750	71.7%	Nissan Versa	$13,790	$8,550	62.0%
Honda CR-V	$24,195	$17,300	71.5%	Dodge Charger	$26,995	$16,750	62.1%
Toyota Highlander	$30,520	$21,650	70.9%	Buick LaCrosse	$33,135	$20,650	62.3%
Ram Pickup	$31,750	$22,500	70.9%	Hyundai Elantra	$19,600	$12,250	62.5%
Toyota Prius	$24,200	$17,150	70.9%	Hyundai Accent	$14,645	$9,175	62.7%
Nissan Frontier	$26,000	$18,300	70.4%	Fiat 500	$16,195	$10,155	62.7%
BMW X5	$52,800	$36,975	70.0%	Hyundai Sonata	$21,450	$13,550	63.2%
Mercedes-Benz E	$51,400	$35,980	70.0%	Volkswagen Golf	$19,995	$12,650	63.3%
Honda Odyssey	$28,825	$20,120	69.8%	Ford Fiesta	$14,600	$9,250	63.4%

CORPORATE TWINS

The term "corporate twins" refers to vehicles that have different names but share the same mechanics, drivetrain, and chassis. In many cases the vehicles are identical. Sometimes the difference is in body style, price, or options as with the Chevrolet Tahoe and the Cadillac Escalade.

While corporate twins share the same basic structure and running gear, some will drive and feel different because of the tuning of the suspension, the standard equipment and options available, and the the comfort and convenience features. One twin may stress a soft ride and luxury while another a tighter, sportier feel.

Historically, corporate twins have been limited mainly to domestic car companies. Today, several Asian and European car companies have started the practice.

CORPORATE TWINS

Chrysler
Chrysler 300
Dodge Charger

Ford
Ford Escape
Lincoln MKC

Ford Expedition
Lincoln Navigator

Ford Fusion
Lincoln MKZ

General Motors
Buick Encore
Chevrolet Trax

Buick Enclave
Chevrolet Traverse

Buick Regal
Chevrolet Malibu

Cadillac Escalade
Chevrolet Tahoe
GMC Yukon

Cadillac Escalade ESV
Chevrolet Suburban
GMC Yukon XL

Cadillac XT5
GMC Acadia

Chevrolet Colorado
GMC Canyon

Chevrolet Equinox
GMC Terrain

Chevrolet Silverado
GMC Sierra

Honda
Acura MDX
Honda Pilot

Hyundai–Kia
Hyundai Accent
Kia Rio

Hyundai Palisade
Kia Telluride

Nissan
Nissan Pathfinder
Infiniti QX60

Toyota
Lexus GX
Toyota 4Runner

Lexus RX
Toyota Highlander

Volkswagen-Audi
Audi A3
Volkswagen Golf

Cadillac Escalade

Chevrolet Tahoe

GMC Yukon

T his section provides an overview of the most important features of this year's new models. Nearly all the information you'll need to make a smart choice is concisely presented on one page. (The data are collected for the model expected to be the most popular.) Here's what you'll find and how to interpret the data we've provided:

The Ratings

These are the ratings in nine important categories, as well as an overall comparative rating. We have adopted the Olympic rating system with "10" being the best.

Overall Crash Test: This rating represents a combination of the front and side crash test ratings and provides a relative comparison of how this year's models did against each other. We give the best performers a 10 and the worst a 1. Remember to compare crash test results relative to other cars in the same size class. For details, see page 16.

Safety Features: This is an evaluation of how much extra safety is built into the car. We give credit for torso and pelvis side airbags, roll-sensing side airbags, a knee bolster bag, crash imminent braking, daytime running lamps, adjustable upper seat belt anchorages, lane keeping assist, pedestrian crash avoidance, automatic crash notification, lane departure warning, dynamic brake support, and frontal collision warning. We also include dynamic head restraints, and blind spot detection among other important safety features. See the "Safety Checklist" descriptions on the following pages.

Rollover: Electronic Stability Control has dramatically reduced the likelihood of rollovers. Due to this, we've reduced the "weight" that the rollover rating has in the vehicle's overall rating. When ESC is not able to prevent the vehicle from getting into a position where a rollover is possible, the vehicle's center of gravity plays a major role in whether or not that vehicle will actually rollover. The government uses a formula which estimates the "risk of rollover" in percentages. Using those percentages, we rated the 2020 vehicles on a relative basis. Again, the good news is that ESC is often able to prevent a vehicle from getting into a position where it is likely to roll over.

Preventive Maintenance: Each manufacturer suggests a preventive maintenance schedule designed to keep the car in good shape and to protect your rights under the warranty. Those with the lowest estimated PM costs get a 10 and the highest a 1. See pages 31-34 for the estimated costs and more information.

Repair Costs: It is virtually impossible to predict exactly what any new car will cost you in repairs. As such, we take nine typical repairs that you are likely to experience after your warranty expires and compare those costs among this year's models. Those with the lowest cost get a 10 and the highest a 1. See pages 31-34 for specific part repair cost and more information.

Warranty: This is an overall assessment of the manufacturer's basic, powertrain, corrosion, and roadside assistance warranties compared to all other manufacturer warranties. We also give credit for perks like free scheduled maintenance. We give the highest-rated warranties a 10 and the lowest a 1. For details, see page 28.

Fuel Economy: Here we compare the EPA mileage ratings of each car. The misers get a 10 and the guzzlers get a 1. For the purposes of the overall rating we pick the fuel economy rating of what is expected to be the most popular engine and drive train configuration. See pages 25-26 for details.

Complaints: This is where you'll find how each vehicle stacks up against hundreds of others on the road, based on the U.S. government complaint data for that vehicle. If the car has not been around long enough to have developed a complaint history, it is given a 5 (average). The least complained about cars get a 10, and the most problematic a 1. See page 41 for details.

Insurance Costs: Insurance companies rate vehicles to determine how much they plan to charge for insurance. While each insurer may have slightly different methods of rating, vehicles typically get a discount (max and min), a surcharge (max and min) or neither (average or typical). We looked at data from the insurance rating program of the largest insurer in America. This rating can predict the cost of insuring that vehicle. However, your location, age, driving record, and other factors also play a significant role in your cost of insurance. (See The Insurance Section pages 36-38.) Vehicles with a low rating (1 or 3) are more expensive to insure than other vehicles in that class or category. On the other hand, vehicles with a high rating (8 or 10) would be less expensive to insure in that particular class of vehicles. Because insurance companies may rate vehicles differently, it's important to compare prices between companies before you buy the car.

Overall Rating: This is the "bottom line." Using a combination of all of the key ratings, this tells how this vehicle stacks up against the others on a scale of 1 to 10. Due to the importance of safety, the combined crash test rating is 20 percent of the overall rating while the other eight ratings are 10 percent each. Vehicles with no front or side crash test results, as of our publication date, cannot be given an overall rating. In other categories, if information is unavailable, an "average" is included in order to develop an overall rating.

At-a-Glance

Status: Here we tell you if a vehicle is all-new, unchanged, or has received an appearance change. All-new vehicles (the minority) are brand new from the ground up. Unchanged vehicles are essentially the same, but could have some different color or feature options. Vehicles with an appearance change are those whose internal workings stayed

essentially the same, but have updated body panels.

Year Series Started: Each year the model is made, the production usually improves, and as a result there are fewer defects. Therefore, the longer a car has been made, the less likely you are to be plagued with manufacturing and design defects. On the other hand, the newer a car is, the more likely it is to have the latest in features and safety.

Twins: These are cars with different make and model names but share the same mechanics, drive train, and chassis. In some cases the vehicles are identical, in other cases the body style, pricing or options are different.

Body Styles: This is a listing of the various body styles available such as coupe, sedan, wagon, etc. SUVs and minivans are only offered in one body style. Data on the page are for the first style listed.

Seating: This is the number of seating positions in the most popular model. When more than one number is listed (for example, 5/6) it means that different seat configurations are available

Anti-theft Device: This lists the anti-theft devices standard for the vehicle. An immobilizer is an electronic device fitted to an automobile which prevents the engine from running unless the correct key (or other token) is present. This prevents the car from being "hot-wired" and driven away. A car alarm is an electronic device that emits high-volume sound and can sometimes flash the vehicles headlights in an attempt to discourage theft of the vehicle itself, its contents, or both. Passive devices automatically enter an armed state after the ignition

is turned off and doors are closed. Active devices require the user to perform some action like pressing a button to arm and disarm the system.

Parking Index Rating: Using the car's length, wheelbase, and turning circle, we have calculated how easy it will be to maneuver this car in tight spots. This rating of "very easy" to "very hard" is an indicator of how much difficulty you may have parking.

Where Made: Here we tell you where the car was assembled. You'll find that traditional domestic companies often build their vehicles in other countries. Also, many foreign companies build their cars in the U.S.

Fuel Factor

MPG Rating (city/hwy): This is the EPA-rated fuel economy for city and highway driving measured in miles per gallon. Most models have a variety of fuel economy ratings because of different engine and transmission options. We've selected the combination expected to be most popular.

Driving Range: Given the car's expected fuel economy and gas tank size, this value gives you an idea of the number of miles you can expect to go on a tank of gas.
Fuel: The type of fuel specified by the manufacturer: regular, premium, E85.

Annual Fuel Cost: This is an estimate based on driving 15,000 miles per year at $2.15/gallon for regular and $2.68/gallon for premium. If the vehicle takes E85 (85% ethanol and 15% gasoline) or gasoline, we calculated the annual cost using regular gasoline.

Gas Guzzler Tax: Auto companies are required to pay a gas guzzler tax on the sale of cars with exceptionally low fuel economy.

This tax does not apply to light trucks.

Greenhouse Gas Emissions: This shows the amount (in tons) of greenhouse gases (carbon dioxide, nitrous oxide, and methane) that a vehicle emits per year, along with the CO2 emitted in the production and distribution of the fuel.

Barrels of Oil Used Per Year: This is the number of barrels of petroleum the vehicle will likely use each year. One barrel, once refined, makes about 19.5 gallons of gas.

Competition

Here we tell you how the car stacks up with some of its key competitors. Use this information to broaden your choice of new car possibilities. This list is only a guideline, not an all-inclusive list of every possible alternative.

Price Range

This box contains information on the manufactuer's suggested retail price (MSRP). When available, we offer a variety of prices between the base and the most luxurious version of the car. The difference is often substantial. Usually the more expensive versions have fancy trim, larger engines, and lots of automatic equipment. The least expensive versions usually have manual transmissions and few extra features. In addition to the price range, we provide the estimated dealer markup. Remember, prices and dealer costs can change during the year. Use these figures for general reference and comparisons, not as a precise indication of exactly how much the car you are interested in will cost. See page 50 for a buying service designed to ensure that you get the very best price.

Safety Checklist

Crash Tests

Frontal and Side Crash Test Ratings: Here's where we tell you if the front or side crash test index was Very Good, Good, Average, Poor or Very Poor when compared to 2020 cars tested to date. To provide this rating we use the crash test for the vehicles with the best available safety equipment among the models when multiple models were tested. Unfortunately, not all of the 2020 models have been crash tested. If the car was previously tested and the 2020 model is unchanged, we can carry those results forward. For details about the crash test programs, see page 20.

Airbags

All vehicles have dual front airbags and head airbags that deploy across the side windows.

TYPES OF AIRBAGS

Airbags were introduced over 40 years ago and have been so successful in saving lives that car makers now include a variety of types. Here's a rundown of the basic types of airbags you'll find in today's vehicles. Manufacturers have various marketing names for these airbags.

Front: These deploy toward the front occupants and are now standard in all vehicles.

Head: These deploy from above the doors and are often called curtain airbags. They can reduce head injuries, shield from spraying glass, and provide protection in rollovers. Some form of these are in all vehicles.

Side: These deploy from the side of the seat or door and protect both the front and rear passengers in a side impact. Bags mounted in seats offer protection in a wider range of seating positions. Not all vehicles have these.

Rollover Protection: These head curtain airbags remain inflated for five seconds to protect in a sustained rollover. Not all vehicles have these.

Knee Bolster: These fill space between the front occupant's knees and instrument panel protecting the knees and legs. Not all vehicles have these.

We've identified three additional types of airbags that the vehicle may have. The side airbags have historically been two separate bag systems. Recently, most manufacturers have been combining torso and pelvis protection into one bag. When the two are combined, we list *Front Pelvis/Torso from Seat* after each airbag type. Otherwise we identify specific bag type (or not) that comes with the vehicle.

Torso Side Airbag: This airbag protects the chest from serious injury in a side impact crash.

Pelvis Side Airbag: Provides extra protection around the pelvis and hip area, the portion of the body that is usually closest to the vehicle's exterior.

Rollover Sensing Airbags: This is a special side airbag system which keeps the side airbags inflated longer in the event of a rollover. These are standard in many 2020 models.

Knee Bolster Airbag: This airbag fills the space between the front passenger's knees and the dashboard.

Crash Avoidance

Collision Avoidance: Great new technology is available that can react faster than you in the event of a frontal collision. There are three basic systems available: Crash Imminent Braking (CIB), Dynamic Brake Support (DBS), and Frontal Collision Warning (FCW). All of these systems use radar or laser sensors to either alert the driver (FCW) or actively intervene to apply the brakes prior to a crash. CIB will actually apply the brakes if you are about to experience a frontal crash. DBS will increase your braking force if the sensors determine that you are not applying enough force to stop in time. FCW will merely sound an alarm in the event of an imminent frontal collision. Whenever a vehicle has CIB or DBS, it will also have a Frontal Crash Warning. We believe that Crash Imminent Braking and Dynamic Brake Support are more useful than just a Frontal Collision Warning (and thus rated higher), however FCW is still a useful safety feature. The government has set standards for FCW and we've used a ^ to indicate which systems DON'T meet the FCW requirements.

Blind Spot Detection: This is a blind spot monitor that uses radar or other technologies to detect objects in the driver's blind spot. When switching lanes a visible, audible, or vibrating alert warns if a vehicle has entered your blind spot.

Lane Keeping Assist: Going one step beyond a Lane Departure Warning, cars with Lane Keeping Assist will actually apply pressure to the brakes or adjust the steering when it senses that a car is drifting out of its lane. Lane Departure Warning (LDW) will simply alert the driver. If the vehicle has Land Keeping Assist, it will also have LDW. We have combined the two since the technology for Lane Departure Warning is required for Lane Keeping Assist, which we believe to be a better technology. The government has set standards for LDW and we've used an ^ to indicate which systems DON'T meet the low requirements.

TIP

THE BEST SAFETY FEATURES

The good news: automatic crash avoidance features are becoming more available. The bad news: it is hard to determine which ones work the best. Currently, the National Highway Traffic Safety Administration has suggested specifications for two important safety features: Lane Departure Warning, and Frontal Collision Warning. Compliance with these specifications are voluntary. In the tradition of *The Car Book* exposing differences to stimulate market changes, in 2016 we started publishing which of these two safety features meets the government specifications and we continue to do so this year. However, it is important to note that having one of these features that doesn't meet government specifications is better than not having it at all. Unfortunately, in order to get some of these features you often have to buy expensive "option packages" or a more expensive model, which may include things you don't necessarily need or want.

Pedestrian Crash Avoidance: These systems utilize a variety of technologies such as infrared, camera, radar to detect pedestrians and adjust the car's course to avoid a collision.

General

Automatic Crash Notification: Using cellular technology and global positioning systems, some vehicles have the ability to send a call for help in the event of airbag deployment or accident. Often free initially, you'll have to pay extra later for this feature. There are several different types of ACN systems. Some simply dial 911 in the event of a crash while others connect your car to a call center which can determine the severity of the crash and dispatch emergency services. Some systems even send information about the crash to the call center.

Daytime Running Lights: Some cars offer daytime running lights that can reduce your chances of being in a crash by up to 40 percent by increasing the visibility of your vehicle. We indicate whether daytime running lights are standard, optional, or not available.

Safety Belts/Restraints

Dynamic Head Restraints: Many people position their seat and head restraint according to their own body and comfort requirements. This may not be the best position to protect you in a crash. These adjustors, sensing a crash, will automatically move the seat and headrest to the optimal position to help reduce injury during a rear-end crash. The Insurance Institute for Highway Safety (IIHS) has rated the performance of many headrests.

Adjustable Belts: Proper positioning of the safety belt across your chest is critical to obtaining the benefits of buckling up. Some systems allow you to adjust the height of the belt so it crosses your chest properly.

Specifications

Drive: This indicates the type of drive the manufacturer offers. This could be two wheel drive in the front (FWD) or rear (RWD) or all or four wheel drive (AWD/4WD).

Engine: This is the engine size (liters) and type that is expected to be the most popular. The engine types specify V6 or V8 for six or eight cylinders and I3, I4 or I6 for engines with cylinders in-line. For electric vehicles, we indicate the type of auxiliary power offered.

Transmission: This is the type of transmission expected to be the most popular. Most drivers today prefer automatic transmissions. The number listed with the transmission (5-sp.) is the number of gears or speeds. Then we list whether it's automatic or manual and if the transmission is a continuously variable transmission (CVT). CVT changes

smoothly and efficiently between ratios of engine to car speeds and can provide better fuel economy.

Tow Rating: Ratings of very low, low, average, high, and very high indicate the vehicle's relative ability to tow trailers or other loads. Some manufacturers do not provide a tow rating.

Head/Leg Room: This tells how roomy the front seat is. The values are given in inches and rated in comparison to all other vehicles.

Interior Space: This tells how roomy the car's passenger area should feel. This value is given in cubic feet and rated in comparison to all other vehicles. Many SUVs do not provide interior space specifications.

Cargo Space: This gives you the cubic feet available for cargo. For minivans, the volume is behind the last row of seats. In cars, it's the trunk space. We rate the roominess of the cargo space compared to all trucks, SUVs, and cars.

Wheelbase/Length: The distance between the centers of the front and rear wheels is the wheelbase, and the length is the distance from front bumper to rear bumper. Wheelbase can affect the ride and length affects how big the car "feels."

TIP

LOOK FOR THE BEST BETS

The CAR Book BEST BET

Ratings—10 Best, 1 Worst

Combo Crash Tests	—
Safety Features	7
Rollover	6
Preventive Maintenance	9
Repair Costs	7
Warranty	6
Fuel Economy	7
Complaints	10
Insurance Costs	10
OVERALL RATING	**—**

Acura ILX

At-a-Glance

Status/Year Series Started	Unchanged/2018
Twins	—
Body Styles	Sedan
Seating	5
Anti-Theft Device	Std. Pass. Immobil. & Alarm
Parking Index Rating	Easy
Where Made	Marysville, OH
Fuel Factor	
MPG Rating (city/hwy)	Good-25/35
Driving Range (mi.)	Short-379
Fuel Type	Premium
Annual Fuel Cost	Average-$1553
Gas Guzzler Tax	No
Greenhouse Gas Emissions (tons/yr.)	Low-5.1
Barrels of Oil Used per year	Average-11.4

How the Competition Rates

Competitors	Rating	Pg.
Audi A3	5	65
BMW 3 Series		73
Mercedes-Benz C	1	185

Price Range

Price Range	Retail	Markup
Base	$27,990	6%
Premium Package	$29,990	6%
Technology Package	$32,990	6%
Tech Pkg w/A-SPEC	$34,980	6%

Acura ILX

Safety Checklist

Crash Test:
Frontal .... –
Side .... –
Airbags:
Torso ...... Std. Fr. Pelvis/Torso from Seat
Roll Sensing .... Yes
Knee Bolster .... None
Crash Avoidance:
Collision Avoidance .... Optional CIB & DBS
Blind Spot Detection .... Optional
Lane Keeping Assist .... Optional
Pedestrian Crash Avoidance ...... Optional
General:
Auto. Crash Notification..... Op. Assist.-Fee
Day Running Lamps .... Standard
Safety Belt/Restraint:
Dynamic Head Restraints .... None
Adjustable Belt............ Standard Front

^Warning feature does not meet suggested government specifications.

Acura ILX

Specifications

Drive	FWD
Engine	2.4-liter I4
Transmission	8-sp. Automatic
Tow Rating (lbs.)	–
Head/Leg Room (in.)	Cramped-38/42.3
Interior Space (cu. ft.)	Very Cramped-89.3
Cargo Space (cu. ft.)	Very Cramped-12.3
Wheelbase/Length (in.)	105.1/181.9

Ratings—10 Best, 1 Worst

Combo Crash Tests	8
Safety Features	10
Rollover	4
Preventive Maintenance	5
Repair Costs	2
Warranty	6
Fuel Economy	3
Complaints	4
Insurance Costs	10
OVERALL RATING	**7**

Acura MDX

At-a-Glance

Status/Year Series Started. Unchanged/2014
Twins . . . . .Honda Pilot
Body Styles . . . . SUV
Seating 7
Anti-Theft Device . . . . . . Std. Pass. Immobil. & Alarm
Parking Index Rating . . . . Hard
Where Made. . . . . Lincoln, AL
Fuel Factor
  MPG Rating (city/hwy). Poor-18/27
  Driving Range (mi.) Average-413
  Fuel Type. . . . . .Premium
  Annual Fuel Cost . . . . Very High-$2104
  Gas Guzzler Tax . . . . .No
  Greenhouse Gas Emissions (tons/yr.). High-8.6
  Barrels of Oil Used per year High-15.7

How the Competition Rates

Competitors	Rating	Pg.
BMW X5		80
Cadillac XT5	3	90
Infiniti QX60	5	149

Price Range

Price Range	Retail	Markup
Base	$44,050	7%
SH-AWD w/Tech. Pkg	$50,460	7%
Advance w/RES	$56,500	7%
SH-AWD Adv, w/RES	$58,500	7%

Acura MDX

Safety Checklist

Crash Test:
  Frontal . . . . Very Good
  Side . . . . Average
Airbags:
  Torso . . . . . . Std. Fr. Pelvis/Torso from Seat
  Roll Sensing . . . . .Yes
  Knee Bolster . . . . Standard Driver
Crash Avoidance:
  Collision Avoidance . . . Standard CIB & DBS
  Blind Spot Detection . . . . Optional
  Lane Keeping Assist . . . . .Standard
  Pedestrian Crash Avoidance. . . . . . Optional
General:
  Auto. Crash Notification. . . . .Op. Assist.-Fee
  Day Running Lamps . . . . .Standard
Safety Belt/Restraint:
  Dynamic Head Restraints . . . . .None
  Adjustable Belt. . . . . Standard Front

^Warning feature does not meet suggested government specifications.

Acura MDX

Specifications

Drive. . . . . AWD
Engine 3.5-liter V6
Transmission . . . . .6-sp. Automatic
Tow Rating (lbs.) Low-3500
Head/Leg Room (in.) . . . . .Very Cramped-38.1/41.4
Interior Space (cu. ft.). . . . . Very Roomy-132.3
Cargo Space (cu. ft.) Cramped-14.8
Wheelbase/Length (in.) 111/193.6

Ratings—10 Best, 1 Worst

Combo Crash Tests	9
Safety Features	10
Rollover	4
Preventive Maintenance	5
Repair Costs	5
Warranty	6
Fuel Economy	3
Complaints	7
Insurance Costs	10
OVERALL RATING	**9**

Acura RDX

Acura RDX

At-a-Glance

Status/Year Series Started	Unchanged/2019
Twins	—
Body Styles	SUV
Seating	5
Anti-Theft Device	Std. Pass. Immobil. & Alarm
Parking Index Rating	Hard
Where Made	East Liberty, OH
Fuel Factor	
MPG Rating (city/hwy)	Poor-21/27
Driving Range (mi.)	Short-393
Fuel Type	Premium
Annual Fuel Cost	Very High-$2032
Gas Guzzler Tax	No
Greenhouse Gas Emissions (tons/yr.)	High-6.4
Barrels of Oil Used per year	High-14.3

How the Competition Rates

Competitors	Rating	Pg.
Acura RDX	9	63
Buick Encore	10	83
Lexus NX	5	171

Price Range

	Retail	Markup
FWD	37300	5%
AWD	39300	5%
Advance FWD	45400	5%
Advance AWD	47400	5%

Safety Checklist

Crash Test:
　Frontal . . . . Average
　Side . . . . Very Good
Airbags:
　Torso . . . . . . Std. Fr. Pelvis/Torso from Seat
　Roll Sensing . . . . Yes
　Knee Bolster . . . . Standard Front
Crash Avoidance:
　Collision Avoidance . . . Standard CIB & DBS
　Blind Spot Detection . . . . Optional
　Lane Keeping Assist . . . . Standard
　Pedestrian Crash Avoidance . . . . . . Optional
General:
　Auto. Crash Notification . . . . . Op. Assist.-Fee
　Day Running Lamps . . . . Standard
Safety Belt/Restraint:
　Dynamic Head Restraints . . . . None
　Adjustable Belt . . . . Standard Front

^Warning feature does not meet suggested government specifications.

Acura RDX

Specifications

Drive	AWD
Engine	2.0-liter I4
Transmission	10-sp. Automatic
Tow Rating (lbs.)	—
Head/Leg Room (in.)	Cramped-39.6/41.6
Interior Space (cu. ft.)	Roomy-104
Cargo Space (cu. ft.)	Roomy-31.1
Wheelbase/Length (in.)	108.3/186.8

Acura TLX

Ratings—10 Best, 1 Worst

Combo Crash Tests	10
Safety Features	8
Rollover	8
Preventive Maintenance	5
Repair Costs	3
Warranty	6
Fuel Economy	6
Complaints	3
Insurance Costs	10
OVERALL RATING	**9**

Acura TLX

Acura TLX

At-a-Glance

Status/Year Series Started........ Unchanged/2015
Twins . . . . —
Body Styles . . . . .Sedan
Seating 5
Anti-Theft Device . . . . . . Std. Pass. Immobil. & Alarm
Parking Index Rating . . . . Hard
Where Made. . . . . Marysville, OH
Fuel Factor
  MPG Rating (city/hwy) Average-23/33
  Driving Range (mi.) . . . . Very Long-458
  Fuel Type. . . . . .Premium
  Annual Fuel Cost . . . . .High-$1673
  Gas Guzzler Tax . . . . .No
  Greenhouse Gas Emissions (tons/yr.). . Average-6.5
  Barrels of Oil Used per year Average-12.2

How the Competition Rates

Competitors	Rating	Pg.
Audi A6		68
BMW 5 Series	6	75
Lexus ES		167

Price Range

Price Range	Retail	Markup
Base 2.4L	$33,000	5%
Base 3.5L	$36,200	5%
3.5L w/Tech. Package	$39,900	5%
SH-AWD w//Adv. Pkg	$45,750	5%

Safety Checklist

Crash Test:
  Frontal . . . . Very Good
  Side . . . . Very Good
Airbags:
  Torso . . . . . . Std. Fr. Pelvis/Torso from Seat
  Roll Sensing . . . . Yes
  Knee Bolster . . . . Standard Driver
Crash Avoidance:
  Collision Avoidance . . . .Optional CIB & DBS
  Blind Spot Detection . . . . Optional
  Lane Keeping Assist . . . . Optional
  Pedestrian Crash Avoidance. . . . . . Optional
General:
  Auto. Crash Notification. . . . .Op. Assist.-Fee
  Day Running Lamps . . . . .Standard
Safety Belt/Restraint:
  Dynamic Head Restraints . . . . .None
  Adjustable Belt. . . . . Standard Front

^Warning feature does not meet suggested government specifications.

Acura TLX

Specifications

Drive. . . . . FWD
Engine 2.4-liter I4
Transmission . . . . .8-sp. Automatic
Tow Rating (lbs.) . . . . —
Head/Leg Room (in.) Cramped-37.2/42.6
Interior Space (cu. ft.). Cramped-93.3
Cargo Space (cu. ft.) . . . . .Very Cramped-13.2
Wheelbase/Length (in.) 109.3/190.3

Audi A3 Compact

Audi A3

Ratings—10 Best, 1 Worst

Combo Crash Tests	6
Safety Features	7
Rollover	7
Preventive Maintenance	1
Repair Costs	5
Warranty	7
Fuel Economy	6
Complaints	4
Insurance Costs	5
OVERALL RATING	**5**

Audi A3

At-a-Glance

Status/Year Series Started	Unchanged/2015
Twins	Volkswagen Golf
Body Styles	Sedan, Wagon
Seating	5
Anti-Theft Device	Std. Pass. Immobil. & Alarm
Parking Index Rating	Easy
Where Made	Gyor, Hungary
Fuel Factor	
MPG Rating (city/hwy)	Average-24/33
Driving Range (mi.)	Short-397
Fuel Type	Premium
Annual Fuel Cost	Average-$1628
Gas Guzzler Tax	No
Greenhouse Gas Emissions (tons/yr.)	Average-6.6
Barrels of Oil Used per year	Average-12.2

How the Competition Rates

Competitors	Rating	Pg.
BMW 3 Series		72
Lexus IS	8	170
Mercedes-Benz C-Class	1	185

Price Range

	Retail	Markup
Premium Sedan	$31,950	8%
Prem. Plus Sdn Quattro	$38,200	8%
Premium Cabrio	$38,350	8%
Prestige Cabriolet Quattro	$49,500	8%

Safety Checklist

Crash Test:
  Frontal . . . . Average
  Side . . . . Average
Airbags:
  Torso . Std. Fr. & Opt. Rr. Pelvis/Torso from Seat
  Roll Sensing . . . . Yes
  Knee Bolster . . . . Standard Front
Crash Avoidance:
  Collision Avoidance . . . . Optional CIB & DBS
  Blind Spot Detection . . . . Optional
  Lane Keeping Assist . . . . Optional
  Pedestrian Crash Avoidance . . . . None
General:
  Auto. Crash Notification . . . . None
  Day Running Lamps . . . . Standard
Safety Belt/Restraint:
  Dynamic Head Restraints . . . . None
  Adjustable Belt . . . . Standard Front

^Warning feature does not meet suggested government specifications.

Audi A3

Specifications

Drive	AWD
Engine	2.0-liter I4
Transmission	6-sp. Automatic
Tow Rating (lbs.)	–
Head/Leg Room (in.)	Very Cramped-36.5/41.2
Interior Space (cu. ft.)	Very Cramped-86
Cargo Space (cu. ft.)	Very Cramped-10.03
Wheelbase/Length (in.)	103.8/175.4

Ratings—10 Best, 1 Worst

Combo Crash Tests	2
Safety Features	5
Rollover	8
Preventive Maintenance	4
Repair Costs	2
Warranty	7
Fuel Economy	7
Complaints	3
Insurance Costs	5
OVERALL RATING	**2**

Audi A4

At-a-Glance

Status/Year Series Started........ Unchanged/2017
Twins .... —
Body Styles .... Sedan
Seating 5
Anti-Theft Device ..... Std. Pass. Immobil. & Alarm
Parking Index Rating .... Average
Where Made................. Ingolstadt, Germany
Fuel Factor
  MPG Rating (city/hwy).............. Good-25/33
  Driving Range (mi.) Long-429
  Fuel Type......................... Premium
  Annual Fuel Cost .... Average-$1588
  Gas Guzzler Tax .... No
  Greenhouse Gas Emissions (tons/yr.)..... Low-5.2
  Barrels of Oil Used per year Average-11.8

How the Competition Rates

Competitors	Rating	Pg.
Acura ILX		61
BMW 3 Series		72
Mercedes-Benz C-Class	1	185

Price Range

	Retail	Markup
2.0T Premium Sedan	$36,000	8%
2.0T Prem. Sdn Quattro	$40,500	8%
2.0T Prem. Plus Sdn Quattro	$43,700	8%
2.0T Prestige Sdn Quattro	$50,000	8%

Audi A4

Safety Checklist

Crash Test:
  Frontal .... Very Poor
  Side .... Average
Airbags:
  Torso . Std. Fr. & Opt. Rr. Pelvis/Torso from Seat
  Roll Sensing .... No
  Knee Bolster .... None
Crash Avoidance:
  Collision Avoidance . . . Std. CIB & Opt. DBS
  Blind Spot Detection .... Optional
  Lane Keeping Assist .... Optional*
  Pedestrian Crash Avoidance...... Standard
General:
  Auto. Crash Notification..... Dial Assist-Fee
  Day Running Lamps .... Standard
Safety Belt/Restraint:
  Dynamic Head Restraints .... None
  Adjustable Belt............ Standard Front

^Warning feature does not meet suggested government specifications.

Audi A4

Specifications

Drive.................................. AWD
Engine 2.0-liter I4
Transmission .... 8-sp. Automatic
Tow Rating (lbs.) .... —
Head/Leg Room (in.) Cramped-38.9/41.3
Interior Space (cu. ft.).............. Cramped-92
Cargo Space (cu. ft.) .... Very Cramped-13
Wheelbase/Length (in.) 111/186.1

Audi A5 Intermediate

Ratings—10 Best, 1 Worst

Combo Crash Tests	—
Safety Features	9
Rollover	8
Preventive Maintenance	4
Repair Costs	4
Warranty	7
Fuel Economy	7
Complaints	10
Insurance Costs	3
OVERALL RATING	**—**

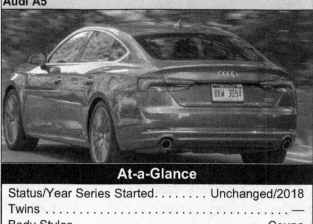
Audi A5

Audi A5

At-a-Glance

Status/Year Series Started........ Unchanged/2018
Twins .... —
Body Styles ....Coupe
Seating 4
Anti-Theft Device ...... Std. Pass. Immobil. & Alarm
Parking Index Rating .... Average
Where Made..................Ingolstadt, Germany
Fuel Factor
  MPG Rating (city/hwy).............. Good-24/34
  Driving Range (mi.) Long-423
  Fuel Type.............................Premium
  Annual Fuel Cost ....Average-$1611
  Gas Guzzler Tax ....No
  Greenhouse Gas Emissions (tons/yr.)..... Low-5.4
  Barrels of Oil Used per year Average-12.2

How the Competition Rates

Competitors	Rating	Pg.
BMW 5 Series	6	75
Infiniti Q50	3	147
Lexus ES		167

Price Range

	Retail	Markup
2.0T Prem. Cpe Quattro	$42,800	8%
2.0T Prem. Plus Cpe Quattro	$45,800	8%
2.0T Prem. Cabrio Quattro	$49,600	8%
2.0T Prem. Plus Cabrio Quattro	$52,600	8%

Safety Checklist

Crash Test:
  Frontal .... —
  Side .... —
Airbags:
  Torso ...... Std. Fr. Pelvis/Torso from Seat
  Roll Sensing .... Yes
  Knee Bolster .... Standard Front
Crash Avoidance:
  Collision Avoidance . . Standard CIB & DBS*
  Blind Spot Detection .... Optional
  Lane Keeping Assist .... Warning Only Opt.
  Pedestrian Crash Avoidance......Standard
General:
  Auto. Crash Notification..... Dial Assist-Fee
  Day Running Lamps ....Standard
Safety Belt/Restraint:
  Dynamic Head Restraints ....None
  Adjustable Belt............Standard Front

^Warning feature does not meet suggested government specifications.

Audi A5

Specifications

Drive................................... AWD
Engine 2.0-liter I4
Transmission ....7-sp. Automatic
Tow Rating (lbs.) .... —
Head/Leg Room (in.) Cramped-39.4/41.3
Interior Space (cu. ft.).......... Very Cramped-84
Cargo Space (cu. ft.) ....Very Cramped-11.6
Wheelbase/Length (in.) 111.2/186.3

Ratings—10 Best, 1 Worst

Combo Crash Tests	—
Safety Features	8
Rollover	9
Preventive Maintenance	4
Repair Costs	1
Warranty	7
Fuel Economy	5
Complaints	10
Insurance Costs	3
OVERALL RATING	**7**

Audi A6

Audi A6

At-a-Glance

```
Status/Year Series Started . . . . . . . Unchanged/2019
Twins . . . . . . . . . . . . . . . . . . . . . . . . . . . . . . . . . . . —
Body Styles . . . . . . . . . . . . . . . . . . . . . . . . . . . Sedan
Seating . . . . . . . . . . . . . . . . . . . . . . . . . . . . . . . . . . . 5
Anti-Theft Device . . . . . . Std. Pass. Immobil. & Alarm
Parking Index Rating . . . . . . . . . . . . . . . . . . . Average
Where Made . . . . . . . . . . . . . . Neckarsulm, Germany
Fuel Factor
  MPG Rating (city/hwy) . . . . . . . . . . . Average-22/29
  Driving Range (mi.) . . . . . . . . . . . . Very Long-482
  Fuel Type . . . . . . . . . . . . . . . . . . . . . . . . . .Premium
  Annual Fuel Cost . . . . . . . . . . . . . . . . . .High-$1862
  Gas Guzzler Tax . . . . . . . . . . . . . . . . . . . . . . . . .No
  Greenhouse Gas Emissions (tons/yr.) . . Average-6.0
  Barrels of Oil Used per year . . . . . . . . . . High-13.2
```

How the Competition Rates

Competitors	Rating	Pg.
Acura TLX	9	64
Lincoln MKZ	4	176
Volvo S60		237

Price Range

	Retail	Markup
3.0T Premium	$58,900	7%
3.0 Pre. Plus Quattro	$62,700	8%
3.0 Prestige Quattro	$67,100	8%

Safety Checklist

```
Crash Test:
  Frontal . . . . . . . . . . . . . . . . . . . . . . . . . . . . . . −
  Side . . . . . . . . . . . . . . . . . . . . . . . . . . . . . . . . −
Airbags:
  Torso . . . Std. Fr. & Rear Pelvis/Torso from Seat
  Roll Sensing . . . . . . . . . . . . . . . . . . . . . . Yes
  Knee Bolster . . . . . . . . . . . . Standard Front
Crash Avoidance:
  Collision Avoidance . . . Standard CIB & DBS
  Blind Spot Detection . . . . . . . . . . . Optional
  Lane Keeping Assist . . . . . . . . . . .Optional*
  Pedestrian Crash Avoidance . . . . . . . . .None
General:
  Auto. Crash Notification . . . . . . . . . . . .None
  Day Running Lamps . . . . . . . . . . .Standard
Safety Belt/Restraint:
  Dynamic Head Restraints . . . . . . . . . .None
  Adjustable Belt . . . . . . . . . . . Standard Front
```

^Warning feature does not meet suggested government specifications.

Audi A6

Specifications

```
Drive . . . . . . . . . . . . . . . . . . . . . . . . . . . . . . AWD
Engine . . . . . . . . . . . . . . . . . . . . . . . . .3.0-liter V6
Transmission . . . . . . . . . . . . . . . .7-sp. Automatic
Tow Rating (lbs.) . . . . . . . . . . . . . . . . . . . . . . . . −
Head/Leg Room (in.) . . . . . . Very Cramped-38/41.3
Interior Space (cu. ft.) . . . . . . . . . . . . . . Average-99
Cargo Space (cu. ft.) . . . . . . . . . . . . Cramped-13.7
Wheelbase/Length (in.) . . . . . . . . . . . 115.1/194.4
```

Audi Q3 — Small SUV

Ratings—10 Best, 1 Worst

Combo Crash Tests	—
Safety Features	7
Rollover	4
Preventive Maintenance	4
Repair Costs	3
Warranty	7
Fuel Economy	4
Complaints	10
Insurance Costs	10
OVERALL RATING	—

Audi Q3

Audi Q3

At-a-Glance

Status/Year Series Started. All-New/2020
Twins . . . . —
Body Styles . . . . SUV
Seating 5
Anti-Theft Device . . . . . . Std. Pass. Immobil. & Alarm
Parking Index Rating . . . . Average
Where Made. . . . . Martorell, Spain
Fuel Factor
  MPG Rating (city/hwy). Poor-19/27
  Driving Range (mi.) . . . . Very Short-350
  Fuel Type. . . . . .Premium
  Annual Fuel Cost . . . . .High-$1676
  Gas Guzzler Tax . . . . .No
  Greenhouse Gas Emissions (tons/yr.). . Average-6.6
  Barrels of Oil Used per year High-15.0

How the Competition Rates

Competitors	Rating	Pg.
Acura RDX	9	61
Buick Encore	10	83
Lexus NX	5	171

Price Range

Price Range	Retail	Markup
2.0T Premium	$32,900	8%
2.0T Premium Quattro	$35,000	8%
2.0T Premium Plus	$35,800	8%
2.0T Prem. Plus Quattro	$37,900	8%

Safety Checklist

Crash Test:
  Frontal . . . . –
  Side . . . . –
Airbags:
  Torso . . . . . . Std. Fr. Pelvis/Torso from Seat
  Roll Sensing . . . . .Yes
  Knee Bolster .None
Crash Avoidance:
  Collision Avoidance . . . . .Std.
  Blind Spot Detection . . . . Optional
  Lane Keeping Assist . . . . Optional
  Pedestrian Crash Avoidance. . . . . .Standard
General:
  Auto. Crash Notification. . . . . .None
  Day Running Lamps . . . . .Standard
Safety Belt/Restraint:
  Dynamic Head Restraints . . . . .None
  Adjustable Belt. . . . . Standard Front

^Warning feature does not meet suggested government specifications.

Audi Q3

Specifications

Drive. . . . . AWD
Engine 2.0-liter I4
Transmission . . . . .6-sp. Automatic
Tow Rating (lbs.) . . . . Very Low-1500
Head/Leg Room (in.) . . . . . . Very Cramped-36.3/42
Interior Space (cu. ft.). . . . . –
Cargo Space (cu. ft.) Roomy-23.7
Wheelbase/Length (in.) 106.0/177.0

Audi Q5 | Medium SUV

Ratings—10 Best, 1 Worst

Combo Crash Tests	—
Safety Features	4
Rollover	4
Preventive Maintenance	4
Repair Costs	2
Warranty	7
Fuel Economy	5
Complaints	6
Insurance Costs	5
OVERALL RATING	**—**

Audi Q5

Audi Q5

At-a-Glance

Status/Year Series Started. Unchanged/2018
Twins . . . . —
Body Styles . . . . SUV
Seating 5
Anti-Theft Device . . . . . . Std. Pass. Immobil. & Alarm
Parking Index Rating . . . . Average
Where Made. . . . . .Ingolstadt, Germany
Fuel Factor
  MPG Rating (city/hwy) Average-23/27
  Driving Range (mi.) Long-456
  Fuel Type. . . . . .Premium
  Annual Fuel Cost . . . . .High-$1808
  Gas Guzzler Tax . . . . .No
  Greenhouse Gas Emissions (tons/yr.). . Average-6.0
  Barrels of Oil Used per year High-13.2

How the Competition Rates

Competitors	Rating	Pg.
Acura MDX	7	62
Lexus RX	4	173
Lincoln Nautilis	5	181

Price Range

	Retail	Markup
2.0T Premium	$41,500	8%
2.0T Premium Plus	$45,500	8%
2.0 Prestige	$50,800	8%

Safety Checklist

Crash Test:
  Frontal . . . . —
  Side . . . . —
Airbags:
  Torso . Std. Fr. & Opt. Rr. Pelvis/Torso from Seat
  Roll Sensing . . . . .Yes
  Knee Bolster .None
Crash Avoidance:
  Collision Avoidance . . . .Optional CIB & DBS
  Blind Spot Detection . . . . Optional
  Lane Keeping Assist . . . Warning Only Opt.*
  Pedestrian Crash Avoidance. . . . . .None
General:
  Auto. Crash Notification. . . . . .None
  Day Running Lamps . . . . .Standard
Safety Belt/Restraint:
  Dynamic Head Restraints . . . . .Opt.
  Adjustable Belt. . . . . Standard Front

^W-arning feature does not meet suggested government specifications.

Audi Q5

Specifications

Drive. . . . . .AWD
Engine 2.0-liter I4
Transmission . . . . .7-sp. Automatic
Tow Rating (lbs.) . . . . —
Head/Leg Room (in.) Roomy-41.7/40.9
Interior Space (cu. ft.). —
Cargo Space (cu. ft.) Roomy-26.8
Wheelbase/Length (in.) 111/183.6

Ratings—10 Best, 1 Worst

Combo Crash Tests	6
Safety Features	8
Rollover	4
Preventive Maintenance	3
Repair Costs	1
Warranty	7
Fuel Economy	3
Complaints	4
Insurance Costs	5
OVERALL RATING	**3**

Audi Q7

Audi Q7

At-a-Glance

Status/Year Series Started........ Unchanged/2016
Twins .... —
Body Styles .... SUV
Seating 7
Anti-Theft Device ...... Std. Pass. Immobil. & Alarm
Parking Index Rating .... Very Hard
Where Made................. Bratislava, Slovakia
Fuel Factor
  MPG Rating (city/hwy)............. Poor-19/25
  Driving Range (mi.) .... Very Long-479
  Fuel Type......................... Premium
  Annual Fuel Cost .... Very High-$2092
  Gas Guzzler Tax .... No
  Greenhouse Gas Emissions (tons/yr.).. Average-6.9
  Barrels of Oil Used per year High-15.7

How the Competition Rates

Competitors	Rating	Pg.
BMW X5		80
Cadillac XT5	3	90
Lexus RX	4	173

Price Range

Price Range	Retail	Markup
2.0T Premium	$49,900	8%
2.0T Premium Plus	$53,900	8%
3.0T Premium Plus	$60,400	8%
3.0T Prestige	$65,400	8%

Safety Checklist

Crash Test:
  Frontal .... Average
  Side .... Average
Airbags:
  Torso . Std. Fr. & Opt. Rr. Pelvis/Torso from Seat
  Roll Sensing .... Yes
  Knee Bolster .... None
Crash Avoidance:
  Collision Avoidance . . . Std. CIB & Opt. DBS
  Blind Spot Detection .... Optional
  Lane Keeping Assist .... Optional
  Pedestrian Crash Avoidance...... Standard
General:
  Auto. Crash Notification..... Dial Assist-Fee
  Day Running Lamps .... Standard
Safety Belt/Restraint:
  Dynamic Head Restraints .... None
  Adjustable Belt............ Standard Front

^Warning feature does not meet suggested government specifications.

Audi Q7

Specifications

Drive................................... AWD
Engine 3.0-liter V6
Transmission .... 8-sp. Automatic
Tow Rating (lbs.) High-7700
Head/Leg Room (in.) Cramped-38.4/41.7
Interior Space (cu. ft.)................ —
Cargo Space (cu. ft.) Cramped-14.8
Wheelbase/Length (in.) 117.9/199.6

Ratings—10 Best, 1 Worst

Combo Crash Tests	—
Safety Features	6
Rollover	7
Preventive Maintenance	4
Repair Costs	3
Warranty	9
Fuel Economy	6
Complaints	6
Insurance Costs	1
OVERALL RATING	**—**

BMW 2 Series

BMW 2 Series

At-a-Glance

Status/Year Series Started. Unchanged/2016
Twins . . . . —
Body Styles . . . . .Coupe
Seating 4
Anti-Theft Device . Std. Pass. Immobil. & Active Alarm
Parking Index Rating . . . . Easy
Where Made. . . . . Leipzig, Germany
Fuel Factor
  MPG Rating (city/hwy) Average-23/35
  Driving Range (mi.) . . . . Very Short-373
  Fuel Type. . . . . .Premium
  Annual Fuel Cost . . . . .Average-$1638
  Gas Guzzler Tax . . . . .No
  Greenhouse Gas Emissions (tons/yr.). . Average-6.4
  Barrels of Oil Used per year Average-12.2

How the Competition Rates

Competitors	Rating	Pg.
Audi A3	5	65
Lexus IS	8	170
Toyota Corrolla	7	222

Price Range

Price Range	Retail	Markup
230i Coupe	$34,800	6%
230xi Convertible	$42,600	6%
M240i Coupe	$45,300	6%
M 240xi Coupe	$47,300	6%

Safety Checklist

Crash Test:
  Frontal . . . . −
  Side . . . . −
Airbags:
  Torso . . . . Std. Fr. Torso from Seat
  Roll Sensing . . . . Yes
  Knee Bolster . . . . .Standard Front
Crash Avoidance:
  Collision Avoidance . . . Optional CIB & DBS*
  Blind Spot Detection . . . . .None
  Lane Keeping Assist . . . Warning Only Opt.*
  Pedestrian Crash Avoidance. . . . . . Optional
General:
  Auto. Crash Notif. Op. Assist. & Crash Info-Free
  Day Running Lamps . . . . .Standard
Safety Belt/Restraint:
  Dynamic Head Restraints . . . . .None
  Adjustable Belt. . . . . .None

^Warning feature does not meet suggested government specifications.

BMW 2 Series

Specifications

Drive. . . . . .RWD
Engine 2.0-liter I4
Transmission . . . . .8-sp. Automatic
Tow Rating (lbs.) . . . . —
Head/Leg Room (in.) Average-40.1/41.5
Interior Space (cu. ft.). . . . . Very Cramped-90
Cargo Space (cu. ft.) Cramped-13.8
Wheelbase/Length (in.) 105.9/174.7

Ratings—10 Best, 1 Worst

Combo Crash Tests	—
Safety Features	7
Rollover	9
Preventive Maintenance	4
Repair Costs	2
Warranty	9
Fuel Economy	7
Complaints	9
Insurance Costs	3
OVERALL RATING	**—**

BMW 3 Series

BMW 3 Series

BMW 3 Series

At-a-Glance

Status/Year Series Started........ Unchanged/2019
Twins ....—
Body Styles ....Sedan, Wagon, Convertible
Seating 5
Anti-Theft Device . Std. Pass. Immobil. & Active Alarm
Parking Index Rating .... Average
Where Made..... Munich, Germany / Toluca, Mexico
Fuel Factor
  MPG Rating (city/hwy).............. Good-23/33
  Driving Range (mi.) Average-427
  Fuel Type........................Premium
  Annual Fuel Cost ....Average-$1685
  Gas Guzzler Tax ....No
  Greenhouse Gas Emissions (tons/yr.)..... Low-5.5
  Barrels of Oil Used per year Average-12.2

How the Competition Rates

Competitors	Rating	Pg.
Audi A4	2	66
Lexus IS	8	170
Mercedes-Benz C-Class	1	185

Price Range

Price Range	Retail	Markup
320i	$34,900	6%
328d	$41,750	6%
330xi	$42,250	6%
340xi	$50,950	6%

Safety Checklist

Crash Test:
  Frontal . . . . –
  Side . . . . –
Airbags:
  Torso . . . . Std. Fr. Torso from Seat
  Roll Sensing . . . . .Yes
  Knee Bolster . . . . Standard Front
Crash Avoidance:
  Collision Avoidance . . . Optional CIB & DBS*
  Blind Spot Detection . . . . Optional
  Lane Keeping Assist . . . . Optional
  Pedestrian Crash Avoidance. . . . . . Optional
General:
  Auto. Crash Notif. . Op. Assist. & Crash Info-Free
  Day Running Lamps . . . . .Standard
Safety Belt/Restraint:
  Dynamic Head Restraints . . . . .None
  Adjustable Belt. . . . . .None

^Warning feature does not meet suggested government specifications.

BMW 3 Series

Specifications

Drive. . . . . .RWD
Engine 2.0-liter I4
Transmission . . . . .8-sp. Automatic
Tow Rating (lbs.) . . . . –
Head/Leg Room (in.) Cramped-38.7/42
Interior Space (cu. ft.). Average-102
Cargo Space (cu. ft.) . . . . –
Wheelbase/Length (in.) 112.2/185.7

Ratings—10 Best, 1 Worst

Combo Crash Tests	—
Safety Features	7
Rollover	9
Preventive Maintenance	4
Repair Costs	2
Warranty	9
Fuel Economy	6
Complaints	8
Insurance Costs	1
OVERALL RATING	**—**

BMW 4 Series

BMW 4 Series

At-a-Glance

Status/Year Series Started Unchanged/2014
Twins . . . . —
Body Styles . . . . Coupe, Convertible
Seating 4
Anti-Theft Device . Std. Pass. Immobil. & Active Alarm
Parking Index Rating . . . . Average
Where Made . . . . .Munich, Germany
Fuel Factor
   MPG Rating (city/hwy) Average-23/35
   Driving Range (mi.) Long-430
   Fuel Type . . . . .Premium
   Annual Fuel Cost . . . . .Average-$1638
   Gas Guzzler Tax . . . . .No
   Greenhouse Gas Emissions (tons/yr.) . . Average-6.7
   Barrels of Oil Used per year Average-12.2

How the Competition Rates

Competitors	Rating	Pg.
Infiniti Q50	3	147
Lexus IS	8	170
Mercedes-Benz C-Class	1	185

Price Range	Retail	Markup
430i Coupe	$42,200	6%
430xi Gran Coupe	$44,200	6%
440i Convertible	$57,500	7%
440xi Convertible	$59,500	7%

Safety Checklist

Crash Test:
   Frontal . . . . −
   Side . . . . −
Airbags:
   Torso . . . . Std. Fr. Torso from Seat
   Roll Sensing . . . . .Yes
   Knee Bolster . . . . Standard Front
Crash Avoidance:
   Collision Avoidance . . . Optional CIB & DBS*
   Blind Spot Detection . . . . Optional
   Lane Keeping Assist . . . Warning Only Opt.*
   Pedestrian Crash Avoidance . . . . . . Optional
General:
   Auto. Crash Notif. . Op. Assist. & Crash Info-Free
   Day Running Lamps . . . . .Standard
Safety Belt/Restraint:
   Dynamic Head Restraints . . . . .None
   Adjustable Belt. . . . . .None

^Warning feature does not meet suggested government specifications.

BMW 4 Series

Specifications

Drive . . . . .RWD
Engine 2.0-liter I4
Transmission . . . . .8-sp. Automatic
Tow Rating (lbs.) . . . . —
Head/Leg Room (in.) Average-39.8/42.2
Interior Space (cu. ft.). . . . . Very Cramped-90
Cargo Space (cu. ft.) Cramped-15.7
Wheelbase/Length (in.) 110.6/182.6

BMW 5 Series   Intermediate

Ratings—10 Best, 1 Worst

Combo Crash Tests	4
Safety Features	7
Rollover	9
Preventive Maintenance	9
Repair Costs	1
Warranty	9
Fuel Economy	6
Complaints	7
Insurance Costs	1
OVERALL RATING	**6**

BMW 5 Series

BMW 5 Series

At-a-Glance

Status/Year Series Started. Unchanged/2011
Twins . . . . —
Body Styles . . . . Sedan, Wagon
Seating 5
Anti-Theft Device . Std. Pass. Immobil. & Active Alarm
Parking Index Rating . . . . Hard
Where Made. . .Dingolfing, Germany / Toluca, Mexico
Fuel Factor
　MPG Rating (city/hwy). Average-23/34
　Driving Range (mi.) . . . . Very Long-498
　Fuel Type. . . . . .Premium
　Annual Fuel Cost . . . . .Average-$1655
　Gas Guzzler Tax . . . . .No
　Greenhouse Gas Emissions (tons/yr.). . Average-6.6
　Barrels of Oil Used per year Average-12.2

How the Competition Rates

Competitors	Rating	Pg.
Infiniti Q50	3	147
Lexus ES		167
Volvo S60		237

Price Range

Price Range	Retail	Markup
530i	$52,400	6%
530xe	$54,700	6%
540xi	$60,000	7%
M550i	$73,400	7%

Safety Checklist

Crash Test:
　Frontal . . . . Very Poor
　Side . . . . .Good
Airbags:
　Torso . . . . Std. Fr. Torso from Seat
　Roll Sensing . . . . .Yes
　Knee Bolster .None
Crash Avoidance:
　Collision Avoidance . . . Optional CIB & DBS*
　Blind Spot Detection . . . . Optional
　Lane Keeping Assist . . . Warning Only Opt.*
　Pedestrian Crash Avoidance. . . . . . Optional
General:
　Auto. Crash Notif. . . Op. Assist. & Crash Info-Free
　Day Running Lamps . . . . .Standard
Safety Belt/Restraint:
　Dynamic Head Restraints . . . Standard Front
　Adjustable Belt. . . . . .None

^Warning feature does not meet suggested government specifications.

BMW 5 Series

Specifications

Drive. . . . . RWD
Engine 2.0-liter I4
Transmission . . . . .8-sp. Automatic
Tow Rating (lbs.) . . . . —
Head/Leg Room (in.) Average-40.5/41.4
Interior Space (cu. ft.). Average-102
Cargo Space (cu. ft.) Average-18.4
Wheelbase/Length (in.) 116.9/193.4

BMW 7 Series | Large

Ratings—10 Best, 1 Worst

Combo Crash Tests	—
Safety Features	10
Rollover	7
Preventive Maintenance	1
Repair Costs	1
Warranty	9
Fuel Economy	4
Complaints	5
Insurance Costs	1
OVERALL RATING	—

BMW 7 Series

BMW 7 Series

At-a-Glance

Status/Year Series Started........ Unchanged/2016
Twins .... —
Body Styles ....Sedan
Seating 5
Anti-Theft Device . Std. Pass. Immobil. & Active Alarm
Parking Index Rating ....Very Hard
Where Made...Dingolfing, Germany / Toluca, Mexico
Fuel Factor
  MPG Rating (city/hwy)...............Poor-21/29
  Driving Range (mi.) ....Very Long-494
  Fuel Type............................Premium
  Annual Fuel Cost ....High-$1858
  Gas Guzzler Tax ....No
  Greenhouse Gas Emissions (tons/yr.).. Average-6.1
  Barrels of Oil Used per year High-13.7

How the Competition Rates

Competitors	Rating	Pg.
Cadillac CT6		86
Mercedes-Benz E-Class	3	186
Tesla Model S	10	216

Price Range

Price Range	Retail	Markup
740i	$83,100	8%
740i xDrive	$86,100	8%
750i	$96,400	8%
750i xDrive	$99,400	8%

Safety Checklist

Crash Test:
  Frontal .... —
  Side .... —
Airbags:
  Torso .... Std. Fr. Torso from Seat
  Roll Sensing ....Yes
  Knee Bolster .... Standard Front
Crash Avoidance:
  Collision Avoidance ... Optional CIB & DBS*
  Blind Spot Detection .... Optional
  Lane Keeping Assist ....Optional*
  Pedestrian Crash Avoidance...... Optional
General:
  Auto. Crash Notif... Op. Assist. & Crash Info-Free
  Day Running Lamps ....Standard
Safety Belt/Restraint:
  Dynamic Head Restraints ... Standard Front
  Adjustable Belt....................None

^Warning feature does not meet suggested government specifications.

BMW 7 Series

Specifications

Drive....................................RWD
Engine 6.0-liter V8
Transmission ....8-sp. Automatic
Tow Rating (lbs.) .... —
Head/Leg Room (in.) Average-39.9/41.4
Interior Space (cu. ft.)............... Roomy-107
Cargo Space (cu. ft.) Average-18.2
Wheelbase/Length (in.) 126.4/206.6

Ratings—10 Best, 1 Worst

Combo Crash Tests	—
Safety Features	6
Rollover	4
Preventive Maintenance	4
Repair Costs	10
Warranty	9
Fuel Economy	10
Complaints	4
Insurance Costs	10
OVERALL RATING	**—**

BMW i3

BMW i3

At-a-Glance

Status/Year Series Started. Unchanged/2016
Twins . . . .—
Body Styles . . . . .Coupe
Seating. 4
Anti-Theft Device . Std. Pass. Immobil. & Active Alarm
Parking Index Rating . . . . .Very Easy
Where Made. . . . . .Leipzig, Germany
Fuel Factor
   MPG Rating (city/hwy) . . . . Very Good-137/111
   Driving Range (mi.) 180
   Fuel Type. . . . . .Premium
   Annual Fuel Cost . . . . .Very Low-$650
   Gas Guzzler Tax . . . . .No
   Greenhouse Gas Emissions (tons/yr.). Very Low-0.5
   Barrels of Oil Used per year . . . . Very Low-1.2

How the Competition Rates

Competitors	Rating	Pg.
Chevrolet Bolt		93
Tesla Model 3		215
Toyota Prius Prime		226

Price Range

Price Range	Retail	Markup
60 Ah Hatchback	$42,400	6%
90 Ah Hatchback	$43,600	6%
90 Ah HB w/Range Ext	$47,450	6%

Safety Checklist

Crash Test:
   Frontal . . . . —
   Side . . . . —
Airbags:
   Torso . . . . Std. Fr. Torso from Seat
   Roll Sensing . . . . .Yes
   Knee Bolster . . . . .Standard Front
Crash Avoidance:
   Collision Avoidance . . . Optional CIB & DBS*
   Blind Spot Detection . . . . .None
   Lane Keeping Assist . . . Warning Only Opt.*
   Pedestrian Crash Avoidance. . . . . . . Optional
General:
   Auto. Crash Notif. . . Op. Assist. & Crash Info-Free
   Day Running Lamps . . . . .Standard
Safety Belt/Restraint:
   Dynamic Head Restraints . . . . .None
   Adjustable Belt. . . . . .None

^Warning feature does not meet suggested government specifications.

BMW i3

Specifications

Drive. . . . . RWD
Engine . . . . Electric
Transmission . . . . .CVT
Tow Rating (lbs.) . . . . —
Head/Leg Room (in.) Cramped-39.6/40.5
Interior Space (cu. ft.). . . . . .Very Cramped-83.1
Cargo Space (cu. ft.) . . . . .Very Cramped-11.8
Wheelbase/Length (in.) 101/157

Ratings—10 Best, 1 Worst

Combo Crash Tests	—
Safety Features	6
Rollover	4
Preventive Maintenance	7
Repair Costs	1
Warranty	9
Fuel Economy	6
Complaints	4
Insurance Costs	3
OVERALL RATING	—

BMW X1

BMW X1

At-a-Glance

Status/Year Series Started. . Apperance Change/2016
Twins . . . . —
Body Styles . . . . SUV
Seating 5
Anti-Theft Device . Std. Pass. Immobil. & Active Alarm
Parking Index Rating . . . . Easy
Where Made. . . . . .Leipzig, Germany
Fuel Factor
  MPG Rating (city/hwy) Average-22/32
  Driving Range (mi.) Average-412
  Fuel Type. . . . . .Premium
  Annual Fuel Cost . . . . .High-$1740
  Gas Guzzler Tax . . . . .No
  Greenhouse Gas Emissions (tons/yr.) Low-5.7
  Barrels of Oil Used per year Average-12.7

How the Competition Rates

Competitors	Rating	Pg.
Acura RDX	9	63
Buick Encore	10	83
Lexus NX	5	171

Price Range	Retail	Markup
sDrive28i	$33,900	6%
XDrive28i	$35,900	6%
sDrive28i	$39,250	6%
XDrive28i	$41,250	6%

Safety Checklist

Crash Test:
  Frontal . . . . —
  Side . . . . —
Airbags:
  Torso . . . . Std. Fr. Torso from Seat
  Roll Sensing . . . . .Yes
  Knee Bolster . . . . Standard Front
Crash Avoidance:
  Collision Avoidance . . . .Optional CIB & DBS
  Blind Spot Detection . . . . .None
  Lane Keeping Assist . . . Warning Only Opt.*
  Pedestrian Crash Avoidance. . . . . . Optional
General:
  Auto. Crash Notif. . Op. Assist. & Crash Info-Free
  Day Running Lamps . . . . .Standard
Safety Belt/Restraint:
  Dynamic Head Restraints . . . . .None
  Adjustable Belt. . . . . .None

^Warning feature does not meet suggested government specifications.

BMW X1

Specifications

Drive. . . . . .RWD
Engine 2.0-liter I4
Transmission . . . . .8-sp. Automatic
Tow Rating (lbs.) Low-4400
Head/Leg Room (in.) Average-41.9/40.4
Interior Space (cu. ft.). Average-101
Cargo Space (cu. ft.) Roomy-27.1
Wheelbase/Length (in.) 105.1/174.8

Ratings—10 Best, 1 Worst

Combo Crash Tests	—
Safety Features	8
Rollover	3
Preventive Maintenance	1
Repair Costs	1
Warranty	9
Fuel Economy	5
Complaints	1
Insurance Costs	5
OVERALL RATING	**—**

BMW X3

BMW X3

At-a-Glance

```
Status/Year Series Started........ Unchanged/2018
Twins ...................................—
Body Styles .............................. SUV
Seating....................................5
Anti-Theft Device . Std. Pass. Immobil. & Active Alarm
Parking Index Rating ...................... Hard
Where Made.............................—
Fuel Factor
  MPG Rating (city/hwy)............. Average-22/29
  Driving Range (mi.) ................. Long-425
  Fuel Type.......................Premium
  Annual Fuel Cost ..................High-$1805
  Gas Guzzler Tax .........................No
  Greenhouse Gas Emissions (tons/yr.). . Average-5.9
  Barrels of Oil Used per year .......... High-13.2
```

How the Competition Rates

Competitors	Rating	Pg.
Acura MDX	7	62
Infiniti QX60	5	149
Lexus RX	4	173

Price Range

Price Range	Retail	Markup
XDrive28d	$42,750	6%
XDrive35i	$47,950	6%

Safety Checklist

```
Crash Test:
  Frontal ............................ −
  Side .............................. −
Airbags:
  Torso .......... Std. Fr. Torso from Seat
  Roll Sensing ..................... Yes
  Knee Bolster ........... Standard Driver
Crash Avoidance:
  Collision Avoidance . . . Optional CIB & DBS*
  Blind Spot Detection ............ Optional
  Lane Keeping Assist . . . Warning Only Opt.*
  Pedestrian Crash Avoidance...... Optional
General:
  Auto. Crash Notif... Op. Assist. & Crash Info-Free
  Day Running Lamps ...........Standard
Safety Belt/Restraint:
  Dynamic Head Restraints . . . Standard Front
  Adjustable Belt.................None
```

^Warning feature does not meet suggested government specifications.

BMW X3

Specifications

```
Drive................................. AWD
Engine ..........................2.0-liter I4
Transmission .................5-sp. Automatic
Tow Rating (lbs.) .............. Very Low-1000
Head/Leg Room (in.) .........Average-41.1/40.3
Interior Space (cu. ft.)............Cramped-93.7
Cargo Space (cu. ft.) ..............Roomy-28.7
Wheelbase/Length (in.) ..........112.8/185.9
```

Ratings—10 Best, 1 Worst

Combo Crash Tests	—
Safety Features	8
Rollover	3
Preventive Maintenance	3
Repair Costs	1
Warranty	9
Fuel Economy	3
Complaints	9
Insurance Costs	1
OVERALL RATING	**—**

BMW X5

BMW X5

At-a-Glance

Status/Year Series Started. Unchanged/2019
Twins . . . . —
Body Styles . . . . SUV
Seating 5
Anti-Theft Device . Std. Pass. Immobil. & Active Alarm
Parking Index Rating . . . . .Very Hard
Where Made. . . . . . .Spartanburg, SC / Toluca, Mexico
Fuel Factor
  MPG Rating (city/hwy). Averge-20/26
  Driving Range (mi.) . . . . Very Long-481
  Fuel Type. . . . . .Premium
  Annual Fuel Cost . . . . Very High-$2052
  Gas Guzzler Tax . . . . .No
  Greenhouse Gas Emissions (tons/yr.). . Average-6.5
  Barrels of Oil Used per year High-15

How the Competition Rates

Competitors	Rating	Pg.
Acura MDX	7	62
Audi Q7	3	71
Cadillac XT5	3	90

Price Range

Price Range	Retail	Markup
XDrive40i	$60,700	7%
XDrive50i	$75,750	7%

Safety Checklist

Crash Test:
  Frontal . . . . −
  Side . . . . −
Airbags:
  Torso . . . . Std. Fr. Torso from Seat
  Roll Sensing . . . . .Yes
  Knee Bolster . . . . .Standard Front
Crash Avoidance:
  Collision Avoidance . . . Optional CIB & DBS*
  Blind Spot Detection . . . . .None
  Lane Keeping Assist . . . . Optional
  Pedestrian Crash Avoidance. . . . . . Optional
General:
  Auto. Crash Notif. . . Op. Assist. & Crash Info-Free
  Day Running Lamps . . . . .Standard
Safety Belt/Restraint:
  Dynamic Head Restraints . . . Standard Front
  Adjustable Belt. . . . . .None

^Warning feature does not meet suggested government specifications.

BMW X5

Specifications

Drive. . . . . AWD
Engine 3.0-liter V6
Transmission . . . . .8-sp. Automatic
Tow Rating (lbs.) Average-6600
Head/Leg Room (in.) Cramped-40.8/39.8
Interior Space (cu. ft.). . . . . −
Cargo Space (cu. ft.) . . . . Very Roomy-33.9
Wheelbase/Length (in.) 117.1/194.3

BMW X6   Medium SUV

Ratings—10 Best, 1 Worst

Combo Crash Tests	—
Safety Features	6
Rollover	2
Preventive Maintenance	2
Repair Costs	1
Warranty	9
Fuel Economy	2
Complaints	—
Insurance Costs	1
OVERALL RATING	**—**

BMW X6

At-a-Glance

Status/Year Series Started. All-New/2020
Twins . . . .—
Body Styles . . . . SUV
Seating 5
Anti-Theft Device . Std. Pass. Immobil. & Active Alarm
Parking Index Rating . . . . .Very Hard
Where Made. . . . . Spartanburg, SC
Fuel Factor
  MPG Rating (city/hwy) . . . . .Very Poor-18/24
  Driving Range (mi.) Long-454
  Fuel Type. . . . . .Premium
  Annual Fuel Cost . . . . Very High-$2197
  Gas Guzzler Tax . . . . .No
  Greenhouse Gas Emissions (tons/yr.). . Average-7.0
  Barrels of Oil Used per year High-15.7

How the Competition Rates

Competitors	Rating	Pg.
Audi Q7	3	71
Cadillac XT5	3	90
Lincoln Nautilis	5	181

Price Range

	Retail	Markup
XDrive35i	$60,500	7%
sDrive35i	$62,700	7%
XDrive50i	$77,450	7%
M	$104,100	7%

BMW X6

Safety Checklist

Crash Test:
  Frontal . . . . —
  Side . . . . —
Airbags:
  Torso . . . . Std. Fr. Torso from Seat
  Roll Sensing . . . . .Yes
  Knee Bolster .None
Crash Avoidance:
  Collision Avoidance . . . Optional CIB & DBS*
  Blind Spot Detection . . . . .Standard
  Lane Keeping Assist . . . Warning Only Opt.*
  Pedestrian Crash Avoidance. . . . . .Standard
General:
  Auto. Crash Notif. . . Op. Assist. & Crash Info-Free
  Day Running Lamps . . . . .Standard
Safety Belt/Restraint:
  Dynamic Head Restraints . . . Standard Front
  Adjustable Belt. . . . . .None

^Warning feature does not meet suggested government specifications.

BMW X6

Specifications

Drive. . . . . AWD
Engine 3.0-liter V6
Transmission . . . . .8-sp. Automatic
Tow Rating (lbs.) High-7200
Head/Leg Room (in.) Cramped-39.3/40.4
Interior Space (cu. ft.). . . . .—
Cargo Space (cu. ft.) . . . .—
Wheelbase/Length (in.) 117.0/194.8

Ratings—10 Best, 1 Worst

Combo Crash Tests	5
Safety Features	5
Rollover	4
Preventive Maintenance	2
Repair Costs	3
Warranty	8
Fuel Economy	3
Complaints	6
Insurance Costs	10
OVERALL RATING	**4**

Buick Enclave

Buick Enclave

At-a-Glance

Status/Year Series Started	Unchanged/2018
Twins	Chevrolet Traverse
Body Styles	SUV
Seating	7
Anti-Theft Device	Std. Pass. Immobil. & Active Alarm
Parking Index Rating	Very Hard
Where Made	Lansing, MI

Fuel Factor
MPG Rating (city/hwy)	Poor-18/26
Driving Range (mi.)	Average-405
Fuel Type	Regular
Annual Fuel Cost	High-$1759
Gas Guzzler Tax	No
Greenhouse Gas Emissions (tons/yr.)	Average-7.0
Barrels of Oil Used per year	High-15.7

How the Competition Rates

Competitors	Rating	Pg.
Chevrolet Tahoe	4	104
Chevrolet Traverse	4	105
Volvo XC90	8	240

Price Range

	Retail	Markup
Base FWD	$39,995	1%
Essence FWD	$44,215	5%
Premium AWD	$50,315	5%
Avenir AWD	$55,715	5%

Safety Checklist

Crash Test:
Frontal	Average
Side	Poor

Airbags:
Torso	Std. Fr. Pelvis/Torso from Seat
Roll Sensing	Yes
Knee Bolster	None

Crash Avoidance:
Collision Avoidance	Optional CIB & DBS
Blind Spot Detection	Optional
Lane Keeping Assist	Warning Only Opt.
Pedestrian Crash Avoidance	Optional

General:
Auto. Crash Notif.	Op. Assist. & Crash Info-Free
Day Running Lamps	Standard

Safety Belt/Restraint:
Dynamic Head Restraints	None
Adjustable Belt	Optional Rear

^Warning feature does not meet suggested government specifications.

Buick Enclave

Specifications

Drive	FWD
Engine	3.6-liter V6
Transmission	9-sp. Automatic
Tow Rating (lbs.)	Low-5000
Head/Leg Room (in.)	Average-41/41.2
Interior Space (cu. ft.)	–
Cargo Space (cu. ft.)	Roomy-23.6
Wheelbase/Length (in.)	120.9/204.3

Buick Encore — Small SUV

Ratings—10 Best, 1 Worst

Combo Crash Tests	8
Safety Features	7
Rollover	3
Preventive Maintenance	7
Repair Costs	8
Warranty	8
Fuel Economy	6
Complaints	10
Insurance Costs	5
OVERALL RATING	**10**

Buick Encore

At-a-Glance

Status/Year Series Started........ Unchanged/2013
Twins .... Chevrolet Trax
Body Styles .... SUV
Seating 5
Anti-Theft Device . Std. Pass. Immobil. & Active Alarm
Parking Index Rating .... Easy
Where Made.............. Bupyeong, South Korea
Fuel Factor
  MPG Rating (city/hwy) Average-23/30
  Driving Range (mi.) .... Very Short-360
  Fuel Type.............................Regular
  Annual Fuel Cost .... Low-$1430
  Gas Guzzler Tax ....No
  Greenhouse Gas Emissions (tons/yr.).. Average-6.9
  Barrels of Oil Used per year Average-12.7

How the Competition Rates

Competitors	Rating	Pg.
Acura RDX	9	63
Ford Escape	5	116
Honda CR-V	10	134

Price Range

Price Range	Retail	Markup
Preferred FWD	$24,365	4%
Sport Touring FWD	$25,565	4%
Essence AWD	$30,565	4%
Premium AWD	$32,015	4%

Buick Encore

Safety Checklist

Crash Test:
  Frontal .... Very Good
  Side .... Average
Airbags:
  Torso Std. Fr. & Rear Pelvis/Torso from Seat
  Roll Sensing .... Yes
  Knee Bolster .... Standard Front
Crash Avoidance:
  Collision Avoidance ..... Warning Only Opt.
  Blind Spot Detection .... Optional
  Lane Keeping Assist .... Warning Only Opt.
  Pedestrian Crash Avoidance.........None
General:
  Auto. Crash Notif... Op. Assist. & Crash Info-Free
  Day Running Lamps ....Standard
Safety Belt/Restraint:
  Dynamic Head Restraints ....None
  Adjustable Belt...... Optional Front & Rear

^Warning feature does not meet suggested government specifications.

Buick Encore

Specifications

Drive................................. AWD
Engine 1.4-liter I4
Transmission .... 6-sp. Automatic
Tow Rating (lbs.) .... –
Head/Leg Room (in.) Cramped-39.6/40.8
Interior Space (cu. ft.)............ Cramped-92.8
Cargo Space (cu. ft.) Average-18.8
Wheelbase/Length (in.) 100.6/168.4

83

Buick Envision

Ratings—10 Best, 1 Worst

Combo Crash Tests	—
Safety Features	10
Rollover	2
Preventive Maintenance	2
Repair Costs	4
Warranty	8
Fuel Economy	4
Complaints	4
Insurance Costs	8
OVERALL RATING	—

Buick Envision

Safety Checklist

Crash Test:
 Frontal . . . . –
 Side . . . . –
Airbags:
 Torso Std. Fr. & Rear Pelvis/Torso from Seat
 Roll Sensing . . . . .Yes
 Knee Bolster . . . . .Standard Front
Crash Avoidance:
 Collision Avoidance . . . Optional CIB & DBS*
 Blind Spot Detection . . . . Optional
 Lane Keeping Assist . . . . Warning Only Opt.
 Pedestrian Crash Avoidance . . . . . . Optional
General:
 Auto. Crash Notif. . . Op. Assist. & Crash Info-Free
 Day Running Lamps . . . . .Standard
Safety Belt/Restraint:
 Dynamic Head Restraints . . . . .None
 Adjustable Belt. . . . . . Optional Front & Rear

^Warning feature does not meet suggested government specifications.

Buick Envision

At-a-Glance

Status/Year Series Started. Unchanged/2016
Twins . . . . —
Body Styles . . . . SUV
Seating 5
Anti-Theft Device . Std. Pass. Immobil. & Active Alarm
Parking Index Rating . . . . Hard
Where Made. . . . . .Yantai, Shandong
Fuel Factor
 MPG Rating (city/hwy). Poor-21/27
 Driving Range (mi.) Average-404
 Fuel Type. . . . . .Regular
 Annual Fuel Cost . . . . .Average-$1575
 Gas Guzzler Tax . . . . .No
 Greenhouse Gas Emissions (tons/yr.). . Average-6.2
 Barrels of Oil Used per year High-13.7

How the Competition Rates

Competitors	Rating	Pg.
Acura MDX	7	62
Audi Q7	3	71
BMW X5		79

Price Range

Price Range	Retail	Markup
Preferred FWD	$35,870	5%
Essence FWD	$37,720	5%
Premium I AWD	$42,320	5%
Premium II AWD	$44,960	5%

Specifications

Drive. . . . . AWD
Engine 2.5-liter I4
Transmission . . . . .6-sp. Automatic
Tow Rating (lbs.) . . . . Very Low-1500
Head/Leg Room (in.) Cramped-40/40.9
Interior Space (cu. ft.). Average-100.6
Cargo Space (cu. ft.) Roomy-26.9
Wheelbase/Length (in.) 108.2/183.7

Buick Regal

Ratings—10 Best, 1 Worst

Combo Crash Tests	—
Safety Features	10
Rollover	7
Preventive Maintenance	1
Repair Costs	3
Warranty	8
Fuel Economy	6
Complaints	9
Insurance Costs	8
OVERALL RATING	**—**

Buick Regal

Buick Regal

At-a-Glance

Status/Year Series Started	Unchanged/2018
Twins	Chevrolet Malibu
Body Styles	Sedan, Wagon
Seating	5
Anti-Theft Device	Std. Pass. Immobil. & Active Alarm
Parking Index Rating	Average
Where Made	Oshawa, Ontario
Fuel Factor	
MPG Rating (city/hwy)	Average-22/32
Driving Range (mi.)	Average-417
Fuel Type	Premium
Annual Fuel Cost	High-$1740
Gas Guzzler Tax	No
Greenhouse Gas Emissions (tons/yr.)	Average-6.7
Barrels of Oil Used per year	High-15.0

How the Competition Rates

Competitors	Rating	Pg.
Acura TLX	9	64
Lincoln MKZ	4	176
Mazda 6	5	183

Price Range

	Retail	Markup
1SV	$27,065	1%
Sport Touring	$28,615	4%
Leather	$31,465	4%
GS AWD	$36,540	4%

Safety Checklist

Crash Test:
  Frontal . . . . −
  Side . . . . −
Airbags:
  Torso Std. Fr. & Rear Pelvis/Torso from Seat
  Roll Sensing . . . . Yes
  Knee Bolster . . . . Standard Front
Crash Avoidance:
  Collision Avoidance . . . . Optional CIB & DBS
  Blind Spot Detection . . . . Optional
  Lane Keeping Assist . . . . Optional
  Pedestrian Crash Avoidance . . . . . . Optional
General:
  Auto. Crash Notif. . . Op. Assist. & Crash Info-Free
  Day Running Lamps . . . . Standard
Safety Belt/Restraint:
  Dynamic Head Restraints . . . . None
  Adjustable Belt . . . . Optional Rear

^Warning feature does not meet suggested government specifications.

Buick Regal

Specifications

Drive	FWD
Engine	3.6-liter V6
Transmission	9-sp. Automatic
Tow Rating (lbs.)	−
Head/Leg Room (in.)	Cramped-38.8/42.1
Interior Space (cu. ft.)	Average-98
Cargo Space (cu. ft.)	Very Roomy-31.5
Wheelbase/Length (in.)	111.4/192.9

Ratings—10 Best, 1 Worst

Combo Crash Tests	—
Safety Features	9
Rollover	7
Preventive Maintenance	2
Repair Costs	2
Warranty	10
Fuel Economy	3
Complaints	8
Insurance Costs	3
\OVERALL RATING	—

Cadillac CT6

Cadillac CT6

At-a-Glance

Status/Year Series Started. Unchanged/2016
Twins . . . . —
Body Styles . . . . .Sedan
Seating 5
Anti-Theft Device . Std. Pass. Immobil. & Active Alarm
Parking Index Rating . . . . .Very Hard
Where Made. . . . . .Hamtramck, MI
Fuel Factor
  MPG Rating (city/hwy). Poor-18/27
  Driving Range (mi.) Average-413
  Fuel Type. . . . . .Regular
  Annual Fuel Cost . . . . .High-$1735
  Gas Guzzler Tax . . . . .No
  Greenhouse Gas Emissions (tons/yr.). . Average-6.9
  Barrels of Oil Used per year High-15.7

How the Competition Rates

Competitors	Rating	Pg.
Lincoln Continental	6	174
Mercedes-Benz E-Class	3	186
Tesla Model S	10	216

Price Range

Price Range	Retail	Markup
Base 2.0L RWD	$54,095	5%
Luxury 3.6L AWD	$61,195	5%
Prem. Luxury 3.6L AWD	$65,295	5%
Platinum 3.0L TT AWD	$88,295	5%

Safety Checklist

Crash Test:
  Frontal . . . . −
  Side . . . . −
Airbags:
  Torso . . . . . . Std. Fr. Pelvis/Torso from Seat
  Roll Sensing . . . . .Yes
  Knee Bolster . . . . Standard Front
Crash Avoidance:
  Collision Avoidance . . . .Optional CIB & DBS
  Blind Spot Detection . . . . Optional
  Lane Keeping Assist . . . . Optional
  Pedestrian Crash Avoidance. . . . . . Optional
General:
  Auto. Crash Notif. . . Op. Assist. & Crash Info-Free
  Day Running Lamps . . . . .Standard
Safety Belt/Restraint:
  Dynamic Head Restraints . . . . .None
  Adjustable Belt. . . . . . Optional Front & Rear

^Warning feature does not meet suggested government specifications.

Cadillac CT6

Specifications

Drive. . . . . AWD
Engine 3.6-liter V6
Transmission . . . . .5-sp. Automatic
Tow Rating (lbs.) . . . . −
Head/Leg Room (in.) Average-40.1/42.3
Interior Space (cu. ft.). Roomy-110
Cargo Space (cu. ft.) Cramped-15.3
Wheelbase/Length (in.) 122.4/204

Cadillac Escalade

Ratings—10 Best, 1 Worst

Combo Crash Tests	7
Safety Features	5
Rollover	2
Preventive Maintenance	1
Repair Costs	3
Warranty	10
Fuel Economy	2
Complaints	7
Insurance Costs	5
OVERALL RATING	**3**

Cadillac Escalade

Cadillac Escalade

At-a-Glance

Status/Year Series Started........ Unchanged/2015
Twins . . . . .Chevrolet Suburban, GMC Yukon
Body Styles . . . . SUV
Seating 6/9
Anti-Theft Device . Std. Pass. Immobil. & Active Alarm
Parking Index Rating . . . . .Very Hard
Where Made. . . . . Arlington, TX
Fuel Factor
  MPG Rating (city/hwy) . . . . .Very Poor-16/22
  Driving Range (mi.) . . . . Very Long-474
  Fuel Type. . . . . .Regular
  Annual Fuel Cost . . . . Very High-$2015
  Gas Guzzler Tax . . . . .No
  Greenhouse Gas Emissions (tons/yr.). High-8.2
  Barrels of Oil Used per year . . . . . . .Very High-18.3

How the Competition Rates

Competitors	Rating	Pg.
Chevrolet Tahoe	4	104
Lincoln Navigator		178
Volvo XC90	8	240

Price Range

	Retail	Markup
Base 2WD	$76,995	7%
Luxury 2WD	$83,690	7%
Premium Luxury 4WD	$88,290	7%
Platinum 4WD	$97,390	7%

Safety Checklist

Crash Test:
  Frontal . . . . .Poor
  Side . . . . Very Good
Airbags:
  Torso . . . . . . Std. Fr. Pelvis/Torso from Seat
  Roll Sensing . . . . .Yes
  Knee Bolster . . . . .None
Crash Avoidance:
  Collision Avoidance . . . .Optional CIB & DBS
  Blind Spot Detection . . . . Optional
  Lane Keeping Assist . . . . Optional
  Pedestrian Crash Avoidance. . . . . .None
General:
  Auto. Crash Notif. . . Op. Assist. & Crash Info-Free
  Day Running Lamps . . . . .Standard
Safety Belt/Restraint:
  Dynamic Head Restraints . . . . .None
  Adjustable Belt. . . . . . Optional Front & Rear

^Warning feature does not meet suggested government specifications.

Cadillac Escalade

Specifications

Drive. . . . . AWD
Engine 6.2-liter V8
Transmission . . . . .6-sp. Automatic
Tow Rating (lbs.) High-8100
Head/Leg Room (in.) . . . . . . Very Roomy-42.8/45.3
Interior Space (cu. ft.). Roomy-120.8
Cargo Space (cu. ft.) Cramped-15.2
Wheelbase/Length (in.) 116/203.9

Cadillac Escalade ESV | Large SUV

Ratings—10 Best, 1 Worst

Combo Crash Tests	5
Safety Features	5
Rollover	2
Preventive Maintenance	1
Repair Costs	5
Warranty	10
Fuel Economy	1
Complaints	10
Insurance Costs	10
OVERALL RATING	**4**

Cadillac Escalade ESV

At-a-Glance

Status/Year Series Started Unchanged/2015
Twins . . . . Chevrolet Tahoe, GMC Yukon XL
Body Styles . . . . SUV
Seating 6/9
Anti-Theft Device . Std. Pass. Immobil. & Active Alarm
Parking Index Rating . . . . Very Hard
Where Made . . . . Arlington, TX
Fuel Factor
  MPG Rating (city/hwy) . . . . .Very Poor-15/22
  Driving Range (mi.) . . . . Very Long-543
  Fuel Type . . . . Regular
  Annual Fuel Cost . . . . Very High-$2099
  Gas Guzzler Tax . . . . .No
  Greenhouse Gas Emissions (tons/yr.)Very High-10.0
  Barrels of Oil Used per year . . . . Very High-18.3

How the Competition Rates

Competitors	Rating	Pg.
Land Rover Range Rover		164
Linlcoln Navigator		178
Volvo XC90	8	240

Price Range

Price Range	Retail	Markup
Base 2WD	$79,490	7%
Luxury 2WD	$85,090	7%
Premium Luxury 4WD	$92,490	7%
Platinum 4WD	$101,590	7%

Cadillac Escalade ESV

Safety Checklist

Crash Test:
  Frontal . . . . Average
  Side . . . . Average
Airbags:
  Torso . . . . . . Std. Fr. Pelvis/Torso from Seat
  Roll Sensing . . . . Yes
  Knee Bolster .None
Crash Avoidance:
  Collision Avoidance . . . . Optional CIB & DBS
  Blind Spot Detection . . . . Optional
  Lane Keeping Assist . . . . Optional
  Pedestrian Crash Avoidance . . . . .None
General:
  Auto. Crash Notif . . . Op. Assist. & Crash Info-Free
  Day Running Lamps . . . . .Standard
Safety Belt/Restraint:
  Dynamic Head Restraints . . . . .None
  Adjustable Belt . . . . . . Optional Front & Rear

^Warning feature does not meet suggested government specifications.

Cadillac Escalade ESV

Specifications

Drive . . . . AWD
Engine 6.2-liter V8
Transmission . . . . .6-sp. Automatic
Tow Rating (lbs.) High-7900
Head/Leg Room (in.) . . . . . . Very Roomy-42.8/45.3
Interior Space (cu. ft.) Roomy-122.4
Cargo Space (cu. ft.) . . . . Very Roomy-39.3
Wheelbase/Length (in.) 130/224.3

Cadillac XT4   Small SUV

Ratings—10 Best, 1 Worst

Combo Crash Tests	—
Safety Features	8
Rollover	8
Preventive Maintenance	2
Repair Costs	4
Warranty	10
Fuel Economy	5
Complaints	9
Insurance Costs	8
OVERALL RATING	**—**

Cadillac XT4

Cadillac XT4

At-a-Glance

Status/Year Series Started........ Unchanged/2019
Twins . . . .—
Body Styles . . . . SUV
Seating 5
Anti-Theft Device . Std. Pass. Immobil. & Active Alarm
Parking Index Rating . . . . .Very Easy
Where Made. Spring Hill, TN
Fuel Factor
  MPG Rating (city/hwy) Average-22/29
  Driving Range (mi.) Short-391
  Fuel Type . . . . .Premium
  Annual Fuel Cost . . . . .High-$1862
  Gas Guzzler Tax . . . . .No
  Greenhouse Gas Emissions (tons/yr.). . Average-6.1
  Barrels of Oil Used per year High-13.7

How the Competition Rates

Competitors	Rating	Pg.
Acura RDX	9	63
Buick Encore	10	83
Hyundai Tucson	8	145

Price Range

Price Range	Retail	Markup
Luxury FWD	$34,795	5%
Luxury AWD	$38,195	5%
Premium Luxury AWD	$42,295	5%

Safety Checklist

Crash Test:
  Frontal . . . .–
  Side . . . .–
Airbags:
  Torso . . . . . . Std. Fr. Pelvis/Torso from Seat
  Roll Sensing . . . . .Yes
  Knee Bolster .None
Crash Avoidance:
  Collision Avoidance . . . .Optional CIB & DBS
  Blind Spot Detection . . . . Optional
  Lane Keeping Assist . . . . Optional
  Pedestrian Crash Avoidance. . . . . .Standard
General:
  Auto. Crash Notif... Op. Assist. & Crash Info-Free
  Day Running Lamps . . . . .Standard
Safety Belt/Restraint:
  Dynamic Head Restraints . . . . .None
  Adjustable Belt. . . . . . Optional Front & Rear

^Warning feature does not meet suggested government specifications.

Cadillac XT4

Specifications

Drive. . . . . FWD
Engine 2.0-liter I4
Transmission . . . . 9-Speed Automatic
Tow Rating (lbs.) Low-3500
Head/Leg Room (in.) Average-39.4/42.5
Interior Space (cu. ft.). . . . .—
Cargo Space (cu. ft.) Roomy-26.5
Wheelbase/Length (in.) 109.0/181.0

Ratings—10 Best, 1 Worst

Combo Crash Tests	3
Safety Features	8
Rollover	3
Preventive Maintenance	1
Repair Costs	4
Warranty	10
Fuel Economy	3
Complaints	2
Insurance Costs	8
OVERALL RATING	**3**

Cadillac XT5

Cadillac XT5

Safety Checklist

Crash Test:
  Frontal . . . . Average
  Side . . . . Very Poor
Airbags:
  Torso . . . . . . Std. Fr. Pelvis/Torso from Seat
  Roll Sensing . . . . Yes
  Knee Bolster . . . . Standard Driver
Crash Avoidance:
  Collision Avoidance . . . . Optional CIB & DBS
  Blind Spot Detection . . . . Optional
  Lane Keeping Assist . . . . Optional
  Pedestrian Crash Avoidance . . . . . . Standard
General:
  Auto. Crash Notif. . . Op. Assist. & Crash Info-Free
  Day Running Lamps . . . . Standard
Safety Belt/Restraint:
  Dynamic Head Restraints . . . . .None
  Adjustable Belt. . . . . .Standard Front & Rear

^Warning feature does not meet suggested government specifications.

At-a-Glance

Status/Year Series Started. Unchanged/2017
Twins . . . . .GMC Acadia
Body Styles . . . . SUV
Seating 5
Anti-Theft Device . Std. Pass. Immobil. & Active Alarm
Parking Index Rating . . . . .Very Easy
Where Made. . . . . Spring Hill, TN
Fuel Factor
  MPG Rating (city/hwy). Poor-19/25
  Driving Range (mi.) Average-405
  Fuel Type. . . . . .Regular
  Annual Fuel Cost . . . . .High-$1725
  Gas Guzzler Tax . . . . .No
  Greenhouse Gas Emissions (tons/yr.). . Average-6.5
  Barrels of Oil Used per year High-15.0

How the Competition Rates

Competitors	Rating	Pg.
Acura MDX	7	62
Audi Q7	3	71
Lexus RX	4	173

Price Range

Price Range	Retail	Markup
Base FWD	$39,995	5%
Luxury FWD	$45,995	5%
Premium Luxury AWD	$54,995	5%
Platinum AWD	$62,995	5%

Cadillac XT5

Specifications

Drive. . . . . .FWD
Engine 3.6-liter V6
Transmission . . . . .8-sp. Automatic
Tow Rating (lbs.) Low-3500
Head/Leg Room (in.) Cramped-38.4/41.2
Interior Space (cu. ft.). Roomy-104.5
Cargo Space (cu. ft.) Roomy-30
Wheelbase/Length (in.) 112.5/189.5

Ratings—10 Best, 1 Worst

Combo Crash Tests	—
Safety Features	8
Rollover	5
Preventive Maintenance	1
Repair Costs	3
Warranty	10
Fuel Economy	2
Complaints	—
Insurance Costs	10
OVERALL RATING	—

Cadillac XT6

Cadillac XT6

At-a-Glance

Status/Year Series Started. All-New/2020
Twins . . . . —
Body Styles . . . . SUV
Seating 7
Anti-Theft Device . Std. Pass. Immobil. & Active Alarm
Parking Index Rating . . . . Average
Where Made. . . . . Spring Hill, TN
Fuel Factor
  MPG Rating (city/hwy). 17/24
  Driving Range (mi.) Average-440
  Fuel Type. . . . . .Regular
  Annual Fuel Cost . . . . .High-$1859
  Gas Guzzler Tax . . . . .No
  Greenhouse Gas Emissions (tons/yr.). High-7.4
  Barrels of Oil Used per year High-16

How the Competition Rates

Competitors	Rating	Pg.
Acura MDX	7	62
Ford Edge	9	115
Hyundai Pilot	8	138

Price Range

Price Range	Retail	Markup
Premium Luxury FWD	52,695.00	5%
Premium Luxury AWD	54,695.00	5%
Premium Luxury AWD	57,095.00	5%

Safety Checklist

Crash Test:
  Frontal . . . .—
  Side . . . .—
Airbags:
  Torso . . . . . . Std. Fr. Pelvis/Torso from Seat
  Roll Sensing . . . . .Yes
  Knee Bolster . . . . Standard Driver
Crash Avoidance:
  Collision Avoidance . . . .Optional CIB & DBS
  Blind Spot Detection . . . . .Standard
  Lane Keeping Assist . . . . .Standard
  Pedestrian Crash Avoidance. . . . . .Standard
General:
  Auto. Crash Notif. . . Op. Assist. & Crash Info-Free
  Day Running Lamps . . . . .Standard
Safety Belt/Restraint:
  Dynamic Head Restraints . . . . .None
  Adjustable Belt. . . . . .Standard Front & Rear

^Warning feature does not meet suggested government specifications.

Cadillac XT6

Specifications

Drive. . . . . FWD
Engine 3.6-liter V6
Transmission . . . . .9-Speed Automatic
Tow Rating (lbs.) . . . . —
Head/Leg Room (in.) Average-39.8/41.2
Interior Space (cu. ft.). . . . . —
Cargo Space (cu. ft.) Cramped-12.6
Wheelbase/Length (in.) 112.7/198.8

Chevrolet Blazer

Medium SUV

Ratings—10 Best, 1 Worst

Combo Crash Tests	—
Safety Features	7
Rollover	3
Preventive Maintenance	1
Repair Costs	7
Warranty	6
Fuel Economy	4
Complaints	9
Insurance Costs	8
OVERALL RATING	**—**

Chevrolet Blazer

Chevrolet Blazer

Safety Checklist

Crash Test:
  Frontal . . . . −
  Side . . . . −
Airbags:
  Torso . . . . . . Std. Fr. Pelvis/Torso from Seat
  Roll Sensing . . . . Yes
  Knee Bolster . . . . Standard Driver
Crash Avoidance:
  Collision Avoidance . . . . Optional CIB & DBS
  Blind Spot Detection . . . . Optional
  Lane Keeping Assist . . . . Optional
  Pedestrian Crash Avoidance. . . . . . Optional
General:
  Auto. Crash Notif. . . Op. Assist. & Crash Info-Free
  Day Running Lamps . . . . Standard
Safety Belt/Restraint:
  Dynamic Head Restraints . . . . .None
  Adjustable Belt. . . . . .Standard Front & Rear

^Warning feature does not meet suggested government specifications.

At-a-Glance

Status/Year Series Started. All-New/2020
Twins . . . . —
Body Styles . . . . SUV
Seating 5
Anti-Theft Device . . . . . . Std. Pass. Immobil. & Alarm
Parking Index Rating . . . . .Very Easy
Where Made. . . . . —
Fuel Factor
  MPG Rating (city/hwy) Poor-21/27
  Driving Range (mi.) Short-499
  Fuel Type. . . . . Regular
  Annual Fuel Cost . . . . .Average-$1575
  Gas Guzzler Tax .No
  Greenhouse Gas Emissions (tons/yr.). High-6.2
  Barrels of Oil Used per year High-14.3

How the Competition Rates

Competitors	Rating	Pg.
Dodge Durango	2	111
Ford Edge	9	115
Kia Sorento	6	160

Price Range

Price Range	Retail	Markup
L FWD	$29,995	2%
2LT FWD	$31,995	5%
3LT AWD	$38,195	5%
Premier AWD	$44,795	5%

Chevrolet Blazer

Specifications

Drive. . . . . FWD
Engine 2.5-leter I4
Transmission . . . . 9-Speed Automatic
Tow Rating (lbs.) . . . . —
Head/Leg Room (in.) Average-39.8/41.0
Interior Space (cu. ft.). Roomy-107.8
Cargo Space (cu. ft.) Roomy-30.5
Wheelbase/Length (in.) 112.7/191.4

Chevrolet Bolt EV — Compact

Ratings—10 Best, 1 Worst

Combo Crash Tests	—
Safety Features	9
Rollover	3
Preventive Maintenance	6
Repair Costs	10
Warranty	6
Fuel Economy	6
Complaints	2
Insurance Costs	5
OVERALL RATING	—

Chevrolet Bolt EV

Chevrolet Bolt EV

At-a-Glance

Status/Year Series Started Unchanged/2017
Twins . . . . —
Body Styles . . . . Hatchback
Seating 5
Anti-Theft Device . . . . . . Std. Pass. Immobil. & Alarm
Parking Index Rating . . . . .Very Easy
Where Made. . . . . Orion Township, MI
Fuel Factor
 MPG Rating (city/hwy) . . . . Very Good-128/110
 Driving Range (mi.) . . . . —
 Fuel Type. . . . . Electricity
 Annual Fuel Cost . . . . .Very Low-$550
 Gas Guzzler Tax . . . . .No
 Greenhouse Gas Emissions (tons/yr.). Very Low-0.0
 Barrels of Oil Used per year . . . . Very Low-0.0

How the Competition Rates

Competitors	Rating	Pg.
BMW i3		77
Nissan Leaf		199
Tesla Model 3		215

Price Range

	Retail	Markup
LT	$36,620	4%
Premier	$40,905	4%

Safety Checklist

Crash Test:
 Frontal . . . .–
 Side . . . .–
Airbags:
 Torso . . . . . . Std. Fr. Pelvis/Torso from Seat
 Roll Sensing . . . . .Yes
 Knee Bolster . . . . Standard Front
Crash Avoidance:
 Collision Avoidance . . . .Optional CIB & DBS
 Blind Spot Detection . . . . Optional
 Lane Keeping Assist . . . . .Optional*
 Pedestrian Crash Avoidance. . . . . . Optional
General:
 Auto. Crash Notif. . . Op. Assist. & Crash Info-Free
 Day Running Lamps . . . . .Standard
Safety Belt/Restraint:
 Dynamic Head Restraints . . . . .None
 Adjustable Belt. . . . . Optional Rear

^Warning feature does not meet suggested government specifications.

Chevrolet Bolt EV

Specifications

Drive. . . . . FWD
Engine . . . . Electric
Transmission . . . . .1-sp. Automatic
Tow Rating (lbs.) . . . . Very Low-0
Head/Leg Room (in.) Average-39.7/41.6
Interior Space (cu. ft.). Cramped-95
Cargo Space (cu. ft.) Average-16.9
Wheelbase/Length (in.) 102.4/164

Chevrolet Camaro

Ratings—10 Best, 1 Worst

Combo Crash Tests	7
Safety Features	4
Rollover	10
Preventive Maintenance	1
Repair Costs	5
Warranty	6
Fuel Economy	3
Complaints	8
Insurance Costs	1
OVERALL RATING	**4**

Chevrolet Camaro

Chevrolet Camaro

At-a-Glance

Status/Year Series Started	Unchanged/2016
Twins	—
Body Styles	Coupe, Convertible
Seating	4
Anti-Theft Device	Std. Pass. Immobil. & Active Alarm
Parking Index Rating	Hard
Where Made	Lansing, MI
Fuel Factor	
MPG Rating (city/hwy)	Poor-19/28
Driving Range (mi.)	Average-422
Fuel Type	Premium
Annual Fuel Cost	Very High-$2006
Gas Guzzler Tax	No
Greenhouse Gas Emissions (tons/yr.)	Average-6.5
Barrels of Oil Used per year	High-14.3

How the Competition Rates

Competitors	Rating	Pg.
Chevrolet Corvette		96
Dodge Challenger	4	111
Ford Mustang	6	123

Price Range

Price Range	Retail	Markup
1LT Coupe	$26,700	4%
2LT Convertible	$35,700	4%
1SS Coupe	$37,000	4%
2SS Coupe	$42,000	4%

Safety Checklist

Crash Test:
Frontal . . . . Average
Side . . . . Very Good
Airbags:
Torso . . . . . . Std. Fr. Pelvis/Torso from Seat
Roll Sensing . . . . Yes
Knee Bolster . . . . Standard Front
Crash Avoidance:
Collision Avoidance . . . . .None
Blind Spot Detection . . . . Optional
Lane Keeping Assist . . . . .None
Pedestrian Crash Avoidance . . . . .None
General:
Auto. Crash Notif. . . Op. Assist. & Crash Info-Free
Day Running Lamps . . . . .Standard
Safety Belt/Restraint:
Dynamic Head Restraints . . . . .None
Adjustable Belt. . . . . .Optional Rear

^W-arning feature does not meet suggested government specifications.

Chevrolet Camaro

Specifications

Drive	RWD
Engine	3.6-liter V6
Transmission	8-sp. Automatic
Tow Rating (lbs.)	—
Head/Leg Room (in.)	Very Cramped-36.6/42.6
Interior Space (cu. ft.)	Very Cramped-77
Cargo Space (cu. ft.)	Very Cramped-9.1
Wheelbase/Length (in.)	110.7/188.3

Ratings—10 Best, 1 Worst

Combo Crash Tests	3
Safety Features	2
Rollover	2
Preventive Maintenance	1
Repair Costs	8
Warranty	6
Fuel Economy	4
Complaints	5
Insurance Costs	10
OVERALL RATING	**2**

Chevrolet Colorado

Chevrolet Colorado

At-a-Glance

Status/Year Series Started........ Unchanged/2015
Twins . . . . .GMC Canyon
Body Styles . . . . Pickup
Seating 5
Anti-Theft Device . Std. Pass. Immobil. & Active Alarm
Parking Index Rating . . . . .Very Hard
Where Made. . . . . .Wentzville, MO
Fuel Factor
  MPG Rating (city/hwy) Poor-20/27
  Driving Range (mi.) . . . . Very Long-475
  Fuel Type. . . . . .Regular
  Annual Fuel Cost . . . . .Average-$1623
  Gas Guzzler Tax . . . . .No
  Greenhouse Gas Emissions (tons/yr.) High-8.2
  Barrels of Oil Used per year High-15.0

How the Competition Rates

Competitors	Rating	Pg.
Ford Ranger		
Nissan Frontier	1	204
Toyota Tacoma	1	230

Price Range

	Retail	Markup
Base Ext. Cab 2WD	$20,000	1%
W/T Crew Cab 4WD	$31,220	5%
Z71 Crew Cab 4WD	$32,775	5%
LT Crew Cab 4WD	$33,775	5%

Safety Checklist

Crash Test:
  Frontal . . . . Poor
  Side . . . . Poor
Airbags:
  Torso . . . . . . Std. Fr. Pelvis/Torso from Seat
  Roll Sensing . . . . .Yes
  Knee Bolster .None
Crash Avoidance:
  Collision Avoidance . . . . . Warning Only Opt.
  Blind Spot Detection . . . . .None
  Lane Keeping Assist . . . . Warning Only Opt.
  Pedestrian Crash Avoidance. . . . . .None
General:
  Auto. Crash Notif. . . Op. Assist. & Crash Info-Free
  Day Running Lamps . . . . .Standard
Safety Belt/Restraint:
  Dynamic Head Restraints . . . . .None
  Adjustable Belt. . . . . . Optional Front & Rear

^W-arning feature does not meet suggested government specifications.

Chevrolet Colorado

Specifications

Drive. . . . . .RWD
Engine 2.5-liter I4
Transmission . . . . .6-sp. Automatic
Tow Rating (lbs.) Low-3500
Head/Leg Room (in.) . . . . .Very Roomy-41.4/45
Interior Space (cu. ft.). . . . . –
Cargo Space (cu. ft.) . . . . Very Roomy-49.9
Wheelbase/Length (in.) 128.3/212.7

Ratings—10 Best, 1 Worst

Combo Crash Tests	—
Safety Features	1
Rollover	10
Preventive Maintenance	1
Repair Costs	1
Warranty	6
Fuel Economy	2
Complaints	6
Insurance Costs	10
OVERALL RATING	—

Chevrolet Corvette

Chevrolet Corvette

Safety Checklist

Crash Test:
  Frontal . . . . −
  Side . . . . −
Airbags:
  Torso . . . . Std. Fr. Torso from Seat
  Roll Sensing . . . . .No
  Knee Bolster . . . . .None
Crash Avoidance:
  Collision Avoidance . . . . .None
  Blind Spot Detection . . . . .None
  Lane Keeping Assist . . . . .None
  Pedestrian Crash Avoidance. . . . . .None
General:
  Auto. Crash Notif. . . Op. Assist. & Crash Info-Free
  Day Running Lamps . . . . .Standard
Safety Belt/Restraint:
  Dynamic Head Restraints . . . . .None
  Adjustable Belt. . . . . .None

At-a-Glance

Status/Year Series Started. All-New/2020
Twins . . . . —
Body Styles . . . . Coupe, Convertible
Seating 2
Anti-Theft Device . Std. Pass. Immobil. & Active Alarm
Parking Index Rating . . . . Average
Where Made. . . . . .Bowling Green, KY
Fuel Factor
  MPG Rating (city/hwy) . . . . .Very Poor-15/25
  Driving Range (mi.) . . . . .Very Short-338
  Fuel Type. . . . . .Premium
  Annual Fuel Cost . . . . Very High-$2435
  Gas Guzzler Tax . . . . .No
  Greenhouse Gas Emissions (tons/yr.). High-8.1
  Barrels of Oil Used per year . . . . . . .Very High-18.3

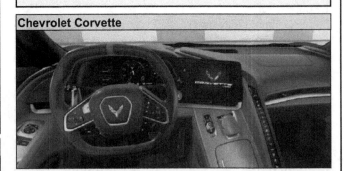

Chevrolet Corvette

How the Competition Rates

Competitors	Rating	Pg.
Chevrolet Camaro	4	94
Dodge Challenger	4	111
Ford Mustang	6	123

Price Range

	Retail	Markup
Base Coupe	$55,495	8%
Z51 Convertible	$64,495	8%
Grand Sport Coupe	$65,495	8%
Z06 Convertible	$83,495	8%

Specifications

Drive. . . . . .RWD
Engine 6.2-liter V8
Transmission . . . . .8-sp. Automatic
Tow Rating (lbs.) . . . . —
Head/Leg Room (in.) Average-37.9/42.8
Interior Space (cu. ft.). . . . . Very Cramped-52
Cargo Space (cu. ft.) Cramped-12.6
Wheelbase/Length (in.) 107.2/182.3

Chevrolet Equinox

Ratings—10 Best, 1 Worst

Combo Crash Tests	6
Safety Features	5
Rollover	2
Preventive Maintenance	1
Repair Costs	3
Warranty	6
Fuel Economy	7
Complaints	2
Insurance Costs	8
OVERALL RATING	**3**

Chevrolet Equinox

Chevrolet Equinox

At-a-Glance

Status/Year Series Started........ Unchanged/2018
Twins .... GMC Terrain
Body Styles .... SUV
Seating 5
Anti-Theft Device . Std. Pass. Immobil. & Active Alarm
Parking Index Rating .... Average
Where Made...... Oshawa, Ontario / Spring Hill, TN
Fuel Factor
  MPG Rating (city/hwy)............. Good-26/32
  Driving Range (mi.) Average-417
  Fuel Type.......................Regular
  Annual Fuel Cost ....Low-$1294
  Gas Guzzler Tax ....No
  Greenhouse Gas Emissions (tons/yr.)..... Low-5.2
  Barrels of Oil Used per year Average-11.8

How the Competition Rates

Competitors	Rating	Pg.
Dodge Journey	1	114
Ford Escape	5	116
Honda Pilot	8	143

Price Range

Price Range	Retail	Markup
L FWD	$23,580	1%
LS FWD	$25,510	5%
LT AWD 2.0	$32,840	5%
Premier AWD 2.0	$37,230	5%

Safety Checklist

Crash Test:
  Frontal .... Very Good
  Side ....Very Poor
Airbags:
  Torso ...... Std. Fr. Pelvis/Torso from Seat
  Roll Sensing ....Yes
  Knee Bolster ....None
Crash Avoidance:
  Collision Avoidance ....Optional CIB
  Blind Spot Detection .... Optional
  Lane Keeping Assist .... Optional
  Pedestrian Crash Avoidance.........None
General:
  Auto. Crash Notif... Op. Assist. & Crash Info-Free
  Day Running Lamps ....Standard
Safety Belt/Restraint:
  Dynamic Head Restraints ....None
  Adjustable Belt...... Optional Front & Rear

Chevrolet Equinox

Specifications

Drive................................... FWD
Engine 1.5-liter I4
Transmission ....6-sp. Automatic
Tow Rating (lbs.) Low-3500
Head/Leg Room (in.) Cramped-40/40.9
Interior Space (cu. ft.)............Average-103.2
Cargo Space (cu. ft.) Roomy-29.9
Wheelbase/Length (in.) 107.3/183.1

Chevrolet Impala | Large

Ratings—10 Best, 1 Worst

Combo Crash Tests	6
Safety Features	6
Rollover	6
Preventive Maintenance	1
Repair Costs	6
Warranty	6
Fuel Economy	3
Complaints	8
Insurance Costs	3
OVERALL RATING	**4**

Chevrolet Impala

Chevrolet Impala

At-a-Glance

Status/Year Series Started	Unchanged/2014
Twins	Cadillac XTS
Body Styles	Sedan
Seating	5
Anti-Theft Device	Std. Pass. Immobil. & Active Alarm
Parking Index Rating	Hard
Where Made	Detroit, MI / Oshawa, Ontario

Fuel Factor

MPG Rating (city/hwy)	Poor-18/28
Driving Range (mi.)	Short-397
Fuel Type	Regular
Annual Fuel Cost	High-$1714
Gas Guzzler Tax	No
Greenhouse Gas Emissions (tons/yr.)	High-8.6
Barrels of Oil Used per year	High-15.7

How the Competition Rates

Competitors	Rating	Pg.
Chrysler 300	1	107
Dodge Charger	4	110
Toyota Avalon	8	220

Price Range

	Retail	Markup
LS	$27,985	5%
LT	$30,220	4%
Premier	$36,420	4%

Safety Checklist

Crash Test:
  Frontal . . . . .Good
  Side . . . . Poor
Airbags:
  Torso . Std. Fr. & Opt. Rr. Pelvis/Torso from Seat
  Roll Sensing . . . . .Yes
  Knee Bolster . . . . Standard Front
Crash Avoidance:
  Collision Avoidance . . . . .Optional CIB
  Blind Spot Detection . . . . Optional
  Lane Keeping Assist . . . . Warning Only Opt.
  Pedestrian Crash Avoidance . . . . .None
General:
  Auto. Crash Notif . . . Op. Assist. & Crash Info-Free
  Day Running Lamps . . . . .Standard
Safety Belt/Restraint:
  Dynamic Head Restraints . . . . .None
  Adjustable Belt . . . . . . Optional Front & Rear

^Warning feature does not meet suggested government specifications.

Chevrolet Impala

Specifications

Drive	FWD
Engine	3.6-liter V6
Transmission	6-sp. Automatic
Tow Rating (lbs.)	Very Low-1000
Head/Leg Room (in.)	Very Roomy-39.9/45.8
Interior Space (cu. ft.)	Roomy-105
Cargo Space (cu. ft.)	Average-18.8
Wheelbase/Length (in.)	111.7/201.3

Ratings—10 Best, 1 Worst

Combo Crash Tests	5
Safety Features	9
Rollover	8
Preventive Maintenance	7
Repair Costs	8
Warranty	6
Fuel Economy	8
Complaints	10
Insurance Costs	3
OVERALL RATING	**9**

Chevrolet Malibu

Chevrolet Malibu

At-a-Glance

Status/Year Series Started	Unchanged/2016
Twins	Buick Regal
Body Styles	Sedan
Seating	5
Anti-Theft Device	Std. Pass. Immobil. & Active Alarm
Parking Index Rating	Average
Where Made	Fairfax, KS
Fuel Factor	
MPG Rating (city/hwy)	Good-27/36
Driving Range (mi.)	Short-395
Fuel Type	Regular
Annual Fuel Cost	Low-$1208
Gas Guzzler Tax	No
Greenhouse Gas Emissions (tons/yr.)	Low-4.8
Barrels of Oil Used per year	Average-11.0

How the Competition Rates

Competitors	Rating	Pg.
Ford Fusion	4	121
Nissan Altima		196
Toyota Camry	8	221

Price Range

	Retail	Markup
L	$21,680	1%
LS	$23,225	4%
LT	$25,125	4%
Hybrid	$27,875	4%

Safety Checklist

Crash Test:
Frontal . . . . Poor
Side . . . . Very Good
Airbags:
Torso Std. Fr. & Rear Pelvis/Torso from Seat
Roll Sensing . . . . Yes
Knee Bolster . . . . Standard Front
Crash Avoidance:
Collision Avoidance . . . . Optional CIB & DBS
Blind Spot Detection . . . . Optional
Lane Keeping Assist . . . . Optional
Pedestrian Crash Avoidance . . . . . . Optional
General:
Auto. Crash Notif. . . Op. Assist. & Crash Info-Free
Day Running Lamps . . . . Standard
Safety Belt/Restraint:
Dynamic Head Restraints . . . . None
Adjustable Belt . . . . Optional Rear

^Warning feature does not meet suggested government specifications.

Chevrolet Malibu

Specifications

Drive	FWD
Engine	1.5-liter I4
Transmission	6-sp. Automatic
Tow Rating (lbs.)	–
Head/Leg Room (in.)	Average-39.1/42
Interior Space (cu. ft.)	Average-102.9
Cargo Space (cu. ft.)	Cramped-15.8
Wheelbase/Length (in.)	111.4/193.8

Chevrolet Silverado   Standard Pickup

Ratings—10 Best, 1 Worst

Combo Crash Tests	—
Safety Features	3
Rollover	3
Preventive Maintenance	1
Repair Costs	5
Warranty	6
Fuel Economy	2
Complaints	4
Insurance Costs	10
OVERALL RATING	**—**

Chevrolet Silverado

Chevrolet Silverado

At-a-Glance

Status/Year Series Started. Unchanged/2019
Twins . . . . GMC Sierra
Body Styles . . . . Pickup
Seating 5/6
Anti-Theft Device . Std. Pass. Immobil. & Active Alarm
Parking Index Rating . . . . Very Hard
Where Made. Fort Wayne, IN
Fuel Factor
  MPG Rating (city/hwy). . . . . .Very Poor-16/22
  Driving Range (mi.) Long-432
  Fuel Type. . . . . .Regular
  Annual Fuel Cost . . . . Very High-$2015
  Gas Guzzler Tax . . . . .No
  Greenhouse Gas Emissions (tons/yr.). High-8.1
  Barrels of Oil Used per year . . . . Very High-18.3

How the Competition Rates

Competitors	Rating	Pg.
Ford F-150	9	119
Ram 1500		208
Toyota Tundra		231

Price Range

Price Range	Retail	Markup
W/T Reg. Cab 2WD	$28,300	5%
LT Dbl. Cab 4WD	$40,200	7%
LTZ Crew Cab 4WD	$48,700	7%
High Cntry Crew Cab 4WD	$56,600	7%

Safety Checklist

Crash Test:
  Frontal . . . . —
  Side . . . . —
Airbags:
  Torso . . . . . . Std. Fr. Pelvis/Torso from Seat
  Roll Sensing . . . . .Yes
  Knee Bolster .None
Crash Avoidance:
  Collision Avoidance . . . . .Optional CIB
  Blind Spot Detection . . . . Optional
  Lane Keeping Assist . . . . Optional
  Pedestrian Crash Avoidance. . . . . .None
General:
  Auto. Crash Notif. . . Op. Assist. & Crash Info-Free
  Day Running Lamps . . . . .Standard
Safety Belt/Restraint:
  Dynamic Head Restraints . . . . .None
  Adjustable Belt. . . . . . Optional Front & Rear

^Warning feature does not meet suggested government specifications.

Chevrolet Silverado

Specifications

Drive. 4WD
Engine 5.3-liter V8
Transmission . . . . .8-sp. Automatic
Tow Rating (lbs.) . . . . Very High-9,900
Head/Leg Room (in.) . . . . .Very Roomy-43/44.5
Interior Space (cu. ft.). . . . . —
Cargo Space (cu. ft.) . . . . Very Roomy-71.7
Wheelbase/Length (in.) 147.4/231.8

Ratings—10 Best, 1 Worst

Combo Crash Tests	7
Safety Features	7
Rollover	8
Preventive Maintenance	9
Repair Costs	9
Warranty	6
Fuel Economy	7
Complaints	6
Insurance Costs	1
OVERALL RATING	**9**

Chevrolet Sonic

Chevrolet Sonic

At-a-Glance

Status/Year Series Started........ Unchanged/2012
Twins .... —
Body Styles .... Sedan, Hatchback
Seating 5
Anti-Theft Device . Std. Pass. Immobil. & Active Alarm
Parking Index Rating .... Very Easy
Where Made................. Orion Township, MI
Fuel Factor
  MPG Rating (city/hwy)............. Good-25/34
  Driving Range (mi.) .... Very Short-346
  Fuel Type............................... Regular
  Annual Fuel Cost .... Low-$1295
  Gas Guzzler Tax .... No
  Greenhouse Gas Emissions (tons/yr.). . Average-6.5
  Barrels of Oil Used per year Average-11.8

How the Competition Rates

Competitors	Rating	Pg.
Nissan Versa	1	206
Honda Fit	9	135
Kia Rio		158

Price Range

	Retail	Markup
LS Sedan MT	$15,295	4%
LT Sedan MT	$17,695	4%
LT Hatchback AT	$19,195	4%
Premier Hatchback AT	$21,295	4%

Safety Checklist

Crash Test:
  Frontal .... Very Good
  Side .... Very Poor
Airbags:
  Torso Std. Fr. & Rear Pelvis/Torso from Seat
  Roll Sensing .... Yes
  Knee Bolster .... Standard Front
Crash Avoidance:
  Collision Avoidance ..... Warning Only Opt.
  Blind Spot Detection .... None
  Lane Keeping Assist .... Warning Only Opt.
  Pedestrian Crash Avoidance......... None
General:
  Auto. Crash Notif... Op. Assist. & Crash Info-Free
  Day Running Lamps .... Standard
Safety Belt/Restraint:
  Dynamic Head Restraints .... None
  Adjustable Belt...... Optional Front & Rear

^Warning feature does not meet suggested government specifications.

Chevrolet Sonic

Specifications

Drive.................................... FWD
Engine 1.8-liter I4
Transmission .... 6-sp. Automatic
Tow Rating (lbs.) .... –
Head/Leg Room (in.) Cramped-38.7/41.8
Interior Space (cu. ft.)............ Cramped-90.6
Cargo Space (cu. ft.) Average-19
Wheelbase/Length (in.) 99.4/159

Chevrolet Spark | Subcompact

Ratings—10 Best, 1 Worst

Rating	
Combo Crash Tests	2
Safety Features	7
Rollover	3
Preventive Maintenance	9
Repair Costs	8
Warranty	6
Fuel Economy	9
Complaints	4
Insurance Costs	1
OVERALL RATING	**5**

Chevrolet Spark

Chevrolet Spark

At-a-Glance

Status/Year Series Started......Unchanged/2016
Twins...............................—
Body Styles...................Hatchback
Seating...............................4
Anti-Theft Device . Std. Pass. Immobil. & Active Alarm
Parking Index Rating................Very Easy
Where Made............Changwon, South Korea
Fuel Factor
  MPG Rating (city/hwy)..........Very Good-29/38
  Driving Range (mi.)...........Very Short-292
  Fuel Type.........................Regular
  Annual Fuel Cost.............Very Low-$1132
  Gas Guzzler Tax.....................No
  Greenhouse Gas Emissions (tons/yr.). Very Low-4.2
  Barrels of Oil Used per year...........Low-9.4

How the Competition Rates

Competitors	Rating	Pg.
Honda Fit	9	135
Mitsubishi Mirage	3	193
Nissan Versa	1	206

Price Range

	Retail	Markup
LS MT	$13,050	4%
1LT MT	$14,875	4%
1LT AT	$15,975	4%
2LT AT	$17,475	4%

Safety Checklist

Crash Test:
  Frontal.....................Very Poor
  Side.........................Poor
Airbags:
  Torso Std. Fr. & Rear Pelvis/Torso from Seat
  Roll Sensing...................Yes
  Knee Bolster...........Standard Front
Crash Avoidance:
  Collision Avoidance.....Warning Only Opt.
  Blind Spot Detection...............None
  Lane Keeping Assist....Warning Only Opt.
  Pedestrian Crash Avoidance.........None
General:
  Auto. Crash Notif... Op. Assist. & Crash Info-Free
  Day Running Lamps...........Standard
Safety Belt/Restraint:
  Dynamic Head Restraints...........None
  Adjustable Belt............Optional Rear

^Warning feature does not meet suggested government specifications.

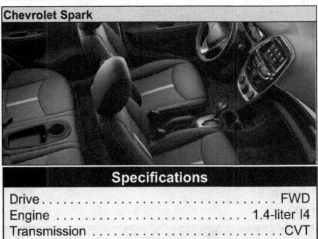
Chevrolet Spark

Specifications

Drive...................................FWD
Engine........................1.4-liter I4
Transmission............................CVT
Tow Rating (lbs.)........................—
Head/Leg Room (in.).........Cramped-39/41.7
Interior Space (cu. ft.).........Very Cramped-83
Cargo Space (cu. ft.).........Very Cramped-11.1
Wheelbase/Length (in.)..........93.9/143.1

Ratings—10 Best, 1 Worst

Combo Crash Tests	6
Safety Features	4
Rollover	2
Preventive Maintenance	1
Repair Costs	5
Warranty	6
Fuel Economy	1
Complaints	3
Insurance Costs	10
OVERALL RATING	**2**

Chevrolet Suburban

Chevrolet Suburban

At-a-Glance

Status/Year Series Started Unchanged/2015
Twins . . . . . . Cadillac Escalade ESV, GMC Yukon XL
Body Styles . . . . SUV
Seating 6/9
Anti-Theft Device . Std. Pass. Immobil. & Active Alarm
Parking Index Rating . . . . Very Hard
Where Made. Arlington, TX
Fuel Factor
  MPG Rating (city/hwy) . . . . Very Poor-15/22
  Driving Range (mi.) . . . . Very Long-543
  Fuel Type . . . . Regular
  Annual Fuel Cost . . . . Very High-$2099
  Gas Guzzler Tax . . . . No
  Greenhouse Gas Emissions (tons/yr.)Very High-10.0
  Barrels of Oil Used per year . . . . Very High-18.3

How the Competition Rates

Competitors	Rating	Pg.
Buick Enclave	4	82
Ford Expedition		117
Volvo XC90	8	240

Price Range	Retail	Markup
1500 LS RWD	$50,150	6%
1500 LT RWD	$55,280	6%
1500 LT 4WD	$58,280	6%
1500 Premier 4WD	$67,830	6%

Safety Checklist

Crash Test:
  Frontal . . . . Average
  Side . . . . Average
Airbags:
  Torso . . . . . . Std. Fr. Pelvis/Torso from Seat
  Roll Sensing . . . . Yes
  Knee Bolster . . . . None
Crash Avoidance:
  Collision Avoidance . . . . Optional CIB
  Blind Spot Detection . . . . Optional
  Lane Keeping Assist . . . . Optional
  Pedestrian Crash Avoidance. . . . . None
General:
  Auto. Crash Notif. . . Op. Assist. & Crash Info-Free
  Day Running Lamps . . . . Standard
Safety Belt/Restraint:
  Dynamic Head Restraints . . . . None
  Adjustable Belt. . . . . . Optional Front & Rear

^Warning feature does not meet suggested government specifications.

Chevrolet Suburban

Specifications

Drive 4WD
Engine 5.3-liter V8
Transmission . . . . 6-sp. Automatic
Tow Rating (lbs.) High-8000
Head/Leg Room (in.) . . . . . . Very Roomy-42.8/45.3
Interior Space (cu. ft.). Roomy-120.8
Cargo Space (cu. ft.) . . . . Very Roomy-39.3
Wheelbase/Length (in.) 130/224.4

Chevrolet Tahoe — Large SUV

Ratings—10 Best, 1 Worst

Combo Crash Tests	8
Safety Features	4
Rollover	2
Preventive Maintenance	1
Repair Costs	3
Warranty	6
Fuel Economy	2
Complaints	5
Insurance Costs	10
OVERALL RATING	**4**

Chevrolet Tahoe

Chevrolet Tahoe

At-a-Glance

Status/Year Series Started Unchanged/2015
Twins . . . . .Cadillac Escalade, GMC Yukon
Body Styles . . . . SUV
Seating 6/9
Anti-Theft Device . Std. Pass. Immobil. & Active Alarm
Parking Index Rating . . . . .Very Hard
Where Made. . . . . Arlington, TX
Fuel Factor
  MPG Rating (city/hwy) . . . . .Very Poor-16/22
  Driving Range (mi.) . . . . Very Long-474
  Fuel Type. . . . . .Regular
  Annual Fuel Cost . . . . Very High-$2015
  Gas Guzzler Tax . . . . .No
  Greenhouse Gas Emissions (tons/yr.) High-8.2
  Barrels of Oil Used per year . . . . . . .Very High-18.3

How the Competition Rates

Competitors	Rating	Pg.
Buick Enclave	4	82
Infiniti QX80		150
Volvo XC90	8	240

Price Range

Price Range	Retail	Markup
LS RWD	$47,450	6%
LT RWD	$52,580	6%
LT4WD	$55,580	6%
Premier 4WD	$65,130	6%

Safety Checklist

Crash Test:
  Frontal . . . . .Good
  Side . . . . Very Good
Airbags:
  Torso . . . . . . Std. Fr. Pelvis/Torso from Seat
  Roll Sensing . . . . .Yes
  Knee Bolster .None
Crash Avoidance:
  Collision Avoidance . . . . .Optional CIB
  Blind Spot Detection . . . . Optional
  Lane Keeping Assist . . . . Optional
  Pedestrian Crash Avoidance. . . . . .None
General:
  Auto. Crash Notif... Op. Assist. & Crash Info-Free
  Day Running Lamps . . . . .Standard
Safety Belt/Restraint:
  Dynamic Head Restraints . . . . .None
  Adjustable Belt. . . . . . Optional Front & Rear

^Warning feature does not meet suggested government specifications.

Chevrolet Tahoe

Specifications

Drive. 4WD
Engine 5.3-liter V8
Transmission . . . . .6-sp. Automatic
Tow Rating (lbs.) . . . . .Very High-8400
Head/Leg Room (in.) . . . . . . Very Roomy-42.8/45.3
Interior Space (cu. ft.). Roomy-120.8
Cargo Space (cu. ft.) Cramped-15.3
Wheelbase/Length (in.) 116/204

Chevrolet Traverse   Large SUV

Ratings—10 Best, 1 Worst

Combo Crash Tests	5
Safety Features	6
Rollover	4
Preventive Maintenance	2
Repair Costs	5
Warranty	6
Fuel Economy	3
Complaints	6
Insurance Costs	10
OVERALL RATING	**4**

Chevrolet Traverse

Chevrolet Traverse

At-a-Glance

Status/Year Series Started. Unchanged/2018
Twins . . . . .Buick Enclave
Body Styles . . . . SUV
Seating 7/8
Anti-Theft Device . Std. Pass. Immobil. & Active Alarm
Parking Index Rating . . . . .Very Hard
Where Made. . . . . Lansing, Michigan
Fuel Factor
  MPG Rating (city/hwy) Poor-18/27
  Driving Range (mi.) Average-411
  Fuel Type. . . . . .Regular
  Annual Fuel Cost . . . . .High-$1735
  Gas Guzzler Tax . . . . .No
  Greenhouse Gas Emissions (tons/yr.). . Average-6.9
  Barrels of Oil Used per year High-15.7

How the Competition Rates

Competitors	Rating	Pg.
Buick Enclave	4	82
Ford Flex		120
Volvo XC90	8	240

Price Range	Retail	Markup
LS FWD	$32,050	5%
LT FWD	$34,550	5%
Premier AWD	$47,350	5%
High Country AWD	$52,050	5%

Safety Checklist

Crash Test:
  Frontal . . . . Average
  Side . . . . Poor
Airbags:
  Torso . . . . . . Std. Fr. Pelvis/Torso from Seat
  Roll Sensing . . . . .Yes
  Knee Bolster .None
Crash Avoidance:
  Collision Avoidance . . . Optional CIB & DBS*
  Blind Spot Detection . . . . Optional
  Lane Keeping Assist . . . . Optional
  Pedestrian Crash Avoidance. . . . . . Optional
General:
  Auto. Crash Notif. . . Op. Assist. & Crash Info-Free
  Day Running Lamps . . . . .Standard
Safety Belt/Restraint:
  Dynamic Head Restraints . . . . .None
  Adjustable Belt. . . . . .Optional Rear

^Warning feature does not meet suggested government specifications.

Chevrolet Traverse

Specifications

Drive. . . . . FWD
Engine 3.6-liter V6
Transmission . . . . .9-sp. Automatic
Tow Rating (lbs.) Low-5000
Head/Leg Room (in.) Average-41.3/41
Interior Space (cu. ft.). . . . . Very Roomy-157.3
Cargo Space (cu. ft.) Roomy-23
Wheelbase/Length (in.) 120.9/204.3

Ratings—10 Best, 1 Worst

Combo Crash Tests	8
Safety Features	7
Rollover	3
Preventive Maintenance	7
Repair Costs	5
Warranty	6
Fuel Economy	6
Complaints	10
Insurance Costs	10
OVERALL RATING	**10**

Chevrolet Trax

Chevrolet Trax

At-a-Glance

Status/Year Series Started........ Unchanged/2015
Twins .... Buick Encore
Body Styles .... SUV
Seating 5
Anti-Theft Device . Std. Pass. Immobil. & Active Alarm
Parking Index Rating .... Easy
Where Made.. South Korea / San Luis Potosi, Mexico
Fuel Factor
  MPG Rating (city/hwy)............ Average-24/30
  Driving Range (mi.) ....Very Short-369
  Fuel Type...........................Regular
  Annual Fuel Cost .... Low-$1393
  Gas Guzzler Tax ....No
  Greenhouse Gas Emissions (tons/yr.)..... Low-5.5
  Barrels of Oil Used per year Average-12.2

How the Competition Rates

Competitors	Rating	Pg.
Ford Escape	5	116
Honda HR-V	5	136
Jeep Compass	4	152

Price Range

Price Range	Retail	Markup
LS FWD	$21,000	4%
LT FWD	$22,900	4%
LT AWD	$24,400	4%
Premier AWD	$28,795	4%

Safety Checklist

Crash Test:
  Frontal .... Very Good
  Side .... Average
Airbags:
  Torso Std. Fr. & Rear Pelvis/Torso from Seat
  Roll Sensing ....Yes
  Knee Bolster .... Standard Front
Crash Avoidance:
  Collision Avoidance ..... Warning Only Opt.
  Blind Spot Detection .... Optional
  Lane Keeping Assist .... Warning Only Opt.
  Pedestrian Crash Avoidance.........None
General:
  Auto. Crash Notif... Op. Assist. & Crash Info-Free
  Day Running Lamps ....Standard
Safety Belt/Restraint:
  Dynamic Head Restraints ....None
  Adjustable Belt...... Optional Front & Rear

^Warning feature does not meet suggested government specifications.

Chevrolet Trax

Specifications

Drive...................................AWD
Engine 1.4-liter I4
Transmission ....6-sp. Automatic
Tow Rating (lbs.) .... –
Head/Leg Room (in.) Cramped-39.6/40.8
Interior Space (cu. ft.)............Cramped-92.8
Cargo Space (cu. ft.) Average-18.7
Wheelbase/Length (in.) 100.6/168.5

Chrysler 300 Large

Ratings—10 Best, 1 Worst

Combo Crash Tests	2
Safety Features	5
Rollover	6
Preventive Maintenance	8
Repair Costs	2
Warranty	4
Fuel Economy	4
Complaints	3
Insurance Costs	1
OVERALL RATING	**1**

Chrysler 300

Chrysler 300

At-a-Glance

Status/Year Series Started	Unchanged/2011
Twins	Dodge Charger
Body Styles	Sedan
Seating	5
Anti-Theft Device	Std. Pass. Immobil. & Alarm
Parking Index Rating	Very Hard
Where Made	Brampton, Ontario
Fuel Factor	
MPG Rating (city/hwy)	Poor-19/30
Driving Range (mi.)	Average-421
Fuel Type	Regular
Annual Fuel Cost	Average-$1615
Gas Guzzler Tax	No
Greenhouse Gas Emissions (tons/yr.)	High-7.8
Barrels of Oil Used per year	High-14.3

How the Competition Rates

Competitors	Rating	Pg.
Cadillac XT5	3	90
Toyota Avalon	8	220

Price Range

	Retail	Markup
Touring RWD	$28,995	1%
Limited RWD	$36,595	3%
S V6 AWD	$38,295	4%
C V8	$40,995	4%

Safety Checklist

Crash Test:
  Frontal . . . . Very Poor
  Side . . . . Poor
Airbags:
  Torso . . . . . . Std. Fr. Pelvis/Torso from Seat
  Roll Sensing . . . . Yes
  Knee Bolster . . . . Standard Driver
Crash Avoidance:
  Collision Avoidance . . . . Optional CIB & DBS
  Blind Spot Detection . . . . Optional
  Lane Keeping Assist . . . . Optional*
  Pedestrian Crash Avoidance . . . . None
General:
  Auto. Crash Notification. . . . . None
  Day Running Lamps . . . . Standard
Safety Belt/Restraint:
  Dynamic Head Restraints . . . . None
  Adjustable Belt. . . . . Standard Front

^Warning feature does not meet suggested government specifications.

Chrysler 300

Specifications

Drive	RWD
Engine	3.6-liter V6
Transmission	8-sp. Automatic
Tow Rating (lbs.)	–
Head/Leg Room (in.)	Cramped-38.6/41.8
Interior Space (cu. ft.)	Roomy-106.3
Cargo Space (cu. ft.)	Cramped-16.3
Wheelbase/Length (in.)	120.2/198.6

Chrysler Pacifica   Minivan

Ratings—10 Best, 1 Worst

Combo Crash Tests	8
Safety Features	7
Rollover	6
Preventive Maintenance	10
Repair Costs	6
Warranty	4
Fuel Economy	3
Complaints	1
Insurance Costs	10
OVERALL RATING	**8**

Chrysler Pacifica

Chrysler Pacifica

At-a-Glance

Status/Year Series Started. Unchanged/2017
Twins . . . . —
Body Styles . . . . Minivan
Seating 7/8
Anti-Theft Device . . . . . . Std. Pass. Immobil. & Alarm
Parking Index Rating . . . . Very Hard
Where Made . . . . Windsor, Ontario
Fuel Factor
  MPG Rating (city/hwy). Poor-18/28
  Driving Range (mi.) Average-407
  Fuel Type . . . . Regular
  Annual Fuel Cost . . . . High-$1714
  Gas Guzzler Tax . . . . No
  Greenhouse Gas Emissions (tons/yr.). . Average-6.9
  Barrels of Oil Used per year High-15.0

How the Competition Rates

Competitors	Rating	Pg.
Honda Odyssey	9	137
Kia Sedona		159
Toyota Sienna	2	229

Price Range

	Retail	Markup
LX	$26,995	0%
Touring L	$35,495	3%
Touring L Plus	$38,695	4%
Limited	$43,695	4%

Safety Checklist

Crash Test:
  Frontal . . . . Very Good
  Side . . . . Poor
Airbags:
  Torso . . . . . . Std. Fr. Pelvis/Torso from Seat
  Roll Sensing . . . . Yes
  Knee Bolster . . . . Standard Front
Crash Avoidance:
  Collision Avoidance . . . . Optional CIB & DBS
  Blind Spot Detection . . . . Optional
  Lane Keeping Assist . . . . Optional
  Pedestrian Crash Avoidance . . . . None
General:
  Auto. Crash Notification. . . . . None
  Day Running Lamps . . . . Standard
Safety Belt/Restraint:
  Dynamic Head Restraints . . . . None
  Adjustable Belt. . . . . . Standard Front & Rear

^Warning feature does not meet suggested government specifications.

Chrysler Pacifica

Specifications

Drive . . . . FWD
Engine 3.6-liter V6
Transmission . . . . 9-sp. Automatic
Tow Rating (lbs.) Low-3600
Head/Leg Room (in.) Average-40.1/41.1
Interior Space (cu. ft.). . . . . Very Roomy-165
Cargo Space (cu. ft.) . . . . Very Roomy-32.3
Wheelbase/Length (in.) 121.6/203.8

Ratings—10 Best, 1 Worst

Combo Crash Tests	7
Safety Features	2
Rollover	7
Preventive Maintenance	8
Repair Costs	3
Warranty	4
Fuel Economy	4
Complaints	9
Insurance Costs	1
OVERALL RATING	**4**

Dodge Challenger

At-a-Glance

Status/Year Series Started	Apperance Change/2015
Twins	—
Body Styles	Coupe
Seating	5
Anti-Theft Device	Std. Pass. Immobil. & Alarm
Parking Index Rating	Hard
Where Made	Brampton, Ontario
Fuel Factor	
MPG Rating (city/hwy)	Poor-19/30
Driving Range (mi.)	Average-421
Fuel Type	Regular
Annual Fuel Cost	Average-$1615
Gas Guzzler Tax	No
Greenhouse Gas Emissions (tons/yr.)	High-7.8
Barrels of Oil Used per year	High-14.3

How the Competition Rates

Competitors	Rating	Pg.
Chevrolet Camaro	4	94
Chevrolet Corvette		96
Ford Mustang	6	123

Price Range

	Retail	Markup
SXT	$26,995	1%
R/T	$33,495	2%
R/T 392	$38,995	4%
SRT Hellcat	$63,795	3%

Dodge Challenger

Safety Checklist

Crash Test:
  Frontal . . . . Average
  Side . . . . Very Good
Airbags:
  Torso . . . . . . Std. Fr. Pelvis/Torso from Seat
  Roll Sensing . . . . Yes
  Knee Bolster . . . . None
Crash Avoidance:
  Collision Avoidance . . . . . Warning Only Opt.
  Blind Spot Detection . . . . Optional
  Lane Keeping Assist . . . . None
  Pedestrian Crash Avoidance . . . . None
General:
  Auto. Crash Notification . . . . None
  Day Running Lamps . . . . Standard
Safety Belt/Restraint:
  Dynamic Head Restraints . . . . None
  Adjustable Belt . . . . None

^Warning feature does not meet suggested government specifications.

Dodge Challenger

Specifications

Drive	RWD
Engine	3.6-liter V6
Transmission	8-sp. Automatic
Tow Rating (lbs.)	Very Low-1000
Head/Leg Room (in.)	Average-39.3/42
Interior Space (cu. ft.)	Cramped-93.9
Cargo Space (cu. ft.)	Cramped-16.2
Wheelbase/Length (in.)	116.2/197.9

Ratings—10 Best, 1 Worst

Combo Crash Tests	3
Safety Features	5
Rollover	8
Preventive Maintenance	8
Repair Costs	7
Warranty	4
Fuel Economy	4
Complaints	3
Insurance Costs	1
OVERALL RATING	**2**

Dodge Charger

At-a-Glance

Status/Year Series Started	Apperance Change/2011
Twins	Chrysler 300
Body Styles	Sedan
Seating	5
Anti-Theft Device	Std. Pass. Immobil. & Alarm
Parking Index Rating	Hard
Where Made	Brampton, Ontario
Fuel Factor	
MPG Rating (city/hwy)	Poor-19/31
Driving Range (mi.)	Long-426
Fuel Type	Regular
Annual Fuel Cost	Average-$1597
Gas Guzzler Tax	No
Greenhouse Gas Emissions (tons/yr.)	High-7.8
Barrels of Oil Used per year	High-14.3

How the Competition Rates

Competitors	Rating	Pg.
Chevrolet Impala	4	98
Chrysler 300	1	107
Genesis G80		125

Price Range

Price Range	Retail	Markup
SXT	$28,495	1%
AWD GT	$32,495	3%
R/T	$34,995	3%
SRT Hellcat	$66,295	4%

Dodge Charger

Safety Checklist

Crash Test:
  Frontal . . . . Very Poor
  Side . . . . Average
Airbags:
  Torso . . . . . . Std. Fr. Pelvis/Torso from Seat
  Roll Sensing . . . . Yes
  Knee Bolster . . . . Standard Driver
Crash Avoidance:
  Collision Avoidance . . . . Optional CIB & DBS
  Blind Spot Detection . . . . Optional
  Lane Keeping Assist . . . . Optional
  Pedestrian Crash Avoidance . . . . None
General:
  Auto. Crash Notification. . . . . None
  Day Running Lamps . . . . Standard
Safety Belt/Restraint:
  Dynamic Head Restraints . . . . None
  Adjustable Belt. . . . . Standard Front

^Warning feature does not meet suggested government specifications.

Dodge Charger

Specifications

Drive	RWD
Engine	3.6-liter V6
Transmission	8-sp. Automatic
Tow Rating (lbs.)	Very Low-1000
Head/Leg Room (in.)	Cramped-38.6/41.8
Interior Space (cu. ft.)	Roomy-104.7
Cargo Space (cu. ft.)	Cramped-16.1
Wheelbase/Length (in.)	120.2/198.4

Dodge Durango | Medium SUV

Dodge Durango

Ratings—10 Best, 1 Worst

Combo Crash Tests	3
Safety Features	7
Rollover	2
Preventive Maintenance	5
Repair Costs	6
Warranty	4
Fuel Economy	3
Complaints	1
Insurance Costs	10
OVERALL RATING	**2**

Dodge Durango

At-a-Glance

Status/Year Series Started........ Unchanged/2011
Twins ....—
Body Styles .... SUV
Seating.. 6/7
Anti-Theft Device Std. Pass. Immob. & Opt. Pass. Alarm
Parking Index Rating .... Hard
Where Made..Detroit, MI
Fuel Factor
　MPG Rating (city/hwy)............... Poor-18/25
　Driving Range (mi.) .... Very Long-507
　Fuel Type................................Regular
　Annual Fuel Cost ....High-$1784
　Gas Guzzler Tax ....No
　Greenhouse Gas Emissions (tons/yr.).. Average-7.1
　Barrels of Oil Used per year High-15.7

How the Competition Rates

Competitors	Rating	Pg.
Ford Edge	9	115
GMC Acadia	2	126
Jeep Grand Cherokee	4	153

Price Range

Price Range	Retail	Markup
SXT RWD	$29,995	0%
GT RWD	$37,795	3%
R/T AWD	$46,295	4%
SRT AWD	$62,995	3%

Safety Checklist

Crash Test:
　Frontal .... Very Poor
　Side .... Average
Airbags:
　Torso ...... Std. Fr. Pelvis/Torso from Seat
　Roll Sensing ....Yes
　Knee Bolster .... Standard Driver
Crash Avoidance:
　Collision Avoidance . . . Optional CIB & DBS*
　Blind Spot Detection .... Optional
　Lane Keeping Assist .... Warning Only Opt.
　Pedestrian Crash Avoidance.........None
General:
　Auto. Crash Notification...........None
　Day Running Lamps ....Standard
Safety Belt/Restraint:
　Dynamic Head Restraints ... Standard Front
　Adjustable Belt............Standard Front

^Warning feature does not meet suggested government specifications.

Dodge Durango

Specifications

Drive.................................... AWD
Engine 3.6-liter V6
Transmission ....8-sp. Automatic
Tow Rating (lbs.) .... Very Low-1350
Head/Leg Room (in.) Cramped-39.9/40.3
Interior Space (cu. ft.)......... Very Roomy-133.9
Cargo Space (cu. ft.) Average-17.2
Wheelbase/Length (in.) 119.8/201.2

Dodge Journey | Medium SUV

Ratings—10 Best, 1 Worst

Combo Crash Tests	2
Safety Features	3
Rollover	2
Preventive Maintenance	9
Repair Costs	4
Warranty	4
Fuel Economy	3
Complaints	1
Insurance Costs	8
OVERALL RATING	**1**

Dodge Journey

Dodge Journey

At-a-Glance

Status/Year Series Started Unchanged/2009
Twins . . . . —
Body Styles . . . . SUV
Seating 5/7
Anti-Theft Device . . . . . . Std. Pass. Immobil. & Alarm
Parking Index Rating . . . . Hard
Where Made . . . . Toluca, Mexico
Fuel Factor
  MPG Rating (city/hwy) Poor-19/25
  Driving Range (mi.) Long-437
  Fuel Type . . . . Regular
  Annual Fuel Cost . . . . High-$1725
  Gas Guzzler Tax . . . . .No
  Greenhouse Gas Emissions (tons/yr.) Very High-9.4
  Barrels of Oil Used per year . . . . Very High-17.3

How the Competition Rates

Competitors	Rating	Pg.
Chevrolet Equinox	4	97
Ford Edge	9	115
GMC Acadia	2	126

Price Range

Price Range	Retail	Markup
SE FWD	$22,495	1%
SXT FWD	$25,695	3%
Crossroad AWD	$31,395	4%
GT AWD	$34,395	4%

Safety Checklist

Crash Test:
  Frontal . . . . Poor
  Side . . . . Very Poor
Airbags:
  Torso . . . . . . Std. Fr. Pelvis/Torso from Seat
  Roll Sensing . . . . .Yes
  Knee Bolster . . . . Standard Driver
Crash Avoidance:
  Collision Avoidance . . . . .None
  Blind Spot Detection . . . . .None
  Lane Keeping Assist . . . . .None
  Pedestrian Crash Avoidance . . . . .None
General:
  Auto. Crash Notification . . . . .None
  Day Running Lamps . . . . .Standard
Safety Belt/Restraint:
  Dynamic Head Restraints . . . Standard Front
  Adjustable Belt . . . . Standard Front

^Warning feature does not meet suggested government specifications.

Dodge Journey
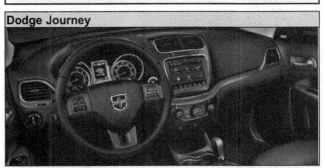

Specifications

Drive . . . . FWD
Engine 3.6-liter V6
Transmission . . . . 4-sp. Automatic
Tow Rating (lbs.) . . . . Very Low-2500
Head/Leg Room (in.) Average-40.8/40.8
Interior Space (cu. ft.) Roomy-123.7
Cargo Space (cu. ft.) . . . . .Very Cramped-10.7
Wheelbase/Length (in.) 113.8/192.4

Ratings—10 Best, 1 Worst

Combo Crash Tests	—
Safety Features	4
Rollover	4
Preventive Maintenance	8
Repair Costs	9
Warranty	5
Fuel Economy	5
Complaints	3
Insurance Costs	5
OVERALL RATING	—

Fiat 500X

Fiat 500X

At-a-Glance

Status/Year Series Started........ Unchanged/2015
Twins .... —
Body Styles .... SUV
Seating 5
Anti-Theft Device ...... Std. Pass. Immobil. & Alarm
Parking Index Rating .... Easy
Where Made......................... Melfi, Italy
Fuel Factor
  MPG Rating (city/hwy)........... Average-22/31
  Driving Range (mi.) .... Very Short-321
  Fuel Type......................... Regular
  Annual Fuel Cost .... Low-$1452
  Gas Guzzler Tax .... No
  Greenhouse Gas Emissions (tons/yr.)..... Low-5.8
  Barrels of Oil Used per year High-13.2

How the Competition Rates

Competitors	Rating	Pg.
Honda HR-V	5	136
Jeep Compass	4	152
Mazda CX-3	10	179

Price Range

Price Range	Retail	Markup
Pop FWD	$19,995	1%
Trekking FWD	$23,335	3%
Trekking AWD	$25,235	3%
Lounge AWD	$27,035	3%

Safety Checklist

Crash Test:
  Frontal .... −
  Side .... −
Airbags:
  Torso ...... Std. Fr. Pelvis/Torso from Seat
  Roll Sensing .... Yes
  Knee Bolster .... Standard Driver
Crash Avoidance:
  Collision Avoidance . . . Optional CIB & DBS*
  Blind Spot Detection .... Optional
  Lane Keeping Assist .... Optional*
  Pedestrian Crash Avoidance........ None
General:
  Auto. Crash Notification........... None
  Day Running Lamps .... Standard
Safety Belt/Restraint:
  Dynamic Head Restraints .... None
  Adjustable Belt............ Standard Front

^Warning feature does not meet suggested government specifications.

Fiat 500X

Specifications

Drive................................. FWD
Engine 2.4-liter I4
Transmission .... 9-sp. Automatic
Tow Rating (lbs.) .... Very Low-1000
Head/Leg Room (in.) Cramped-39.1/41.4
Interior Space (cu. ft.)........... Cramped-91.7
Cargo Space (cu. ft.) .... Very Cramped-12.2
Wheelbase/Length (in.) 101.2/167.2

Ford EcoSport

Ratings—10 Best, 1 Worst

Combo Crash Tests	—
Safety Features	4
Rollover	2
Preventive Maintenance	7
Repair Costs	7
Warranty	4
Fuel Economy	7
Complaints	8
Insurance Costs	8
OVERALL RATING	**—**

Ford EcoSport

Ford EcoSport

At-a-Glance

Status/Year Series Started. Unchanged/2018
Twins . . . . —
Body Styles . . . . SUV
Seating 5
Anti-Theft Device . . . . . . Std. Pass. Immobil. & Alarm
Parking Index Rating . . . . .Very Easy
Where Made. . . . . Chennai, India
Fuel Factor
  MPG Rating (city/hwy). Good-27/29
  Driving Range (mi.) Short-379
  Fuel Type. . . . . .Regular
  Annual Fuel Cost . . . . Low-$1319
  Gas Guzzler Tax . . . . .No
  Greenhouse Gas Emissions (tons/yr.). Low-5.2
  Barrels of Oil Used per year Average-11.8

How the Competition Rates

Competitors	Rating	Pg.
Chevrolet Trax	10	106
Jeep Compass	4	152
Mazda CX-3	10	179

Price Range

Price Range	Retail	Markup
S	$19,995	4%
SE	$22,905	4%
Titanium	$25,740	4%
SES	$26,740	4%

Safety Checklist

Crash Test:
  Frontal . . . . −
  Side . . . . −
Airbags:
  Torso Std. Fr. & Rear Pelvis/Torso from Seat
  Roll Sensing . . . . Yes
  Knee Bolster . . . . Standard Front
Crash Avoidance:
  Collision Avoidance . . . . .None
  Blind Spot Detection . . . . Optional
  Lane Keeping Assist . . . . .None
  Pedestrian Crash Avoidance. . . . . .None
General:
  Auto. Crash Notification. . . . Dial Assist.-Free
  Day Running Lamps . . . . .Standard
Safety Belt/Restraint:
  Dynamic Head Restraints . . . . .None
  Adjustable Belt. . . . . Standard Front

^Warning feature does not meet suggested government specifications.

Ford EcoSport

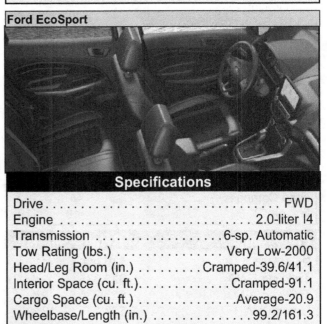

Specifications

Drive. . . . . FWD
Engine 2.0-liter I4
Transmission . . . . .6-sp. Automatic
Tow Rating (lbs.) . . . . Very Low-2000
Head/Leg Room (in.) Cramped-39.6/41.1
Interior Space (cu. ft.). Cramped-91.1
Cargo Space (cu. ft.) Average-20.9
Wheelbase/Length (in.) 99.2/161.3

114

Ratings—10 Best, 1 Worst

Combo Crash Tests	10
Safety Features	8
Rollover	4
Preventive Maintenance	6
Repair Costs	6
Warranty	4
Fuel Economy	4
Complaints	4
Insurance Costs	10
OVERALL RATING	**9**

Ford Edge

Ford Edge

Ford Edge

At-a-Glance

Status/Year Series Started........ Unchanged/2015
Twins .... —
Body Styles .... SUV
Seating 5
Anti-Theft Device ...... Std. Pass. Immobil. & Alarm
Parking Index Rating .... Very Easy
Where Made................... Oakville, Ontario
Fuel Factor
  MPG Rating (city/hwy)............ Poor-20/30
  Driving Range (mi.) Long-431
  Fuel Type........................... Regular
  Annual Fuel Cost .... Average-$1562
  Gas Guzzler Tax .... No
  Greenhouse Gas Emissions (tons/yr.).. Average-7.1
  Barrels of Oil Used per year High-15.7

How the Competition Rates

Competitors	Rating	Pg.
Chevrolet Equinox	4	97
Dodge Journey	1	114
Infiniti QX60	5	149

Price Range

Price Range	Retail	Markup
SE FWD	$29,220	4%
SEL FWD	$31,955	5%
Titanium AWD	$37,925	5%
Sport AWD	$40,675	5%

Safety Checklist

Crash Test:
  Frontal .... Very Good
  Side .... Good
Airbags:
  Torso ...... Std. Fr. Pelvis/Torso from Seat
  Roll Sensing .... Yes
  Knee Bolster .... Standard Front
Crash Avoidance:
  Collision Avoidance .... Optional CIB & DBS
  Blind Spot Detection .... Optional
  Lane Keeping Assist .... Optional
  Pedestrian Crash Avoidance......... None
General:
  Auto. Crash Notification.... Dial Assist.-Free
  Day Running Lamps .... Standard
Safety Belt/Restraint:
  Dynamic Head Restraints .... None
  Adjustable Belt............ Standard Front

^Warning feature does not meet suggested government specifications.

Specifications

Drive................................. FWD
Engine 3.5-liter V6
Transmission .... 6-sp. Automatic
Tow Rating (lbs.) .... Very Low-1500
Head/Leg Room (in.) Roomy-40.2/42.6
Interior Space (cu. ft.)............. Roomy-113.9
Cargo Space (cu. ft.) .... Very Roomy-39.2
Wheelbase/Length (in.) 112.2/188.1

Ratings—10 Best, 1 Worst

Combo Crash Tests	—
Safety Features	5
Rollover	2
Preventive Maintenance	7
Repair Costs	3
Warranty	4
Fuel Economy	5
Complaints	—
Insurance Costs	5
OVERALL RATING	—

Ford Escape

Ford Escape

At-a-Glance

Status/Year Series Started. All-New/2020
Twins . . . . .Lincoln MKC
Body Styles . . . . SUV
Seating 5
Anti-Theft Device . . . . . . Std. Pass. Immobil. & Alarm
Parking Index Rating . . . . Average
Where Made. . . . . Louisville, Kentucky
Fuel Factor
  MPG Rating (city/hwy). Average-23/31
  Driving Range (mi.) Short-390
  Fuel Type. . . . . .Regular
  Annual Fuel Cost . . . . .High-$1612
  Gas Guzzler Tax . . . . .No
  Greenhouse Gas Emissions (tons/yr.). Low-5.7
  Barrels of Oil Used per year Average-12.7

How the Competition Rates

Competitors	Rating	Pg.
Honda HR-V	5	136
Jeep Cherokee	5	151
Toyota RAV4		227

Price Range

Price Range	Retail	Markup
S FWD	$23,850	4%
SE FWD	$26,955	5%
SEL 4WD	$29,335	5%
Titanium 4WD	$33,395	5%

Safety Checklist

Crash Test:
  Frontal . . . . −
  Side . . . . −
Airbags:
  Torso . . . . . . Std. Fr. Pelvis/Torso from Seat
  Roll Sensing . . . . .Yes
  Knee Bolster . . . . Standard Driver
Crash Avoidance:
  Collision Avoidance . . . Standard CIB & DBS
  Blind Spot Detection . . . . .Standard
  Lane Keeping Assist . . . . .Standard
  Pedestrian Crash Avoidance. . . . . .Standard
General:
  Auto. Crash Notification. . . .Dial Assist.-Free
  Day Running Lamps . . . . .Standard
Safety Belt/Restraint:
  Dynamic Head Restraints . . . . .None
  Adjustable Belt. . . . . Standard Front

^Warning feature does not meet suggested government specifications.

Ford Escape

Specifications

Drive. . . . . FWD
Engine 2.0-liter I4
Transmission . . . . .8-sp. Automatic
Tow Rating (lbs.) . . . . Very Low-1500
Head/Leg Room (in.) Roomy-39.9/42.4
Interior Space (cu. ft.). Average-104.0
Cargo Space (cu. ft.) . . . . Very Roomy-37.5
Wheelbase/Length (in.) 106.7/180.5

Ratings—10 Best, 1 Worst

Combo Crash Tests	—
Safety Features	7
Rollover	1
Preventive Maintenance	2
Repair Costs	9
Warranty	4
Fuel Economy	2
Complaints	7
Insurance Costs	10
OVERALL RATING	**—**

Ford Expedition

Ford Expedition

At-a-Glance

Status/Year Series Started. Unchanged/2003
Twins . . . . Lincoln Navigator
Body Styles . . . . SUV
Seating 7/8
Anti-Theft Device . . . . . . Std. Pass. Immobil. & Alarm
Parking Index Rating . . . . Very Hard
Where Made. . . . . Louisville, Kentucky
Fuel Factor
  MPG Rating (city/hwy) . . . . Very Poor-17/22
  Driving Range (mi.) . . . . Very Long-530
  Fuel Type. . . . . .Regular
  Annual Fuel Cost . . . . .High-$1941
  Gas Guzzler Tax . . . . .No
  Greenhouse Gas Emissions (tons/yr.). High-7.7
  Barrels of Oil Used per year . . . . Very High-17.3

How the Competition Rates

Competitors	Rating	Pg.
Buick Enclave	4	82
Chevrolet Suburban	2	103
Toyota 4Runner	2	219

Price Range

Price Range	Retail	Markup
XL RWD	$48,095	5%
XLT RWD	$54,705	5%
Limited 4WD	$65,705	5%
Platinum 4WD	$75,855	5%

Safety Checklist

Crash Test:
  Frontal . . . . –
  Side . . . . –
Airbags:
  Torso . . . . Std. Fr. Torso from Seat
  Roll Sensing . . . . .Yes
  Knee Bolster .None
Crash Avoidance:
  Collision Avoidance . . . .Optional CIB & DBS
  Blind Spot Detection . . . . Optional
  Lane Keeping Assist . . . . Optional
  Pedestrian Crash Avoidance. . . . . . Optional
General:
  Auto. Crash Notification. . . .Dial Assist.-Free
  Day Running Lamps . . . . .Standard
Safety Belt/Restraint:
  Dynamic Head Restraints . . . . .None
  Adjustable Belt. . . . . .Standard Front

^Warning feature does not meet suggested government specifications.

Ford Expedition

Specifications

Drive. 4WD
Engine 3.5-liter V6
Transmission . . . . 10-sp. Automatic
Tow Rating (lbs.) . . . . .Very High-9300
Head/Leg Room (in.) . . . . Very Roomy-42/43.9
Interior Space (cu. ft.). . . . . Very Roomy-171.9
Cargo Space (cu. ft.) Average-20.9
Wheelbase/Length (in.) 122.5/210

Ford Explorer — Medium SUV

Ratings—10 Best, 1 Worst

Combo Crash Tests	—
Safety Features	5
Rollover	3
Preventive Maintenance	5
Repair Costs	6
Warranty	4
Fuel Economy	2
Complaints	—
Insurance Costs	10
OVERALL RATING	**—**

Ford Explorer

Ford Explorer

At-a-Glance

Status/Year Series Started. All-New/2020
Twins . . . . —
Body Styles . . . . SUV
Seating 6/7
Anti-Theft Device . . . . . . Std. Pass. Immobil. & Alarm
Parking Index Rating . . . . Hard
Where Made. . . . . Chicago, IL
Fuel Factor
  MPG Rating (city/hwy). Poor-20/27
  Driving Range (mi.) Long-442
  Fuel Type. . . . . .Regular
  Annual Fuel Cost . . . . .Average-$1623
  Gas Guzzler Tax . . . . .No
  Greenhouse Gas Emissions (tons/yr.). . Average-6.4
  Barrels of Oil Used per year High-14.3

How the Competition Rates

Competitors	Rating	Pg.
Dodge Journey	1	114
Honda Pilot	8	143
Toyota Highlander	8	224

Price Range

	Retail	Markup
Base FWD	$31,660	4%
XLT FWD	$33,775	5%
Limited 4WD	$43,825	5%
Platinum 4WD	$53,235	5%

Safety Checklist

Crash Test:
  Frontal . . . . −
  Side . . . . −
Airbags:
  Torso . . . . . . Std. Fr. Pelvis/Torso from Seat
  Roll Sensing . . . . .Yes
  Knee Bolster . . . . .Std. Passenger
Crash Avoidance:
  Collision Avoidance . . . Standard CIB & DBS
  Blind Spot Detection . . . . .Standard
  Lane Keeping Assist . . . . .Standard
  Pedestrian Crash Avoidance. . . . . .Standard
General:
  Auto. Crash Notification. . . .Dial Assist.-Free
  Day Running Lamps . . . . .Standard
Safety Belt/Restraint:
  Dynamic Head Restraints . . . . .None
  Adjustable Belt. . . . . Standard Front

^Warning feature does not meet suggested government specifications.

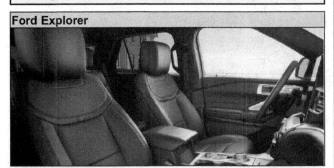
Ford Explorer

Specifications

Drive. . . . . AWD
Engine 3.0-liter V6
Transmission . . . . 10-sp. Automatic
Tow Rating (lbs.) Low-5000
Head/Leg Room (in.) . . . . . . Very Roomy-40.7/43.0
Interior Space (cu. ft.). . . . . Very Roomy-152.7
Cargo Space (cu. ft.) Average-18.2
Wheelbase/Length (in.) 119.1/198.8

Ratings—10 Best, 1 Worst

Combo Crash Tests	10
Safety Features	3
Rollover	2
Preventive Maintenance	8
Repair Costs	8
Warranty	4
Fuel Economy	2
Complaints	10
Insurance Costs	8
OVERALL RATING	**9**

Ford F-150

Ford F-150

At-a-Glance

Status/Year Series Started........ Unchanged/2015
Twins .... —
Body Styles .... Pickup
Seating 5/6
Anti-Theft Device ...... Std. Pass. Immobil. & Alarm
Parking Index Rating .... Very Hard
Where Made...................... Dearborn, MI
Fuel Factor
  MPG Rating (city/hwy)........... Very Poor-17/23
  Driving Range (mi.) .... Very Long-693
  Fuel Type........................... Regular
  Annual Fuel Cost .... High-$1908
  Gas Guzzler Tax .... No
  Greenhouse Gas Emissions (tons/yr.) Very High-9.5
  Barrels of Oil Used per year .... Very High-17.3

How the Competition Rates

Competitors	Rating	Pg.
Chevrolet Silverado		100
Ram 1500		208
Toyota Tundra		231

Price Range

Price Range	Retail	Markup
XL Reg. Cab 2WD	$27,680	5%
XLT Supercab 2WD	$37,185	8%
Lariat Supercrew 4WD	$48,220	8%
Platinum Supercrew 4WD	$57,880	8%

Safety Checklist

Crash Test:
  Frontal .... Very Good
  Side .... Very Good
Airbags:
  Torso ...... Std. Fr. Pelvis/Torso from Seat
  Roll Sensing .... Yes
  Knee Bolster .... None
Crash Avoidance:
  Collision Avoidance ..... Warning Only Opt.
  Blind Spot Detection .... Optional
  Lane Keeping Assist .... Optional
  Pedestrian Crash Avoidance......... None
General:
  Auto. Crash Notification. . . . Dial Assist.-Free
  Day Running Lamps .... Standard
Safety Belt/Restraint:
  Dynamic Head Restraints .... None
  Adjustable Belt............ Standard Front

^Warning feature does not meet suggested government specifications.

Ford F-150

Specifications

Drive................................. 4WD
Engine 3.5-liter V6
Transmission .... 6-sp. Automatic
Tow Rating (lbs.) .... Very High-10700
Head/Leg Room (in.) ...... Very Roomy-40.8/43.9
Interior Space (cu. ft.)........... Roomy-116
Cargo Space (cu. ft.) .... Very Roomy-62.3
Wheelbase/Length (in.) 141.1/231.9

Ratings—10 Best, 1 Worst

Combo Crash Tests	—
Safety Features	2
Rollover	3
Preventive Maintenance	6
Repair Costs	6
Warranty	4
Fuel Economy	2
Complaints	3
Insurance Costs	5
OVERALL RATING	**—**

Ford Flex

At-a-Glance

Status/Year Series Started........ Unchanged/2009
Twins .... —
Body Styles .... SUV
Seating 6/7
Anti-Theft Device ...... Std. Pass. Immobil. & Alarm
Parking Index Rating .... Very Hard
Where Made..................... Oakville, Ontario
Fuel Factor
  MPG Rating (city/hwy)........... Very Poor-16/23
  Driving Range (mi.) .... Very Short-345
  Fuel Type........................... Regular
  Annual Fuel Cost .... Very High-$1982
  Gas Guzzler Tax .... No
  Greenhouse Gas Emissions (tons/yr.)..... High-7.7
  Barrels of Oil Used per year .... Very High-17.3

How the Competition Rates

Competitors	Rating	Pg.
Buick Enclave	4	82
Chevrolet Tahoe	4	104
Volvo XC90	8	240

Price Range

Price Range	Retail	Markup
SE FWD	$30,025	4%
SEL AWD	$34,680	5%
Limited FWD	$38,230	5%
Limited AWD	$40,180	5%

Ford Flex

Safety Checklist

Crash Test:
  Frontal .... —
  Side .... —
Airbags:
  Torso .... Std. Fr. Torso from Seat
  Roll Sensing .... Yes
  Knee Bolster .... None
Crash Avoidance:
  Collision Avoidance ..... Warning Only Opt.
  Blind Spot Detection .... Optional
  Lane Keeping Assist .... None
  Pedestrian Crash Avoidance......... None
General:
  Auto. Crash Notification.... Dial Assist.-Free
  Day Running Lamps .... None
Safety Belt/Restraint:
  Dynamic Head Restraints .... None
  Adjustable Belt............ Standard Front

^W-arning feature does not meet suggested government specifications.

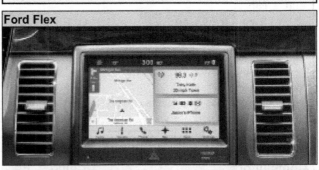
Ford Flex

Specifications

Drive................................... FWD
Engine 3.5-liter V6
Transmission .... 6-sp. Automatic
Tow Rating (lbs.) Low-4500
Head/Leg Room (in.) Roomy-41.8/40.8
Interior Space (cu. ft.)........ Very Roomy-155.8
Cargo Space (cu. ft.) Average-20
Wheelbase/Length (in.) 117.9/201.8

Ford Fusion Intermediate

Ratings—10 Best, 1 Worst

Combo Crash Tests	3
Safety Features	8
Rollover	7
Preventive Maintenance	8
Repair Costs	9
Warranty	4
Fuel Economy	5
Complaints	4
Insurance Costs	1
OVERALL RATING	**4**

Ford Fusion

At-a-Glance

Status/Year Series Started	Unchanged/2013
Twins	Lincoln MKZ
Body Styles	Sedan
Seating	5
Anti-Theft Device	Std. Pass. Immobil. & Alarm
Parking Index Rating	Average
Where Made	Hermosillo, Mexico
Fuel Factor	
MPG Rating (city/hwy)	Average-21/32
Driving Range (mi.)	Average-410
Fuel Type	Regular
Annual Fuel Cost	Average-$1479
Gas Guzzler Tax	No
Greenhouse Gas Emissions (tons/yr.)	Average-6.9
Barrels of Oil Used per year	Average-12.7

How the Competition Rates

Competitors	Rating	Pg.
Chevrolet Malibu	9	99
Infiniti Q50	3	147
Toyota Camry	8	221

Price Range	Retail	Markup
S	$22,120	5%
SE AWD	$27,045	6%
Sport	$33,605	6%
Platinum	$36,750	6%

Ford Fusion

Safety Checklist

Crash Test:
  Frontal . . . . Very Poor
  Side . . . . Average
Airbags:
  Torso . . . . . . Std. Fr. Pelvis/Torso from Seat
  Roll Sensing . . . . Yes
  Knee Bolster . . . . Standard Front
Crash Avoidance:
  Collision Avoidance . . . . Optional CIB & DBS
  Blind Spot Detection . . . . Optional
  Lane Keeping Assist . . . . Optional
  Pedestrian Crash Avoidance . . . . None
General:
  Auto. Crash Notification . . . . Dial Assist.-Free
  Day Running Lamps . . . . Standard
Safety Belt/Restraint:
  Dynamic Head Restraints . . . . None
  Adjustable Belt . . . . Standard Front

^W-arning feature does not meet suggested government specifications.

Ford Fusion

Specifications

Drive	FWD
Engine	2.5-liter I4
Transmission	6-sp. Automatic
Tow Rating (lbs.)	–
Head/Leg Room (in.)	Roomy-39.2/44.3
Interior Space (cu. ft.)	Roomy-118.8
Cargo Space (cu. ft.)	Cramped-16
Wheelbase/Length (in.)	112.2/191.8

Ford Fusion Energi — Intermediate

Ratings—10 Best, 1 Worst

Combo Crash Tests	7
Safety Features	8
Rollover	7
Preventive Maintenance	6
Repair Costs	10
Warranty	4
Fuel Economy	9
Complaints	1
Insurance Costs	5
OVERALL RATING	**8**

Ford Fusion Energi

At-a-Glance

Status/Year Series Started........ Unchanged/2016
Twins .... —
Body Styles .... Sedan
Seating 5
Anti-Theft Device ...... Std. Pass. Immobil. & Alarm
Parking Index Rating .... Average
Where Made.................. Hermosillo, Mexico
Fuel Factor
  MPG Rating (city/hwy).......... Very Good-40/36
  Driving Range (mi.) .... Very Long-533
  Fuel Type............................. Regular
  Annual Fuel Cost .... Very Low-$965
  Gas Guzzler Tax .... No
  Greenhouse Gas Emissions (tons/yr.). Very Low-2.1
  Barrels of Oil Used per year .... Very Low-4.9

How the Competition Rates

Competitors	Rating	Pg.
Hyundai Sonata	9	144
Nissan Altima		196
Subaru Legacy	7	219

Price Range

Price Range	Retail	Markup
SE Luxury Energi	$33,120	6%
Titanium Energi	$34,120	6%
Platinum Energi	$41,120	6%

Ford Fusion Energi

Safety Checklist

Crash Test:
  Frontal .... Very Good
  Side .... Very Poor
Airbags:
  Torso ...... Std. Fr. Pelvis/Torso from Seat
  Roll Sensing .... Yes
  Knee Bolster .... Standard Front
Crash Avoidance:
  Collision Avoidance .... Optional CIB & DBS
  Blind Spot Detection .... Optional
  Lane Keeping Assist .... Optional
  Pedestrian Crash Avoidance......... None
General:
  Auto. Crash Notification.... Dial Assist.-Free
  Day Running Lamps .... Standard
Safety Belt/Restraint:
  Dynamic Head Restraints .... None
  Adjustable Belt............ Standard Front

^W-arning feature does not meet suggested government specifications.

Ford Fusion Energi

Specifications

Drive.................................... FWD
Engine 2.0-liter I4
Transmission .... CVT
Tow Rating (lbs.) .... –
Head/Leg Room (in.) Roomy-39.2/44.3
Interior Space (cu. ft.)........... Average-102.8
Cargo Space (cu. ft.) .... Very Cramped-8.2
Wheelbase/Length (in.) 112.2/191.8

Ratings—10 Best, 1 Worst

Combo Crash Tests	8
Safety Features	2
Rollover	10
Preventive Maintenance	8
Repair Costs	6
Warranty	4
Fuel Economy	3
Complaints	6
Insurance Costs	3
OVERALL RATING	**6**

Ford Mustang

At-a-Glance

Status/Year Series Started. Unchanged/2015
Twins . . . . —
Body Styles . . . . Coupe, Convertible
Seating 4
Anti-Theft Device . . . . . . Std. Pass. Immobil. & Alarm
Parking Index Rating . . . . Easy
Where Made. Flat Rock, MI
Fuel Factor
  MPG Rating (city/hwy). Poor-19/28
  Driving Range (mi.) . . . . Very Short-355
  Fuel Type. . . . . .Regular
  Annual Fuel Cost . . . . .Average-$1654
  Gas Guzzler Tax . . . . .No
  Greenhouse Gas Emissions (tons/yr.). High-8.1
  Barrels of Oil Used per year High-15.0

How the Competition Rates

Competitors	Rating	Pg.
Chevrolet Camaro	4	94
Chevrolet Corvette		96
Dodge Challenger	4	111

Price Range

	Retail	Markup
Base Coupe	$24,645	4%
Eco Premium Coupe	$29,645	6%
GT Premium Convertible	$42,145	6%
Shelby GT350	$54,295	6%

Ford Mustang

Safety Checklist

Crash Test:
  Frontal . . . . Very Good
  Side . . . . Poor
Airbags:
  Torso . . . . . . Std. Fr. Pelvis/Torso from Seat
  Roll Sensing . . . . .No
  Knee Bolster . . . . Standard Front
Crash Avoidance:
  Collision Avoidance . . . . . Warning Only Opt.
  Blind Spot Detection . . . . Optional
  Lane Keeping Assist . . . . .None
  Pedestrian Crash Avoidance. . . . . .None
General:
  Auto. Crash Notification. . . .Dial Assist.-Free
  Day Running Lamps . . . . .None
Safety Belt/Restraint:
  Dynamic Head Restraints . . . . .None
  Adjustable Belt. . . . . .None

^W-arning feature does not meet suggested government specifications.

Ford Mustang

Specifications

Drive. . . . . RWD
Engine 3.7-liter V6
Transmission . . . . .6-sp. Automatic
Tow Rating (lbs.) . . . . —
Head/Leg Room (in.) Average-37.6/44.5
Interior Space (cu. ft.). . . . . . . .Very Cramped-84.5
Cargo Space (cu. ft.) . . . . .Very Cramped-13.5
Wheelbase/Length (in.) 107.1/188.5

Ratings—10 Best, 1 Worst

Combo Crash Tests	—
Safety Features	9
Rollover	2
Preventive Maintenance	2
Repair Costs	6
Warranty	4
Fuel Economy	4
Complaints	4
Insurance Costs	5
OVERALL RATING	**—**

Ford Ranger

Ford Ranger

At-a-Glance

Status/Year Series Started........ Unchanged/2019
Twins . . . . —
Body Styles . . . . Pickup
Seating 4/5
Anti-Theft Device . . . . . . Std. Pass. Immobil. & Alarm
Parking Index Rating . . . . Very Hard
Where Made. . . . . Wayne, Michigan
Fuel Factor
  MPG Rating (city/hwy). Poor-21/26
  Driving Range (mi.) Long-432
  Fuel Type. . . . . .Regular
  Annual Fuel Cost . . . . .Average-$1553
  Gas Guzzler Tax . . . . .No
  Greenhouse Gas Emissions (tons/yr.). . Average-6.4
  Barrels of Oil Used per year High-14.3

How the Competition Rates

Competitors	Rating	Pg.
Chevrolet Colorado	2	95
Nissan Frontier	1	198
Toyota Tacoma	1	230

Price Range	Retail	Markup
XL 2WD	$25,495	6%
XLT 2WD	$27,940	6%
XLT 4WD	$31,940	6%
Lariat 4WD	$36,210	6%

Safety Checklist

Crash Test:
  Frontal . . . . —
  Side . . . . —
Airbags:
  Torso . . . . . . Std. Fr. Pelvis/Torso from Seat
  Roll Sensing . . . . .Yes
  Knee Bolster . . . . .Standard Front
Crash Avoidance:
  Collision Avoidance . . . Standard CIB & DBS
  Blind Spot Detection . . . . Optional
  Lane Keeping Assist . . . . Optional
  Pedestrian Crash Avoidance. . . . . .Standard
General:
  Auto. Crash Notification. . . .Dial Assist.-Free
  Day Running Lamps . . . . .Standard
Safety Belt/Restraint:
  Dynamic Head Restraints . . . . .None
  Adjustable Belt. . . . . .Standard Front

^Warning feature does not meet suggested government specifications.

Ford Ranger

Specifications

Drive. . . . . RWD
Engine 2.3-liter I4
Transmission . . . . 10-sp. Automatic
Tow Rating (lbs.) High-7500
Head/Leg Room (in.) Average-39.8/43.1
Interior Space (cu. ft.). . . . . .Very Cramped-89.2
Cargo Space (cu. ft.) . . . . Very Roomy-43.3
Wheelbase/Length (in.) 126.8/210.8

Genesis G80

Ratings—10 Best, 1 Worst

Combo Crash Tests	—
Safety Features	10
Rollover	7
Preventive Maintenance	3
Repair Costs	4
Warranty	10
Fuel Economy	3
Complaints	10
Insurance Costs	—
OVERALL RATING	**—**

Genesis G80

Genesis G80

At-a-Glance

Status/Year Series Started........ Unchanged/2017
Twins .... -
Body Styles ....Sedan
Seating 5
Anti-Theft Device . Std. Pass. Immobil. & Active Alarm
Parking Index Rating .... Average
Where Made................. Ulsan, South Korea
Fuel Factor
  MPG Rating (city/hwy)................ Poor-19/27
  Driving Range (mi.) Long-445
  Fuel Type........................Regular
  Annual Fuel Cost ....High-$1676
  Gas Guzzler Tax ....No
  Greenhouse Gas Emissions (tons/yr.).. Average-6.8
  Barrels of Oil Used per year High-15.0

How the Competition Rates

Competitors	Rating	Pg.
Acura TLX	9	64
Lexus ES		167
Lincoln MKZ	4	176

Price Range

	Retail	Markup
3.8L V6	$42,050	6%
3.8L V6 AWD	$44,550	6%
3.3L Turbo V6 Sport	$55,250	7%
5.0L V8 AWD	$59,500	7%

Safety Checklist

Crash Test:
  Frontal............................ −
  Side.............................. −
Airbags:
  Torso . Std. Fr. & Opt. Rr. Pelvis/Torso from Seat
  Roll Sensing ....Yes
  Knee Bolster .... Standard Driver
Crash Avoidance:
  Collision Avoidance... Standard CIB & DBS
  Blind Spot Detection ....Standard
  Lane Keeping Assist ....Standard
  Pedestrian Crash Avoidance ....None
General:
  Auto. Crash Notification ....Op. Assist.-Fee
  Day Running Lamps ....Standard
Safety Belt/Restraint:
  Dynamic Head Restraints ....None
  Adjustable Belt ....Standard Front

^Warning feature does not meet suggested government specifications.

Genesis G80

Specifications

Drive...................................RWD
Engine 3.8-liter V6
Transmission ....8-sp. Automatic
Tow Rating (lbs.) .... −
Head/Leg Room (in.) ...... Very Roomy-41.1/45.7
Interior Space (cu. ft.)............ Roomy-107.7
Cargo Space (cu. ft.) Cramped-15.3
Wheelbase/Length (in.) 118.5/196.5

125

GMC Acadia | Medium SUV

Ratings—10 Best, 1 Worst

Combo Crash Tests	3
Safety Features	7
Rollover	4
Preventive Maintenance	2
Repair Costs	3
Warranty	5
Fuel Economy	3
Complaints	2
Insurance Costs	10
OVERALL RATING	**2**

GMC Acadia

GMC Acadia

At-a-Glance

Status/Year Series Started Unchanged/2017
Twins . . . . .Cadillac XT5
Body Styles . . . . SUV
Seating 5/6/7
Anti-Theft Device . Std. Pass. Immobil. & Active Alarm
Parking Index Rating . . . . Hard
Where Made . . . . .Lansing, MI
Fuel Factor
  MPG Rating (city/hwy) Poor-18/25
  Driving Range (mi.) Short-391
  Fuel Type . . . . .Regular
  Annual Fuel Cost . . . . .High-$1784
  Gas Guzzler Tax . . . . .No
  Greenhouse Gas Emissions (tons/yr.) . . Average-7.0
  Barrels of Oil Used per year High-15.7

How the Competition Rates

Competitors	Rating	Pg.
Lincoln Nautilis	5	181
Mitsubishi Outlander	4	194
Nissan Rogue	3	203

Price Range

	Retail	Markup
SLE1 FWD	$32,800	5%
SLT1 FWD	$38,000	5%
SLT2 AWD	$43,900	5%
Denali AWD	$47,500	5%

Safety Checklist

Crash Test:
  Frontal . . . . .Poor
  Side . . . . .Very Poor
Airbags:
  Torso . . . . . . Std. Fr. Pelvis/Torso from Seat
  Roll Sensing . . . . .Yes
  Knee Bolster . . . . Standard Driver
Crash Avoidance:
  Collision Avoidance. . . .Optional CIB & DBS
  Blind Spot Detection . . . . Optional
  Lane Keeping Assist . . . . Optional
  Pedestrian Crash Avoidance . . . . . Optional
General:
  Auto. Crash Notif.. . . Op. Assist. & Crash Info-Fee
  Day Running Lamps . . . . .Standard
Safety Belt/Restraint:
  Dynamic Head Restraints . . . . .None
  Adjustable Belt . . . . .Optional Rear

^Warning feature does not meet suggested government specifications.

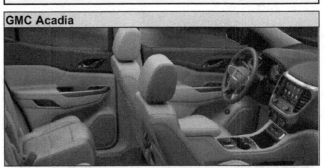

GMC Acadia

Specifications

Drive . . . . FWD
Engine 3.6-liter V6
Transmission . . . . .6-sp. Automatic
Tow Rating (lbs.) Low-4000
Head/Leg Room (in.) Average-40.3/41
Interior Space (cu. ft.) . . . . Very Roomy-143.8
Cargo Space (cu. ft.) . . . . .Very Cramped-12.8
Wheelbase/Length (in.) 112.5/193.6

Ratings—10 Best, 1 Worst

Combo Crash Tests	—
Safety Features	3
Rollover	2
Preventive Maintenance	2
Repair Costs	1
Warranty	8
Fuel Economy	5
Complaints	4
Insurance Costs	3
OVERALL RATING	**—**

GMC Canyon

GMC Canyon

At-a-Glance

Status/Year Series Started Unchanged/2015
Twins . . . . Chevrolet Colorado
Body Styles . . . . Pickup
Seating 5
Anti-Theft Device . Std. Pass. Immobil. & Active Alarm
Parking Index Rating . . . . Very Hard
Where Made. Wentzville, MO
Fuel Factor
  MPG Rating (city/hwy) Poor-20/27
  Driving Range (mi.) . . . . Very Long-475
  Fuel Type . . . . Regular
  Annual Fuel Cost . . . . Average-$1623
  Gas Guzzler Tax . . . . No
  Greenhouse Gas Emissions (tons/yr.) High-8.2
  Barrels of Oil Used per year High-15.0

How the Competition Rates

Competitors	Rating	Pg.
Chevrolet Colorado	2	95
Nissan Frontier	1	198
Toyota Tacoma	1	230

Price Range

Price Range	Retail	Markup
SL Ext. Cab 2WD	$21,400	3%
SLE Crew Cab 2WD	$35,900	4%
SLT Crew Cab 4WD	$36,400	4%
Denali Crew Cab 4WD	$44,100	5%

Safety Checklist

Crash Test:
  Frontal . . . . Poor
  Side . . . . Poor
Airbags:
  Torso . . . . . . Std. Fr. Pelvis/Torso from Seat
  Roll Sensing . . . . Yes
  Knee Bolster . . . . None
Crash Avoidance:
  Collision Avoidance. . . . . Warning Only Opt.
  Blind Spot Detection . . . . None
  Lane Keeping Assist . . . . Warning Only Opt.
  Pedestrian Crash Avoidance . . . . None
General:
  Auto. Crash Notif. . . . Op. Assist. & Crash Info-Fee
  Day Running Lamps . . . . Standard
Safety Belt/Restraint:
  Dynamic Head Restraints . . . . None
  Adjustable Belt . . . . . Optional Front & Rear

^Warning feature does not meet suggested government specifications.

GMC Canyon

Specifications

Drive . . . . RWD
Engine 2.5-liter I4
Transmission . . . . 6-sp. Automatic
Tow Rating (lbs.) Low-3500
Head/Leg Room (in.) . . . . Very Roomy-41.4/45
Interior Space (cu. ft.). . . . . —
Cargo Space (cu. ft.) . . . . Very Roomy-49.9
Wheelbase/Length (in.) 128.3/212.7

GMC Sierra
Standard Pickup

Ratings—10 Best, 1 Worst

Combo Crash Tests	—
Safety Features	3
Rollover	3
Preventive Maintenance	1
Repair Costs	5
Warranty	5
Fuel Economy	2
Complaints	3
Insurance Costs	10
OVERALL RATING	**—**

GMC Sierra

GMC Sierra

At-a-Glance

Status/Year Series Started. Unchanged/2019
Twins . . . . Chevrolet Silverado
Body Styles . . . . Pickup
Seating. 5/6
Anti-Theft Device . Std. Pass. Immobil. & Active Alarm
Parking Index Rating . . . . Very Hard
Where Made. . . . . Fort Wayne, IN
Fuel Factor
  MPG Rating (city/hwy). . . . . Very Poor-16/22
  Driving Range (mi.) Long-432
  Fuel Type. . . . . Regular
  Annual Fuel Cost . . . . Very High-$2015
  Gas Guzzler Tax . . . . No
  Greenhouse Gas Emissions (tons/yr.). High-8.1
  Barrels of Oil Used per year . . . . Very High-18.3

How the Competition Rates

Competitors	Rating	Pg.
Chevrolet Silverado		100
Ford F-150	9	119
Toyota Tundra		231

Price Range

Price Range	Retail	Markup
Base Reg. Cab 2WD	$29,600	5%
SLE Dbl. Cab 2WD	$37,800	7%
SLT Dbl. Cab 4WD	$47,600	7%
Denali Crew Cab 4WD	$58,300	7%

Safety Checklist

Crash Test:
  Frontal . . . . —
  Side. . . . . —
Airbags:
  Torso. . . . . . Std. Fr. Pelvis/Torso from Seat
  Roll Sensing . . . . Yes
  Knee Bolster . . . . None
Crash Avoidance:
  Collision Avoidance. . . . . Optional CIB
  Blind Spot Detection . . . . None
  Lane Keeping Assist . . . . Optional
  Pedestrian Crash Avoidance . . . . None
General:
  Auto. Crash Notif.. . . Op. Assist. & Crash Info-Fee
  Day Running Lamps . . . . Standard
Safety Belt/Restraint:
  Dynamic Head Restraints . . . . None
  Adjustable Belt . . . . . Optional Front & Rear

^Warning feature does not meet suggested government specifications.

GMC Sierra

Specifications

Drive. 4WD
Engine 5.3-liter V8
Transmission . . . . .8-sp. Automatic
Tow Rating (lbs.) . . . . Very High-9900
Head/Leg Room (in.) . . . . .Very Roomy-43/44.5
Interior Space (cu. ft.). . . . . —
Cargo Space (cu. ft.) . . . . Very Roomy-71.7
Wheelbase/Length (in.) 147.4/231.8

Ratings—10 Best, 1 Worst

Combo Crash Tests	6
Safety Features	4
Rollover	4
Preventive Maintenance	1
Repair Costs	3
Warranty	5
Fuel Economy	7
Complaints	8
Insurance Costs	10
OVERALL RATING	**5**

GMC Terrrain

At-a-Glance

Status/Year Series Started	Unchanged/2010
Twins	Chevrolet Equinox
Body Styles	SUV
Seating	5
Anti-Theft Device	Std. Pass. Immobil. & Active Alarm
Parking Index Rating	Average
Where Made	Ingersoll, Ontario
Fuel Factor	
MPG Rating (city/hwy)	Good-26/30
Driving Range (mi.)	Average-412
Fuel Type	Regular
Annual Fuel Cost	Low-$1329
Gas Guzzler Tax	No
Greenhouse Gas Emissions (tons/yr.)	Low-5.2
Barrels of Oil Used per year	Average-11.8

How the Competition Rates

Competitors	Rating	Pg.
Ford Escape	5	116
Honda CR-V	10	134
Hyundai Tucson	8	145

Price Range

Price Range	Retail	Markup
SL FWD	$24,995	1%
SLE FWD	$27,820	5%
SLT AWD	$33,070	5%
Denali AWD	$39,270	5%

GMC Terrrain

Safety Checklist

Crash Test:
  Frontal . . . . Very Good
  Side . . . . Very Poor
Airbags:
  Torso . . . . . . Std. Fr. Pelvis/Torso from Seat
  Roll Sensing . . . . Yes
  Knee Bolster . . . . None
Crash Avoidance:
  Collision Avoidance . . . . Optional CIB
  Blind Spot Detection . . . . Optional
  Lane Keeping Assist . . . . Optional
  Pedestrian Crash Avoidance . . . . None
General:
  Auto. Crash Notif. . . . Op. Assist. & Crash Info-Fee
  Day Running Lamps . . . . Standard
Safety Belt/Restraint:
  Dynamic Head Restraints . . . . None
  Adjustable Belt . . . . Std. Rear

^Warning feature does not meet suggested government specifications.

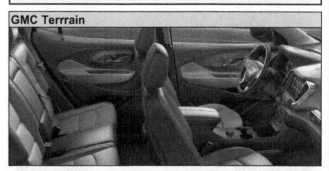

GMC Terrrain

Specifications

Drive	FWD
Engine	1.5-liter I4
Transmission	6-sp. Automatic
Tow Rating (lbs.)	Very Low-1500
Head/Leg Room (in.)	Cramped-40/40.9
Interior Space (cu. ft.)	Average-103.2
Cargo Space (cu. ft.)	Roomy-29.6
Wheelbase/Length (in.)	107.3/182.3

GMC Yukon

Ratings—10 Best, 1 Worst

Combo Crash Tests	—
Safety Features	6
Rollover	4
Preventive Maintenance	2
Repair Costs	5
Warranty	6
Fuel Economy	5
Complaints	1
Insurance Costs	6
OVERALL RATING	**5**

GMC Yukon

GMC Yukon

At-a-Glance

Status/Year Series Started	Unchanged/2015
Twins	Chevrolet Tahoe, GMC Yukon
Body Styles	SUV
Seating	6/9
Anti-Theft Device	Std. Pass. Immobil. & Active Alarm
Parking Index Rating	Very Hard
Where Made	Arlington, TX

Fuel Factor
MPG Rating (city/hwy)	Very Poor-16/22
Driving Range (mi.)	Very Long-474
Fuel Type	Regular
Annual Fuel Cost	Very High-$2015
Gas Guzzler Tax	No
Greenhouse Gas Emissions (tons/yr.)	High-8.2
Barrels of Oil Used per year	Very High-18.3

How the Competition Rates

Competitors	Rating	Pg.
Chevrolet Tahoe	4	104
Lincoln Navigator		178
Volvo XC90	8	240

Price Range

Price Range	Retail	Markup
SLE RWD	$49,500	6%
Standard Edition RWD	$54,700	6%
SLT AWD	$60,500	6%
Denali AWD	$66,600	7%

Safety Checklist

Crash Test:
- Frontal...Good
- Side...Very Good

Airbags:
- Torso...Std. Fr. Pelvis/Torso from Seat
- Roll Sensing...Yes
- Knee Bolster...None

Crash Avoidance:
- Collision Avoidance...Optional CIB
- Blind Spot Detection...Optional
- Lane Keeping Assist...Optional
- Pedestrian Crash Avoidance...None

General:
- Auto. Crash Notif....Op. Assist. & Crash Info-Fee
- Day Running Lamps...Standard

Safety Belt/Restraint:
- Dynamic Head Restraints...None
- Adjustable Belt...Optional Front & Rear

^Warning feature does not meet suggested government specifications.

Specifications

Drive	4WD
Engine	5.3-liter V8
Transmission	6-sp. Automatic
Tow Rating (lbs.)	Very High-8400
Head/Leg Room (in.)	Very Roomy-42.8/45.3
Interior Space (cu. ft.)	Roomy-120.8
Cargo Space (cu. ft.)	Cramped-15.3
Wheelbase/Length (in.)	116/204

Ratings—10 Best, 1 Worst

Combo Crash Tests	—
Safety Features	6
Rollover	4
Preventive Maintenance	2
Repair Costs	5
Warranty	6
Fuel Economy	5
Complaints	1
Insurance Costs	6
OVERALL RATING	**4**

GMC Yukon XL

At-a-Glance

Status/Year Series Started Unchanged/2015
Twins . . Cadillac Escalade ESV, Chevrolet Saburban
Body Styles . . . . SUV
Seating 6/9
Anti-Theft Device . Std. Pass. Immobil. & Active Alarm
Parking Index Rating . . . . Very Hard
Where Made. . . . . Arlington, TX
Fuel Factor
  MPG Rating (city/hwy) . . . . .Very Poor-15/22
  Driving Range (mi.) . . . . Very Long-543
  Fuel Type. . . . . .Regular
  Annual Fuel Cost . . . . Very High-$2099
  Gas Guzzler Tax . . . . .No
  Greenhouse Gas Emissions (tons/yr.)Very High-10.0
  Barrels of Oil Used per year . . . . . . .Very High-18.3

How the Competition Rates

Competitors	Rating	Pg.
Land Rover Range Rover		164
LinIcoln Navigator		178
Volvo XC90	8	240

Price Range	Retail	Markup
SLE RWD	$51,500	6%
Standard Edition RWD	$56,700	6%
SLT AWD	$62,500	6%
Denali AWD	$68,600	7%

GMC Yukon XL

Safety Checklist

Crash Test:
  Frontal . . . . Average
  Side . . . . Average
Airbags:
  Torso . . . . . . Std. Fr. Pelvis/Torso from Seat
  Roll Sensing . . . . .Yes
  Knee Bolster .None
Crash Avoidance:
  Collision Avoidance. . . . . .Optional CIB
  Blind Spot Detection . . . . Optional
  Lane Keeping Assist . . . . Optional
  Pedestrian Crash Avoidance . . . . .None
General:
  Auto. Crash Notif. . . . Op. Assist. & Crash Info-Fee
  Day Running Lamps . . . . .Standard
Safety Belt/Restraint:
  Dynamic Head Restraints . . . . .None
  Adjustable Belt . . . . . Optional Front & Rear

^Warning feature does not meet suggested government specifications.

Specifications

Drive 4WD
Engine 5.3-liter V8
Transmission . . . . .6-sp. Automatic
Tow Rating (lbs.) High-8000
Head/Leg Room (in.) . . . . . . Very Roomy-42.8/45.3
Interior Space (cu. ft.). Roomy-120.8
Cargo Space (cu. ft.) . . . . Very Roomy-39.3
Wheelbase/Length (in.) 130/224.4

Ratings—10 Best, 1 Worst

Combo Crash Tests	—
Safety Features	9
Rollover	7
Preventive Maintenance	10
Repair Costs	6
Warranty	2
Fuel Economy	6
Complaints	3
Insurance Costs	8
OVERALL RATING	**—**

Honda Accord

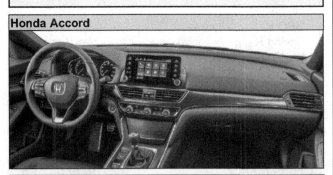

Honda Accord

At-a-Glance

Status/Year Series Started	Unchanged/2018
Twins	-
Body Styles	Sedan
Seating	5
Anti-Theft Device	Std. Pass. Immobil. & Alarm
Parking Index Rating	Hard
Where Made	Marysville, OH

Fuel Factor
MPG Rating (city/hwy)	Average-23/34
Driving Range (mi.)	Short-398
Fuel Type	Regular
Annual Fuel Cost	Low-$1365
Gas Guzzler Tax	No
Greenhouse Gas Emissions (tons/yr.)	Low-5.5
Barrels of Oil Used per year	Average-12.2

How the Competition Rates

Competitors	Rating	Pg.
Nissan Alimta		196
Subaru Legacy	7	213
Volvo S60		237

Price Range

	Retail	Markup
LX Sedan MT	$22,335	9%
EX Sedan AT	$26,530	9%
EX-L Coupe V6 AT	$31,175	9%
Touring Sedan V6 AT	$34,830	9%

Honda Accord

Safety Checklist

Crash Test:
Frontal . . . . –
Side . . . . –
Airbags:
Torso . . . . . . Std. Fr. Pelvis/Torso from Seat
Roll Sensing . . . . Yes
Knee Bolster . . . . Standard Front
Crash Avoidance:
Collision Avoidance. . . Optional CIB & DBS*
Blind Spot Detection . . . . Optional
Lane Keeping Assist . . . . Optional
Pedestrian Crash Avoidance . . . . . Standard
General:
Auto. Crash Notification . . . Dial Assist.-Free
Day Running Lamps . . . . Standard
Safety Belt/Restraint:
Dynamic Head Restraints . . . . None
Adjustable Belt . . . . Standard Front

Specifications

Drive	FWD
Engine	2.0-liter I4
Transmission	CVT
Tow Rating (lbs.)	–
Head/Leg Room (in.)	Average-39.5/42.3
Interior Space (cu. ft.)	Roomy-105.6
Cargo Space (cu. ft.)	Cramped-16.7
Wheelbase/Length (in.)	111.4/192.2

Honda Civic   Compact

Ratings—10 Best, 1 Worst

Combo Crash Tests	5
Safety Features	6
Rollover	9
Preventive Maintenance	10
Repair Costs	8
Warranty	2
Fuel Economy	9
Complaints	8
Insurance Costs	10
OVERALL RATING	**10**

Honda Civic

Honda Civic

At-a-Glance

Status/Year Series Started Unchanged/2016
Twins . . . . -
Body Styles . . . . .Coupe
Seating 5
Anti-Theft Device . . . . . . Std. Pass. Immobil. & Alarm
Parking Index Rating . . . . Easy
Where Made . . . . . . Greensburg, IN / Alliston, Ontario
Fuel Factor
  MPG Rating (city/hwy) . . . . Very Good-31/41
  Driving Range (mi.) Long-432
  Fuel Type . . . . .Regular
  Annual Fuel Cost . . . . Very Low-$1055
  Gas Guzzler Tax . . . . .No
  Greenhouse Gas Emissions (tons/yr.). Very Low-4.2
  Barrels of Oil Used per year Low-9.4

How the Competition Rates

Competitors	Rating	Pg.
Ford Fusion	4	121
Nissan Altima		196
Toyota Camry	8	221

Price Range

Price Range	Retail	Markup
LX Coupe MT	$19,150	8%
EX Sedan AT	$21,140	8%
EX-L Sedan w/Sensing	$24,800	8%
Touring Sedan	$26,600	8%

Safety Checklist

Crash Test:
  Frontal . . . . Average
  Side . . . . Poor
Airbags:
  Torso . . . . . . Std. Fr. Pelvis/Torso from Seat
  Roll Sensing . . . . .Yes
  Knee Bolster .None
Crash Avoidance:
  Collision Avoidance. . . .Optional CIB & DBS
  Blind Spot Detection . . . . .None
  Lane Keeping Assist . . . . Optional
  Pedestrian Crash Avoidance . . . . . Optional
General:
  Auto. Crash Notification . . .Dial Assist.-Free
  Day Running Lamps . . . . .Standard
Safety Belt/Restraint:
  Dynamic Head Restraints . . . . .None
  Adjustable Belt . . . . Standard Front

Honda Civic

Specifications

Drive . . . . FWD
Engine 1.8-liter I4
Transmission . . . . .CVT
Tow Rating (lbs.) . . . . –
Head/Leg Room (in.) Average-39.3/42.3
Interior Space (cu. ft.) Cramped-94.8
Cargo Space (cu. ft.) Cramped-15.1
Wheelbase/Length (in.) 106.3/179.4

Ratings—10 Best, 1 Worst

Combo Crash Tests	9
Safety Features	7
Rollover	4
Preventive Maintenance	10
Repair Costs	8
Warranty	2
Fuel Economy	7
Complaints	7
Insurance Costs	10
OVERALL RATING	**10**

Honda CR-V

Honda CR-V

At-a-Glance

Status/Year Series Started . . Apperance Change/2017
Twins . . . . -
Body Styles . . . . SUV
Seating 5
Anti-Theft Device . . . . . . Std. Pass. Immobil. & Alarm
Parking Index Rating . . . . Easy
Where Made. . . . . .East Liberty, OH
Fuel Factor
  MPG Rating (city/hwy) Good-26/32
  Driving Range (mi.) Short-398
  Fuel Type. . . . . .Regular
  Annual Fuel Cost . . . . Low-$1294
  Gas Guzzler Tax . . . . .No
  Greenhouse Gas Emissions (tons/yr.). Low-5.2
  Barrels of Oil Used per year Average-11.8

How the Competition Rates

Competitors	Rating	Pg.
Nissan Sentra	5	204
Toyota Corolla	7	222
Volkswagen Jetta		234

Price Range	Retail	Markup
LX 2WD	$24,045	6%
EX 2WD	$26,695	7%
EX-L AWD	$30,495	7%
Touring AWD	$33,695	7%

Safety Checklist

Crash Test:
  Frontal. . . . . Very Good
  Side. . . . . .Good
Airbags:
  Torso. . . . . . . Std. Fr. Pelvis/Torso from Seat
  Roll Sensing . . . . .Yes
  Knee Bolster . . . . .None
Crash Avoidance:
  Collision Avoidance. . . . .Optional CIB & DBS
  Blind Spot Detection . . . . Optional
  Lane Keeping Assist . . . . Optional
  Pedestrian Crash Avoidance . . . . . Optional
General:
  Auto. Crash Notification . . .Dial Assist.-Free
  Day Running Lamps . . . . .Standard
Safety Belt/Restraint:
  Dynamic Head Restraints . . . . .None
  Adjustable Belt . . . . Standard Front

^Warning feature does not meet suggested government specifications.

Honda CR-V

Specifications

Drive. . . . . .FWD
Engine 2.4-liter I4
Transmission . . . . .CVT
Tow Rating (lbs.) . . . . Very Low-1500
Head/Leg Room (in.) . . . . . . Very Cramped-38/41.3
Interior Space (cu. ft.). Average-102.9
Cargo Space (cu. ft.) . . . . Very Roomy-39.2
Wheelbase/Length (in.) 104.7/180.6

Ratings—10 Best, 1 Worst

Combo Crash Tests	9
Safety Features	2
Rollover	4
Preventive Maintenance	10
Repair Costs	9
Warranty	2
Fuel Economy	9
Complaints	8
Insurance Costs	5
OVERALL RATING	**9**

Honda Fit

Honda Fit

At-a-Glance

Status/Year Series Started Unchanged2015
Twins . . . . -
Body Styles . . . . Sedan, Hatchback
Seating 5
Anti-Theft Device . . . . . . Std. Pass. Immobil. & Alarm
Parking Index Rating . . . . .Very Easy
Where Made .Celaya, Mexico
Fuel Factor
  MPG Rating (city/hwy) . . . . Very Good-31/36
  Driving Range (mi.) . . . . .Very Short-350
  Fuel Type . . . . .Regular
  Annual Fuel Cost . . . . .Very Low-$1151
  Gas Guzzler Tax . . . . .No
  Greenhouse Gas Emissions (tons/yr.). Very Low-4.4
  Barrels of Oil Used per year . . . . Very Low-9.1

How the Competition Rates

Competitors	Rating	Pg.
Ford Escape	5	116
Jeep Cherokee	5	151
Toyota RAV4		227

Price Range

Price Range	Retail	Markup
LX MT	$16,190	3%
EX MT	$18,160	3%
EX AT	$18,960	3%
EX-L AT w/Nav	$21,520	3%

Safety Checklist

Crash Test:
  Frontal . . . . .Good
  Side . . . . .Good
Airbags:
  Torso . . . . . . Std. Fr. Pelvis/Torso from Seat
  Roll Sensing . . . . .Yes
  Knee Bolster . . . . .None
Crash Avoidance:
  Collision Avoidance. . . .Optional CIB & DBS
  Blind Spot Detection . . . . .None
  Lane Keeping Assist . . . . Optional
  Pedestrian Crash Avoidance . . . . .None
General:
  Auto. Crash Notification . . .Dial Assist.-Free
  Day Running Lamps . . . . .None
Safety Belt/Restraint:
  Dynamic Head Restraints . . . . .None
  Adjustable Belt . . . . Standard Front

^Warning feature does not meet suggested government specifications.

Honda Fit

Specifications

Drive . . . . FWD
Engine 1.5-liter I4
Transmission . . . . .CVT
Tow Rating (lbs.) . . . . –
Head/Leg Room (in.) Cramped-39.5/41.4
Interior Space (cu. ft.) Cramped-95.7
Cargo Space (cu. ft.) Cramped-16.6
Wheelbase/Length (in.) 99.6/161.4

Ratings—10 Best, 1 Worst

Combo Crash Tests	3
Safety Features	2
Rollover	4
Preventive Maintenance	7
Repair Costs	8
Warranty	2
Fuel Economy	8
Complaints	6
Insurance Costs	10
OVERALL RATING	**5**

Honda HR-V

At-a-Glance

Status/Year Series Started. Unchanged/2016
Twins . . . . -
Body Styles . . . . SUV
Seating 5
Anti-Theft Device . . . . . . Std. Pass. Immobil. & Alarm
Parking Index Rating . . . . Easy
Where Made. .Celaya, Mexico
Fuel Factor
  MPG Rating (city/hwy) Good-28/34
  Driving Range (mi.) Average-401
  Fuel Type. . . . . .Regular
  Annual Fuel Cost . . . . Low-$1208
  Gas Guzzler Tax . . . . .No
  Greenhouse Gas Emissions (tons/yr.). Low-4.7
  Barrels of Oil Used per year Average-10.6

How the Competition Rates

Competitors	Rating	Pg.
Chevrolet Spark	5	102
Nissan Versa	1	206
Toyota RAV4		227

Price Range

	Retail	Markup
LX FWD MT	$19,570	3%
LX AWD AT	$21,670	3%
EX FWD AT	$22,420	3%
EX-L AWD w/Nav	$26,340	3%

Honda HR-V

Honda HR-V

Safety Checklist

Crash Test:
  Frontal. . . . . Poor
  Side . . . . Average
Airbags:
  Torso . . . . . . Std. Fr. Pelvis/Torso from Seat
  Roll Sensing . . . . .Yes
  Knee Bolster . . . . .None
Crash Avoidance:
  Collision Avoidance. . . . . .None
  Blind Spot Detection . . . . .None
  Lane Keeping Assist . . . . .None
  Pedestrian Crash Avoidance . . . . .None
General:
  Auto. Crash Notification . . .Dial Assist.-Free
  Day Running Lamps . . . . .Standard
Safety Belt/Restraint:
  Dynamic Head Restraints . . . . .None
  Adjustable Belt . . . . Standard Front

^Warning feature does not meet suggested government specifications.

Specifications

Drive. . . . . FWD
Engine 1.8-liter I4
Transmission . . . . .CVT
Tow Rating (lbs.) . . . . –
Head/Leg Room (in.) Cramped-39.5/41.2
Interior Space (cu. ft.). Average-100.1
Cargo Space (cu. ft.) Roomy-24.3
Wheelbase/Length (in.) 102.8/169.1

Honda Odyssey   Minivan

Ratings—10 Best, 1 Worst

Combo Crash Tests	7
Safety Features	10
Rollover	5
Preventive Maintenance	9
Repair Costs	8
Warranty	2
Fuel Economy	3
Complaints	2
Insurance Costs	10
OVERALL RATING	**8**

Honda Odyssey

Honda Odyssey

At-a-Glance

Status/Year Series Started........ Unchanged/2018
Twins .... -
Body Styles .... Minivan
Seating 7
Anti-Theft Device ...... Std. Pass. Immobil. & Alarm
Parking Index Rating .... Very Hard
Where Made.................... Lincoln, Alabama
Fuel Factor
  MPG Rating (city/hwy)............. Poor-19/28
  Driving Range (mi.) Long-433
  Fuel Type......................... Regular
  Annual Fuel Cost .... Average-$1654
  Gas Guzzler Tax .... No
  Greenhouse Gas Emissions (tons/yr.).. Average-6.7
  Barrels of Oil Used per year High-15.0

How the Competition Rates

Competitors	Rating	Pg.
Chevrolet Trax	10	106
Jeep Renegade	1	154
Mazda CX-5	4	180

Price Range

	Retail	Markup
LX	$29,990	9%
EX	$33,860	9%
EX-L w/Nav	$39,360	9%
Touring	$44,510	9%

Safety Checklist

Crash Test:
  Frontal.........................Good
  Side............................Good
Airbags:
  Torso...... Std. Fr. Pelvis/Torso from Seat
  Roll Sensing ....Yes
  Knee Bolster .... Standard Front
Crash Avoidance:
  Collision Avoidance... Standard CIB & DBS
  Blind Spot Detection .... Optional
  Lane Keeping Assist .... Optional
  Pedestrian Crash Avoidance ..... Optional
General:
  Auto. Crash Notification ...Dial Assist.-Free
  Day Running Lamps ....Standard
Safety Belt/Restraint:
  Dynamic Head Restraints... Standard Front
  Adjustable Belt .... Standard Front

^Warning feature does not meet suggested government specifications.

Honda Odyssey

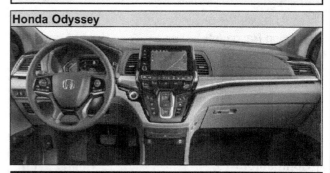

Specifications

Drive................................ FWD
Engine 3.5-liter V6
Transmission .... 9-sp. Automatic
Tow Rating (lbs.) .... –
Head/Leg Room (in.) Average-40.7/40.9
Interior Space (cu. ft.)....... Very Roomy-163.6
Cargo Space (cu. ft.) .... Very Roomy-32.8
Wheelbase/Length (in.) 118.1/203.2

137

Honda Pilot — Medium SUV

Ratings—10 Best, 1 Worst

Combo Crash Tests	8
Safety Features	6
Rollover	4
Preventive Maintenance	10
Repair Costs	7
Warranty	2
Fuel Economy	3
Complaints	4
Insurance Costs	10
OVERALL RATING	**8**

Honda Pilot

Honda Pilot

At-a-Glance

Status/Year Series Started........ Unchanged/2016
Twins.............................Acura MDX
Body Styles............................. SUV
Seating.....................................8
Anti-Theft Device...... Std. Pass. Immobil. & Alarm
Parking Index Rating.................... Hard
Where Made........................Lincoln, AL
Fuel Factor
  MPG Rating (city/hwy)..............Poor-19/27
  Driving Range (mi.).................. Long-428
  Fuel Type.........................Regular
  Annual Fuel Cost.................High-$1676
  Gas Guzzler Tax.......................No
  Greenhouse Gas Emissions (tons/yr.).. Average-6.4
  Barrels of Oil Used per year.......... High-14.3

How the Competition Rates

Competitors	Rating	Pg.
Chrysler Pacifica	8	110
Kia Sedona		159
Toyota Sienna	2	229

Price Range

Price Range	Retail	Markup
LX 2WD	$30,595	9%
EX AWD	$34,830	9%
EX-L AWD	$38,255	9%
Touring AWD	$43,470	9%

Honda Pilot

Safety Checklist

Crash Test:
  Frontal...........................Good
  Side....................... Very Good
Airbags:
  Torso...... Std. Fr. Pelvis/Torso from Seat
  Roll Sensing ....Yes
  Knee Bolster.....................None
Crash Avoidance:
  Collision Avoidance.....Optional CIB & DBS
  Blind Spot Detection .... Optional
  Lane Keeping Assist............ Optional
  Pedestrian Crash Avoidance ..... Optional
General:
  Auto. Crash Notification ...Dial Assist.-Free
  Day Running Lamps ....Standard
Safety Belt/Restraint:
  Dynamic Head Restraints...........None
  Adjustable Belt ....Standard Front

^Warning feature does not meet suggested government specifications.

Honda Pilot

Specifications

Drive................................... AWD
Engine 3.5-liter V6
Transmission ....6-sp. Automatic
Tow Rating (lbs.) Low-3500
Head/Leg Room (in.) Average-40.1/40.9
Interior Space (cu. ft.)......... Very Roomy-152.9
Cargo Space (cu. ft.) Cramped-16.5
Wheelbase/Length (in.) 111/194.5

Ratings—10 Best, 1 Worst

Combo Crash Tests	—
Safety Features	2
Rollover	—
Preventive Maintenance	6
Repair Costs	10
Warranty	10
Fuel Economy	8
Complaints	8
Insurance Costs	1
OVERALL RATING	**—**

Hyundai Accent

At-a-Glance

Status/Year Series Started........ Unchanged/2018
Twins .... Kia Rio
Body Styles .... Sedan, Hatchback
Seating 5
Anti-Theft Device . Std. Pass. Immobil. & Active Alarm
Parking Index Rating ....Very Easy
Where Made.................. Ulsan, South Korea
Fuel Factor
  MPG Rating (city/hwy).............. Good-28/38
  Driving Range (mi.) ....Very Short-362
  Fuel Type.............................Regular
  Annual Fuel Cost .... Very Low-$1157
  Gas Guzzler Tax ....No
  Greenhouse Gas Emissions (tons/yr.). Very Low-4.6
  Barrels of Oil Used per year Low-10.3

How the Competition Rates

Competitors	Rating	Pg.
Ford Edge	9	115
Mitsubishi Outlander	4	194
Subaru Outback	8	214

Price Range	Retail	Markup
SE Sedan MT	$14,745	3%
SE Hatchback AT	$16,195	3%
Value Edition AT	$16,450	3%
Sport Hatchback AT	$17,495	3%

Hyundai Accent

Safety Checklist

Crash Test:
  Frontal............................−
  Side................................−
Airbags:
  Torso...... Std. Fr. Pelvis/Torso from Seat
  Roll Sensing ....Yes
  Knee Bolster ....None
Crash Avoidance:
  Collision Avoidance.....Optional CIB & DBS
  Blind Spot Detection ....None
  Lane Keeping Assist...............None
  Pedestrian Crash Avoidance ....None
General:
  Auto. Crash Notification ....Op. Assist.-Fee
  Day Running Lamps .... Optional
Safety Belt/Restraint:
  Dynamic Head Restraints ....None
  Adjustable Belt ....Standard Front

^Warning feature does not meet suggested government specifications.

Hyundai Accent

Specifications

Drive...................................FWD
Engine 1.6-liter I4
Transmission ....6-sp. Automatic
Tow Rating (lbs.) ....−
Head/Leg Room (in.) Average-39.2/41.8
Interior Space (cu. ft.)........Very Cramped-89.7
Cargo Space (cu. ft.) Cramped-13.7
Wheelbase/Length (in.) 101.6/172

Hyundai Elantra | Compact

Hyundai Elantra

Ratings—10 Best, 1 Worst

Combo Crash Tests	—
Safety Features	7
Rollover	7
Preventive Maintenance	4
Repair Costs	10
Warranty	10
Fuel Economy	8
Complaints	6
Insurance Costs	1
OVERALL RATING	**—**

Hyundai Elantra

At-a-Glance

Status/Year Series Started. Unchanged/2017
Twins . . . . .Kia Forte
Body Styles . . . . .Sedan, Coupe, Hatchback
Seating 5
Anti-Theft Device . Std. Pass. Immobil. & Active Alarm
Parking Index Rating . . . . Easy
Where Made. . . . . .Montgomery, AL
Fuel Factor
  MPG Rating (city/hwy). Good-28/37
  Driving Range (mi.) Long-440
  Fuel Type. . . . . .Regular
  Annual Fuel Cost . . . . .Very Low-$1169
  Gas Guzzler Tax . . . . .No
  Greenhouse Gas Emissions (tons/yr.). Low-4.7
  Barrels of Oil Used per year Low-10.3

How the Competition Rates

Competitors	Rating	Pg.
Honda Civic	10	133
Nissan Sentra	5	204
Toyota Corolla	7	222

Price Range

Price Range	Retail	Markup
SE MT	$16,950	3%
SEL AT	$18,850	3%
Eco AT	$20,550	4%
Limited AT	$22,100	5%

Safety Checklist

Crash Test:
  Frontal . . . .−
  Side . . . .−
Airbags:
  Torso. . . . . . . Std. Fr. Pelvis/Torso from Seat
  Roll Sensing . . . . Yes
  Knee Bolster . . . . Standard Driver
Crash Avoidance:
  Collision Avoidance. . . .Optional CIB & DBS
  Blind Spot Detection . . . . Optional
  Lane Keeping Assist . . . . Optional
  Pedestrian Crash Avoidance . . . . . Optional
General:
  Auto. Crash Notification . . . .Op. Assist.-Fee
  Day Running Lamps . . . . .Standard
Safety Belt/Restraint:
  Dynamic Head Restraints . . . . .None
  Adjustable Belt . . . . Standard Front

^Warning feature does not meet suggested government specifications.

Hyundai Elantra

Specifications

Drive. . . . . FWD
Engine 2.0-liter I4
Transmission . . . . .6-sp. Automatic
Tow Rating (lbs.) . . . . −
Head/Leg Room (in.) Average-38.8/42.2
Interior Space (cu. ft.). Cramped-95.8
Cargo Space (cu. ft.) Cramped-14.4
Wheelbase/Length (in.) 106.3/179.9

Hyundai Kona

Ratings—10 Best, 1 Worst

Combo Crash Tests	—
Safety Features	7
Rollover	8
Preventive Maintenance	6
Repair Costs	9
Warranty	10
Fuel Economy	8
Complaints	9
Insurance Costs	8
OVERALL RATING	**—**

Hyundai Kona

At-a-Glance

Status/Year Series Started........ Unchanged/2018
Twins .... -
Body Styles .... SUV
Seating 5
Anti-Theft Device . Std. Pass. Immobil. & Active Alarm
Parking Index Rating ....Very Easy
Where Made................. Ulsan, South Korea
Fuel Factor
  MPG Rating (city/hwy).............. Good-28/32
  Driving Range (mi.) Short-396
  Fuel Type........................Regular
  Annual Fuel Cost .... Low-$1224
  Gas Guzzler Tax ....No
  Greenhouse Gas Emissions (tons/yr.)..... Low-5.0
  Barrels of Oil Used per year Low-11.0

How the Competition Rates

Competitors	Rating	Pg.
Buick Encore	10	83
Chevrolet Trax	10	106
Honda HR-V	5	136

Price Range

	Retail	Markup
SE 2.0L FWD	$19,990	3%
SEL 2.0L FWD	$21,800	4%
Limited 2.6L AWD	$26,950	4%
Ultimate 2.6L AWD	$28,900	5%

Hyundai Kona

Safety Checklist

Crash Test:
  Frontal........................... −
  Side.............................. −
Airbags:
  Torso...... Std. Fr. Pelvis/Torso from Seat
  Roll Sensing ....Yes
  Knee Bolster ....None
Crash Avoidance:
  Collision Avoidance... Optional CIB & DBS*
  Blind Spot Detection .... Optional
  Lane Keeping Assist ....Optional*
  Pedestrian Crash Avoidance ..... Optional
General:
  Auto. Crash Notification ....Op. Assist.-Fee
  Day Running Lamps ....Standard
Safety Belt/Restraint:
  Dynamic Head Restraints ....None
  Adjustable Belt ....Standard Front

^Warning feature does not meet suggested government specifications.

Hyundai Kona

Specifications

Drive............................... FWD
Engine 1.6-liter I4
Transmission ....7-sp. Automatic
Tow Rating (lbs.) .... Very Low-2755
Head/Leg Room (in.) Average-39.6/41.5
Interior Space (cu. ft.).............. Cramped-94
Cargo Space (cu. ft.) Cramped-14.2
Wheelbase/Length (in.) 102.4/164

Hyundai Palisade   Medium SUV

Ratings—10 Best, 1 Worst

Combo Crash Tests	—
Safety Features	10
Rollover	4
Preventive Maintenance	5
Repair Costs	7
Warranty	10
Fuel Economy	3
Complaints	—
Insurance Costs	8
OVERALL RATING	—

Hyundai Palisade

Hyundai Palisade

At-a-Glance

Status/Year Series Started. All-New/2020
Twins . . . . Kia Telluride
Body Styles . . . . SUV
Seating 7/8
Anti-Theft Device . Std. Pass. Immobil. & Active Alarm
Parking Index Rating . . . . Hard
Where Made. . . . . —
Fuel Factor
  MPG Rating (city/hwy) Poor-19/24
  Driving Range (mi.) Average-394
  Fuel Type . . . . Regular
  Annual Fuel Cost . . . . .High-$1700
  Gas Guzzler Tax . . . . .No
  Greenhouse Gas Emissions (tons/yr.). . Average-7.0
  Barrels of Oil Used per year High-15.7

How the Competition Rates

Competitors	Rating	Pg.
Ford Edge	9	115
Kia Telluride		163
Lexus RX	4	173

Price Range

Price Range	Retail	Markup
SE FWD	$31,775	5%
SEL FWD	$33,725	5%
SEL AWD	$35,425	5%
Limited AWD	$46,625	5%

Safety Checklist

Crash Test:
  Frontal . . . . –
  Side . . . . –
Airbags:
  Torso . . . . . . Std. Fr. Pelvis/Torso from Seat
  Roll Sensing . . . . .Yes
  Knee Bolster .None
Crash Avoidance:
  Collision Avoidance. . Standard CIB & DBS*
  Blind Spot Detection . . . . .Standard
  Lane Keeping Assist . . . . .Standard
  Pedestrian Crash Avoidance . . . . .Standard
General:
  Auto. Crash Notification . . . .Op. Assist.-Fee
  Day Running Lamps . . . . .Standard
Safety Belt/Restraint:
  Dynamic Head Restraints . . . . .None
  Adjustable Belt . . . . Standard Front

^Warning feature does not meet suggested government specifications.

Hyundai Palisade

Specifications

Drive . . . . FWD
Engine 3.8-liter V6
Transmission . . . . 8-speed Automatic
Tow Rating (lbs.) Low-5000
Head/Leg Room (in.) . . . . . . Very Roomy-40.7/44.1
Interior Space (cu. ft.) . . . . Very Roomy-155.3
Cargo Space (cu. ft.) Average-18.0
Wheelbase/Length (in.) 114.2/196.1

Hyundai Santa Fe — Medium SUV

Ratings—10 Best, 1 Worst

Combo Crash Tests	—
Safety Features	6
Rollover	4
Preventive Maintenance	4
Repair Costs	7
Warranty	10
Fuel Economy	5
Complaints	4
Insurance Costs	5
OVERALL RATING	**—**

Hyundai Santa Fe

Hyundai Santa Fe

At-a-Glance

Status/Year Series Started Unchanged/2019
Twins . . . . -
Body Styles . . . . SUV
Seating 5
Anti-Theft Device . Std. Pass. Immobil. & Active Alarm
Parking Index Rating . . . . Average
Where Made . . . . West Point, GA
Fuel Factor
  MPG Rating (city/hwy) Average-22/29
  Driving Range (mi.) . . . . Very Long-470
  Fuel Type . . . . .Regular
  Annual Fuel Cost . . . . .Average-$1458
  Gas Guzzler Tax . . . . .No
  Greenhouse Gas Emissions (tons/yr.) . . Average-6.0
  Barrels of Oil Used per year High-13.2

How the Competition Rates

Competitors	Rating	Pg.
Kia Sorento	6	160
Mazda CX-5	4	180
Mitsubishi Outlander Sport	3	195

Price Range

Price Range	Retail	Markup
SE FWD	$25,500	5%
SEL Plus FWD	$39,800	5%
Limited 2.0T AWD	$35,900	5%
Ultimate 2.0T Turbo AWD	$38,800	5%

Safety Checklist

Crash Test:
  Frontal . . . . –
  Side . . . . –
Airbags:
  Torso . . . . . . Std. Fr. Pelvis/Torso from Seat
  Roll Sensing . . . . Yes
  Knee Bolster . . . . Standard Driver
Crash Avoidance:
  Collision Avoidance. . . Standard CIB & DBS
  Blind Spot Detection . . . . Optional
  Lane Keeping Assist . . . . .Standard
  Pedestrian Crash Avoidance . . . . .Standard
General:
  Auto. Crash Notification . . . .Op. Assist.-Fee
  Day Running Lamps . . . . .Standard
Safety Belt/Restraint:
  Dynamic Head Restraints . . . . .None
  Adjustable Belt . . . . Standard Front

^Warning feature does not meet suggested government specifications.

Hyundai Santa Fe

Specifications

Drive . . . . FWD
Engine 2.4-liter I4
Transmission . . . . .8-sp. Automatic
Tow Rating (lbs.) . . . . Very Low-2000
Head/Leg Room (in.) . . . . . . Very Roomy-41.2/44.1
Interior Space (cu. ft.) Roomy-110.7
Cargo Space (cu. ft.) . . . . Very Roomy-35.9
Wheelbase/Length (in.) 108.9/187.8

Hyundai Sonata   Intermediate

Ratings—10 Best, 1 Worst

Combo Crash Tests	—
Safety Features	6
Rollover	7
Preventive Maintenance	5
Repair Costs	8
Warranty	10
Fuel Economy	7
Complaints	—
Insurance Costs	5
OVERALL RATING	—

Hyundai Sonata

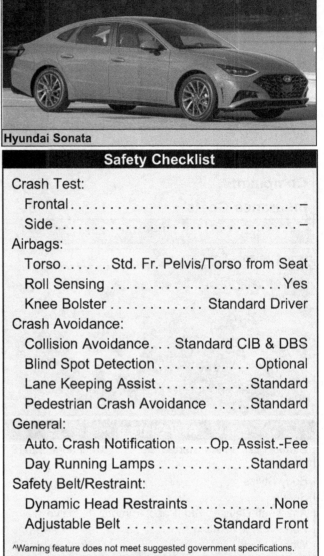

Hyundai Sonata

At-a-Glance

Status/Year Series Started. All-New/2020
Twins . . . . -
Body Styles . . . . .Sedan
Seating 5
Anti-Theft Device . Std. Pass. Immobil. & Active Alarm
Parking Index Rating . . . . Easy
Where Made. . . . . .Montgomery, AL
Fuel Factor
  MPG Rating (city/hwy). Good-28/38
  Driving Range (mi.) . . . . Very Long-473
  Fuel Type. . . . . .Regular
  Annual Fuel Cost . . . . .Very Low-$1157
  Gas Guzzler Tax . . . . .No
  Greenhouse Gas Emissions (tons/yr.). Very Low-4.7
  Barrels of Oil Used per year Low-10.3

How the Competition Rates

Competitors	Rating	Pg.
Mazda 6	5	183
Toyota Camry	8	221
Volkswagen Passat	4	235

Price Range

Price Range	Retail	Markup
SE 2.4L	$22,050	4%
SEL 2.4L	$23,700	6%
Sport 2.0L Turbo	$26,600	2%
Limited 2.0L Turbo	$32,450	6%

Safety Checklist

Crash Test:
  Frontal . . . . -
  Side . . . . -
Airbags:
  Torso . . . . . . Std. Fr. Pelvis/Torso from Seat
  Roll Sensing . . . . .Yes
  Knee Bolster . . . . Standard Driver
Crash Avoidance:
  Collision Avoidance. . . Standard CIB & DBS
  Blind Spot Detection . . . . Optional
  Lane Keeping Assist. . . . . .Standard
  Pedestrian Crash Avoidance . . . . .Standard
General:
  Auto. Crash Notification . . . .Op. Assist.-Fee
  Day Running Lamps . . . . .Standard
Safety Belt/Restraint:
  Dynamic Head Restraints . . . . .None
  Adjustable Belt . . . . Standard Front

^Warning feature does not meet suggested government specifications.

Hyundai Sonata

Specifications

Drive. . . . . .FWD
Engine 2.5-liter I4
Transmission . . . . .8-sp. Automatic
Tow Rating (lbs.) . . . . -
Head/Leg Room (in.) . . . . . . Very Roomy-40.0/46.1
Interior Space (cu. ft.). -
Cargo Space (cu. ft.) Cramped-16.3
Wheelbase/Length (in.) 111.8/192.9

Hyundai Tucson   Small SUV

Ratings—10 Best, 1 Worst

Combo Crash Tests	4
Safety Features	8
Rollover	4
Preventive Maintenance	4
Repair Costs	10
Warranty	10
Fuel Economy	6
Complaints	1
Insurance Costs	10
OVERALL RATING	**8**

Hyundai Tucson

At-a-Glance

Status/Year Series Started........ Unchanged/2016
Twins . . . . -
Body Styles . . . . SUV
Seating 5
Anti-Theft Device . Std. Pass. Immobil. & Active Alarm
Parking Index Rating . . . . Very Easy
Where Made. . . . . Ulsan, South Korea
Fuel Factor
  MPG Rating (city/hwy) Average-24/28
  Driving Range (mi.) Average-421
  Fuel Type. . . . . .Regular
  Annual Fuel Cost . . . . Low-$1433
  Gas Guzzler Tax . . . . .No
  Greenhouse Gas Emissions (tons/yr.) Low-5.8
  Barrels of Oil Used per year Average-12.7

How the Competition Rates

Competitors	Rating	Pg.
Ford Escape	5	116
Honda HR-V	5	136
Toyota RAV4		227

Price Range

	Retail	Markup
SE FWD	$22,700	4%
Eco AWD	$25,550	5%
Sport AWD	$27,300	5%
Limited AWD	$31,175	5%

Hyundai Tucson

Safety Checklist

Crash Test:
  Frontal . . . . Poor
  Side . . . . Average
Airbags:
  Torso . . . . . . Std. Fr. Pelvis/Torso from Seat
  Roll Sensing . . . . .Yes
  Knee Bolster .None
Crash Avoidance:
  Collision Avoidance. . . .Optional CIB & DBS
  Blind Spot Detection . . . . Optional
  Lane Keeping Assist . . . . Warning Only Opt.
  Pedestrian Crash Avoidance . . . . . Optional
General:
  Auto. Crash Notification . . . .Op. Assist.-Fee
  Day Running Lamps . . . . Optional
Safety Belt/Restraint:
  Dynamic Head Restraints . . . Standard Front
  Adjustable Belt . . . . Standard Front

^Warning feature does not meet suggested government specifications.

Hyundai Tucson

Specifications

Drive. . . . . FWD
Engine 2.0-liter I4
Transmission . . . . .6-sp. Automatic
Tow Rating (lbs.) . . . . –
Head/Leg Room (in.) Average-39.6/41.5
Interior Space (cu. ft.). Average-102.2
Cargo Space (cu. ft.) . . . . .Very Roomy-31
Wheelbase/Length (in.) 105.1/176.2

Hyundai Veloster | Subcompact

Ratings—10 Best, 1 Worst

Combo Crash Tests	—
Safety Features	3
Rollover	7
Preventive Maintenance	5
Repair Costs	9
Warranty	10
Fuel Economy	8
Complaints	7
Insurance Costs	3
OVERALL RATING	**6**

Hyundai Veloster

Hyundai Veloster

At-a-Glance

Status/Year Series Started. Unchanged/2019
Twins . . . . -
Body Styles . . . . .Coupe
Seating 5
Anti-Theft Device . Std. Pass. Immobil. & Active Alarm
Parking Index Rating . . . . .Very Easy
Where Made. . . . . Ulsan, South Korea
Fuel Factor
  MPG Rating (city/hwy) Good-27/34
  Driving Range (mi.) Short-396
  Fuel Type. . . . . .Regular
  Annual Fuel Cost . . . . Low-$1242
  Gas Guzzler Tax . . . . .No
  Greenhouse Gas Emissions (tons/yr.). Low-4.9
  Barrels of Oil Used per year Average-11.0

How the Competition Rates

Competitors	Rating	Pg.
Chevrolet Sonic	9	101
Mini Hardtop	6	192
Nissan Versa	1	206

Price Range

Price Range	Retail	Markup
Base MT	$18,500	4%
Premium AT	$22,750	4%
Turbo AT	$25,400	5%
Turbo Ultimate AT	$28,150	5%

Safety Checklist

Crash Test:
  Frontal . . . . –
  Side . . . . –
Airbags:
  Torso . . . . . . Std. Fr. Pelvis/Torso from Seat
  Roll Sensing . . . . .Yes
  Knee Bolster .None
Crash Avoidance:
  Collision Avoidance. . . Standard CIB & DBS
  Blind Spot Detection . . . . Optional
  Lane Keeping Assist . . . . .Standard
  Pedestrian Crash Avoidance . . . . .None
General:
  Auto. Crash Notification . . . .Op. Assist.-Fee
  Day Running Lamps . . . . .Standard
Safety Belt/Restraint:
  Dynamic Head Restraints . . . Standard Front
  Adjustable Belt . . . . Standard Front

^W-arning feature does not meet suggested government specifications.

Hyundai Veloster

Specifications

Drive. . . . . .FWD
Engine 2.0-liter I4
Transmission . . . . .6-sp. Automatic
Tow Rating (lbs.) . . . . –
Head/Leg Room (in.) Cramped-38.1/42.6
Interior Space (cu. ft.). . . . . .Very Cramped-89.9
Cargo Space (cu. ft.) Average-19.9
Wheelbase/Length (in.) 104.3/166.9

Infiniti Q50 — Intermediate

Ratings—10 Best, 1 Worst

Combo Crash Tests	4
Safety Features	5
Rollover	8
Preventive Maintenance	5
Repair Costs	3
Warranty	9
Fuel Economy	4
Complaints	8
Insurance Costs	1
OVERALL RATING	**3**

Infiniti Q50

Infiniti Q50

At-a-Glance

Status/Year Series Started........ Unchanged/2014
Twins .... -
Body Styles ....Sedan
Seating.......................................5
Anti-Theft Device ...... Std. Pass. Immobil. & Alarm
Parking Index Rating .... Average
Where Made.................... Tochigi, Japan
Fuel Factor
  MPG Rating (city/hwy)..............Poor-20/29
  Driving Range (mi.) .... Very Long-465
  Fuel Type........................Premium
  Annual Fuel Cost ....High-$1916
  Gas Guzzler Tax ....No
  Greenhouse Gas Emissions (tons/yr.)..... High-7.8
  Barrels of Oil Used per year High-14.3

How the Competition Rates

Competitors	Rating	Pg.
BMW 3 Series		72
Lexus IS	8	170
Lincoln MKZ	4	176

Price Range

	Retail	Markup
Base RWD 2.0T	$34,200	8%
Luxe RWD 3.0T	$38,950	8%
Sport AWD 3.0T	$42,650	8%
Hybrid Luxe AWD	$52,600	8%

Safety Checklist

Crash Test:
  Frontal...................... Very Poor
  Side........................ Very Good
Airbags:
  Torso. Std. Fr. & Opt. Rr. Pelvis/Torso from Seat
  Roll Sensing ....Yes
  Knee Bolster ....None
Crash Avoidance:
  Collision Avoidance.... Optional CIB & DBS
  Blind Spot Detection .... Optional
  Lane Keeping Assist.... Warning Only Opt.
  Pedestrian Crash Avoidance ....None
General:
  Auto. Crash Notification ....Op. Assist.-Fee
  Day Running Lamps ....Standard
Safety Belt/Restraint:
  Dynamic Head Restraints ....None
  Adjustable Belt ....Standard Front

^W-arning feature does not meet suggested government specifications.

Infiniti Q50

Specifications

Drive...................................RWD
Engine 3.0-liter V6
Transmission ....7-sp. Automatic
Tow Rating (lbs.) .... –
Head/Leg Room (in.) ...... Very Roomy-39.5/44.5
Interior Space (cu. ft.).............Average-100
Cargo Space (cu. ft.) ....Very Cramped-13.5
Wheelbase/Length (in.) 112.2/189.6

Ratings—10 Best, 1 Worst

Combo Crash Tests	—
Safety Features	3
Rollover	4
Preventive Maintenance	9
Repair Costs	2
Warranty	9
Fuel Economy	2
Complaints	5
Insurance Costs	10
OVERALL RATING	**—**

Infiniti QX50

Infiniti QX50

At-a-Glance

Status/Year Series Started Unchanged/2019
Twins . . . . -
Body Styles . . . . SUV
Seating 5
Anti-Theft Device . . . . . . Std. Pass. Immobil. & Alarm
Parking Index Rating . . . . Average
Where Made . . . . Tochigi, Japan
Fuel Factor
  MPG Rating (city/hwy) Average-24/31
  Driving Range (mi.) Long-432
  Fuel Type . . . . Premium
  Annual Fuel Cost . . . . Average-$1689
  Gas Guzzler Tax . . . . No
  Greenhouse Gas Emissions (tons/yr.) . . Average-6.2
  Barrels of Oil Used per year Average-12.2

How the Competition Rates

Competitors	Rating	Pg.
Buick Encore	10	83
Mazda CX-5	4	180
Subaru Forester		211

Price Range

Price Range	Retail	Markup
Pure FWD	$36,550	8%
Luxe FWD	$39,400	8%
Luxe AWD	$41,200	8%
Essential AWD	$45,150	8%

Safety Checklist

Crash Test:
  Frontal . . . . —
  Side . . . . —
Airbags:
  Torso . . . . . . Std. Fr. Pelvis/Torso from Seat
  Roll Sensing . . . . Yes
  Knee Bolster . . . . None
Crash Avoidance:
  Collision Avoidance . . . Standard CIB & DBS
  Blind Spot Detection . . . . Optional
  Lane Keeping Assist . . . . Optional
  Pedestrian Crash Avoidance . . . . None
General:
  Auto. Crash Notification . . . . Op. Assist.-Fee
  Day Running Lamps . . . . Standard
Safety Belt/Restraint:
  Dynamic Head Restraints . . . Standard Front
  Adjustable Belt . . . . Standard Front

^Warning feature does not meet suggested government specifications.

Infiniti QX50

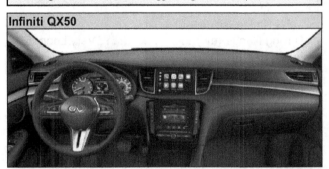

Specifications

Drive . . . . FWD
Engine 2.0-liter I4
Transmission . . . . 8-sp. Automatic
Tow Rating (lbs.) . . . . —
Head/Leg Room (in.) Cramped-41.0/39.6
Interior Space (cu. ft.) . . . . —
Cargo Space (cu. ft.) Roomy-31.4
Wheelbase/Length (in.) 110.2/184.7

Ratings—10 Best, 1 Worst

Combo Crash Tests	6
Safety Features	5
Rollover	3
Preventive Maintenance	3
Repair Costs	3
Warranty	9
Fuel Economy	3
Complaints	5
Insurance Costs	8
OVERALL RATING	**5**

Infiniti QX60

Infiniti QX60

At-a-Glance

Status/Year Series Started........ Unchanged/2013
Twins .Nissan Pathfinder
Body Styles . . . . SUV
Seating 7
Anti-Theft Device . . . . . . Std. Pass. Immobil. & Alarm
Parking Index Rating . . . . Hard
Where Made. Smyrna, TN
Fuel Factor
  MPG Rating (city/hwy) Poor-19/26
  Driving Range (mi.) Average-422
  Fuel Type. . . . . .Premium
  Annual Fuel Cost . . . . Very High-$2061
  Gas Guzzler Tax . . . . .No
  Greenhouse Gas Emissions (tons/yr.). High-8.2
  Barrels of Oil Used per year High-15.0

How the Competition Rates

Competitors	Rating	Pg.
Acura MDX	7	62
Audi Q7	3	71
BMW X5		79

Price Range	Retail	Markup
RWD	$43,100	8%
AWD	$44,900	8%

Safety Checklist

Crash Test:
  Frontal . . . . Average
  Side . . . . Average
Airbags:
  Torso . . . . . . Std. Fr. Pelvis/Torso from Seat
  Roll Sensing . . . . .Yes
  Knee Bolster .None
Crash Avoidance:
  Collision Avoidance. . . .Optional CIB & DBS
  Blind Spot Detection . . . . Optional
  Lane Keeping Assist . . . . Warning Only Opt.
  Pedestrian Crash Avoidance . . . . . Optional
General:
  Auto. Crash Notification . . . .Op. Assist.-Fee
  Day Running Lamps . . . . .Standard
Safety Belt/Restraint:
  Dynamic Head Restraints . . . . .None
  Adjustable Belt . . . Standard Front and Rear

^Warning feature does not meet suggested government specifications.

Infiniti QX60

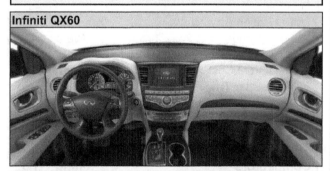

Specifications

Drive . . . . AWD
Engine 3.5-liter V6
Transmission . . . . .7-sp. Automatic
Tow Rating (lbs.) Low-5000
Head/Leg Room (in.) Roomy-40.7/42.3
Interior Space (cu. ft.). . . . . Very Roomy-149.8
Cargo Space (cu. ft.) Cramped-15.8
Wheelbase/Length (in.) 114.2/196.4

Ratings—10 Best, 1 Worst

Combo Crash Tests	—
Safety Features	7
Rollover	2
Preventive Maintenance	3
Repair Costs	4
Warranty	9
Fuel Economy	1
Complaints	7
Insurance Costs	5

OVERALL RATING   —

Infiniti QX80

Infiniti QX80

At-a-Glance

Status/Year Series Started. Unchanged/2011
Twins . . . . -
Body Styles . . . . SUV
Seating. 7/8
Anti-Theft Device . . . . . . Std. Pass. Immobil. & Alarm
Parking Index Rating . . . . Very Hard
Where Made. Kyushu, Japan
Fuel Factor
  MPG Rating (city/hwy) . . . . Very Poor-14/20
  Driving Range (mi.) Average-421
  Fuel Type . . . . .Premium
  Annual Fuel Cost . . . . Very High-$2753
  Gas Guzzler Tax . . . . .No
  Greenhouse Gas Emissions (tons/yr.)Very High-11.2
  Barrels of Oil Used per year . . . . Very High-20.6

How the Competition Rates

Competitors	Rating	Pg.
Buick Enclave	4	82
Chevrolet Tahoe	4	104
Volvo XC90	8	240

Price Range	Retail	Markup
Base RWD	$63,850	8%
Base AWD	$66,950	8%
Signature AWD	$70,435	8%
Limited AWD	$89,450	8%

Safety Checklist

Crash Test:
  Frontal . . . . –
  Side . . . . –
Airbags:
  Torso . . . . . . Std. Fr. Pelvis/Torso from Seat
  Roll Sensing . . . . .Yes
  Knee Bolster . . . . .None
Crash Avoidance:
  Collision Avoidance. . . .Optional CIB & DBS
  Blind Spot Detection . . . . Optional
  Lane Keeping Assist . . . . Warning Only Opt.
  Pedestrian Crash Avoidance . . . . . Optional
General:
  Auto. Crash Notification . . . .Op. Assist.-Fee
  Day Running Lamps . . . . .Standard
Safety Belt/Restraint:
  Dynamic Head Restraints . . . Standard Front
  Adjustable Belt . . . . .Standard Front & Rear

^Warning feature does not meet suggested government specifications.

Infiniti QX80

Specifications

Drive. . . . . AWD
Engine 5.6-liter V8
Transmission . . . . .7-sp. Automatic
Tow Rating (lbs.) . . . . .Very High-8500
Head/Leg Room (in.) . . . . .Very Cramped-39.9/39.6
Interior Space (cu. ft.). . . . . Very Roomy-151.3
Cargo Space (cu. ft.) Cramped-16.6
Wheelbase/Length (in.) 121.1/208.9

Jeep Cherokee | Medium SUV

Ratings—10 Best, 1 Worst

Combo Crash Tests	5
Safety Features	7
Rollover	3
Preventive Maintenance	10
Repair Costs	5
Warranty	3
Fuel Economy	4
Complaints	1
Insurance Costs	10
OVERALL RATING	**5**

Jeep Cherokee

At-a-Glance

Status/Year Series Started........ Unchanged/2014
Twins .... -
Body Styles .... SUV
Seating..5
Anti-Theft DeviceStd. Pass. Immobil. & Opt. Pass. Alarm
Parking Index Rating .... Average
Where Made.........................Toldeo, OH
Fuel Factor
  MPG Rating (city/hwy)............. Poor-21/28
  Driving Range (mi.) Short-376
  Fuel Type...........................Regular
  Annual Fuel Cost ....Average-$1553
  Gas Guzzler Tax ....No
  Greenhouse Gas Emissions (tons/yr.).. Average-6.3
  Barrels of Oil Used per year High-14.3

How the Competition Rates

Competitors	Rating	Pg.
Ford Escape	5	116
Mazda CX-5	4	180
Toyota RAV4		227

Price Range

	Retail	Markup
Latitude FWD	$24,395	1%
Trailhawk 4WD	$30,995	2%
Limited 4WD	$31,295	2%
Overland 4WD	$37,340	3%

Jeep Cherokee

Safety Checklist

Crash Test:
  Frontal...................... Very Poor
  Side........................ Very Good
Airbags:
  Torso. Std. Fr. & Opt. Rr. Pelvis/Torso from Seat
  Roll Sensing ....Yes
  Knee Bolster .... Standard Front
Crash Avoidance:
  Collision Avoidance.....Optional CIB & DBS
  Blind Spot Detection .... Optional
  Lane Keeping Assist ....Optional*
  Pedestrian Crash Avoidance ....None
General:
  Auto. Crash Notification ....None
  Day Running Lamps ....Standard
Safety Belt/Restraint:
  Dynamic Head Restraints ....None
  Adjustable Belt ....Standard Front

^Warning feature does not meet suggested government specifications.

Jeep Cherokee

Specifications

Drive................................. AWD
Engine 2.4-liter I4
Transmission ....9-sp. Automatic
Tow Rating (lbs.) .... Very Low-2000
Head/Leg Room (in.) Cramped-39.4/41.1
Interior Space (cu. ft.)........... Average-103.4
Cargo Space (cu. ft.) Roomy-24.6
Wheelbase/Length (in.) 106.2/182

Jeep Compass — Small SUV

Jeep Compass

Ratings—10 Best, 1 Worst

Combo Crash Tests	2
Safety Features	2
Rollover	2
Preventive Maintenance	10
Repair Costs	10
Warranty	3
Fuel Economy	5
Complaints	3
Insurance Costs	10
OVERALL RATING	**4**

Jeep Compass

At-a-Glance

Status/Year Series Started. Unchanged/2007
Twins . . . . -
Body Styles . . . . SUV
Seating 5
Anti-Theft DeviceStd. Pass. Immobil. & Opt. Pass. Alarm
Parking Index Rating . . . . Easy
Where Made. .Toluca, Mexico
Fuel Factor
  MPG Rating (city/hwy) Average-22/30
  Driving Range (mi.) . . . . .Very Short-338
  Fuel Type. . . . . .Regular
  Annual Fuel Cost . . . . .Average-$1470
  Gas Guzzler Tax . . . . .No
  Greenhouse Gas Emissions (tons/yr.). . Average-5.9
  Barrels of Oil Used per year High-13.2

How the Competition Rates

Competitors	Rating	Pg.
Acura RDX	9	63
GMC Acadia	2	129
Honda HR-V	5	136

Price Range

	Retail	Markup
Sport FWD	$20,995	1%
Latitude FWD	$24,295	2%
Trailhawk 4WD	$28,695	2%
Limited 4WD	$29,095	3%

Safety Checklist

Crash Test:
  Frontal. . . . . .Poor
  Side. . . . . .Very Poor
Airbags:
  Torso. . . . . . . Std. Fr. Pelvis/Torso from Seat
  Roll Sensing . . . . .Yes
  Knee Bolster .None
Crash Avoidance:
  Collision Avoidance. . . Optional CIB & DBS*
  Blind Spot Detection . . . . Optional
  Lane Keeping Assist . . . . Optional
  Pedestrian Crash Avoidance . . . . .None
General:
  Auto. Crash Notification . . . . .None
  Day Running Lamps . . . . .Standard
Safety Belt/Restraint:
  Dynamic Head Restraints . . . Standard Front
  Adjustable Belt . . . . Standard Front

^Warning feature does not meet suggested government specifications.

Jeep Compass

Specifications

Drive. . . . . AWD
Engine 2.4-liter I4
Transmission . . . . .6-sp. Automatic
Tow Rating (lbs.) . . . . Very Low-2000
Head/Leg Room (in.) Average-39.2/41.8
Interior Space (cu. ft.). Roomy-126.7
Cargo Space (cu. ft.) Roomy-27.2
Wheelbase/Length (in.) 103.8/173

Jeep Grand Cherokee   Medium SUV

Ratings—10 Best, 1 Worst

Combo Crash Tests	6
Safety Features	7
Rollover	3
Preventive Maintenance	8
Repair Costs	6
Warranty	3
Fuel Economy	1
Complaints	2
Insurance Costs	8
OVERALL RATING	**4**

Jeep Grand Cherokee

Jeep Grand Cherokee

At-a-Glance

Status/Year Series Started Unchanged/2011
Twins . . . . -
Body Styles . . . . SUV
Seating 5
Anti-Theft Device Std. Pass. Immobil. & Opt. Pass. Alarm
Parking Index Rating . . . . Average
Where Made . . . . .Detroit, MI
Fuel Factor
  MPG Rating (city/hwy) . . . . .Very Poor-14/22
  Driving Range (mi.) Average-412
  Fuel Type . . . . .Regular
  Annual Fuel Cost . . . . Very High-$2195
  Gas Guzzler Tax . . . . .No
  Greenhouse Gas Emissions (tons/yr.) Very High-8.8
  Barrels of Oil Used per year . . . . Very High-19.4

How the Competition Rates

Competitors	Rating	Pg.
Chevrolet Equinox	4	97
Honda CR-V	10	134
Lexus NX	5	171

Price Range

	Retail	Markup
Laredo RWD	$30,595	0%
Limited RWD	$38,195	3%
Trailhawk 4WD	$43,295	4%
Overland 4WD	$47,995	4%

Safety Checklist

Crash Test:
  Frontal . . . . .Good
  Side . . . . Poor
Airbags:
  Torso . . . . . . Std. Fr. Pelvis/Torso from Seat
  Roll Sensing . . . . Yes
  Knee Bolster . . . . Standard Driver
Crash Avoidance:
  Collision Avoidance . . . .Optional CIB & DBS
  Blind Spot Detection . . . . Optional
  Lane Keeping Assist . . . . .Optional*
  Pedestrian Crash Avoidance . . . . .None
General:
  Auto. Crash Notification . . . . .None
  Day Running Lamps . . . . .Standard
Safety Belt/Restraint:
  Dynamic Head Restraints . . . Standard Front
  Adjustable Belt . . . . Standard Front

^Warning feature does not meet suggested government specifications.

Jeep Grand Cherokee

Specifications

Drive 4WD
Engine 5.7-liter V8
Transmission . . . . .8-sp. Automatic
Tow Rating (lbs.) High-7200
Head/Leg Room (in.) Cramped-39.9/40.3
Interior Space (cu. ft.) Average-103.9
Cargo Space (cu. ft.) . . . . Very Roomy-36.3
Wheelbase/Length (in.) 114.8/189.8

Ratings—10 Best, 1 Worst

Combo Crash Tests	2
Safety Features	4
Rollover	3
Preventive Maintenance	4
Repair Costs	7
Warranty	3
Fuel Economy	5
Complaints	2
Insurance Costs	5
OVERALL RATING	**1**

Jeep Renegade

At-a-Glance

Status/Year Series Started	Unchanged/2015
Twins	-
Body Styles	SUV
Seating	5
Anti-Theft Device	Std. Pass. Immobil. & Opt. Pass. Alarm
Parking Index Rating	Easy
Where Made	Melfi, Italy
Fuel Factor	
MPG Rating (city/hwy)	Average-22/31
Driving Range (mi.)	Very Short-321
Fuel Type	Premium
Annual Fuel Cost	High-$1760
Gas Guzzler Tax	No
Greenhouse Gas Emissions (tons/yr.)	Average-6.1
Barrels of Oil Used per year	Average-12.9

How the Competition Rates

Competitors	Rating	Pg.
Chevrolet Equinox	4	97
Ford Edge	9	115
Hyundai Tucson	8	145

Price Range

	Retail	Markup
Sport FWD	$17,995	1%
Latitude FWD	$21,495	2%
Trailhawk 4WD	$26,645	2%
Limited 4WD	$27,195	2%

Jeep Renegade

Safety Checklist

Crash Test:
  Frontal . . . . Poor
  Side . . . . Very Poor
Airbags:
  Torso . . . . . . Std. Fr. Pelvis/Torso from Seat
  Roll Sensing . . . . Yes
  Knee Bolster . . . . Standard Driver
Crash Avoidance:
  Collision Avoidance. . . Optional CIB & DBS*
  Blind Spot Detection . . . . Optional
  Lane Keeping Assist . . . . .Optional*
  Pedestrian Crash Avoidance . . . . .None
General:
  Auto. Crash Notification . . . . .None
  Day Running Lamps . . . . Optional
Safety Belt/Restraint:
  Dynamic Head Restraints . . . . .None
  Adjustable Belt . . . . Standard Front

^Warning feature does not meet suggested government specifications.

Jeep Renegade

Specifications

Drive	FWD
Engine	1.4-liter I4
Transmission	9-sp. Automatic
Tow Rating (lbs.)	Very Low-2000
Head/Leg Room (in.)	Average-41.1/41.2
Interior Space (cu. ft.)	Average-100.1
Cargo Space (cu. ft.)	Average-18.5
Wheelbase/Length (in.)	101.2/166.6

Ratings—10 Best, 1 Worst

Combo Crash Tests	—
Safety Features	1
Rollover	1
Preventive Maintenance	10
Repair Costs	9
Warranty	3
Fuel Economy	2
Complaints	1
Insurance Costs	3
OVERALL RATING	—

Jeep Wrangler

At-a-Glance

```
Status/Year Series Started........ Unchanged/2018
Twins . . . . . . . . . . . . . . . . . . . . . . . . . . . . . . . . . -
Body Styles . . . . . . . . . . . . . . . . . . . . . . . . . . . SUV
Seating . . . . . . . . . . . . . . . . . . . . . . . . . . . . . . . 5
Anti-Theft DeviceStd. Pass. Immobil. & Opt. Pass. Alarm
Parking Index Rating . . . . . . . . . . . . . . . . . . . . Hard
Where Made. . . . . . . . . . . . . . . . . . . . . .Toledo, Ohio
Fuel Factor
  MPG Rating (city/hwy) . . . . . . . . . . .Very Poor-17/21
  Driving Range (mi.) . . . . . . . . . . . . . . .Average-418
  Fuel Type. . . . . . . . . . . . . . . . . . . . . . . . .Regular
  Annual Fuel Cost . . . . . . . . . . . . . Very High-$1976
  Gas Guzzler Tax . . . . . . . . . . . . . . . . . . . . . .No
  Greenhouse Gas Emissions (tons/yr.). . . . . High-8.0
  Barrels of Oil Used per year . . . . . . .Very High-18.3
```

How the Competition Rates

Competitors	Rating	Pg.
Mazda CX-5	4	180
Mitsubishi Outlander Sport	3	195
Subaru Forester		211

Price Range

	Retail	Markup
Sport	$23,995	1%
Rubicon	$33,645	5%
Unlimited Sahara	$34,245	5%
Unlimited Rubicon	$37,445	5%

Jeep Wrangler

Safety Checklist

```
Crash Test:
  Frontal . . . . . . . . . . . . . . . . . . . . . . . . . . . . . –
  Side . . . . . . . . . . . . . . . . . . . . . . . . . . . . . . . . –
Airbags:
  Torso. . . . . . . . . . . . . . . . . . . . . . . . . .None
  Roll Sensing . . . . . . . . . . . . . . . . . . . . .No
  Knee Bolster . . . . . . . . . . . . . . . . . . . .None
Crash Avoidance:
  Collision Avoidance. . . . . . . . . . . . . . .None
  Blind Spot Detection . . . . . . . . . . . . . .None
  Lane Keeping Assist . . . . . . . . . . . . . .None
  Pedestrian Crash Avoidance . . . . . . . .None
General:
  Auto. Crash Notification . . . . . . . . . . .None
  Day Running Lamps . . . . . . . . . . .Standard
Safety Belt/Restraint:
  Dynamic Head Restraints . . . . . . . . . .None
  Adjustable Belt . . . . . . . . . .Standard Front
```

^Warning feature does not meet suggested government specifications.

Jeep Wrangler

Specifications

```
Drive. . . . . . . . . . . . . . . . . . . . . . . . . . . . . . . 4WD
Engine . . . . . . . . . . . . . . . . . . . . . . . . .3.6-liter V6
Transmission . . . . . . . . . . . . . . . . . .6-sp. Automatic
Tow Rating (lbs.) . . . . . . . . . . . . . . . Very Low-1000
Head/Leg Room (in.) . . . . . . . . . . . Average-41.3/41
Interior Space (cu. ft.). . . . . . . . . . . . . .Average-104
Cargo Space (cu. ft.) . . . . . . . . . Very Roomy-31.5
Wheelbase/Length (in.) . . . . . . . . . . . . . .95.4/184.9
```

Ratings—10 Best, 1 Worst

Combo Crash Tests	—
Safety Features	2
Rollover	7
Preventive Maintenance	9
Repair Costs	10
Warranty	9
Fuel Economy	8
Complaints	3
Insurance Costs	3
OVERALL RATING	—

Kia Forte

Kia Forte

At-a-Glance

Status/Year Series Started	Unchanged/2019
Twins	—
Body Styles	Sedan, Hatchback
Seating	5
Anti-Theft Device	Std. Pass. Immobil. & Active Alarm
Parking Index Rating	Easy
Where Made	Pesquería, Mexico

Fuel Factor
MPG Rating (city/hwy)	Very Good-30/40
Driving Range (mi.)	Very Long-476
Fuel Type	Regular
Annual Fuel Cost	Very Low-$1025
Gas Guzzler Tax	No
Greenhouse Gas Emissions (tons/yr.)	Very Low-4.4
Barrels of Oil Used per year	Low-9.7

How the Competition Rates

Competitors	Rating	Pg.
Honda Civic	10	133
Mazda 3	6	182
Toyota Corolla	7	222

Price Range

	Retail	Markup
FE MT	$17,690	3%
LXS AT	$19,090	4%
S AT	$20,190	5%
EX AT	$21,990	5%

Safety Checklist

Crash Test:
Frontal	—
Side	—

Airbags:
Torso	Std. Fr. Pelvis/Torso from Seat
Roll Sensing	Yes
Knee Bolster	None

Crash Avoidance:
Collision Avoidance	Standard CIB & DBS
Blind Spot Detection	Optional
Lane Keeping Assist	Standard*
Pedestrian Crash Avoidance	Optional

General:
Auto. Crash Notification	Dial Assist.-Free
Day Running Lamps	Optional

Safety Belt/Restraint:
Dynamic Head Restraints	None
Adjustable Belt	Standard Front

^W-arning feature does not meet suggested government specifications.

Kia Forte

Specifications

Drive	FWD
Engine	2.0-liter I4
Transmission	6-sp. Automatic
Tow Rating (lbs.)	—
Head/Leg Room (in.)	Cramped-38.8/42.2
Interior Space (cu. ft.)	Cramped-96
Cargo Space (cu. ft.)	Cramped-15.3
Wheelbase/Length (in.)	106.3/182.7

Kia Optima
Intermediate

Ratings—10 Best, 1 Worst

Combo Crash Tests	7
Safety Features	7
Rollover	8
Preventive Maintenance	6
Repair Costs	10
Warranty	9
Fuel Economy	7
Complaints	6
Insurance Costs	1
OVERALL RATING	**9**

Kia Optima

Kia Optima

At-a-Glance

Status/Year Series Started........ Unchanged/2011
Twins .... -
Body Styles ....Sedan
Seating.......................................5
Anti-Theft Device . Std. Pass. Immobil. & Active Alarm
Parking Index Rating .... Easy
Where Made................... West Point, GA
Fuel Factor
  MPG Rating (city/hwy)............. Good-24/34
  Driving Range (mi.) .... Very Long-512
  Fuel Type........................Regular
  Annual Fuel Cost .... Low-$1329
  Gas Guzzler Tax ....No
  Greenhouse Gas Emissions (tons/yr.)..... Low-5.3
  Barrels of Oil Used per year Average-11.8

How the Competition Rates

Competitors	Rating	Pg.
Mazda 6	5	183
Nissan Altima		196
Toyota Camry	8	221

Price Range

	Retail	Markup
LX	$22,500	4%
S	$23,500	4%
LX Turbo	$24,300	6%
SX Turbo	$30,500	7%

Safety Checklist

Crash Test:
  Frontal.........................Good
  Side........................... Poor
Airbags:
  Torso...... Std. Fr. Pelvis/Torso from Seat
  Roll Sensing ....Yes
  Knee Bolster .... Standard Driver
Crash Avoidance:
  Collision Avoidance....Optional CIB & DBS
  Blind Spot Detection .... Optional
  Lane Keeping Assist.... Warning Only Opt.
  Pedestrian Crash Avoidance ..... Optional
General:
  Auto. Crash Notification ...Dial Assist.-Free
  Day Running Lamps .... Optional
Safety Belt/Restraint:
  Dynamic Head Restraints ....None
  Adjustable Belt ....Standard Front

^Warning feature does not meet suggested government specifications.

Kia Optima

Specifications

Drive................................. FWD
Engine 2.4-liter I4
Transmission ....6-sp. Automatic
Tow Rating (lbs.) .... −
Head/Leg Room (in.) ....Very Roomy-40/45.5
Interior Space (cu. ft.)............ Roomy-117.6
Cargo Space (cu. ft.) Cramped-15.4
Wheelbase/Length (in.) 110/190.7

Kia Rio

Subcompact

Ratings—10 Best, 1 Worst

Combo Crash Tests	—
Safety Features	3
Rollover	6
Preventive Maintenance	7
Repair Costs	10
Warranty	9
Fuel Economy	8
Complaints	9
Insurance Costs	1
OVERALL RATING	**—**

Kia Rio

Kia Rio

Safety Checklist

Crash Test:
  Frontal . . . . −
  Side . . . . −
Airbags:
  Torso . . . . . . Std. Fr. Pelvis/Torso from Seat
  Roll Sensing . . . . Yes
  Knee Bolster .None
Crash Avoidance:
  Collision Avoidance . . . .Optional CIB & DBS
  Blind Spot Detection . . . . .None
  Lane Keeping Assist . . . . .None
  Pedestrian Crash Avoidance . . . . .None
General:
  Auto. Crash Notification . . .Dial Assist.-Free
  Day Running Lamps . . . . Optional
Safety Belt/Restraint:
  Dynamic Head Restraints . . . . .None
  Adjustable Belt . . . . Standard Front

^Warning feature does not meet suggested government specifications.

At-a-Glance

Status/Year Series Started Unchanged/2018
Twins . . . . Hyundai Accent
Body Styles . . . . Sedan, Hatchback
Seating 5
Anti-Theft Device . Std. Pass. Immobil. & Active Alarm
Parking Index Rating . . . . .Very Easy
Where Made . . . . .Gwanmyeong, South Korea
Fuel Factor
  MPG Rating (city/hwy) Good-28/37
  Driving Range (mi.) . . . . .Very Short-374
  Fuel Type . . . . .Regular
  Annual Fuel Cost . . . . Very Low-$1169
  Gas Guzzler Tax . . . . .No
  Greenhouse Gas Emissions (tons/yr.). Very Low-4.6
  Barrels of Oil Used per year Low-10.3

Kia Rio

How the Competition Rates

Competitors	Rating	Pg.
Chevrolet Sonic	9	101
Mitsubishi Mirage	3	193
Nissan Versa	1	206

Price Range	Retail	Markup
LX Sedan MT	$14,165	2%
LX Hatchback AT	$15,495	3%
EX Sedan AT	$17,755	5%
SX Hatchback AT	$20,905	6%

Specifications

Drive . . . . .FWD
Engine 1.6-liter I4
Transmission . . . . .6-sp. Automatic
Tow Rating (lbs.) . . . . −
Head/Leg Room (in.) Average-38.9/42.1
Interior Space (cu. ft.) . . . . .Very Cramped-89.9
Cargo Space (cu. ft.) Cramped-13.7
Wheelbase/Length (in.) 101.6/172.6

Kia Sedona   Minivan

Ratings—10 Best, 1 Worst

Combo Crash Tests	—
Safety Features	4
Rollover	5
Preventive Maintenance	4
Repair Costs	9
Warranty	9
Fuel Economy	3
Complaints	7
Insurance Costs	5
OVERALL RATING	**—**

Kia Sedona

Kia Sedona

At-a-Glance

Status/Year Series Started. Unchanged/2015
Twins . . . . -
Body Styles . . . . .Minivan
Seating 7/8
Anti-Theft Device . Std. Pass. Immobil. & Active Alarm
Parking Index Rating . . . . Hard
Where Made. West Point, GA
Fuel Factor
  MPG Rating (city/hwy). Poor-18/25
  Driving Range (mi.) Long-435
  Fuel Type. . . . . .Regular
  Annual Fuel Cost . . . . .High-$1784
  Gas Guzzler Tax . . . . .No
  Greenhouse Gas Emissions (tons/yr.). . Average-7.2
  Barrels of Oil Used per year High-15.7

How the Competition Rates

Competitors	Rating	Pg.
Chrysler Pacifica	8	110
Honda Odyssey	9	137
Toyota Sienna	2	229

Price Range	Retail	Markup
L	$26,900	3%
EX	$33,600	6%
SX	$36,900	7%
SXL	$41,900	7%

Safety Checklist

Crash Test:
  Frontal. . . . . –
  Side . . . . –
Airbags:
  Torso. . . . . . . Std. Fr. Pelvis/Torso from Seat
  Roll Sensing . . . . .Yes
  Knee Bolster .None
Crash Avoidance:
  Collision Avoidance. . . .Optional CIB & DBS
  Blind Spot Detection . . . . Optional
  Lane Keeping Assist . . . . Warning Only Opt.
  Pedestrian Crash Avoidance . . . . . Optional
General:
  Auto. Crash Notification . . .Dial Assist.-Free
  Day Running Lamps . . . . .None
Safety Belt/Restraint:
  Dynamic Head Restraints . . . . .None
  Adjustable Belt . . . . .Standard Front & Rear

^Warning feature does not meet suggested government specifications.

Kia Sedona

Specifications

Drive. . . . . FWD
Engine 3.3-liter V6
Transmission . . . . .6-sp. Automatic
Tow Rating (lbs.) Low-3500
Head/Leg Room (in.) Roomy-39.8/43.1
Interior Space (cu. ft.). . . . . Very Roomy-172.3
Cargo Space (cu. ft.) . . . . Very Roomy-33.9
Wheelbase/Length (in.) 120.5/201.4

Ratings—10 Best, 1 Worst

Combo Crash Tests	7
Safety Features	4
Rollover	4
Preventive Maintenance	5
Repair Costs	8
Warranty	9
Fuel Economy	4
Complaints	4
Insurance Costs	5
OVERALL RATING	**6**

kia Sorento

kia Sorento

At-a-Glance

Status/Year Series Started. Unchanged/2016
Twins . . . . -
Body Styles . . . . SUV
Seating 5
Anti-Theft Device . Std. Pass. Immobil. & Active Alarm
Parking Index Rating . . . . .Very Easy
Where Made. . . . . West Point, GA
Fuel Factor
  MPG Rating (city/hwy). Poor-21/28
  Driving Range (mi.) Long-445
  Fuel Type. . . . . .Regular
  Annual Fuel Cost . . . . .Average-$1553
  Gas Guzzler Tax . . . . .No
  Greenhouse Gas Emissions (tons/yr.). . Average-6.2
  Barrels of Oil Used per year High-13.7

How the Competition Rates

Competitors	Rating	Pg.
Dodge Durango	2	113
Ford Edge	9	115
Nissan Rogue	3	203

Price Range

Price Range	Retail	Markup
L FWD	$25,800	4%
LX AWD V6	$31,300	4%
SX AWD	$40,400	5%
SXL AWD	$45,700	7%

kia Sorento

Safety Checklist

Crash Test:
  Frontal. . . . . .Good
  Side. . . . . Poor
Airbags:
  Torso. . . . . . . Std. Fr. Pelvis/Torso from Seat
  Roll Sensing . . . . .Yes
  Knee Bolster . . . . .None
Crash Avoidance:
  Collision Avoidance. . . .Optional CIB & DBS
  Blind Spot Detection . . . . Optional
  Lane Keeping Assist . . . . Warning Only Opt.
  Pedestrian Crash Avoidance . . . . . Optional
General:
  Auto. Crash Notification . . .Dial Assist.-Free
  Day Running Lamps . . . . .None
Safety Belt/Restraint:
  Dynamic Head Restraints . . . . .None
  Adjustable Belt . . . . Standard Front

^W-arning feature does not meet suggested government specifications.

kia Sorento

Specifications

Drive. . . . . .FWD
Engine 2.4-liter I4
Transmission . . . . .6-sp. Automatic
Tow Rating (lbs.) . . . . Very Low-2000
Head/Leg Room (in.) Roomy-39.5/44.1
Interior Space (cu. ft.). . . . . Very Roomy-146.4
Cargo Space (cu. ft.) . . . . Very Roomy-38.8
Wheelbase/Length (in.) 109.4/187.4

Ratings—10 Best, 1 Worst

Combo Crash Tests	—
Safety Features	4
Rollover	4
Preventive Maintenance	4
Repair Costs	8
Warranty	9
Fuel Economy	6
Complaints	—
Insurance Costs	1
OVERALL RATING	—

kia Soul

kia Soul

At-a-Glance

Status/Year Series Started	All-New/2020
Twins	-
Body Styles	Wagon
Seating	5
Anti-Theft Device	Std. Pass. Immobil
Parking Index Rating	Very Easy
Where Made	Gwangju, South Korea
Fuel Factor	
MPG Rating (city/hwy)	Average-25/31
Driving Range (mi.)	Short-386
Fuel Type	Regular
Annual Fuel Cost	Low-$1360
Gas Guzzler Tax	No
Greenhouse Gas Emissions (tons/yr.)	Low-5.5
Barrels of Oil Used per year	Average-12.2

How the Competition Rates

Competitors	Rating	Pg.
Chevrolet Spark	5	102
Mini Hardtop	6	192
Toyota Yaris	6	232

Price Range

	Retail	Markup
Base MT	$16,100	2%
!	$22,800	6%
EV e	$32,250	7%
EV +	$35,950	8%

Safety Checklist

Crash Test:
  Frontal . . . . –
  Side . . . . –
Airbags:
  Torso . . . . . . Std. Fr. Pelvis/Torso from Seat
  Roll Sensing . . . . Yes
  Knee Bolster . . . . None
Crash Avoidance:
  Collision Avoidance . . . . Optional CIB & DBS
  Blind Spot Detection . . . . Optional
  Lane Keeping Assist . . . . None
  Pedestrian Crash Avoidance . . . . . Optional
General:
  Auto. Crash Notification . . . Dial Assist.-Free
  Day Running Lamps . . . . Optional
Safety Belt/Restraint:
  Dynamic Head Restraints . . . . None
  Adjustable Belt . . . . Standard Front

^Warning feature does not meet suggested government specifications.

kia Soul

Specifications

Drive	FWD
Engine	2.0-liter I4
Transmission	6-sp. Automatic
Tow Rating (lbs.)	–
Head/Leg Room (in.)	Cramped-39.6/40.9
Interior Space (cu. ft.)	Average-101
Cargo Space (cu. ft.)	Roomy-24.2
Wheelbase/Length (in.)	101.2/163

Ratings—10 Best, 1 Worst

Combo Crash Tests	7
Safety Features	6
Rollover	4
Preventive Maintenance	5
Repair Costs	7
Warranty	9
Fuel Economy	5
Complaints	8
Insurance Costs	8
OVERALL RATING	**9**

Kia Sportage

Kia Sportage

At-a-Glance

Status/Year Series Started	Unchanged/2011
Twins	-
Body Styles	SUV
Seating	5
Anti-Theft Device	Std. Pass. Immobil. & Active Alarm
Parking Index Rating	Very Easy
Where Made	Gwangju, South Korea
Fuel Factor	
MPG Rating (city/hwy)	Average-22/29
Driving Range (mi.)	Very Short-358
Fuel Type	Regular
Annual Fuel Cost	Average-$1489
Gas Guzzler Tax	No
Greenhouse Gas Emissions (tons/yr.)	Average-5.9
Barrels of Oil Used per year	High-13.2

How the Competition Rates

Competitors	Rating	Pg.
Ford Escape	5	116
Honda HR-V	5	136
Toyota RAV4		227

Price Range

	Retail	Markup
LX FWD	$23,500	4%
EX FWD	$26,300	5%
EX AWD	$27,800	5%
SX AWD	$34,300	6%

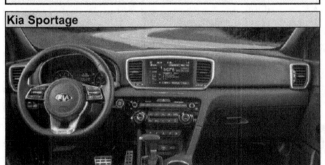

Kia Sportage

Safety Checklist

Crash Test:	
Frontal	Average
Side	Good
Airbags:	
Torso	Std. Fr. Pelvis/Torso from Seat
Roll Sensing	Yes
Knee Bolster	None
Crash Avoidance:	
Collision Avoidance	Optional CIB & DBS
Blind Spot Detection	Optional
Lane Keeping Assist	Warning Only Opt.
Pedestrian Crash Avoidance	Optional
General:	
Auto. Crash Notification	Dial Assist.-Free
Day Running Lamps	Standard
Safety Belt/Restraint:	
Dynamic Head Restraints	None
Adjustable Belt	Standard Front

^Warning feature does not meet suggested government specifications.

Kia Sportage

Specifications

Drive	FWD
Engine	2.4-liter I4
Transmission	6-sp. Automaitc
Tow Rating (lbs.)	Very Low-2000
Head/Leg Room (in.)	Cramped-39.1/41.4
Interior Space (cu. ft.)	Average-100
Cargo Space (cu. ft.)	Roomy-26.1
Wheelbase/Length (in.)	103.9/174.8

Ratings—10 Best, 1 Worst

Combo Crash Tests	—
Safety Features	10
Rollover	4
Preventive Maintenance	5
Repair Costs	7
Warranty	9
Fuel Economy	3
Complaints	—
Insurance Costs	8
OVERALL RATING	**—**

Kia Telluride

Kia Telluride

At-a-Glance

Status/Year Series Started	All-New/2020
Twins	Hyundai Palisade
Body Styles	SUV
Seating	7/8
Anti-Theft Device	Std. Pass. Immobil. & Active Alarm
Parking Index Rating	Hard
Where Made	—
Fuel Factor	
MPG Rating (city/hwy)	Poor-19/24
Driving Range (mi.)	Average-394
Fuel Type	Regular
Annual Fuel Cost	High-$1700
Gas Guzzler Tax	No
Greenhouse Gas Emissions (tons/yr.)	Average-7.0
Barrels of Oil Used per year	High-15.7

How the Competition Rates

Competitors	Rating	Pg.
Ford Edge	9	115
Hyundai Palisade		142
Lexus RX	4	173

Price Range

	Retail	Markup
LX	$31,890	5%
S	$34,290	5%
EX	$37,290	5%
SX	$41,790	6%

Safety Checklist

Crash Test:
  Frontal . . . . –
  Side . . . . –
Airbags:
  Torso . . . . . . Std. Fr. Pelvis/Torso from Seat
  Roll Sensing . . . . Yes
  Knee Bolster . . . . None
Crash Avoidance:
  Collision Avoidance . . Standard CIB & DBS*
  Blind Spot Detection . . . . Standard
  Lane Keeping Assist . . . . Standard
  Pedestrian Crash Avoidance . . . . . Standard
General:
  Auto. Crash Notification . . . . Op. Assist.-Fee
  Day Running Lamps . . . . Standard
Safety Belt/Restraint:
  Dynamic Head Restraints . . . . None
  Adjustable Belt . . . . Standard Front

^Warning feature does not meet suggested government specifications.

Kia Telluride

Specifications

Drive	FWD
Engine	3.8-liter V6
Transmission	8-speed Automatic
Tow Rating (lbs.)	Low-5000
Head/Leg Room (in.)	Very Roomy-40.7/44.1
Interior Space (cu. ft.)	Very Roomy-155.3
Cargo Space (cu. ft.)	Average-18.0
Wheelbase/Length (in.)	114.2/196.1

Ratings—10 Best, 1 Worst

Combo Crash Tests	—
Safety Features	5
Rollover	2
Preventive Maintenance	6
Repair Costs	4
Warranty	7
Fuel Economy	1
Complaints	7
Insurance Costs	5
OVERALL RATING	**—**

Land Rover Range Rover

Land Rover Range Rover

At-a-Glance

Status/Year Series Started Unchanged/2013
Twins . . . . -
Body Styles . . . . SUV
Seating 5
Anti-Theft Device . . . . . . Std. Pass. Immobil. & Alarm
Parking Index Rating . . . . .Very Hard
Where Made . . . . Solihull, England
Fuel Factor
  MPG Rating (city/hwy) . . . . .Very Poor-14/19
  Driving Range (mi.) Long-440
  Fuel Type . . . . .Premium
  Annual Fuel Cost . . . . Very High-$2805
  Gas Guzzler Tax . . . . .No
  Greenhouse Gas Emissions (tons/yr.)Very High-11.3
  Barrels of Oil Used per year . . . . . . .Very High-20.6

How the Competition Rates

Competitors	Rating	Pg.
Buick Enclave	4	82
Chevrolet Suburban	2	103
Toyota 4Runner	2	219

Price Range

	Retail	Markup
Base	$85,650	6%
HSE	$92,650	6%
Supercharged	$103,895	6%
Autobiography	$140,995	6%

Land Rover Range Rover

Safety Checklist

Crash Test:
  Frontal . . . . −
  Side . . . . −
Airbags:
  Torso . . . . . . Std. Fr. Pelvis/Torso from Seat
  Roll Sensing . . . . .Yes
  Knee Bolster .None
Crash Avoidance:
  Collision Avoidance . . .Std. CIB & Opt. DBS*
  Blind Spot Detection . . . . Optional
  Lane Keeping Assist . . . . .Optional*
  Pedestrian Crash Avoidance . . . . .None
General:
  Auto. Crash Notification . . . .Op. Assist.-Fee
  Day Running Lamps . . . . .Standard
Safety Belt/Restraint:
  Dynamic Head Restraints . . . . .None
  Adjustable Belt . . . . .Standard Front

^Warning feature does not meet suggested government specifications.

Land Rover Range Rover

Specifications

Drive 4WD
Engine 5.0-liter V8
Transmission . . . . .6-sp. Automatic
Tow Rating (lbs.) High-7716
Head/Leg Room (in.) Average-42.5/39.1
Interior Space (cu. ft.) . . . . −
Cargo Space (cu. ft.) . . . . Very Roomy-32.1
Wheelbase/Length (in.) 115/196.8

Land Rover Range Rover Evoque

Small SUV

Ratings—10 Best, 1 Worst

Combo Crash Tests	—
Safety Features	6
Rollover	4
Preventive Maintenance	6
Repair Costs	5
Warranty	7
Fuel Economy	5
Complaints	—
Insurance Costs	3
OVERALL RATING	—

Land Rover Range Rover Evoque

At-a-Glance

Status/Year Series Started. All-New/2020
Twins . . . . -
Body Styles . . . . SUV
Seating 5
Anti-Theft Device . . . . . . Std. Pass. Immobil. & Alarm
Parking Index Rating . . . . Easy
Where Made. . . . . Halewood, England
Fuel Factor
  MPG Rating (city/hwy). Average-21/26
  Driving Range (mi.) Long-449
  Fuel Type. . . . . Premium
  Annual Fuel Cost . . . . .High-$1835
  Gas Guzzler Tax . . . . .No
  Greenhouse Gas Emissions (tons/yr.). High-6.4
  Barrels of Oil Used per year High-14.3

How the Competition Rates

Competitors	Rating	Pg.
Lexus NX	5	171
Mazda CX-5	4	180
Subaru Crosstrek	5	210

Price Range

	Retail	Markup
SE	$41,800	6%
SE Premium	$45,700	6%
HSE	$51,000	6%
HSE Dynamic	$54,200	6%

Land Rover Range Rover Evoque

Safety Checklist

Crash Test:
  Frontal. . . . . –
  Side . . . . –
Airbags:
  Torso. . . . . . . Std. Fr. Pelvis/Torso from Seat
  Roll Sensing . . . . .Yes
  Knee Bolster . . . . Standard Driver
Crash Avoidance:
  Collision Avoidance. . .Std. CIB & Opt. DBS*
  Blind Spot Detection . . . . Optional
  Lane Keeping Assist . . . . .Optional*
  Pedestrian Crash Avoidance . . . . .None
General:
  Auto. Crash Notification . . . .Op. Assist.-Fee
  Day Running Lamps . . . . .Standard
Safety Belt/Restraint:
  Dynamic Head Restraints . . . . .None
  Adjustable Belt . . . . .Standard Front

^Warning feature does not meet suggested government specifications.

Land Rover Range Rover Evoque

Specifications

Drive. 4WD
Engine 2.0-liter I4
Transmission . . . . .9-sp. Automatic
Tow Rating (lbs.) . . . . –
Head/Leg Room (in.) Cramped-38.9/40.1
Interior Space (cu. ft.). –
Cargo Space (cu. ft.) Average-21.5
Wheelbase/Length (in.) 105.5/172.1

Land Rover Range Rover Sport — Medium SUV

Ratings—10 Best, 1 Worst

Combo Crash Tests	—
Safety Features	5
Rollover	3
Preventive Maintenance	1
Repair Costs	4
Warranty	7
Fuel Economy	1
Complaints	9
Insurance Costs	1
OVERALL RATING	—

Land Rover Range Rover Sport

At-a-Glance

Status/Year Series Started. . Apperance Change/2014
Twins . . . . -
Body Styles . . . . SUV
Seating 5
Anti-Theft Device . . . . . . Std. Pass. Immobil. & Alarm
Parking Index Rating . . . . Hard
Where Made. . . . . Solihull, England
Fuel Factor
  MPG Rating (city/hwy) . . . . .Very Poor-14/19
  Driving Range (mi.) Long-440
  Fuel Type. . . . . .Premium
  Annual Fuel Cost . . . . Very High-$2805
  Gas Guzzler Tax . . . . .No
  Greenhouse Gas Emissions (tons/yr.)Very High-11.2
  Barrels of Oil Used per year . . . . . . Very High-20.6

How the Competition Rates

Competitors	Rating	Pg.
Acura MDX	7	62
Audi Q7	3	71
BMW X5		79

Price Range

Price Range	Retail	Markup
SE	$65,650	6%
HSE	$70,650	6%
Supercharged	$80,650	6%
Autobiography	$94,450	6%

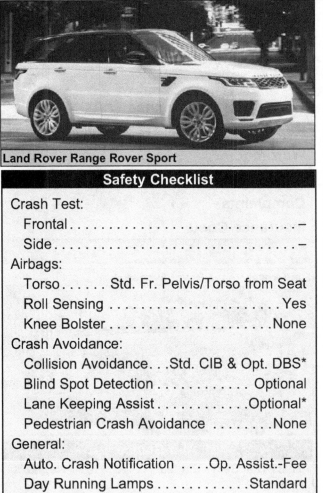

Land Rover Range Rover Sport

Safety Checklist

Crash Test:
  Frontal . . . . –
  Side . . . . –
Airbags:
  Torso . . . . . . Std. Fr. Pelvis/Torso from Seat
  Roll Sensing . . . . .Yes
  Knee Bolster .None
Crash Avoidance:
  Collision Avoidance. . .Std. CIB & Opt. DBS*
  Blind Spot Detection . . . . Optional
  Lane Keeping Assist . . . . .Optional*
  Pedestrian Crash Avoidance . . . . .None
General:
  Auto. Crash Notification . . . .Op. Assist.-Fee
  Day Running Lamps . . . . .Standard
Safety Belt/Restraint:
  Dynamic Head Restraints . . . . .None
  Adjustable Belt . . . . .Standard Front

^Warning feature does not meet suggested government specifications.

Land Rover Range Rover Sport

Specifications

Drive. 4WD
Engine 5.0-liter V8
Transmission . . . . .8-sp. Automatic
Tow Rating (lbs.) High-7716
Head/Leg Room (in.) Average-39.4/42.2
Interior Space (cu. ft.). . . . . –
Cargo Space (cu. ft.) Roomy-27.7
Wheelbase/Length (in.) 115.1/191.8

Lexus ES Intermediate

Ratings—10 Best, 1 Worst

Combo Crash Tests	—
Safety Features	9
Rollover	7
Preventive Maintenance	6
Repair Costs	2
Warranty	7
Fuel Economy	5
Complaints	10
Insurance Costs	1
OVERALL RATING	—

Lexus ES

At-a-Glance

```
Status/Year Series Started........ Unchanged/2019
Twins ....................................... -
Body Styles ...........................Sedan
Seating ........................................5
Anti-Theft Device ...... Std. Pass. Immobil. & Alarm
Parking Index Rating ..................Very Easy
Where Made.................... Kyushu, Japan
Fuel Factor
  MPG Rating (city/hwy)............ Average-22/33
  Driving Range (mi.) ...............Average-413
  Fuel Type.........................Regular
  Annual Fuel Cost ...............Average-$1369
  Gas Guzzler Tax .......................No
  Greenhouse Gas Emissions (tons/yr.)..... Low-5.7
  Barrels of Oil Used per year ........ Average-12.7
```

How the Competition Rates

Competitors	Rating	Pg.
Acura TLX	9	64
Audi A6		68
Volkswagen Passat	4	235

Price Range

	Retail	Markup
Sedan	$39,500	7%
Luxury	$42,155	7%
Ultra Luxury	$43,150	7%
F Sport	$44,035	7%

Lexus ES

Safety Checklist

```
Crash Test:
  Frontal............................. –
  Side................................ –
Airbags:
  Torso Std. Fr. & Rear Pelvis/Torso from Seat
  Roll Sensing ......................Yes
  Knee Bolster ............Standard Front
Crash Avoidance:
  Collision Avoidance... Standard CIB & DBS
  Blind Spot Detection ............ Optional
  Lane Keeping Assist ...........Standard
  Pedestrian Crash Avoidance ........None
General:
  Auto. Crash Notification ....Op. Assist.-Fee
  Day Running Lamps ...........Standard
Safety Belt/Restraint:
  Dynamic Head Restraints ...........None
  Adjustable Belt ..........Standard Front
```

^Warning feature does not meet suggested government specifications.

Lexus ES

Specifications

```
Drive................................. FWD
Engine ........................3.5-liter V6
Transmission ..............8-sp. Automatic
Tow Rating (lbs.) ..................... –
Head/Leg Room (in.) ........Cramped-37.5/42.4
Interior Space (cu. ft.)........... Average-99.9
Cargo Space (cu. ft.) ...........Cramped-16.7
Wheelbase/Length (in.) ........113.0/195.9
```

Ratings—10 Best, 1 Worst

Combo Crash Tests	—
Safety Features	9
Rollover	7
Preventive Maintenance	8
Repair Costs	1
Warranty	7
Fuel Economy	3
Complaints	4
Insurance Costs	1

OVERALL RATING —

Lexus GS

Lexus GS

At-a-Glance

Status/Year Series Started. Unchanged/2012
Twins . . . . -
Body Styles . . . . .Sedan
Seating. 5
Anti-Theft Device . . . . . . Std. Pass. Immobil. & Alarm
Parking Index Rating . . . . Average
Where Made. . . . . Tahara, Japan
Fuel Factor
  MPG Rating (city/hwy). Poor-19/29
  Driving Range (mi.) Short-391
  Fuel Type. . . . . .Premium
  Annual Fuel Cost . . . . Very High-$1981
  Gas Guzzler Tax . . . . .No
  Greenhouse Gas Emissions (tons/yr.). High-7.8
  Barrels of Oil Used per year High-14.3

How the Competition Rates

Competitors	Rating	Pg.
Infiniti Q50	3	147
Lincoln MKZ	4	176
Volvo S60		237

Price Range

	Retail	Markup
200t	$46,310	8%
350	$50,695	8%
200t F Sport	$53,980	8%
350 F Sport AWD	$56,555	8%

Safety Checklist

Crash Test:
  Frontal. . . . . −
  Side. . . . . −
Airbags:
  Torso Std. Fr. & Rear Pelvis/Torso from Seat
  Roll Sensing . . . . .Yes
  Knee Bolster . . . . Standard Front
Crash Avoidance:
  Collision Avoidance. . . . Optional CIB & DBS
  Blind Spot Detection . . . . Optional
  Lane Keeping Assist . . . . Optional
  Pedestrian Crash Avoidance . . . . .None
General:
  Auto. Crash Notification . . . .Op. Assist.-Fee
  Day Running Lamps . . . . .Standard
Safety Belt/Restraint:
  Dynamic Head Restraints . . . . .None
  Adjustable Belt . . . . .Standard Front

^W-arning feature does not meet suggested government specifications.

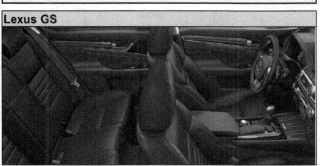

Lexus GS

Specifications

Drive. . . . . RWD
Engine 3.5-liter V6
Transmission . . . . .8-sp. Automatic
Tow Rating (lbs.) . . . . −
Head/Leg Room (in.) Cramped-38/42.3
Interior Space (cu. ft.). Average-99
Cargo Space (cu. ft.) Cramped-14.1
Wheelbase/Length (in.) 112.2/190.7

Lexus GX

Large SUV

Lexus GX

Ratings—10 Best, 1 Worst

Combo Crash Tests	—
Safety Features	9
Rollover	1
Preventive Maintenance	6
Repair Costs	2
Warranty	7
Fuel Economy	1
Complaints	9
Insurance Costs	10
OVERALL RATING	**—**

Lexus GX

Safety Checklist

Crash Test:
 Frontal . . . . –
 Side . . . . –
Airbags:
 Torso . Std. Fr. & Opt. Rr. Pelvis/Torso from Seat
 Roll Sensing . . . . Yes
 Knee Bolster . . . . Standard Front
Crash Avoidance:
 Collision Avoidance . . . . Optional CIB & DBS
 Blind Spot Detection . . . . Optional
 Lane Keeping Assist . . . . Warning Only Opt.
 Pedestrian Crash Avoidance . . . . None
General:
 Auto. Crash Notification . . . . Op. Assist.-Fee
 Day Running Lamps . . . . Standard
Safety Belt/Restraint:
 Dynamic Head Restraints . . . Standard Front
 Adjustable Belt . . . . . Standard Front & Rear

^W-arning feature does not meet suggested government specifications.

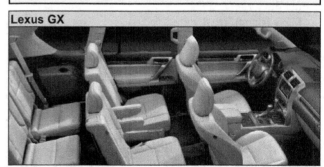

Lexus GX

At-a-Glance

Status/Year Series Started. . Apperance Change/2010
Twins Lexus RX, Toyota 4Runner, Toyota Highlander
Body Styles . . . . SUV
Seating 7
Anti-Theft Device . . . . . . Std. Pass. Immobil. & Alarm
Parking Index Rating . . . . Very Hard
Where Made . . . . Tahara, Japan
Fuel Factor
 MPG Rating (city/hwy) . . . . Very Poor-15/20
 Driving Range (mi.) Short-389
 Fuel Type . . . . Premium
 Annual Fuel Cost . . . . Very High-$2636
 Gas Guzzler Tax . . . . No
 Greenhouse Gas Emissions (tons/yr.)Very High-10.6
 Barrels of Oil Used per year . . . . Very High-19.4

How the Competition Rates

Competitors	Rating	Pg.
Buick Enclave	4	82
Chevrolet Suburban	2	103
Volvo XC90	8	240

Price Range	Retail	Markup
460	$51,680	9%
460 Luxury	$63,380	9%

Specifications

Drive 4WD
Engine 4.6-liter V8
Transmission . . . . 6-sp. Automatic
Tow Rating (lbs.) Average-6500
Head/Leg Room (in.) Cramped-38/41.7
Interior Space (cu. ft.) . . . . Very Roomy-129.7
Cargo Space (cu. ft.) . . . . Very Cramped-11.6
Wheelbase/Length (in.) 109.8/192.1

Ratings—10 Best, 1 Worst

Combo Crash Tests	5
Safety Features	9
Rollover	9
Preventive Maintenance	7
Repair Costs	1
Warranty	7
Fuel Economy	5
Complaints	10
Insurance Costs	5
OVERALL RATING	**8**

Lexus IS

Lexus IS

At-a-Glance

Status/Year Series Started	Unchanged/2014
Twins	-
Body Styles	Sedan, Convertible
Seating	5
Anti-Theft Device	Std. Pass. Immobil. & Alarm
Parking Index Rating	Easy
Where Made	Kyushu, Japan / Tahara, Japan
Fuel Factor	
MPG Rating (city/hwy)	Average-21/30
Driving Range (mi.)	Average-422
Fuel Type	Premium
Annual Fuel Cost	High-$1835
Gas Guzzler Tax	No
Greenhouse Gas Emissions (tons/yr.)	High-7.5
Barrels of Oil Used per year	High-13.7

How the Competition Rates

Competitors	Rating	Pg.
Audi A3	5	65
BMW 3 Series		72
Infiniti Q50	3	147

Price Range

	Retail	Markup
200t	$37,825	8%
300 AWD	$40,200	8%
350	$41,370	8%
350 AWD	$43,535	8%

Lexus IS

Safety Checklist

Crash Test:
   Frontal . . . . Poor
   Side . . . . .Good
Airbags:
   Torso Std. Fr. & Rear Pelvis/Torso from Seat
   Roll Sensing . . . . .Yes
   Knee Bolster . . . . Standard Front
Crash Avoidance:
   Collision Avoidance. . . Optional CIB & DBS*
   Blind Spot Detection . . . . Optional
   Lane Keeping Assist . . . . .Standard
   Pedestrian Crash Avoidance . . . . .None
General:
   Auto. Crash Notification . . . .Op. Assist.-Fee
   Day Running Lamps . . . . .Standard
Safety Belt/Restraint:
   Dynamic Head Restraints . . . . .None
   Adjustable Belt . . . . Standard Front

^Warning feature does not meet suggested government specifications.

Lexus IS

Specifications

Drive	RWD
Engine	2.5-liter V6
Transmission	6-sp. Automatic
Tow Rating (lbs.)	–
Head/Leg Room (in.)	Roomy-38.2/44.8
Interior Space (cu. ft.)	Very Cramped-90.2
Cargo Space (cu. ft.)	Cramped-13.8
Wheelbase/Length (in.)	110.2/183.7

Ratings—10 Best, 1 Worst

Combo Crash Tests	7
Safety Features	8
Rollover	4
Preventive Maintenance	1
Repair Costs	3
Warranty	7
Fuel Economy	5
Complaints	7
Insurance Costs	5
OVERALL RATING	**5**

Lexus NX

Lexus NX

At-a-Glance

Status/Year Series Started Unchanged/2015
Twins . . . . -
Body Styles . . . . SUV
Seating 5
Anti-Theft Device . . . . . . Std. Pass. Immobil. & Alarm
Parking Index Rating . . . . .Very Easy
Where Made. . . . . Kyushu, Japan
Fuel Factor
  MPG Rating (city/hwy). Average-22/28
  Driving Range (mi.) Short-387
  Fuel Type. . . . . .Premium
  Annual Fuel Cost . . . . .High-$1830
  Gas Guzzler Tax . . . . .No
  Greenhouse Gas Emissions (tons/yr.). Very Low-3.5
  Barrels of Oil Used per year High-13.7

How the Competition Rates

Competitors	Rating	Pg.
Acura RDX	9	63
Buick Enclave	4	82
Mazda CX-5	4	180

Price Range

	Retail	Markup
200t FWD	$35,285	7%
200t AWD	$36,685	7%
200t F Sport AWD	$38,785	7%
300h	$39,720	6%

Safety Checklist

Crash Test:
  Frontal . . . . Very Good
  Side . . . . .Very Poor
Airbags:
  Torso . . . . . . Std. Fr. Pelvis/Torso from Seat
  Roll Sensing . . . . .Yes
  Knee Bolster . . . . .Standard Front
Crash Avoidance:
  Collision Avoidance. . . .Optional CIB & DBS
  Blind Spot Detection . . . . Optional
  Lane Keeping Assist . . . . Optional
  Pedestrian Crash Avoidance . . . . .None
General:
  Auto. Crash Notification . . . .Op. Assist.-Fee
  Day Running Lamps . . . . .Standard
Safety Belt/Restraint:
  Dynamic Head Restraints . . . . .None
  Adjustable Belt . . . . .Standard Front

^Warning feature does not meet suggested government specifications.

Lexus NX

Specifications

Drive . . . . AWD
Engine 2.0-liter I4
Transmission . . . . .6-sp. Automatic
Tow Rating (lbs.) . . . . Very Low-2000
Head/Leg Room (in.) Average-38.2/42.8
Interior Space (cu. ft.). . . . . .Very Cramped-71.6
Cargo Space (cu. ft.) Average-17.7
Wheelbase/Length (in.) 104.7/182.3

Ratings—10 Best, 1 Worst

Combo Crash Tests	—
Safety Features	8
Rollover	8
Preventive Maintenance	6
Repair Costs	1
Warranty	7
Fuel Economy	6
Complaints	10
Insurance Costs	3
OVERALL RATING	—

Lexus RC

Lexus RC

At-a-Glance

Status/Year Series Started Unchanged/2016
Twins . . . . -
Body Styles . . . . .Coupe
Seating 4
Anti-Theft Device . . . . . . Std. Pass. Immobil. & Alarm
Parking Index Rating . . . . Easy
Where Made. . . . . Tahara, Japan
Fuel Factor
  MPG Rating (city/hwy) Average-22/32
  Driving Range (mi.) Long-445
  Fuel Type. . . . . .Premium
  Annual Fuel Cost . . . . .High-$1740
  Gas Guzzler Tax . . . . .No
  Greenhouse Gas Emissions (tons/yr.) Low-5.7
  Barrels of Oil Used per year Average-12.7

How the Competition Rates

Competitors	Rating	Pg.
Audi A3	5	65
Mercedes-Benz C-Class	1	185

Price Range

	Retail	Markup
200T	$40,155	8%
300 AWD	$42,770	8%
350	$43,010	8%
350 AWD	$45,175	8%

Safety Checklist

Crash Test:
  Frontal . . . . −
  Side . . . . −
Airbags:
  Torso . . . . . . Std. Fr. Pelvis/Torso from Seat
  Roll Sensing . . . . Yes
  Knee Bolster . . . . Standard Front
Crash Avoidance:
  Collision Avoidance. . . . Optional CIB & DBS
  Blind Spot Detection . . . . .Standard
  Lane Keeping Assist . . . . Warning Only Opt.
  Pedestrian Crash Avoidance . . . . .None
General:
  Auto. Crash Notification . . . .Op. Assist.-Fee
  Day Running Lamps . . . . .Standard
Safety Belt/Restraint:
  Dynamic Head Restraints . . . . .None
  Adjustable Belt . . . . .None

^Warning feature does not meet suggested government specifications.

Lexus RC

Specifications

Drive. . . . . .RWD
Engine 2.0-liter I4
Transmission . . . . .8-sp. Automatic
Tow Rating (lbs.) . . . . −
Head/Leg Room (in.) Roomy-37.8/45.4
Interior Space (cu. ft.). . . . . Very Cramped-82
Cargo Space (cu. ft.) . . . . .Very Cramped-10.4
Wheelbase/Length (in.) 107.5/184.8

Lexus RX | Medium SUV

Ratings—10 Best, 1 Worst

Combo Crash Tests	3
Safety Features	8
Rollover	4
Preventive Maintenance	5
Repair Costs	1
Warranty	7
Fuel Economy	4
Complaints	10
Insurance Costs	5
OVERALL RATING	**4**

Lexus RX

At-a-Glance

Status/Year Series Started. . Apperance Change/2016
Twins Lexus GX, Toyota 4Runner, Toyota Highlander
Body Styles . . . . SUV
Seating 5
Anti-Theft Device . . . . . . Std. Pass. Immobil. & Alarm
Parking Index Rating . . . . Hard
Where Made . . . . Kyushu, Japan / Cambridge, Ontario
Fuel Factor
  MPG Rating (city/hwy) Poor-20/28
  Driving Range (mi.) Long-441
  Fuel Type . . . . Regular
  Annual Fuel Cost . . . . Average-$1601
  Gas Guzzler Tax . . . . No
  Greenhouse Gas Emissions (tons/yr.). . Average-6.4
  Barrels of Oil Used per year High-14.3

How the Competition Rates

Competitors	Rating	Pg.
Audi Q7	3	71
BMW X5		79
Cadillac XT5	3	90

Price Range

	Retail	Markup
350 Base FWD	$43,120	7%
350 Base AWD	$44,520	7%
350 F Sport	$50,420	7%
450 Hybrid AWD	$53,035	6%

Lexus RX

Safety Checklist

Crash Test:
  Frontal . . . . Very Poor
  Side . . . . Good
Airbags:
  Torso . Std. Fr. & Opt. Rr. Pelvis/Torso from Seat
  Roll Sensing . . . . Yes
  Knee Bolster . . . . Standard Driver
Crash Avoidance:
  Collision Avoidance. . . . Optional CIB & DBS
  Blind Spot Detection . . . . Standard
  Lane Keeping Assist . . . . Optional
  Pedestrian Crash Avoidance . . . . None
General:
  Auto. Crash Notification . . . . Op. Assist.-Fee
  Day Running Lamps . . . . Standard
Safety Belt/Restraint:
  Dynamic Head Restraints . . . . None
  Adjustable Belt . . . . Standard Front

^Warning feature does not meet suggested government specifications.

Lexus RX

Specifications

Drive . . . . FWD
Engine 3.5-liter V6
Transmission . . . . 8-sp. Automatic
Tow Rating (lbs.) . . . . –
Head/Leg Room (in.) Roomy-39.4/44.4
Interior Space (cu. ft.). . . . . Very Roomy-139.7
Cargo Space (cu. ft.) Average-18.4
Wheelbase/Length (in.) 109.8/192.5

Lincoln Continental Large

Ratings—10 Best, 1 Worst

Combo Crash Tests	10
Safety Features	8
Rollover	7
Preventive Maintenance	5
Repair Costs	2
Warranty	9
Fuel Economy	2
Complaints	2
Insurance Costs	3
OVERALL RATING	**6**

Lincoln Continental

At-a-Glance

Status/Year Series Started........ Unchanged/2017
Twins . . . . -
Body Styles . . . . .Sedan
Seating 5
Anti-Theft Device . . . . . . Std. Pass. Immobil. & Alarm
Parking Index Rating . . . . .Very Hard
Where Made. . . . . .Chicago, IL
Fuel Factor
  MPG Rating (city/hwy). . . . . .Very Poor-17/26
  Driving Range (mi.) . . . . .Very Short-362
  Fuel Type. . . . . .Regular
  Annual Fuel Cost . . . . .High-$1825
  Gas Guzzler Tax . . . . .No
  Greenhouse Gas Emissions (tons/yr.). High-7.3
  Barrels of Oil Used per year High-16.5

How the Competition Rates

Competitors	Rating	Pg.
Cadillac CT6		86
Mercedes-Benz E-Class	3	186
Tesla Model S	10	216

Price Range

	Retail	Markup
Premiere FWD	$44,560	5%
Select FWD	$47,515	5%
Reserve AWD	$55,915	6%
Black Label AWD	$64,915	6%

Lincoln Continental

Safety Checklist

Crash Test:
  Frontal . . . . Very Good
  Side . . . . Very Good
Airbags:
  Torso . . . . . . Std. Fr. Pelvis/Torso from Seat
  Roll Sensing . . . . .Yes
  Knee Bolster . . . . .Standard Front
Crash Avoidance:
  Collision Avoidance. . . .Optional CIB & DBS
  Blind Spot Detection . . . . Optional
  Lane Keeping Assist . . . . Optional
  Pedestrian Crash Avoidance . . . . .None
General:
  Auto. Crash Notification . . .Dial Assist.-Free
  Day Running Lamps . . . . .Standard
Safety Belt/Restraint:
  Dynamic Head Restraints . . . . .None
  Adjustable Belt . . . . .Standard Front

^W-arning feature does not meet suggested government specifications.

Lincoln Continental

Specifications

Drive. . . . . FWD
Engine 3.7-liter V6
Transmission . . . . .6-sp. Automatic
Tow Rating (lbs.) . . . . –
Head/Leg Room (in.) Roomy-39.3/44.4
Interior Space (cu. ft.). Roomy-106.4
Cargo Space (cu. ft.) Cramped-16.7
Wheelbase/Length (in.) 117.9/201.4

Lincoln Corsair   Small SUV

Ratings—10 Best, 1 Worst

Combo Crash Tests	—
Safety Features	10
Rollover	5
Preventive Maintenance	7
Repair Costs	3
Warranty	9
Fuel Economy	5
Complaints	—
Insurance Costs	8
OVERALL RATING	**—**

Lincoln Corsair

Lincoln Corsair

At-a-Glance

Status/Year Series Started. All-New/2020
Twins . . . . -
Body Styles . . . . SUV
Seating 5
Anti-Theft Device . . . . . . Std. Pass. Immobil. & Alarm
Parking Index Rating . . . . Hard
Where Made. . . . . —
Fuel Factor
  MPG Rating (city/hwy). Average-22/29
  Driving Range (mi.) Average-405
  Fuel Type. . . . . .Regular
  Annual Fuel Cost . . . . .Average-$1458
  Gas Guzzler Tax . . . . .No
  Greenhouse Gas Emissions (tons/yr.). . Average-6.0
  Barrels of Oil Used per year High-13.2

How the Competition Rates

Competitors	Rating	Pg.
Acura RDX	9	63
Buick Encore	10	83
Volkswagen Tiguan		236

Price Range

	Retail	Markup
Standard FWD	$35,945	5%
Standard AWD	$38,145	5%
Reserve FWD	$42,630	6%
Reserve AWD	$44,830	6%

Lincoln Corsair

Safety Checklist

Crash Test:
  Frontal. . . . . −
  Side . . . . −
Airbags:
  Torso . . . . . . Std. Fr. Pelvis/Torso from Seat
  Roll Sensing . . . . .Yes
  Knee Bolster . . . . .Standard Front
Crash Avoidance:
  Collision Avoidance. . . Standard CIB & DBS
  Blind Spot Detection . . . . .Standard
  Lane Keeping Assist . . . . .Standard
  Pedestrian Crash Avoidance . . . . .Standard
General:
  Auto. Crash Notification . . .Dial Assist.-Free
  Day Running Lamps . . . . .Standard
Safety Belt/Restraint:
  Dynamic Head Restraints . . . . .None
  Adjustable Belt . . . . .Standard Front

^Warning feature does not meet suggested government specifications.

Lincoln Corsair

Specifications

Drive. . . . . FWD
Engine 2.0-liter I4
Transmission . . . . .8-sp. Automatic
Tow Rating (lbs.) . . . . −
Head/Leg Room (in.) Roomy-39.5/43.2
Interior Space (cu. ft.). Average-102.5
Cargo Space (cu. ft.) Roomy-27.6
Wheelbase/Length (in.) 106.7/180.6

Lincoln MKZ

Intermediate

Ratings—10 Best, 1 Worst	
Combo Crash Tests	3
Safety Features	6
Rollover	7
Preventive Maintenance	8
Repair Costs	2
Warranty	9
Fuel Economy	3
Complaints	6
Insurance Costs	5
OVERALL RATING	**4**

Lincoln MKZ

Lincoln MKZ

At-a-Glance

Status/Year Series Started	Unchanged/2013
Twins	Ford Fusion
Body Styles	Sedan
Seating	5
Anti-Theft Device	Std. Pass. Immobil. & Alarm
Parking Index Rating	Hard
Where Made	Hermosillo, Mexico
Fuel Factor	
MPG Rating (city/hwy)	Poor-18/27
Driving Range (mi.)	Very Short-349
Fuel Type	Regular
Annual Fuel Cost	High-$1735
Gas Guzzler Tax	No
Greenhouse Gas Emissions (tons/yr.)	High-8.1
Barrels of Oil Used per year	High-15.0

How the Competition Rates

Competitors	Rating	Pg.
Acura TLX	9	64
Audi A6		68
Infiniti Q50	3	147

Price Range	Retail	Markup
Base FWD	$35,010	5%
Hybrid Select	$36,760	5%
Select AWD	$38,650	5%
Black Label Hybrid FWD	$47,670	6%

Safety Checklist

Crash Test:
  Frontal . . . . Very Poor
  Side . . . . Average
Airbags:
  Torso . . . . . . Std. Fr. Pelvis/Torso from Seat
  Roll Sensing . . . . Yes
  Knee Bolster .None
Crash Avoidance:
  Collision Avoidance . . . . Optional CIB & DBS
  Blind Spot Detection . . . . Optional
  Lane Keeping Assist . . . . Optional
  Pedestrian Crash Avoidance . . . . .None
General:
  Auto. Crash Notification . . .Dial Assist.-Free
  Day Running Lamps . . . . .Standard
Safety Belt/Restraint:
  Dynamic Head Restraints . . . . .None
  Adjustable Belt . . . . Standard Front

^Warning feature does not meet suggested government specifications.

Lincoln MKZ

Specifications

Drive	FWD
Engine	3.7-liter V6
Transmission	6-sp. Automatic
Tow Rating (lbs.)	Very Low-1000
Head/Leg Room (in.)	Average-37.9/44.3
Interior Space (cu. ft.)	Cramped-96.5
Cargo Space (cu. ft.)	Cramped-15.4
Wheelbase/Length (in.)	112.2/194.1

Lincoln Nautilis — Medium SUV

Ratings—10 Best, 1 Worst

Combo Crash Tests	2
Safety Features	6
Rollover	5
Preventive Maintenance	7
Repair Costs	6
Warranty	9
Fuel Economy	2
Complaints	3
Insurance Costs	10
OVERALL RATING	**5**

Lincoln Nautilis

Lincoln Nautilis

At-a-Glance

Status/Year Series Started Unchanged/2016
Twins . . . . -
Body Styles . . . . SUV
Seating 5
Anti-Theft Device . . . . . . Std. Pass. Immobil. & Alarm
Parking Index Rating . . . . Hard
Where Made. . . . . .Oakville, Ontario
Fuel Factor
  MPG Rating (city/hwy) . . . . .Very Poor-18/25
  Driving Range (mi.) . . . . .Very Short-357
  Fuel Type. . . . . .Regular
  Annual Fuel Cost . . . . .High-$1850
  Gas Guzzler Tax . . . . .No
  Greenhouse Gas Emissions (tons/yr.). High-7.5
  Barrels of Oil Used per year High-16.5

How the Competition Rates

Competitors	Rating	Pg.
Acura MDX	7	62
Audi Q7	3	71
Lexus RX	4	173

Price Range

	Retail	Markup
Premiere FWD	$39,035	5%
Select FWD	$42,550	6%
Reserve AWD	$49,055	6%
Black Label AWD	$56,725	7%

Safety Checklist

Crash Test:
  Frontal . . . . .Very Poor
  Side . . . . Poor
Airbags:
  Torso . . . . . . Std. Fr. Pelvis/Torso from Seat
  Roll Sensing . . . . .Yes
  Knee Bolster . . . . Standard Front
Crash Avoidance:
  Collision Avoidance. . . . . .Optional CIB
  Blind Spot Detection . . . . Optional
  Lane Keeping Assist . . . . Warning Only Opt.
  Pedestrian Crash Avoidance . . . . . Optional
General:
  Auto. Crash Notification . . .Dial Assist.-Free
  Day Running Lamps . . . . Optional
Safety Belt/Restraint:
  Dynamic Head Restraints . . . . .None
  Adjustable Belt . . . . Standard Front

^Warning feature does not meet suggested government specifications.

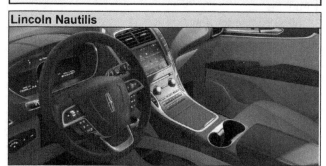
Lincoln Nautilis

Specifications

Drive . . . . FWD
Engine 2.0-liter I4
Transmission . . . . .8-sp. Automatic
Tow Rating (lbs.) . . . . −
Head/Leg Room (in.) Roomy-39.9/42.8
Interior Space (cu. ft.). −
Cargo Space (cu. ft.) . . . . Very Roomy-37.2
Wheelbase/Length (in.) 112.2/190

Lincoln Navigator

Ratings—10 Best, 1 Worst

Combo Crash Tests	—
Safety Features	5
Rollover	1
Preventive Maintenance	2
Repair Costs	6
Warranty	9
Fuel Economy	1
Complaints	9
Insurance Costs	10
OVERALL RATING	—

Lincoln Navigator

Lincoln Navigator

At-a-Glance

Status/Year Series Started Unchanged/2018
Twins . . . . Ford Expedition
Body Styles . . . . SUV
Seating 7/8
Anti-Theft Device . . . . . . Std. Pass. Immobil. & Alarm
Parking Index Rating . . . . Very Hard
Where Made . . . . Louisville, Kentucky
Fuel Factor
  MPG Rating (city/hwy) . . . . Very Poor-16/21
  Driving Range (mi.) Average-412
  Fuel Type . . . . Regular
  Annual Fuel Cost . . . . Very High-$2051
  Gas Guzzler Tax . . . . No
  Greenhouse Gas Emissions (tons/yr.) High-8.3
  Barrels of Oil Used per year . . . . Very High-18.3

How the Competition Rates

Competitors	Rating	Pg.
Buick Enclave	4	82
Chevrolet Suburban	2	103
Volvo XC90	8	240

Price Range

	Retail	Markup
Premier RWD	$72,055	5%
Select 4WD	$78,710	6%
Select L 4WD	$83,905	6%
Black Label 4WD	$93,205	6%

Safety Checklist

Crash Test:
  Frontal . . . . –
  Side . . . . –
Airbags:
  Torso . . . . Std. Fr. Torso from Seat
  Roll Sensing . . . . Yes
  Knee Bolster .None
Crash Avoidance:
  Collision Avoidance . . . . Optional CIB & DBS
  Blind Spot Detection . . . . .Standard
  Lane Keeping Assist . . . . Optional
  Pedestrian Crash Avoidance . . . . . Optional
General:
  Auto. Crash Notification . . .Dial Assist.-Free
  Day Running Lamps . . . . .Standard
Safety Belt/Restraint:
  Dynamic Head Restraints . . . . .None
  Adjustable Belt . . . . .Standard Front

^Warning feature does not meet suggested government specifications.

Lincoln Navigator

Specifications

Drive 4WD
Engine 3.5-liter V6
Transmission . . . . .10-sp. Automatic
Tow Rating (lbs.) . . . . .Very High-8400
Head/Leg Room (in.) . . . . . . Very Roomy-41.8/43.9
Interior Space (cu. ft.) . . . . .Very Roomy-172
Cargo Space (cu. ft.) Average-19.3
Wheelbase/Length (in.) 122.5/210

Mazda CX-3 — Small SUV

Ratings—10 Best, 1 Worst

Combo Crash Tests	9
Safety Features	5
Rollover	5
Preventive Maintenance	7
Repair Costs	9
Warranty	1
Fuel Economy	8
Complaints	9
Insurance Costs	8
OVERALL RATING	**10**

Mazda CX-3

Mazda CX-3

At-a-Glance

Status/Year Series Started........ Unchanged/2016
Twins .... -
Body Styles .... SUV
Seating 5
Anti-Theft Device .... Std. Passive Immobil. Only
Parking Index Rating .... Very Easy
Where Made....... Hiroshima, Japan / Hofu, Japan
Fuel Factor
 MPG Rating (city/hwy) Good-29/34
 Driving Range (mi.) Short-394
 Fuel Type.........................Regular
 Annual Fuel Cost .... Low-$1183
 Gas Guzzler Tax ....No
 Greenhouse Gas Emissions (tons/yr.)..... Low-4.8
 Barrels of Oil Used per year Average-10.6

How the Competition Rates

Competitors	Rating	Pg.
Buick Encore	10	83
Chevrolet Trax	10	106
Honda HR-V	5	136

Price Range

	Retail	Markup
Sport FWD	$19,960	3%
Sport AWD	$21,210	3%
Touring AWD	$23,210	3%
Grand Touring AWD	$26,240	3%

Safety Checklist

Crash Test:
 Frontal..................... Very Good
 Side.............................Good
Airbags:
 Torso...... Std. Fr. Pelvis/Torso from Seat
 Roll Sensing ....Yes
 Knee Bolster ....None
Crash Avoidance:
 Collision Avoidance... Optional CIB & DBS*
 Blind Spot Detection .... Optional
 Lane Keeping Assist...........Optional*
 Pedestrian Crash Avoidance ....None
General:
 Auto. Crash Notification ...Dial Assist.-Free
 Day Running Lamps ....Standard
Safety Belt/Restraint:
 Dynamic Head Restraints..........None
 Adjustable Belt ....Standard Front

^W-arning feature does not meet suggested government specifications.

Mazda CX-3

Specifications

Drive................................. FWD
Engine 2.0-liter I4
Transmission ....6-sp. Automatic
Tow Rating (lbs.) .... −
Head/Leg Room (in.) Cramped-38.4/41.7
Interior Space (cu. ft.)........Very Cramped-87.6
Cargo Space (cu. ft.) ....Very Cramped-12.4
Wheelbase/Length (in.) 101.2/168.3

Ratings—10 Best, 1 Worst

Combo Crash Tests	6
Safety Features	4
Rollover	3
Preventive Maintenance	7
Repair Costs	10
Warranty	1
Fuel Economy	7
Complaints	8
Insurance Costs	1
OVERALL RATING	**4**

Mazda CX-5

Mazda CX-5

At-a-Glance

Status/Year Series Started	Unchanged/2013
Twins	-
Body Styles	SUV
Seating	5
Anti-Theft Device	Std. Passive Immobil. Only
Parking Index Rating	Average
Where Made	Hiroshima, Japan

Fuel Factor

MPG Rating (city/hwy)	Good-26/32
Driving Range (mi.)	Average-420
Fuel Type	Regular
Annual Fuel Cost	Low-$1294
Gas Guzzler Tax	No
Greenhouse Gas Emissions (tons/yr.)	Average-6.2
Barrels of Oil Used per year	Average-11.4

How the Competition Rates

Competitors	Rating	Pg.
Buick Enclave	4	82
Honda CR-V	10	134
Mitsubishi Outlander Sport	3	195

Price Range

	Retail	Markup
Sport FWD	$24,045	3%
Touring FWD	$25,915	3%
Grand Select AWD	$30,195	3%
Grand Touring AWD	$30,695	3%

Mazda CX-5

Safety Checklist

Crash Test:
Frontal	Good
Side	Very Poor

Airbags:
Torso	Std. Fr. Pelvis/Torso from Seat
Roll Sensing	Yes
Knee Bolster	None

Crash Avoidance:
Collision Avoidance	Optional CIB & DBS*
Blind Spot Detection	Optional
Lane Keeping Assist	Optional*
Pedestrian Crash Avoidance	None

General:
Auto. Crash Notification	Dial Assist.-Free
Day Running Lamps	Standard

Safety Belt/Restraint:
Dynamic Head Restraints	None
Adjustable Belt	Standard Front

^Warning feature does not meet suggested government specifications.

Mazda CX-5

Specifications

Drive	FWD
Engine	2.0-liter I4
Transmission	6-sp. Automatic
Tow Rating (lbs.)	Very Low-2000
Head/Leg Room (in.)	Average-40.1/41
Interior Space (cu. ft.)	Average-103.8
Cargo Space (cu. ft.)	Very Roomy-34.1
Wheelbase/Length (in.)	106.3/178.7

Ratings—10 Best, 1 Worst

Combo Crash Tests	—
Safety Features	5
Rollover	3
Preventive Maintenance	7
Repair Costs	3
Warranty	1
Fuel Economy	3
Complaints	9
Insurance Costs	10
OVERALL RATING	**—**

Mazda CX-9

At-a-Glance

Status/Year Series Started	Unchanged/2016
Twins	-
Body Styles	SUV
Seating	7
Anti-Theft Device	Std. Passive Immobil. Only
Parking Index Rating	Hard
Where Made	Hiroshima, Japan
Fuel Factor	
MPG Rating (city/hwy)	Poor-20/26
Driving Range (mi.)	Long-424
Fuel Type	Regular
Annual Fuel Cost	Average-$1647
Gas Guzzler Tax	No
Greenhouse Gas Emissions (tons/yr.)	Very High-10.0
Barrels of Oil Used per year	Very High-18.3

How the Competition Rates

Competitors	Rating	Pg.
Infiniti QX60	5	149
Kia Sorento		165
Lexus RX	4	173

Price Range

	Retail	Markup
Sport FWD	$31,520	6%
Touring FWD	$35,970	6%
Grand Touring AWD	$42,270	6%
Signature AWD	$44,315	6%

Mazda CX-9

Safety Checklist

Crash Test:
Frontal . . . . –
Side . . . . –
Airbags:
Torso . . . . . . Std. Fr. Pelvis/Torso from Seat
Roll Sensing . . . . Yes
Knee Bolster . . . . None
Crash Avoidance:
Collision Avoidance. . . Optional CIB & DBS*
Blind Spot Detection . . . . Optional
Lane Keeping Assist . . . . Optional*
Pedestrian Crash Avoidance . . . . None
General:
Auto. Crash Notification . . . Dial Assist.-Free
Day Running Lamps . . . . Standard
Safety Belt/Restraint:
Dynamic Head Restraints . . . . None
Adjustable Belt . . . . Standard Front

^Warning feature does not meet suggested government specifications.

Mazda CX-9

Specifications

Drive	AWD
Engine	3.7-liter I4
Transmission	6-sp. Automatic
Tow Rating (lbs.)	Low-3500
Head/Leg Room (in.)	Cramped-39.3/40.9
Interior Space (cu. ft.)	Very Roomy-135.1
Cargo Space (cu. ft.)	Cramped-14.4
Wheelbase/Length (in.)	115.3/199.4

Ratings—10 Best, 1 Worst

Combo Crash Tests	4
Safety Features	5
Rollover	7
Preventive Maintenance	7
Repair Costs	9
Warranty	1
Fuel Economy	8
Complaints	10
Insurance Costs	3
OVERALL RATING	**6**

Mazda 3

At-a-Glance

Status/Year Series Started. Unchanged/2019
Twins . . . . -
Body Styles . . . . Sedan, Hatchback
Seating 5
Anti-Theft Device . . . . Std. Passive Immobil. Only
Parking Index Rating . . . . Easy
Where Made. . . . . Hofu, Japan
Fuel Factor
  MPG Rating (city/hwy). Good-27/36
  Driving Range (mi.) Average-415
  Fuel Type. . . . . .Regular
  Annual Fuel Cost . . . . .Very Low-$1169
  Gas Guzzler Tax . . . . .No
  Greenhouse Gas Emissions (tons/yr.) Low-4.7
  Barrels of Oil Used per year Average-10.6

How the Competition Rates

Competitors	Rating	Pg.
Nissan Sentra	5	204
Toyota Yaris	6	232
Volkswagen Jetta		234

Price Range

	Retail	Markup
Sport Sedan MT	$18,095	4%
Touring Sedan AT	$21,140	4%
Touring Hatchback AT	$21,890	5%
Grand Touring HB AT	$24,945	5%

Mazda 3

Safety Checklist

Crash Test:
  Frontal. . . . . Poor
  Side. . . . . Poor
Airbags:
  Torso. . . . . . . Std. Fr. Pelvis/Torso from Seat
  Roll Sensing . . . . .Yes
  Knee Bolster . . . . .None
Crash Avoidance:
  Collision Avoidance. . . Optional CIB & DBS*
  Blind Spot Detection . . . . Optional
  Lane Keeping Assist . . . . Optional
  Pedestrian Crash Avoidance . . . . .None
General:
  Auto. Crash Notification . . .Dial Assist.-Free
  Day Running Lamps . . . . .Standard
Safety Belt/Restraint:
  Dynamic Head Restraints . . . . .None
  Adjustable Belt . . . . Standard Front

^Warning feature does not meet suggested government specifications.

Mazda3

Specifications

Drive. . . . . .FWD
Engine 2.5-liter I4
Transmission . . . . .6-sp. Automatic
Tow Rating (lbs.) . . . . –
Head/Leg Room (in.) Cramped-38.0/42.3
Interior Space (cu. ft.). Cramped-92.8
Cargo Space (cu. ft.) . . . . .Very Cramped-13.2
Wheelbase/Length (in.) 107.3/183.5

Mazda 6 Intermediate

Ratings—10 Best, 1 Worst

Combo Crash Tests	7
Safety Features	5
Rollover	8
Preventive Maintenance	6
Repair Costs	8
Warranty	1
Fuel Economy	8
Complaints	7
Insurance Costs	1
OVERALL RATING	**6**

Mazda 6

Mazda 6

At-a-Glance

Status/Year Series Started........ Unchanged/2014
Twins .... -
Body Styles ....Sedan
Seating 5
Anti-Theft Device .... Std. Passive Immobil. Only
Parking Index Rating .... Average
Where Made...................... Flat Rock, MI
Fuel Factor
  MPG Rating (city/hwy)............. Good-26/38
  Driving Range (mi.) .... Very Long-497
  Fuel Type.......................Regular
  Annual Fuel Cost .... Low-$1213
  Gas Guzzler Tax ....No
  Greenhouse Gas Emissions (tons/yr.).. Average-6.0
  Barrels of Oil Used per year Average-11.0

How the Competition Rates

Competitors	Rating	Pg.
Kia Optima	9	162
Nissan Altima		196
Toyota Camry	8	221

Price Range

	Retail	Markup
Sport MT	$21,945	5%
Sport AT	$22,995	5%
Touring AT	$25,245	6%
Grand Touring AT	$30,695	6%

Safety Checklist

Crash Test:
  Frontal.........................Good
  Side.............................Good
Airbags:
  Torso...... Std. Fr. Pelvis/Torso from Seat
  Roll Sensing ....Yes
  Knee Bolster ....None
Crash Avoidance:
  Collision Avoidance.... Optional CIB & DBS
  Blind Spot Detection .... Optional
  Lane Keeping Assist.... Warning Only Opt.
  Pedestrian Crash Avoidance ....None
General:
  Auto. Crash Notification ...Dial Assist.-Free
  Day Running Lamps ....Standard
Safety Belt/Restraint:
  Dynamic Head Restraints...........None
  Adjustable Belt ....Standard Front

^Warning feature does not meet suggested government specifications.

Mazda 6

Specifications

Drive....................................... FWD
Engine 2.5-liter I4
Transmission ....6-sp. Automatic
Tow Rating (lbs.) .... –
Head/Leg Room (in.) Cramped-38.4/42.2
Interior Space (cu. ft.)............. Average-99.7
Cargo Space (cu. ft.) Cramped-14.8
Wheelbase/Length (in.) 111.4/191.5

Mazda MX-5 Miata Subcompact

Ratings—10 Best, 1 Worst

Combo Crash Tests	—
Safety Features	1
Rollover	10
Preventive Maintenance	6
Repair Costs	6
Warranty	1
Fuel Economy	8
Complaints	5
Insurance Costs	10
OVERALL RATING	—

Mazda MX-5 Miata

At-a-Glance

Status/Year Series Started........ Unchanged/2016
Twins .... -
Body Styles .... Coupe, Convertible
Seating 2
Anti-Theft Device .... Std. Passive Immobil. Only
Parking Index Rating ....Very Easy
Where Made................... Hiroshima, Japan
Fuel Factor
　MPG Rating (city/hwy).............. Good-27/36
　Driving Range (mi.) ....Very Short-362
　Fuel Type......................Premium
　Annual Fuel Cost ....Average-$1464
　Gas Guzzler Tax ....No
　Greenhouse Gas Emissions (tons/yr.)..... Low-4.9
　Barrels of Oil Used per year Average-11.0

How the Competition Rates

Competitors	Rating	Pg.
Toyota 86		218

Price Range	Retail	Markup
Sport MT	$24,915	6%
Club AT	$29,530	6%
Grand Touring AT	$31,270	6%
Launch Edition AT	$34,925	6%

Mazda MX-5 Miata

Safety Checklist

Crash Test:
　Frontal..............................−
　Side................................−
Airbags:
　Torso...... Std. Fr. Pelvis/Torso from Seat
　Roll Sensing ....No
　Knee Bolster ....None
Crash Avoidance:
　Collision Avoidance................None
　Blind Spot Detection .... Optional
　Lane Keeping Assist.... Warning Only Opt.
　Pedestrian Crash Avoidance ....None
General:
　Auto. Crash Notification ....None
　Day Running Lamps ....Standard
Safety Belt/Restraint:
　Dynamic Head Restraints ....None
　Adjustable Belt ....None

^Warning feature does not meet suggested government specifications.

Mazda MX-5 Miata

Specifications

Drive....................................RWD
Engine 2.0-liter I4
Transmission ....6-sp. Manual
Tow Rating (lbs.) ....−
Head/Leg Room (in.) Cramped-37.4/43.1
Interior Space (cu. ft.)........................−
Cargo Space (cu. ft.) ....Very Cramped-4.6
Wheelbase/Length (in.) 90.9/154.1

Mercedes-Benz C   Compact

Ratings—10 Best, 1 Worst

Combo Crash Tests	3
Safety Features	9
Rollover	7
Preventive Maintenance	1
Repair Costs	3
Warranty	3
Fuel Economy	5
Complaints	5
Insurance Costs	3
OVERALL RATING	**1**

Mercedes-Benz C-Class

Mercedes-Benz C-Class

At-a-Glance

Status/Year Series Started........ Unchanged/2015
Twins .... -
Body Styles ....Sedan, Coupe, Wagon
Seating..5
Anti-Theft Device . Std. Active Immobil. & Pass. Alarm
Parking Index Rating .... Average
Where Made................... Tuscaloosa, AL
Fuel Factor
  MPG Rating (city/hwy)........... Average-22/30
  Driving Range (mi.) Long-450
  Fuel Type....................... Premium
  Annual Fuel Cost .... High-$1782
  Gas Guzzler Tax ....No
  Greenhouse Gas Emissions (tons/yr.).. Average-7.2
  Barrels of Oil Used per year High-13.2

How the Competition Rates

Competitors	Rating	Pg.
Audi A3	5	65
BMW 3 Series		72
Lexus IS	8	170

Price Range

Price Range	Retail	Markup
C300 Sedan	$39,500	8%
C300 Coupe	$42,650	8%
C300 Coupe 4Matic	$44,650	8%
AMG C63 Coupe	$67,000	8%

Safety Checklist

Crash Test:
  Frontal........................ Average
  Side....................... Very Poor
Airbags:
  Torso . Std. Fr. & Opt. Rr. Pelvis/Torso from Seat
  Roll Sensing ....No
  Knee Bolster .... Standard Driver
Crash Avoidance:
  Collision Avoidance... Standard CIB & DBS
  Blind Spot Detection .... Optional
  Lane Keeping Assist .... Optional
  Pedestrian Crash Avoidance ..... Optional
General:
  Auto. Crash Notif.... Op. Assist. & Crash Info-Fee
  Day Running Lamps ....None
Safety Belt/Restraint:
  Dynamic Head Restraints ... Standard Front
  Adjustable Belt .... Standard Front

^Warning feature does not meet suggested government specifications.

Mercedes-Benz C-Class

Specifications

Drive................................RWD
Engine 2.0-liter I4
Transmission ....9-sp. Automatic
Tow Rating (lbs.) .... –
Head/Leg Room (in.) .....Very Cramped-37.1/41.7
Interior Space (cu. ft.).......... Very Cramped-81
Cargo Space (cu. ft.) ....Very Cramped-12.8
Wheelbase/Length (in.) 111.8/184.5

Mercedes-Benz E | Large

Ratings—10 Best, 1 Worst

Combo Crash Tests	5
Safety Features	10
Rollover	8
Preventive Maintenance	3
Repair Costs	1
Warranty	3
Fuel Economy	5
Complaints	5
Insurance Costs	5
OVERALL RATING	**3**

Mercedes-Benz E-Class

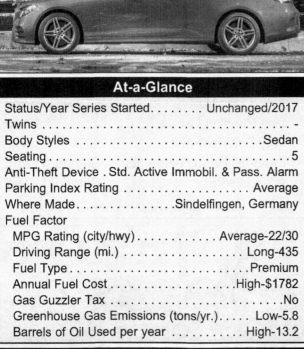

At-a-Glance

Status/Year Series Started........ Unchanged/2017
Twins .... -
Body Styles ....Sedan
Seating.......................................5
Anti-Theft Device . Std. Active Immobil. & Pass. Alarm
Parking Index Rating .... Average
Where Made...............Sindelfingen, Germany
Fuel Factor
  MPG Rating (city/hwy)............ Average-22/30
  Driving Range (mi.) Long-435
  Fuel Type...........................Premium
  Annual Fuel Cost ....High-$1782
  Gas Guzzler Tax ....No
  Greenhouse Gas Emissions (tons/yr.)..... Low-5.8
  Barrels of Oil Used per year High-13.2

How the Competition Rates

Competitors	Rating	Pg.
BMW 7 Series		76
Lincoln Continental	6	174
Tesla Model S	10	216

Price Range

Price Range	Retail	Markup
E300 Sedan	$52,150	8%
E400 Coupe	$54,550	8%
E400 Cabriolet	$62,600	8%
E550 Cabriolet	$69,100	8%

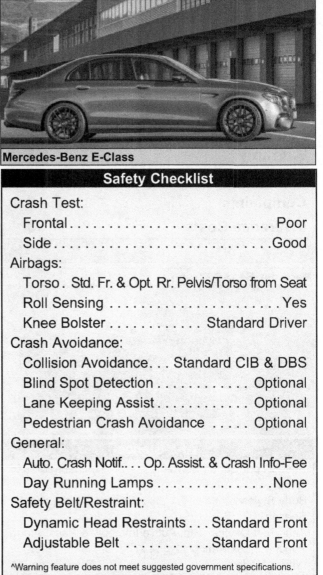

Mercedes-Benz E-Class

Safety Checklist

Crash Test:
  Frontal........................... Poor
  Side.............................Good
Airbags:
  Torso . Std. Fr. & Opt. Rr. Pelvis/Torso from Seat
  Roll Sensing ....Yes
  Knee Bolster .... Standard Driver
Crash Avoidance:
  Collision Avoidance... Standard CIB & DBS
  Blind Spot Detection .... Optional
  Lane Keeping Assist........... Optional
  Pedestrian Crash Avoidance ..... Optional
General:
  Auto. Crash Notif.... Op. Assist. & Crash Info-Fee
  Day Running Lamps ....None
Safety Belt/Restraint:
  Dynamic Head Restraints ... Standard Front
  Adjustable Belt ....Standard Front

^Warning feature does not meet suggested government specifications.

Mercedes-Benz E-Class

Specifications

Drive..................................RWD
Engine 2.0-liter V6
Transmission ....9-sp. Automatic
Tow Rating (lbs.) .... –
Head/Leg Room (in.) .....Very Cramped-37.9/41.3
Interior Space (cu. ft.)............... Average-98
Cargo Space (cu. ft.) ....Very Cramped-13.1
Wheelbase/Length (in.) 115.7/193.8

Mercedes-Benz GLA | Small SUV

Ratings—10 Best, 1 Worst

Combo Crash Tests	—
Safety Features	8
Rollover	5
Preventive Maintenance	10
Repair Costs	2
Warranty	3
Fuel Economy	6
Complaints	6
Insurance Costs	10
OVERALL RATING	—

Mercedes-Benz GLA-Class

Mercedes-Benz GLA-Class

At-a-Glance

```
Status/Year Series Started........ Unchanged/2015
Twins . . . . . . . . . . . . . . . . . . . . . . . . . . . . . . . . . . -
Body Styles . . . . . . . . . . . . . . . . . . . . . . . . . . SUV
Seating . . . . . . . . . . . . . . . . . . . . . . . . . . . . . . . . .5
Anti-Theft Device . Std. Active Immobil. & Pass. Alarm
Parking Index Rating . . . . . . . . . . . . . . . . . Average
Where Made . . . . . . . . . . . . . . . . . . Rastatt, Germany
Fuel Factor
  MPG Rating (city/hwy) . . . . . . . . . . . Average-23/31
  Driving Range (mi.) . . . . . . . . . . . . . . . Short-385
  Fuel Type . . . . . . . . . . . . . . . . . . . . . . . Premium
  Annual Fuel Cost . . . . . . . . . . . . . . . . . High-$1712
  Gas Guzzler Tax . . . . . . . . . . . . . . . . . . . . . . No
  Greenhouse Gas Emissions (tons/yr.) . . . . . Low-5.6
  Barrels of Oil Used per year . . . . . . . . Average-12.7
```

How the Competition Rates

Competitors	Rating	Pg.
Acura RDX	9	63
Infiniti QX50		148
Lexus NX	5	171

Price Range

	Retail	Markup
GLA250	$32,850	8%
GLA250 4Matic	$34,850	8%
AMG GLA45 4Matic	$49,900	8%

Mercedes-Benz GLA-Class

Safety Checklist

```
Crash Test:
  Frontal . . . . . . . . . . . . . . . . . . . . . . . . . . . . . −
  Side . . . . . . . . . . . . . . . . . . . . . . . . . . . . . . . −
Airbags:
  Torso . Std. Fr. & Opt. Rr. Pelvis/Torso from Seat
  Roll Sensing . . . . . . . . . . . . . . . . . . . . . Yes
  Knee Bolster . . . . . . . . . . . . Standard Front
Crash Avoidance:
  Collision Avoidance. . . Standard CIB & DBS
  Blind Spot Detection . . . . . . . . . . . Optional
  Lane Keeping Assist . . . . Warning Only Opt.
  Pedestrian Crash Avoidance . . . . . . . .None
General:
  Auto. Crash Notif. . . . Op. Assist. & Crash Info-Fee
  Day Running Lamps . . . . . . . . . . . . .None
Safety Belt/Restraint:
  Dynamic Head Restraints . . . . . . . . . .None
  Adjustable Belt . . . . . . . . . . . . . . . .None
```

^Warning feature does not meet suggested government specifications.

Mercedes-Benz GLA-Class

Specifications

```
Drive . . . . . . . . . . . . . . . . . . . . . . . . . . . . . . . AWD
Engine . . . . . . . . . . . . . . . . . . . . . . . . 2.0-liter I4
Transmission . . . . . . . . . . . . . . . . .7-sp. Automatic
Tow Rating (lbs.) . . . . . . . . . . . . . . . . . . . . . . . . −
Head/Leg Room (in.) . . . . . . . . .Cramped-38.3/41.9
Interior Space (cu. ft.) . . . . . . . . . . . . . Cramped-91
Cargo Space (cu. ft.) . . . . . . . . . . . . Average-17.2
Wheelbase/Length (in.) . . . . . . . . . . 106.3/173.9
```

Mercedes-Benz GLC Small SUV

Ratings—10 Best, 1 Worst

Combo Crash Tests	—
Safety Features	10
Rollover	8
Preventive Maintenance	3
Repair Costs	2
Warranty	3
Fuel Economy	4
Complaints	1
Insurance Costs	10
OVERALL RATING	—

Mercedes-Benz GLC-Class

Mercedes-Benz GLC-Class

At-a-Glance

Status/Year Series Started . . Apperance Change/2016
Twins . . . . -
Body Styles . . . . SUV
Seating 5
Anti-Theft Device . Std. Active Immobil. & Pass. Alarm
Parking Index Rating . . . . Average
Where Made . . . . Tuscaloosa, AL
Fuel Factor
 MPG Rating (city/hwy) Poor-21/28
 Driving Range (mi.) Average-412
 Fuel Type . . . . .Premium
 Annual Fuel Cost . . . . .High-$1883
 Gas Guzzler Tax . . . . .No
 Greenhouse Gas Emissions (tons/yr.) High-8.6
 Barrels of Oil Used per year High-13.7

How the Competition Rates

Competitors	Rating	Pg.
Audi Q7	3	71
BMW X5		80
Volkswagen Atlas	6	233

Price Range

Price Range	Retail	Markup
GLC300	$39,150	8%
GLC300 4Matic	$41,150	8%
AMG GLC43	$54,900	8%

Safety Checklist

Crash Test:
 Frontal . . . . –
 Side . . . . –
Airbags:
 Torso . Std. Fr. & Opt. Rr. Pelvis/Torso from Seat
 Roll Sensing . . . . .Yes
 Knee Bolster . . . . Standard Driver
Crash Avoidance:
 Collision Avoidance. . . Standard CIB & DBS
 Blind Spot Detection . . . . Optional
 Lane Keeping Assist . . . . Optional
 Pedestrian Crash Avoidance . . . . . Optional
General:
 Auto. Crash Notif. . . . Op. Assist. & Crash Info-Fee
 Day Running Lamps . . . . .None
Safety Belt/Restraint:
 Dynamic Head Restraints . . . Standard Front
 Adjustable Belt . . . . Standard Front

^Warning feature does not meet suggested government specifications.

Mercedes-Benz GLC-Class

Specifications

Drive 4WD
Engine 2.0-liter I4
Transmission . . . . .9-sp. Automatic
Tow Rating (lbs.) Low-3500
Head/Leg Room (in.) . . . . .Very Cramped-37.8/40.8
Interior Space (cu. ft.) . . . . .Very Cramped-79.5
Cargo Space (cu. ft.) Cramped-16.5
Wheelbase/Length (in.) 113.1/183.3

Mercedes-Benz GLE

Ratings—10 Best, 1 Worst

Combo Crash Tests	—
Safety Features	9
Rollover	2
Preventive Maintenance	3
Repair Costs	2
Warranty	3
Fuel Economy	2
Complaints	—
Insurance Costs	8
OVERALL RATING	**—**

Mercedes-Benz GLE-Class

At-a-Glance

Status/Year Series Started. All-New/2020
Twins . . . . -
Body Styles . . . . SUV
Seating 5
Anti-Theft Device . Std. Active Immobil. & Pass. Alarm
Parking Index Rating . . . . Hard
Where Made. . . . . Bremen, Germany
Fuel Factor
  MPG Rating (city/hwy). . . . . Very Poor-19/24
  Driving Range (mi.) . . . . Very Long-472
  Fuel Type. . . . . Premium
  Annual Fuel Cost . . . . Very High-$2233
  Gas Guzzler Tax . . . . .No
  Greenhouse Gas Emissions (tons/yr.) High-7.0
  Barrels of Oil Used per year High-15.7

How the Competition Rates

Competitors	Rating	Pg.
Buick Encore	10	83
Lexus NX	5	171
Tesla Model X	10	217

Price Range

	Retail	Markup
GLE300d 4Matic	$53,400	8%
GLE350 4Matic	$54,500	8%
GLE550e 4Matic	$66,300	8%
GLE63 AMG 4Matic	$101,690	8%

Mercedes-Benz GLE-Class

Safety Checklist

Crash Test:
  Frontal. . . . . –
  Side. . . . . –
Airbags:
  Torso . Std. Fr. & Opt. Rr. Pelvis/Torso from Seat
  Roll Sensing . . . . .Yes
  Knee Bolster . . . . Standard Driver
Crash Avoidance:
  Collision Avoidance. . . Std. CIB & Opt. DBS
  Blind Spot Detection . . . . Optional
  Lane Keeping Assist . . . . Optional
  Pedestrian Crash Avoidance . . . . . Optional
General:
  Auto. Crash Notif. . . . Op. Assist. & Crash Info-Fee
  Day Running Lamps . . . . .None
Safety Belt/Restraint:
  Dynamic Head Restraints . . . . .None
  Adjustable Belt . . . . .Standard Front

^Warning feature does not meet suggested government specifications.

Mercedes-Benz GLE-Class

Specifications

Drive. . . . . .RWD
Engine 3.0-liter I6
Transmission . . . . .9-sp. Automatic
Tow Rating (lbs.) High-7700
Head/Leg Room (in.) Cramped-40.5/39.6
Interior Space (cu. ft.). . . . . –
Cargo Space (cu. ft.) Roomy-29.1
Wheelbase/Length (in.) 114.8/189.1

Ratings—10 Best, 1 Worst

Combo Crash Tests	—
Safety Features	9
Rollover	2
Preventive Maintenance	3
Repair Costs	2
Warranty	3
Fuel Economy	2
Complaints	—
Insurance Costs	10
OVERALL RATING	**—**

Mercedes-Benz GLS-Class

At-a-Glance

Status/Year Series Started	All-New/2020
Twins	-
Body Styles	SUV
Seating	5
Anti-Theft Device	Std. Active Immobil. & Pass. Alarm
Parking Index Rating	Very Hard
Where Made	Tuscaloosa, AL
Fuel Factor	
MPG Rating (city/hwy)	Very Poor-19/23
Driving Range (mi.)	Very Long-500
Fuel Type	Premium
Annual Fuel Cost	Very High-$2353
Gas Guzzler Tax	No
Greenhouse Gas Emissions (tons/yr.)	Average-7.1
Barrels of Oil Used per year	High-15.7

How the Competition Rates

Competitors	Rating	Pg.
Buick Enclave	4	82
Chevrolet Suburban	2	103
Volvo XC90	8	240

Price Range

	Retail	Markup
GLS350	$67,050	8%
GLS450	$68,700	8%
GLS550	$93,850	8%
GLS63 AMG	$124,100	8%

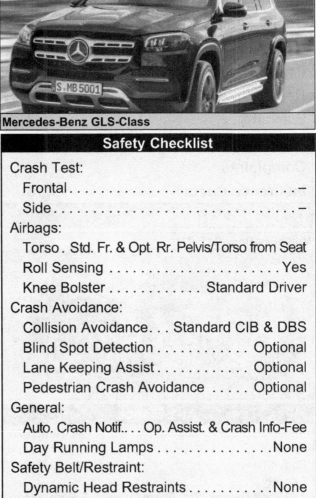

Mercedes-Benz GLS-Class

Safety Checklist

Crash Test:
  Frontal . . . . –
  Side . . . . –
Airbags:
  Torso . Std. Fr. & Opt. Rr. Pelvis/Torso from Seat
  Roll Sensing . . . . Yes
  Knee Bolster . . . . Standard Driver
Crash Avoidance:
  Collision Avoidance. . . Standard CIB & DBS
  Blind Spot Detection . . . . Optional
  Lane Keeping Assist . . . . Optional
  Pedestrian Crash Avoidance . . . . . Optional
General:
  Auto. Crash Notif.. . . Op. Assist. & Crash Info-Fee
  Day Running Lamps . . . . None
Safety Belt/Restraint:
  Dynamic Head Restraints . . . . None
  Adjustable Belt . . . . Standard Front

^Warning feature does not meet suggested government specifications.

Mercedes-Benz GLS-Class

Specifications

Drive	4WD
Engine	3.0-liter V6
Transmission	9-sp. Automatic
Tow Rating (lbs.)	High-7700
Head/Leg Room (in.)	Average-39.4/41.9
Interior Space (cu. ft.)	—
Cargo Space (cu. ft.)	Cramped-17.4
Wheelbase/Length (in.)	123.4/205.0

Mercedes-Benz S — Large

Mercedes-Benz S-Class

Ratings—10 Best, 1 Worst

Combo Crash Tests	—
Safety Features	10
Rollover	7
Preventive Maintenance	3
Repair Costs	1
Warranty	3
Fuel Economy	3
Complaints	7
Insurance Costs	1
OVERALL RATING	—

Mercedes-Benz S-Class

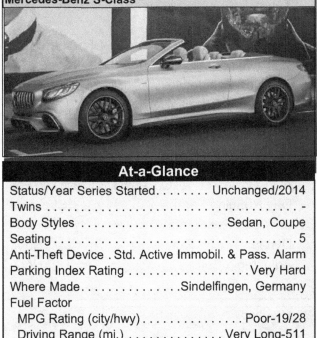

At-a-Glance

Status/Year Series Started Unchanged/2014
Twins . . . . -
Body Styles . . . . Sedan, Coupe
Seating 5
Anti-Theft Device . Std. Active Immobil. & Pass. Alarm
Parking Index Rating . . . . Very Hard
Where Made . . . . Sindelfingen, Germany
Fuel Factor
  MPG Rating (city/hwy) Poor-19/28
  Driving Range (mi.) . . . . Very Long-511
  Fuel Type . . . . Premium
  Annual Fuel Cost . . . . Very High-$2006
  Gas Guzzler Tax . . . . No
  Greenhouse Gas Emissions (tons/yr.) . . Average-6.7
  Barrels of Oil Used per year High-15.0

How the Competition Rates

Competitors	Rating	Pg.
Genesis G80		125
Lincoln Continental	6	174
Tesla Model S	10	216

Price Range

Price Range	Retail	Markup
S450	$89,900	8%
S560	$99,900	8%
S560 4Matic	$102,900	8%
S63 AMG	$147,500	8%

Safety Checklist

Crash Test:
  Frontal . . . . –
  Side . . . . –
Airbags:
  Torso . Std. Fr. & Opt. Rr. Pelvis/Torso from Seat
  Roll Sensing . . . . Yes
  Knee Bolster . . . . Standard Front
Crash Avoidance:
  Collision Avoidance. . . Standard CIB & DBS
  Blind Spot Detection . . . . Optional
  Lane Keeping Assist . . . . Optional
  Pedestrian Crash Avoidance . . . . . Optional
General:
  Auto. Crash Notif. . . . Op. Assist. & Crash Info-Fee
  Day Running Lamps . . . . None
Safety Belt/Restraint:
  Dynamic Head Restraints . . . Standard Front
  Adjustable Belt . . . . Standard Front

^Warning feature does not meet suggested government specifications.

Mercedes-Benz S-Class

Specifications

Drive . . . . RWD
Engine 3.0-liter V6
Transmission . . . . 9-sp. Automatic
Tow Rating (lbs.) . . . . –
Head/Leg Room (in.) Average-39.7/41.4
Interior Space (cu. ft.) Roomy-112
Cargo Space (cu. ft.) Cramped-16.3
Wheelbase/Length (in.) 124.6/206.5

Mini Hardtop

Ratings—10 Best, 1 Worst

Combo Crash Tests	4
Safety Features	4
Rollover	7
Preventive Maintenance	5
Repair Costs	4
Warranty	9
Fuel Economy	8
Complaints	7
Insurance Costs	5
OVERALL RATING	**6**

Mini Hardtop

At-a-Glance

Status/Year Series Started........ Unchanged/2016
Twins . . . . -
Body Styles . . . . .Sedan
Seating 4
Anti-Theft Device . Std. Pass. Immobil. & Active Alarm
Parking Index Rating . . . . .Very Easy
Where Made. Oxford, England
Fuel Factor
  MPG Rating (city/hwy). Good-27/35
  Driving Range (mi.) . . . . .Very Short-349
  Fuel Type. . . . . .Premium
  Annual Fuel Cost . . . . .Average-$1480
  Gas Guzzler Tax . . . . .No
  Greenhouse Gas Emissions (tons/yr.). Low-4.9
  Barrels of Oil Used per year Average-11.0

How the Competition Rates

Competitors	Rating	Pg.
Chevrolet Sonic	9	101
Honda Fit	9	135
Nissan Versa	1	206

Price Range	Retail	Markup
Base Hatchback	$20,950	5%
S Hatchback	$25,400	9%
S Convertible	$29,600	9%
John Cooper Works HB	$30,900	12%

Safety Checklist

Crash Test:
  Frontal. . . . . Average
  Side. . . . . .Very Poor
Airbags:
  Torso. . . . . Std. Fr. Torso from Seat
  Roll Sensing . . . . .Yes
  Knee Bolster . . . . Standard Front
Crash Avoidance:
  Collision Avoidance. . . Optional CIB & DBS*
  Blind Spot Detection . . . . .None
  Lane Keeping Assist. . . . . .None
  Pedestrian Crash Avoidance . . . . .None
General:
  Auto. Crash Notif.. . . Op. Assist. & Crash Info-Fee
  Day Running Lamps . . . . .Standard
Safety Belt/Restraint:
  Dynamic Head Restraints . . . . .None
  Adjustable Belt . . . . .None

^Warning feature does not meet suggested government specifications.

Mini Hardtop

Specifications

Drive. . . . . FWD
Engine 1.5-liter I3
Transmission . . . . .6-sp. Automatic
Tow Rating (lbs.) . . . . –
Head/Leg Room (in.) Average-39.9/41.4
Interior Space (cu. ft.). . . . . Very Cramped-84
Cargo Space (cu. ft.) . . . . .Very Cramped-9.0
Wheelbase/Length (in.) 101.1/157.4

Mitsubishi Mirage — Subcompact

Ratings—10 Best, 1 Worst

Combo Crash Tests	2
Safety Features	1
Rollover	4
Preventive Maintenance	8
Repair Costs	7
Warranty	10
Fuel Economy	9
Complaints	4
Insurance Costs	1
OVERALL RATING	**3**

Mitsubishi Mirage

Mitsubishi Mirage

At-a-Glance

Status/Year Series Started........ Unchanged/2014
Twins .... -
Body Styles .... Hatchback
Seating 5
Anti-Theft Device . Std. Pass. Immobil. & Active Alarm
Parking Index Rating .... Very Easy
Where Made............. Laem Chabang, Thailand
Fuel Factor
  MPG Rating (city/hwy) .... Very Good-37/43
  Driving Range (mi.) .... Very Short-363
  Fuel Type........................... Regular
  Annual Fuel Cost .... Very Low-$931
  Gas Guzzler Tax .... No
  Greenhouse Gas Emissions (tons/yr.). Very Low-3.7
  Barrels of Oil Used per year Low-8.5

How the Competition Rates

Competitors	Rating	Pg.
Chevrolet Sonic	9	101
Honda Fit	9	135
Nissan Versa	1	206

Price Range

Price Range	Retail	Markup
ES MT	$13,395	2%
ES AT	$14,595	2%
SE AT	$16,095	2%
GT AT	$16,595	2%

Safety Checklist

Crash Test:
  Frontal......................... Poor
  Side........................ Very Poor
Airbags:
  Torso...... Std. Fr. Pelvis/Torso from Seat
  Roll Sensing .... Yes
  Knee Bolster .... Standard Driver
Crash Avoidance:
  Collision Avoidance............... None
  Blind Spot Detection .... None
  Lane Keeping Assist.............. None
  Pedestrian Crash Avoidance .... None
General:
  Auto. Crash Notification .... None
  Day Running Lamps .... None
Safety Belt/Restraint:
  Dynamic Head Restraints.......... None
  Adjustable Belt........... Standard Front

^Warning feature does not meet suggested government specifications.

Specifications

Drive................................ FWD
Engine 1.2-liter I3
Transmission .... CVT
Tow Rating (lbs.) .... –
Head/Leg Room (in.) Cramped-39.1/41.7
Interior Space (cu. ft.)........ Very Cramped-86.1
Cargo Space (cu. ft.) Average-17.2
Wheelbase/Length (in.) 96.5/148.8

Mitsubishi Outlander

Ratings—10 Best, 1 Worst

Combo Crash Tests	5
Safety Features	5
Rollover	4
Preventive Maintenance	4
Repair Costs	8
Warranty	10
Fuel Economy	6
Complaints	3
Insurance Costs	1
OVERALL RATING	**4**

Mitsubishi Outlander

Mitsubishi Outlander

At-a-Glance

Status/Year Series Started	All-New/2020
Twins	-
Body Styles	SUV
Seating	7
Anti-Theft Device	Std. Pass. Immobil. & Active Alarm
Parking Index Rating	Easy
Where Made	Okazaki, Japan
Fuel Factor	
MPG Rating (city/hwy)	Average-24/30
Driving Range (mi.)	Average-411
Fuel Type	Regular
Annual Fuel Cost	Low-$1393
Gas Guzzler Tax	No
Greenhouse Gas Emissions (tons/yr.)	Low-5.5
Barrels of Oil Used per year	Average-12.2

How the Competition Rates

Competitors	Rating	Pg.
Ford Edge	9	115
Kia Sorento	6	160
Nissan Rogue	3	203

Price Range	Retail	Markup
ES FWD	$23,495	3%
SE FWD	$24,495	3%
SEL AWD	$27,495	3%
GT AWD	$31,695	3%

Safety Checklist

Crash Test:
  Frontal . . . . –
  Side . . . . –
Airbags:
  Torso . . . . . . Std. Fr. Pelvis/Torso from Seat
  Roll Sensing . . . . Yes
  Knee Bolster . . . . Standard Driver
Crash Avoidance:
  Collision Avoidance . . . . Optional CIB & DBS
  Blind Spot Detection . . . . Optional
  Lane Keeping Assist . . . . Warning Only Opt.
  Pedestrian Crash Avoidance . . . . . Optional
General:
  Auto. Crash Notification . . . . None
  Day Running Lamps . . . . Standard
Safety Belt/Restraint:
  Dynamic Head Restraints . . . . None
  Adjustable Belt . . . . Standard Front

^Warning feature does not meet suggested government specifications.

Mitsubishi Outlander

Specifications

Drive	4WD
Engine	2.4-liter I4
Transmission	CVT
Tow Rating (lbs.)	Very Low-1500
Head/Leg Room (in.)	Average-40.6/40.5
Interior Space (cu. ft.)	Very Roomy-128.2
Cargo Space (cu. ft.)	Very Cramped-10.3
Wheelbase/Length (in.)	105.0/185.0

Ratings—10 Best, 1 Worst

Combo Crash Tests	4
Safety Features	2
Rollover	2
Preventive Maintenance	7
Repair Costs	5
Warranty	10
Fuel Economy	5
Complaints	7
Insurance Costs	1
OVERALL RATING	**3**

Mitsubishi Outlander Sport

At-a-Glance

Status/Year Series Started. All-New/2020
Twins . . . . -
Body Styles . . . . SUV
Seating 5
Anti-Theft Device . Std. Pass. Immobil. & Active Alarm
Parking Index Rating . . . . .Very Easy
Where Made. . . . . Okazaki, Japan
Fuel Factor
  MPG Rating (city/hwy) Average-24/30
  Driving Range (mi.) Average-411
  Fuel Type. . . . . .Regular
  Annual Fuel Cost . . . . Low-$1393
  Gas Guzzler Tax . . . . .No
  Greenhouse Gas Emissions (tons/yr.) Low-5.5
  Barrels of Oil Used per year Average-12.2

How the Competition Rates

Competitors	Rating	Pg.
Acura RDX	9	63
Hyundai Santa Fe		143
Jeep Cherokee	5	151

Price Range

	Retail	Markup
ES 2.0L FWD MT	$19,795	3%
ES 2.0L AWD AT	$22,495	3%
SEL 2.4L FWD AT	$24,195	3%
GT 2.4L 4WD	$27,695	3%

Mitsubishi Outlander Sport

Safety Checklist

Crash Test:
  Frontal. . . . . –
  Side . . . . –
Airbags:
  Torso. . . . . . . Std. Fr. Pelvis/Torso from Seat
  Roll Sensing . . . . .Yes
  Knee Bolster . . . . Standard Driver
Crash Avoidance:
  Collision Avoidance. . . .Optional CIB & DBS
  Blind Spot Detection . . . . Optional
  Lane Keeping Assist . . . . Warning Only Opt.
  Pedestrian Crash Avoidance . . . . . Optional
General:
  Auto. Crash Notification . . . . .None
  Day Running Lamps . . . . Optional
Safety Belt/Restraint:
  Dynamic Head Restraints . . . . .None
  Adjustable Belt . . . . Standard Front

^Warning feature does not meet suggested government specifications.

Mitsubishi Outlander Sport

Specifications

Drive. . . . . FWD
Engine 2.0-liter I4
Transmission . . . . .CVT
Tow Rating (lbs.) . . . . –
Head/Leg Room (in.) Average-39.4/41.6
Interior Space (cu. ft.). Average-97.5
Cargo Space (cu. ft.) Roomy-21.7
Wheelbase/Length (in.) 105.1/169.1

Nissan Altima | Intermediate

Ratings—10 Best, 1 Worst

Combo Crash Tests	—
Safety Features	3
Rollover	8
Preventive Maintenance	4
Repair Costs	9
Warranty	1
Fuel Economy	8
Complaints	5
Insurance Costs	1
OVERALL RATING	**—**

Nissan Altima

Nissan Altima

At-a-Glance

Status/Year Series Started........ Unchanged/2019
Twins .... -
Body Styles .... Sedan, Coupe
Seating 5
Anti-Theft Device ...... Std. Pass. Immobil. & Alarm
Parking Index Rating .... Average
Where Made............ Smyrna, TN / Canton, MS
Fuel Factor
  MPG Rating (city/hwy)............... Good-28/39
  Driving Range (mi.) .... Very Long-518
  Fuel Type............................Regular
  Annual Fuel Cost .... Very Low-$1146
  Gas Guzzler Tax ....No
  Greenhouse Gas Emissions (tons/yr.). Very Low-4.6
  Barrels of Oil Used per year Low-10.3

How the Competition Rates

Competitors	Rating	Pg.
Chevrolet Malibu	9	99
Ford Fusion	4	121
Kia Optima	9	157

Price Range

Price Range	Retail	Markup
S 2.5L	$23,750	7%
SV 2.5L	$27,930	7%
SR 2.5L	$26,450	7%
Platinum 2.0L AWD	$33,130	7%

Safety Checklist

Crash Test:
  Frontal............................... −
  Side................................ −
Airbags:
  Torso...... Std. Fr. Pelvis/Torso from Seat
  Roll Sensing ....Yes
  Knee Bolster ....None
Crash Avoidance:
  Collision Avoidance... Standard CIB & DBS
  Blind Spot Detection .... Optional
  Lane Keeping Assist............ Optional
  Pedestrian Crash Avoidance ....None
General:
  Auto. Crash Notification ....Op. Assist.-Fee
  Day Running Lamps .... Optional
Safety Belt/Restraint:
  Dynamic Head Restraints...........None
  Adjustable Belt............Standard Front

^Warning feature does not meet suggested government specifications.

Nissan Altima

Specifications

Drive................................. FWD
Engine 2.5-liter I4
Transmission ....CVT
Tow Rating (lbs.) .... −
Head/Leg Room (in.) ...... Very Roomy-39.2/43.8
Interior Space (cu. ft.)............ Average-100.8
Cargo Space (cu. ft.) Cramped-15.4
Wheelbase/Length (in.) 111.2/192.9

Nissan Armada — Large SUV

Ratings—10 Best, 1 Worst

Combo Crash Tests	—
Safety Features	7
Rollover	2
Preventive Maintenance	3
Repair Costs	5
Warranty	1
Fuel Economy	1
Complaints	7
Insurance Costs	10
OVERALL RATING	—

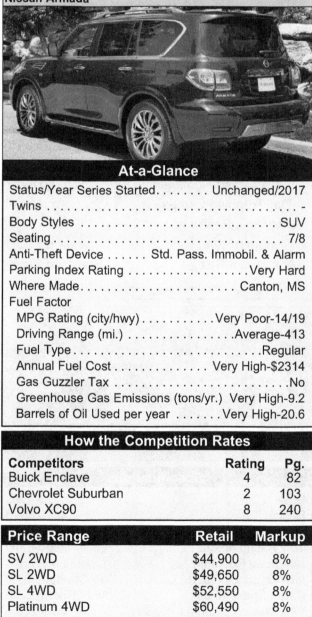
Nissan Armada

At-a-Glance

Status/Year Series Started........ Unchanged/2017
Twins .... -
Body Styles .... SUV
Seating.................................... 7/8
Anti-Theft Device ...... Std. Pass. Immobil. & Alarm
Parking Index Rating .... Very Hard
Where Made...................... Canton, MS
Fuel Factor
  MPG Rating (city/hwy)........... Very Poor-14/19
  Driving Range (mi.) Average-413
  Fuel Type.......................... Regular
  Annual Fuel Cost .... Very High-$2314
  Gas Guzzler Tax .... No
  Greenhouse Gas Emissions (tons/yr.) Very High-9.2
  Barrels of Oil Used per year .... Very High-20.6

How the Competition Rates

Competitors	Rating	Pg.
Buick Enclave	4	82
Chevrolet Suburban	2	103
Volvo XC90	8	240

Price Range

	Retail	Markup
SV 2WD	$44,900	8%
SL 2WD	$49,650	8%
SL 4WD	$52,550	8%
Platinum 4WD	$60,490	8%

Nissan Armada

Safety Checklist

Crash Test:
  Frontal............................. –
  Side............................... –
Airbags:
  Torso...... Std. Fr. Pelvis/Torso from Seat
  Roll Sensing .... Yes
  Knee Bolster .... None
Crash Avoidance:
  Collision Avoidance.... Optional CIB & DBS
  Blind Spot Detection .... Optional
  Lane Keeping Assist.... Warning Only Opt.
  Pedestrian Crash Avoidance .... None
General:
  Auto. Crash Notification ....Op. Assist.-Fee
  Day Running Lamps .... Standard
Safety Belt/Restraint:
  Dynamic Head Restraints ... Standard Front
  Adjustable Belt.... Standard Front and Rear

^Warning feature does not meet suggested government specifications.

Nissan Armada

Specifications

Drive................................. RWD
Engine 5.6-liter V8
Transmission .... 7-sp. Automatic
Tow Rating (lbs.) .... Very High-8500
Head/Leg Room (in.) Roomy-40.9/41.9
Interior Space (cu. ft.)........ Very Roomy-154.5
Cargo Space (cu. ft.) Cramped-16.2
Wheelbase/Length (in.) 121.1/208.9

Ratings—10 Best, 1 Worst

Combo Crash Tests	4
Safety Features	2
Rollover	2
Preventive Maintenance	3
Repair Costs	7
Warranty	1
Fuel Economy	1
Complaints	6
Insurance Costs	5
OVERALL RATING	1

Nissan Frontier

Nissan Frontier

Safety Checklist

Crash Test:
Frontal . . . . Very Poor
Side . . . . Very Good
Airbags:
Torso . . . . . . Std. Fr. Pelvis/Torso from Seat
Roll Sensing . . . . Yes
Knee Bolster . . . . None
Crash Avoidance:
Collision Avoidance . . . . None
Blind Spot Detection . . . . None
Lane Keeping Assist . . . . None
Pedestrian Crash Avoidance . . . . None
General:
Auto. Crash Notification . . . . None
Day Running Lamps . . . . None
Safety Belt/Restraint:
Dynamic Head Restraints . . . Standard Front
Adjustable Belt . . . . Standard Front

^Warning feature does not meet suggested government specifications.

At-a-Glance

Status/Year Series Started Unchanged/2005
Twins . . . . -
Body Styles . . . . Pickup
Seating 5
Anti-Theft Device . . . . . . Std. Pass. Immobil. & Alarm
Parking Index Rating . . . . .Very Hard
Where Made . . . . Canton, MS
Fuel Factor
MPG Rating (city/hwy) . . . . .Very Poor-15/21
Driving Range (mi.) . . . . .Very Short-363
Fuel Type . . . . .Regular
Annual Fuel Cost . . . . Very High-$2135
Gas Guzzler Tax . . . . .No
Greenhouse Gas Emissions (tons/yr.)Very High-10.5
Barrels of Oil Used per year . . . . . . .Very High-19.4

How the Competition Rates

Competitors	Rating	Pg.
Chevrolet Colorado	2	95
Ford Ranger		
Toyota Tacoma	1	230

Price Range

Price Range	Retail	Markup
S King Cab I4 2WD MT	$18,390	3%
SV Crew Cab V6 2WD AT	$25,950	4%
PRO-4X Crew Cab 4WD AT	$33,390	6%
SL Crew Cab 4WD AT	$35,550	7%

Nissan Frontier

Specifications

Drive 4WD
Engine 4.0-liter V6
Transmission . . . . .5-sp. Automatic
Tow Rating (lbs.) Average-6300
Head/Leg Room (in.) Average-39.7/42.4
Interior Space (cu. ft.) . . . . .Very Cramped-87.7
Cargo Space (cu. ft.) . . . . Very Roomy-33.5
Wheelbase/Length (in.) 125.9/205.5

Nissan Leaf

Compact

Ratings—10 Best, 1 Worst	
Combo Crash Tests	—
Safety Features	7
Rollover	7
Preventive Maintenance	8
Repair Costs	10
Warranty	1
Fuel Economy	10
Complaints	9
Insurance Costs	10
OVERALL RATING	**—**

Nissan Leaf

Nissan Leaf

At-a-Glance

```
Status/Year Series Started........ Unchanged/2018
Twins ....................................... -
Body Styles ........................ Hatchback
Seating ....................................... 5
Anti-Theft Device ...... Std. Pass. Immobil. & Alarm
Parking Index Rating .................. Very Easy
Where Made....................... Smyrna, TN
Fuel Factor
  MPG Rating (city/hwy)........ Very Good-126/101
  Driving Range (mi.) ............. Very Short-150
  Fuel Type........................... Electricity
  Annual Fuel Cost ............... Very Low-$600
  Gas Guzzler Tax ......................... No
  Greenhouse Gas Emissions (tons/yr.). Very Low-0.0
  Barrels of Oil Used per year ........ Very Low-0.0
```

How the Competition Rates

Competitors	Rating	Pg.
BMW i3		77
Chevrolet Bolt		93

Price Range	Retail	Markup
S	$30,680	6%
SV	$34,200	6%
SL	$36,790	6%

Safety Checklist

```
Crash Test:
  Frontal............................. −
  Side................................ −
Airbags:
  Torso...... Std. Fr. Pelvis/Torso from Seat
  Roll Sensing ....................... No
  Knee Bolster ..................... None
Crash Avoidance:
  Collision Avoidance... Standard CIB & DBS
  Blind Spot Detection ............ Optional
  Lane Keeping Assist ............ Optional
  Pedestrian Crash Avoidance ..... Optional
General:
  Auto. Crash Notification ....Op. Assist.-Fee
  Day Running Lamps .............. None
Safety Belt/Restraint:
  Dynamic Head Restraints........... None
  Adjustable Belt ........... Standard Front
```

^Warning feature does not meet suggested government specifications.

Nissan Leaf

Specifications

```
Drive................................. FWD
Engine ........................... Electric
Transmission ................. 1-sp. Automatic
Tow Rating (lbs.) ..................... −
Head/Leg Room (in.) .......... Roomy-41.2/42.1
Interior Space (cu. ft.)............ Cramped-92.4
Cargo Space (cu. ft.) .............. Roomy-24
Wheelbase/Length (in.) ........ 106.3/176.4
```

Nissan Maxima — Intermediate

Ratings—10 Best, 1 Worst

Combo Crash Tests	7
Safety Features	3
Rollover	9
Preventive Maintenance	6
Repair Costs	6
Warranty	1
Fuel Economy	5
Complaints	8
Insurance Costs	1
OVERALL RATING	**4**

Nissan Maxima

Nissan Maxima

At-a-Glance

Status/Year Series Started. . Apperance Change/2016
Twins . . . . -
Body Styles . . . . .Sedan
Seating 5
Anti-Theft Device . . . . . . Std. Pass. Immobil. & Alarm
Parking Index Rating . . . . Hard
Where Made. . . . . Smyrna, TN
Fuel Factor
  MPG Rating (city/hwy) Average-22/30
  Driving Range (mi.) Long-450
  Fuel Type. . . . . .Premium
  Annual Fuel Cost . . . . .High-$1782
  Gas Guzzler Tax . . . . .No
  Greenhouse Gas Emissions (tons/yr.). . Average-6.0
  Barrels of Oil Used per year High-13.2

How the Competition Rates

Competitors	Rating	Pg.
Hyundai Sonata	9	144
Mazda 6	5	183
Toyota Camry	8	221

Price Range

Price Range	Retail	Markup
S	$32,910	7%
SV	$34,890	7%
SR	$38,030	7%
Platinum	$40,340	7%

Safety Checklist

Crash Test:
  Frontal . . . . .Good
  Side. . . . . Average
Airbags:
  Torso . . . . . . Std. Fr. Pelvis/Torso from Seat
  Roll Sensing . . . . .Yes
  Knee Bolster .None
Crash Avoidance:
  Collision Avoidance. . . .Optional CIB & DBS
  Blind Spot Detection . . . . Optional
  Lane Keeping Assist. . . . . .None
  Pedestrian Crash Avoidance . . . . .None
General:
  Auto. Crash Notification . . . .Op. Assist.-Fee
  Day Running Lamps . . . . .Standard
Safety Belt/Restraint:
  Dynamic Head Restraints . . . . .None
  Adjustable Belt . . . . .Standard Front

^Warning feature does not meet suggested government specifications.

Nissan Maxima

Specifications

Drive. . . . . FWD
Engine 3.5-liter V6
Transmission . . . . .CVT
Tow Rating (lbs.) . . . . –
Head/Leg Room (in.) . . . . .Very Roomy-39.4/45
Interior Space (cu. ft.). Average-98.6
Cargo Space (cu. ft.) Cramped-14.3
Wheelbase/Length (in.) 109.3/192.8

Nissan Murano

Ratings—10 Best, 1 Worst

Combo Crash Tests	—
Safety Features	4
Rollover	4
Preventive Maintenance	8
Repair Costs	3
Warranty	1
Fuel Economy	4
Complaints	8
Insurance Costs	10
OVERALL RATING	**—**

Nissan Murano

Nissan Murano

At-a-Glance

Status/Year Series Started........ Unchanged/2015
Twins .... -
Body Styles .... SUV
Seating 5
Anti-Theft Device ...... Std. Pass. Immobil. & Alarm
Parking Index Rating .... Hard
Where Made...................... Canton, MS
Fuel Factor
  MPG Rating (city/hwy)............. Poor-21/28
  Driving Range (mi.) Long-450
  Fuel Type........................... Regular
  Annual Fuel Cost .... Average-$1553
  Gas Guzzler Tax .... No
  Greenhouse Gas Emissions (tons/yr.)..... High-7.5
  Barrels of Oil Used per year High-13.7

How the Competition Rates

Competitors	Rating	Pg.
Cadillac XT5	3	90
Ford Edge	9	115
Jeep Grand Cherokee	4	153

Price Range

Price Range	Retail	Markup
S FWD	$29,740	6%
SV FWD	$32,800	7%
SL AWD	$38,730	7%
Platinum AWD	$40,780	7%

Safety Checklist

Crash Test:
  Frontal............................. −
  Side............................... −
Airbags:
  Torso...... Std. Fr. Pelvis/Torso from Seat
  Roll Sensing .... Yes
  Knee Bolster .... Standard Driver
Crash Avoidance:
  Collision Avoidance..... Optional CIB & DBS
  Blind Spot Detection .... Optional
  Lane Keeping Assist .... None
  Pedestrian Crash Avoidance .... None
General:
  Auto. Crash Notification .... Op. Assist.-Fee
  Day Running Lamps .... Standard
Safety Belt/Restraint:
  Dynamic Head Restraints .... None
  Adjustable Belt .... Standard Front

^Warning feature does not meet suggested government specifications.

Nissan Murano

Specifications

Drive................................. AWD
Engine 3.5-liter V6
Transmission .... CVT
Tow Rating (lbs.) .... Very Low-1500
Head/Leg Room (in.) Cramped-39.9/40.5
Interior Space (cu. ft.)........... Roomy-108.1
Cargo Space (cu. ft.) .... Very Roomy-39.6
Wheelbase/Length (in.) 111.2/192.4

Nissan Pathfinder

Medium SUV

Nissan Pathfinder

Ratings—10 Best, 1 Worst

Combo Crash Tests	—
Safety Features	3
Rollover	3
Preventive Maintenance	1
Repair Costs	4
Warranty	1
Fuel Economy	3
Complaints	3
Insurance Costs	10
OVERALL RATING	**—**

Nissan Pathfinder

At-a-Glance

Status/Year Series Started	Unchanged/2013
Twins	Infiniti QX60
Body Styles	SUV
Seating	7
Anti-Theft Device	Std. Pass. Immobil. & Alarm
Parking Index Rating	Hard
Where Made	Smyrna, TN
Fuel Factor	
MPG Rating (city/hwy)	Poor-19/26
Driving Range (mi.)	Average-422
Fuel Type	Regular
Annual Fuel Cost	High-$1700
Gas Guzzler Tax	No
Greenhouse Gas Emissions (tons/yr.)	High-8.2
Barrels of Oil Used per year	High-15.0

How the Competition Rates

Competitors	Rating	Pg.
Dodge Durango	2	113
Ford Explorer	3	118
GMC Acadia	2	126

Price Range

	Retail	Markup
S FWD	$29,990	8%
SV FWD	$32,680	8%
SL 4WD	$37,390	8%
Platinum 4WD	$43,560	8%

Safety Checklist

Crash Test:
  Frontal . . . . –
  Side . . . . –
Airbags:
  Torso . . . . . . Std. Fr. Pelvis/Torso from Seat
  Roll Sensing . . . . Yes
  Knee Bolster . . . . .None
Crash Avoidance:
  Collision Avoidance. . . .Optional CIB & DBS
  Blind Spot Detection . . . . Optional
  Lane Keeping Assist . . . . .None
  Pedestrian Crash Avoidance . . . . .None
General:
  Auto. Crash Notification . . . .Op. Assist.-Fee
  Day Running Lamps . . . . .Standard
Safety Belt/Restraint:
  Dynamic Head Restraints . . . . .None
  Adjustable Belt . . . . . .Standard Front & Rear

^Warning feature does not meet suggested government specifications.

Nissan Pathfinder

Specifications

Drive	4WD
Engine	3.5-liter V6
Transmission	CVT
Tow Rating (lbs.)	Low-5000
Head/Leg Room (in.)	Roomy-41.1/42.3
Interior Space (cu. ft.)	Very Roomy-157.8
Cargo Space (cu. ft.)	Cramped-16
Wheelbase/Length (in.)	114.2/197.2

202

Nissan Rogue — Medium SUV

Ratings—10 Best, 1 Worst

Combo Crash Tests	1
Safety Features	5
Rollover	4
Preventive Maintenance	3
Repair Costs	4
Warranty	1
Fuel Economy	7
Complaints	10
Insurance Costs	10
OVERALL RATING	**3**

Nissan Rogue

Nissan Rogue

At-a-Glance

Status/Year Series Started........ Unchanged/2014
Twins . . . . -
Body Styles . . . . SUV
Seating 5/7
Anti-Theft Device . . . . . . Std. Pass. Immobil. & Alarm
Parking Index Rating . . . . Average
Where Made. . . . . Smyrna, TN
Fuel Factor
  MPG Rating (city/hwy) Good-25/32
  Driving Range (mi.) Average-402
  Fuel Type. . . . . .Regular
  Annual Fuel Cost . . . . Low-$1325
  Gas Guzzler Tax . . . . .No
  Greenhouse Gas Emissions (tons/yr.) . . Average-6.4
  Barrels of Oil Used per year Average-11.8

How the Competition Rates

Competitors	Rating	Pg.
Kia Sorento	6	160
Mazda CX-5	4	180
Subaru Outback	8	214

Price Range

	Retail	Markup
S FWD	$23,820	6%
SV FWD	$25,240	6%
SV AWD	$26,590	6%
SL AWD	$31,310	6%

Safety Checklist

Crash Test:
  Frontal . . . . Very Poor
  Side . . . . Very Poor
Airbags:
  Torso . . . . . . Std. Fr. Pelvis/Torso from Seat
  Roll Sensing . . . . .Yes
  Knee Bolster .None
Crash Avoidance:
  Collision Avoidance. . . .Optional CIB & DBS
  Blind Spot Detection . . . . Optional
  Lane Keeping Assist . . . . Warning Only Opt.
  Pedestrian Crash Avoidance . . . . . Optional
General:
  Auto. Crash Notification . . . .Op. Assist.-Fee
  Day Running Lamps . . . . .Standard
Safety Belt/Restraint:
  Dynamic Head Restraints . . . . .None
  Adjustable Belt . . . . .Standard Front

^Warning feature does not meet suggested government specifications.

Nissan Rogue

Specifications

Drive. . . . . AWD
Engine 2.5-liter I4
Transmission . . . . .CVT
Tow Rating (lbs.) . . . . Very Low-1000
Head/Leg Room (in.) . . . . .Very Roomy-41.6/43
Interior Space (cu. ft.). Roomy-105.8
Cargo Space (cu. ft.) . . . . .Very Cramped-9.4
Wheelbase/Length (in.) 106.5/182.3

203

Nissan Sentra

Compact

Nissan Sentra

Ratings—10 Best, 1 Worst

Combo Crash Tests	2
Safety Features	2
Rollover	6
Preventive Maintenance	8
Repair Costs	9
Warranty	1
Fuel Economy	9
Complaints	9
Insurance Costs	5
OVERALL RATING	**5**

Nissan Sentra

At-a-Glance

Status/Year Series Started........ Unchanged/2013
Twins .... -
Body Styles ....Sedan
Seating 5
Anti-Theft Device ...... Std. Pass. Immobil. & Alarm
Parking Index Rating .... Easy
Where Made Aguascalientes, Mexico / Kyushu, Japan
Fuel Factor
  MPG Rating (city/hwy)........... Very Good-30/39
  Driving Range (mi.) Long-442
  Fuel Type.............................Regular
  Annual Fuel Cost ....Very Low-$1098
  Gas Guzzler Tax ....No
  Greenhouse Gas Emissions (tons/yr.)..... Low-5.3
  Barrels of Oil Used per year Low-9.7

How the Competition Rates

Competitors	Rating	Pg.
Honda Civic	10	133
Toyota Corolla	7	222
Volkswagen Jetta		234

Price Range	Retail	Markup
S MT	$16,990	3%
SV	$18,840	5%
SR	$19,990	5%
SL	$21,500	5%

Safety Checklist

Crash Test:
  Frontal .... Very Poor
  Side .... Average
Airbags:
  Torso...... Std. Fr. Pelvis/Torso from Seat
  Roll Sensing ....Yes
  Knee Bolster ....None
Crash Avoidance:
  Collision Avoidance.... Optional CIB & DBS
  Blind Spot Detection .... Optional
  Lane Keeping Assist...............None
  Pedestrian Crash Avoidance ....None
General:
  Auto. Crash Notification ....Op. Assist.-Fee
  Day Running Lamps ....None
Safety Belt/Restraint:
  Dynamic Head Restraints ....None
  Adjustable Belt............Standard Front

^Warning feature does not meet suggested government specifications.

Nissan Sentra

Specifications

Drive...................................FWD
Engine 2.0-liter I4
Transmission ....CVT
Tow Rating (lbs.) .... –
Head/Leg Room (in.) Average-39.4/42.5
Interior Space (cu. ft.)............Cramped-95.9
Cargo Space (cu. ft.) Cramped-15.1
Wheelbase/Length (in.) 106.3/182.1

Ratings—10 Best, 1 Worst

Combo Crash Tests	7
Safety Features	2
Rollover	2
Preventive Maintenance	2
Repair Costs	5
Warranty	1
Fuel Economy	1
Complaints	2
Insurance Costs	8
OVERALL RATING	**1**

Nissan Titan

At-a-Glance

Status/Year Series Started	Unchanged/2016
Twins	-
Body Styles	Pickup
Seating	6
Anti-Theft Device	Std. Pass. Immobil. & Alarm
Parking Index Rating	Very Hard
Where Made	Canton, MS

Fuel Factor

MPG Rating (city/hwy)	Very Poor-15/21
Driving Range (mi.)	Long-448
Fuel Type	Regular
Annual Fuel Cost	Very High-$2135
Gas Guzzler Tax	No
Greenhouse Gas Emissions (tons/yr.)	High-8.4
Barrels of Oil Used per year	Very High-18.3

How the Competition Rates

Competitors	Rating	Pg.
Chevrolet Silverado		100
Ford F-150	9	119
Toyota Tundra		231

Price Range

	Retail	Markup
S Crew Cab 2WD	$35,230	4%
SV Crew Cab 4WD	$41,400	6%
SL Crew Cab 4WD	$49,910	6%
Platinum Crew Cab 4WD	$55,850	6%

Nissan Titan

Safety Checklist

Crash Test:
Frontal . . . . Average
Side . . . . Very Good
Airbags:
Torso . . . . . . Std. Fr. Pelvis/Torso from Seat
Roll Sensing . . . . Yes
Knee Bolster . . . . None
Crash Avoidance:
Collision Avoidance . . . . None
Blind Spot Detection . . . . Optional
Lane Keeping Assist . . . . None
Pedestrian Crash Avoidance . . . . None
General:
Auto. Crash Notification . . . . Op. Assist.-Fee
Day Running Lamps . . . . Optional
Safety Belt/Restraint:
Dynamic Head Restraints . . . . None
Adjustable Belt . . . . Standard Front

^Warning feature does not meet suggested government specifications.

Nissan Titan

Specifications

Drive	4WD
Engine	5.0-liter V8
Transmission	6-sp. Automatic
Tow Rating (lbs.)	Very High-12038
Head/Leg Room (in.)	Roomy-41/41.8
Interior Space (cu. ft.)	–
Cargo Space (cu. ft.)	Very Roomy-58.1
Wheelbase/Length (in.)	151.6/242.7

Nissan Versa — Subcompact

Nissan Versa

Ratings—10 Best, 1 Worst

Rating	
Combo Crash Tests	—
Safety Features	1
Rollover	4
Preventive Maintenance	9
Repair Costs	9
Warranty	1
Fuel Economy	9
Complaints	—
Insurance Costs	1
OVERALL RATING	**—**

Nissan Versa

At-a-Glance

Status/Year Series Started	All-New/2020
Twins	-
Body Styles	Sedan, Hatchback
Seating	4
Anti-Theft Device	Std. Pass. Immobil. & Alarm
Parking Index Rating	Very Easy
Where Made	Aguascalientes, Mexico / Kyushu, Japan

Fuel Factor
MPG Rating (city/hwy)	Very Good-32/40
Driving Range (mi.)	Average-395
Fuel Type	Regular
Annual Fuel Cost	Very Low-$1045
Gas Guzzler Tax	No
Greenhouse Gas Emissions (tons/yr.)	Very Low-4.1
Barrels of Oil Used per year	Low-9.4

How the Competition Rates

Competitors	Rating	Pg.
Chevrolet Sonic	9	101
Honda Fit	9	135
Mitsubishi Mirage	3	193

Price Range

Price Range	Retail	Markup
S MT	$11,900	2%
S Plus	$14,130	3%
SV	$15,720	3%

Safety Checklist

Crash Test:
Frontal	−
Side	−

Airbags:
Torso	Std. Fr. Pelvis/Torso from Seat
Roll Sensing	Yes
Knee Bolster	None

Crash Avoidance:
Collision Avoidance	Standard CIB & DBS
Blind Spot Detection	Optional
Lane Keeping Assist	None
Pedestrian Crash Avoidance	Standard

General:
Auto. Crash Notification	None
Day Running Lamps	None

Safety Belt/Restraint:
Dynamic Head Restraints	None
Adjustable Belt	Standard Front

^Warning feature does not meet suggested government specifications.

Nissan Versa

Specifications

Drive	FWD
Engine	1.6-liter I4
Transmission	CVT
Tow Rating (lbs.)	−
Head/Leg Room (in.)	Very Roomy-39.5/44.5
Interior Space (cu. ft.)	Very Cramped-88.9
Cargo Space (cu. ft.)	Cramped-14.7
Wheelbase/Length (in.)	103.1/177.0

Porsche Macan | Medium SUV

Ratings—10 Best, 1 Worst

Combo Crash Tests	—
Safety Features	6
Rollover	5
Preventive Maintenance	3
Repair Costs	1
Warranty	7
Fuel Economy	2
Complaints	10
Insurance Costs	5
OVERALL RATING	**—**

Porsche Macan

Porsche Macan

At-a-Glance

Status/Year Series Started. . Apperance Change/2019
Twins . . . . -
Body Styles . . . . SUV
Seating 5
Anti-Theft Device . Std. Pass. Immobil. & Active Alarm
Parking Index Rating . . . . Hard
Where Made. . . . . Leipzig, Germany
Fuel Factor
  MPG Rating (city/hwy) . . . . Very Poor-17/23
  Driving Range (mi.) Short-381
  Fuel Type. . . . . Premium
  Annual Fuel Cost . . . . Very High-$2313
  Gas Guzzler Tax . . . . .No
  Greenhouse Gas Emissions (tons/yr.). . Average-6.6
  Barrels of Oil Used per year High-15.0

How the Competition Rates

Competitors	Rating	Pg.
BMW X5		79
Cadillac XT5	3	90
Lexus RX	4	173

Price Range	Retail	Markup
Base	$47,800	11%
S	$55,400	11%
GTS	$68,900	11%
Turbo	$77,200	11%

Safety Checklist

Crash Test:
  Frontal . . . . −
  Side . . . . −
Airbags:
  Torso . . . . . Std. Fr. & Rear Torso from Seat
  Roll Sensing . . . . .Yes
  Knee Bolster . . . . .Standard Front
Crash Avoidance:
  Collision Avoidance. . . Optional CIB & DBS*
  Blind Spot Detection . . . . Optional
  Lane Keeping Assist . . . . .Optional*
  Pedestrian Crash Avoidance . . . . .None
General:
  Auto. Crash Notification . . . . .None
  Day Running Lamps . . . . .Standard
Safety Belt/Restraint:
  Dynamic Head Restraints . . . . .None
  Adjustable Belt . . . . . .Standard Front & Rear

^Warning feature does not meet suggested government specifications.

Porsche Macan

Specifications

Drive. . . . . .AWD
Engine 3.0-liter V6
Transmission . . . . .7-sp. Automatic
Tow Rating (lbs.) Low-4400
Head/Leg Room (in.) . . . . −
Interior Space (cu. ft.). . . . . −
Cargo Space (cu. ft.) Average-17.7
Wheelbase/Length (in.) 110.5/184.9

Ratings—10 Best, 1 Worst

Combo Crash Tests	2
Safety Features	1
Rollover	2
Preventive Maintenance	8
Repair Costs	10
Warranty	2
Fuel Economy	1
Complaints	5
Insurance Costs	10
OVERALL RATING	**2**

Ram 1500

Ram 1500

At-a-Glance

Status/Year Series Started. Unchanged/2019
Twins . . . . -
Body Styles . . . . Pickup
Seating 6
Anti-Theft DeviceStd. Pass. Immobil. & Opt. Pass. Alarm
Parking Index Rating . . . . Very Hard
Where Made. . . . . Warren, MI / Saltillo, Mexico
Fuel Factor
  MPG Rating (city/hwy) . . . . Very Poor-17/22
  Driving Range (mi.) Short-494
  Fuel Type. . . . . Regular
  Annual Fuel Cost . . . . High-$1941
  Gas Guzzler Tax . . . . No
  Greenhouse Gas Emissions (tons/yr.) High-7.8
  Barrels of Oil Used per year . . . . Very High-17.3

How the Competition Rates

Competitors	Rating	Pg.
Chevrolet Silverado		100
Ford F-150	9	119
Toyota Tundra		231

Price Range

	Retail	Markup
Tradesman Reg. Cab 2WD	$31,795	4%
Big Horn Quad Cab 2WD	$35,895	6%
Laramie Crew Cab 4WD	$46,295	9%
Limited Crew Cab 4WD	$56,895	10%

Safety Checklist

Crash Test:
  Frontal . . . . Very Poor
  Side. . . . . Poor
Airbags:
  Torso . . . . . . Std. Fr. Pelvis/Torso from Seat
  Roll Sensing . . . . Yes
  Knee Bolster .None
Crash Avoidance:
  Collision Avoidance. . . . Optional CIB & DBS
  Blind Spot Detection . . . . Optional
  Lane Keeping Assist . . . . Optional
  Pedestrian Crash Avoidance . . . . . Optional
General:
  Auto. Crash Notification . . . . .None
  Day Running Lamps . . . . .Standard
Safety Belt/Restraint:
  Dynamic Head Restraints . . . . .None
  Adjustable Belt . . . . .Standard Front

^Warning feature does not meet suggested government specifications.

Ram 1500

Specifications

Drive. 4WD
Engine 5.7-liter V8
Transmission . . . . .8-sp. Automatic
Tow Rating (lbs.) . . . . .Very High-7520
Head/Leg Room (in.) Average-40.9/40.9
Interior Space (cu. ft.). –
Cargo Space (cu. ft.) . . . . Very Roomy-61.5
Wheelbase/Length (in.) 140.5/228.9

Subaru Ascent — Large SUV

Ratings—10 Best, 1 Worst

Combo Crash Tests	—
Safety Features	9
Rollover	4
Preventive Maintenance	3
Repair Costs	9
Warranty	3
Fuel Economy	4
Complaints	3
Insurance Costs	5
OVERALL RATING	**—**

Subaru Ascent

At-a-Glance

Status/Year Series Started Unchanged/2019
Twins . . . . -
Body Styles . . . . SUV
Seating 7/8
Anti-Theft Device . Std. Pass. Immobil. & Active Alarm
Parking Index Rating . . . . Hard
Where Made . . . . .Lafayette, IN
Fuel Factor
  MPG Rating (city/hwy) Poor-21/27
  Driving Range (mi.) . . . . Very Short-443
  Fuel Type . . . . .Regular
  Annual Fuel Cost . . . . .Average-$1575
  Gas Guzzler Tax . . . . .No
  Greenhouse Gas Emissions (tons/yr.) High-6.4
  Barrels of Oil Used per year High-14.3

How the Competition Rates

Competitors	Rating	Pg.
Buick Enclave	4	82
Ford Flex		120
Volvo XC90	8	240

Price Range

	Retail	Markup
Base 8 Passenger	$31,995	7%
Premium 8 Passenger	$35,655	7%
Limited 7 Passenger	$38,995	7%
Touring 7 Passenger	$44,695	7%

Subaru Ascent

Safety Checklist

Crash Test:
  Frontal . . . . Very Good
  Side . . . . Very Good
Airbags:
  Torso . . . . . . Std. Fr. Pelvis/Torso from Seat
  Roll Sensing . . . . Yes
  Knee Bolster . . . . Standard Driver
Crash Avoidance:
  Collision Avoidance. . . Standard CIB & DBS
  Blind Spot Detection . . . . Optional
  Lane Keeping Assist . . . . .Standard
  Pedestrian Crash Avoidance . . . . . Optional
General:
  Auto. Crash Notification . . . .Op. Assist.-Fee
  Day Running Lamps . . . . .Standard
Safety Belt/Restraint:
  Dynamic Head Restraints . . . . .None
  Adjustable Belt . . . . Standard Front

^Warning feature does not meet suggested government specifications.

Subaru Ascent

Specifications

Drive . . . . AWD
Engine 2.4-liter I4
Transmission . . . . .8-sp. Automatic
Tow Rating (lbs.) . . . . —
Head/Leg Room (in.) Roomy-41.3/42.2
Interior Space (cu. ft.) . . . . Very Roomy-153.5
Cargo Space (cu. ft.) Average-17.8
Wheelbase/Length (in.) 113.8/196.8

Ratings—10 Best, 1 Worst

Combo Crash Tests	5
Safety Features	8
Rollover	4
Preventive Maintenance	4
Repair Costs	8
Warranty	3
Fuel Economy	7
Complaints	3
Insurance Costs	5
OVERALL RATING	**5**

Subaru Crosstrek

Subaru Crosstrek

At-a-Glance

Status/Year Series Started. Unchanged/2018
Twins . . . . -
Body Styles . . . . SUV
Seating 5
Anti-Theft Device . Std. Pass. Immobil. & Active Alarm
Parking Index Rating . . . . Easy
Where Made. Gunma, Japan
Fuel Factor
　MPG Rating (city/hwy) Good-27/33
　Driving Range (mi.) . . . . Very Long-488
　Fuel Type. . . . . Regular
　Annual Fuel Cost . . . . Low-$1250
　Gas Guzzler Tax . . . . .No
　Greenhouse Gas Emissions (tons/yr.). Low-5.0
　Barrels of Oil Used per year Average-11.4

How the Competition Rates

Competitors	Rating	Pg.
Chevrolet Traverse	4	105
Jeep Renegade	1	154
Toyota RAV4		227

Price Range

	Retail	Markup
Base MT	$21,795	5%
Premium MT	$22,595	5%
Premium AT	$23,595	6%
Limited	$26,295	6%

Subaru Crosstrek

Safety Checklist

Crash Test:
　Frontal. . . . . Average
　Side . . . . Average
Airbags:
　Torso. . . . . . . Std. Fr. Pelvis/Torso from Seat
　Roll Sensing . . . . .Yes
　Knee Bolster . . . . Standard Driver
Crash Avoidance:
　Collision Avoidance. . . .Optional CIB & DBS
　Blind Spot Detection . . . . Optional
　Lane Keeping Assist . . . . Optional
　Pedestrian Crash Avoidance . . . . . Optional
General:
　Auto. Crash Notification . . . .Op. Assist.-Fee
　Day Running Lamps . . . . .Standard
Safety Belt/Restraint:
　Dynamic Head Restraints . . . . .None
　Adjustable Belt . . . . .Standard Front

^Warning feature does not meet suggested government specifications.

Subaru Crosstrek

Specifications

Drive. . . . . AWD
Engine 2.0-liter I4
Transmission . . . . .CVT
Tow Rating (lbs.) . . . . –
Head/Leg Room (in.) Average-39/43.1
Interior Space (cu. ft.). Average-100.9
Cargo Space (cu. ft.) Average-20.8
Wheelbase/Length (in.) 104.9/175.8

Ratings—10 Best, 1 Worst

Combo Crash Tests	—
Safety Features	8
Rollover	3
Preventive Maintenance	3
Repair Costs	7
Warranty	3
Fuel Economy	6
Complaints	1
Insurance Costs	1
OVERALL RATING	**—**

Subaru Forester

Subaru Forester

At-a-Glance

Status/Year Series Started........ Unchanged/2019
Twins .... -
Body Styles .... SUV
Seating...................................... 5
Anti-Theft Device . Std. Pass. Immobil. & Active Alarm
Parking Index Rating .... Easy
Where Made...................... Lafayette, IN
Fuel Factor
  MPG Rating (city/hwy)............. Good-26/33
  Driving Range (mi.) .... Very Long-481
  Fuel Type............................Regular
  Annual Fuel Cost .... Low-$1263
  Gas Guzzler Tax ....No
  Greenhouse Gas Emissions (tons/yr.)..... Low-5.1
  Barrels of Oil Used per year Average-11.4

How the Competition Rates

Competitors	Rating	Pg.
Chevrolet Trax	10	106
Mazda CX-3	10	183
Mitsubishi Outlander Sport	3	195

Price Range	Retail	Markup
2.5i	$24,295	6%
2.5i Premium	$26,695	6%
2.5i Limited	$30,795	7%
2.5i XT Touring	$34,295	7%

Safety Checklist

Crash Test:
  Frontal............................... –
  Side................................. –
Airbags:
  Torso...... Std. Fr. Pelvis/Torso from Seat
  Roll Sensing ....Yes
  Knee Bolster .... Standard Driver
Crash Avoidance:
  Collision Avoidance. . . Standard CIB & DBS
  Blind Spot Detection .... Optional
  Lane Keeping Assist........... Optional
  Pedestrian Crash Avoidance ..... Optional
General:
  Auto. Crash Notification ....Op. Assist.-Fee
  Day Running Lamps ....Standard
Safety Belt/Restraint:
  Dynamic Head Restraints...........None
  Adjustable Belt............Standard Front

^Warning feature does not meet suggested government specifications.

Subaru Forester

Specifications

Drive................................... AWD
Engine 2.5-liter I4
Transmission ....CVT
Tow Rating (lbs.) .... Very Low-1500
Head/Leg Room (in.) ...... Very Roomy-41.2/43.3
Interior Space (cu. ft.)............ Roomy-111.9
Cargo Space (cu. ft.) .... Very Roomy-35.4
Wheelbase/Length (in.) 105.1/182.1

Subaru Impreza   Compact

Ratings—10 Best, 1 Worst

Combo Crash Tests	6
Safety Features	8
Rollover	9
Preventive Maintenance	4
Repair Costs	8
Warranty	3
Fuel Economy	4
Complaints	6
Insurance Costs	1
OVERALL RATING	**5**

Subaru Impreza

Subaru Impreza

At-a-Glance

Status/Year Series Started........ Unchanged/2017
Twins .... -
Body Styles .... Sedan, Hatchback
Seating 5
Anti-Theft Device . Std. Pass. Immobil. & Active Alarm
Parking Index Rating .... Easy
Where Made................... Gunma, Japan
Fuel Factor
  MPG Rating (city/hwy)............... Poor-20/27
  Driving Range (mi.) Average-419
  Fuel Type...........................Regular
  Annual Fuel Cost ....Average-$1623
  Gas Guzzler Tax ....No
  Greenhouse Gas Emissions (tons/yr.).. Average-6.5
  Barrels of Oil Used per year High-15.0

How the Competition Rates

Competitors	Rating	Pg.
Mazda 3	6	182
Toyota Corolla	7	222
Volkswagen Jetta		234

Price Range

Price Range	Retail	Markup
Base Sedan MT	$18,495	5%
Premium Wagon	$21,795	5%
Sport Sedan AT	$22,895	5%
Limited Wagon	$24,695	6%

Safety Checklist

Crash Test:
  Frontal.........................Good
  Side............................ Poor
Airbags:
  Torso...... Std. Fr. Pelvis/Torso from Seat
  Roll Sensing ....Yes
  Knee Bolster .... Standard Driver
Crash Avoidance:
  Collision Avoidance....Optional CIB & DBS
  Blind Spot Detection .... Optional
  Lane Keeping Assist........... Optional
  Pedestrian Crash Avoidance ..... Optional
General:
  Auto. Crash Notification ....Op. Assist.-Fee
  Day Running Lamps ....Standard
Safety Belt/Restraint:
  Dynamic Head Restraints ....None
  Adjustable Belt............ Standard Front

^Warning feature does not meet suggested government specifications.

Subaru Impreza

Specifications

Drive...................................AWD
Engine 2.0-liter I4
Transmission ....CVT
Tow Rating (lbs.) .... –
Head/Leg Room (in.) Roomy-39.8/43.1
Interior Space (cu. ft.)..............Average-100
Cargo Space (cu. ft.) ....Very Cramped-12.3
Wheelbase/Length (in.) 105.1/182.1

Subaru Legacy
Intermediate

Ratings—10 Best, 1 Worst	
Combo Crash Tests	—
Safety Features	7
Rollover	8
Preventive Maintenance	2
Repair Costs	9
Warranty	3
Fuel Economy	7
Complaints	—
Insurance Costs	1
OVERALL RATING	—

Subaru Legacy

Subaru Legacy

At-a-Glance

Status/Year Series Started	All-New/2020
Twins	-
Body Styles	Sedan
Seating	5
Anti-Theft Device	Std. Pass. Immobil. & Active Alarm
Parking Index Rating	Average
Where Made	Lafayette, IN
Fuel Factor	
MPG Rating (city/hwy)	Good-27/35
Driving Range (mi.)	Very Long-555
Fuel Type	Premium
Annual Fuel Cost	Average-$1480
Gas Guzzler Tax	No
Greenhouse Gas Emissions (tons/yr.)	Low-4.9
Barrels of Oil Used per year	Average-11.0

How the Competition Rates

Competitors	Rating	Pg.
Ford Fusion	4	121
Nissan Maxima	4	200
Toyota Camry	8	221

Price Range

	Retail	Markup
Base	$22,195	6%
Premium	$24,295	6%
Limited	$29,095	7%
3.6R Limited	$31,945	7%

Safety Checklist

Crash Test:
Frontal . . . . –
Side . . . . –
Airbags:
Torso . . . . . . Std. Fr. Pelvis/Torso from Seat
Roll Sensing . . . . Yes
Knee Bolster .None
Crash Avoidance:
Collision Avoidance. . . Standard CIB & DBS
Blind Spot Detection . . . . Optional
Lane Keeping Assist . . . . .Standard
Pedestrian Crash Avoidance . . . . .Standard
General:
Auto. Crash Notification . . . .Op. Assist.-Fee
Day Running Lamps . . . . .Standard
Safety Belt/Restraint:
Dynamic Head Restraints . . . . .None
Adjustable Belt . . . . Standard Front

^Warning feature does not meet suggested government specifications.

Subaru Legacy

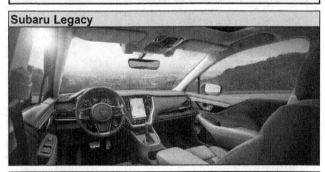

Specifications

Drive	AWD
Engine	2.5-liter I4
Transmission	8-sp. Automatic
Tow Rating (lbs.)	–
Head/Leg Room (in.)	Roomy-39.4/42.8
Interior Space (cu. ft.)	Roomy-105.5
Cargo Space (cu. ft.)	Cramped-15.1
Wheelbase/Length (in.)	108.3/190.6

213

Subaru Outback | Medium SUV

Ratings—10 Best, 1 Worst

Combo Crash Tests	—
Safety Features	7
Rollover	3
Preventive Maintenance	2
Repair Costs	9
Warranty	3
Fuel Economy	7
Complaints	—
Insurance Costs	5
OVERALL RATING	**—**

Subaru Outback

Subaru Outback

At-a-Glance

Status/Year Series Started. All-New/2020
Twins . . . . -
Body Styles . . . . Wagon
Seating 5
Anti-Theft Device . Std. Pass. Immobil. & Active Alarm
Parking Index Rating . . . . Easy
Where Made. .Lafayette, IN
Fuel Factor
  MPG Rating (city/hwy). Good-26/33
  Driving Range (mi.) . . . . Very Long-536
  Fuel Type. . . . . .Regular
  Annual Fuel Cost . . . . Low-$1263
  Gas Guzzler Tax . . . . .No
  Greenhouse Gas Emissions (tons/yr.). Low-5.1
  Barrels of Oil Used per year Average-11.4

How the Competition Rates

Competitors	Rating	Pg.
Kia Sorento	6	160
Toyota Highlander	8	224
Volkswagen Atlas	6	233

Price Range

Price Range	Retail	Markup
Base	$25,895	6%
Premium	$27,995	6%
Limited	$32,695	7%
3.6R Limited	$35,395	7%

Safety Checklist

Crash Test:
  Frontal. . . . . –
  Side. . . . . –
Airbags:
  Torso. . . . . . . Std. Fr. Pelvis/Torso from Seat
  Roll Sensing . . . . .Yes
  Knee Bolster .None
Crash Avoidance:
  Collision Avoidance. . . Standard CIB & DBS
  Blind Spot Detection . . . . Optional
  Lane Keeping Assist . . . . .Standard
  Pedestrian Crash Avoidance . . . . .Standard
General:
  Auto. Crash Notification . . . .Op. Assist.-Fee
  Day Running Lamps . . . . .Standard
Safety Belt/Restraint:
  Dynamic Head Restraints . . . . .None
  Adjustable Belt . . . . .Standard Front

^Warning feature does not meet suggested government specifications.

Subaru Outback

Specifications

Drive. . . . . AWD
Engine 2.5-liter I4
Transmission . . . . .8-sp. Automatic
Tow Rating (lbs.) . . . . Very Low-2700
Head/Leg Room (in.) Roomy-40.1/42.9
Interior Space (cu. ft.). Roomy-109.0
Cargo Space (cu. ft.) . . . . Very Roomy-32.5
Wheelbase/Length (in.) 108.1/191.3

Tesla Model 3 — Compact

Ratings—10 Best, 1 Worst

Combo Crash Tests	—
Safety Features	7
Rollover	7
Preventive Maintenance	8
Repair Costs	10
Warranty	10
Fuel Economy	10
Complaints	1
Insurance Costs	5
OVERALL RATING	—

Tesla Model 3

At-a-Glance

Status/Year Series Started........ Unchanged/2018
Twins .... -
Body Styles ....Sedan
Seating...............................5
Anti-Theft Device .... Std. Passive Alarm Only
Parking Index Rating ....Very Easy
Where Made.......................Fremont, CA
Fuel Factor
  MPG Rating (city/hwy)........ Very Good-131/120
  Driving Range (mi.) ....Very Short-310
  Fuel Type........................ Electricity
  Annual Fuel Cost ....Very Low-$500
  Gas Guzzler Tax ....No
  Greenhouse Gas Emissions (tons/yr.). Very Low-0.0
  Barrels of Oil Used per year .... Very Low-0.0

How the Competition Rates

Competitors	Rating	Pg.
BMW i3		77
Chevrolet Bolt		93

Price Range

	Retail	Markup
Base	$35,000	6%
Premium	$40,000	6%
Prem. w/Enh. Autopilot	$45,000	6%

Tesla Model 3

Safety Checklist

Crash Test:
  Frontal............................. −
  Side.............................. −
Airbags:
  Torso...... Std. Fr. Pelvis/Torso from Seat
  Roll Sensing ....Yes
  Knee Bolster .... Standard Front
Crash Avoidance:
  Collision Avoidance... Optional CIB & DBS*
  Blind Spot Detection .... Optional
  Lane Keeping Assist............ Optional
  Pedestrian Crash Avoidance ....None
General:
  Auto. Crash Notification ....None
  Day Running Lamps ....Standard
Safety Belt/Restraint:
  Dynamic Head Restraints...........None
  Adjustable Belt ....None

^Warning feature does not meet suggested government specifications.

Tesla Model 3

Specifications

Drive....................................RWD
Engine .... Electric
Transmission ....CVT
Tow Rating (lbs.) .... −
Head/Leg Room (in.) .... −
Interior Space (cu. ft.).................... −
Cargo Space (cu. ft.) Cramped-15
Wheelbase/Length (in.) 113.2/184.8

Tesla Model S — Large

Ratings—10 Best, 1 Worst

Combo Crash Tests	9
Safety Features	9
Rollover	10
Preventive Maintenance	8
Repair Costs	10
Warranty	10
Fuel Economy	10
Complaints	1
Insurance Costs	1
OVERALL RATING	**10**

Tesla Model S

At-a-Glance

Status/Year Series Started	Unchanged/2015
Twins	-
Body Styles	Sedan
Seating	5
Anti-Theft Device	Std. Passive Alarm Only
Parking Index Rating	Hard
Where Made	Fremont, CA
Fuel Factor	
MPG Rating (city/hwy)	Very Good-88/90
Driving Range (mi.)	Very Short-335
Fuel Type	Electricity
Annual Fuel Cost	Very Low-$650
Gas Guzzler Tax	No
Greenhouse Gas Emissions (tons/yr.)	Very Low-0.0
Barrels of Oil Used per year	Very Low-0.0

How the Competition Rates

Competitors	Rating	Pg.
Cadillac CT6		86
Mercedes-Benz E-Class	3	186
Lincoln MKZ	4	176

Price Range

	Retail	Markup
75 kWh	$69,500	6%
75D kWh	$74,500	6%
90D kWh	$87,500	6%
P100D kWh	$135,000	6%

Tesla Model S

Safety Checklist

Crash Test:
  Frontal............................Good
  Side......................... Very Good
Airbags:
  Torso...... Std. Fr. Pelvis/Torso from Seat
  Roll Sensing ....Yes
  Knee Bolster .... Standard Front
Crash Avoidance:
  Collision Avoidance... Standard CIB & DBS
  Blind Spot Detection ....Standard
  Lane Keeping Assist............ Optional
  Pedestrian Crash Avoidance ....None
General:
  Auto. Crash Notification ....None
  Day Running Lamps ....Standard
Safety Belt/Restraint:
  Dynamic Head Restraints...........None
  Adjustable Belt ....None

^Warning feature does not meet suggested government specifications.

Tesla Model S

Specifications

Drive	RWD
Engine	Electric
Transmission	CVT
Tow Rating (lbs.)	–
Head/Leg Room (in.)	Average-38.8/42.7
Interior Space (cu. ft.)	Cramped-94
Cargo Space (cu. ft.)	Very Roomy-31.6
Wheelbase/Length (in.)	116.5/196

Tesla Model X — Medium SUV

Ratings—10 Best, 1 Worst

Combo Crash Tests	10
Safety Features	9
Rollover	9
Preventive Maintenance	8
Repair Costs	10
Warranty	10
Fuel Economy	10
Complaints	2
Insurance Costs	8
OVERALL RATING	**10**

Tesla Model X

Tesla Model X

At-a-Glance

Status/Year Series Started........ Unchanged/2017
Twins .... -
Body Styles .... SUV
Seating....................................... 7
Anti-Theft Device .... Std. Passive Alarm Only
Parking Index Rating .... Very Hard
Where Made....................... Fremont, CA
Fuel Factor
  MPG Rating (city/hwy)......... Very Good-89/90
  Driving Range (mi.) .... Very Short-295
  Fuel Type......................... Electricity
  Annual Fuel Cost .... Very Low-$700
  Gas Guzzler Tax .... No
  Greenhouse Gas Emissions (tons/yr). Very Low-0.0
  Barrels of Oil Used per year .... Very Low-0.0

How the Competition Rates

Competitors	Rating	Pg.
Audi Q7	3	71
BMW X5		79
Buick Enclave	4	82

Price Range

Price Range	Retail	Markup
75D kWh	$79,500	6%
90D kWh	$93,500	6%
100D kWh	$96,000	6%
P100D kWh	$140,000	6%

Tesla Model X

Safety Checklist

Crash Test:
  Frontal...................... Very Good
  Side........................ Very Good
Airbags:
  Torso...... Std. Fr. Pelvis/Torso from Seat
  Roll Sensing .... Yes
  Knee Bolster .... Standard Front
Crash Avoidance:
  Collision Avoidance... Standard CIB & DBS
  Blind Spot Detection .... Standard
  Lane Keeping Assist........... Optional
  Pedestrian Crash Avoidance .... None
General:
  Auto. Crash Notification .... None
  Day Running Lamps .... Standard
Safety Belt/Restraint:
  Dynamic Head Restraints.......... None
  Adjustable Belt .... None

^Warning feature does not meet suggested government specifications.

Tesla Model X

Specifications

Drive.................................. AWD
Engine .... Electric
Transmission .... CVT
Tow Rating (lbs.) .... –
Head/Leg Room (in.) Roomy-41.7/41.2
Interior Space (cu. ft.)............. Roomy-120
Cargo Space (cu. ft.) Roomy-26
Wheelbase/Length (in.) 116.7/198.3

Toyota 86 — Compact

Ratings—10 Best, 1 Worst

Combo Crash Tests	—
Safety Features	2
Rollover	9
Preventive Maintenance	4
Repair Costs	3
Warranty	2
Fuel Economy	7
Complaints	9
Insurance Costs	1
OVERALL RATING	**—**

Toyota 86

Toyota 86

At-a-Glance

Status/Year Series Started. Unchanged/2017
Twins . . . . -
Body Styles . . . . .Coupe
Seating 4
Anti-Theft Device . Std. Pass. Immobil. & Active Alarm
Parking Index Rating . . . . .Very Easy
Where Made. . . . . Gunma, Japan
Fuel Factor
MPG Rating (city/hwy). Good-25/34
Driving Range (mi.) . . . . .Very Short-375
Fuel Type. . . . . .Premium
Annual Fuel Cost . . . . .Average-$1570
Gas Guzzler Tax . . . . .No
Greenhouse Gas Emissions (tons/yr.). . .Average-6.4
Barrels of Oil Used per year Average-11.8

How the Competition Rates

Competitors	Rating	Pg.
Mazda MX-5		184

Price Range

	Retail	Markup
Base MT	$26,255	5%
Base AT	$26,975	5%
Special Edition MT	$29,155	5%
Special Edition AT	$29,875	5%

Safety Checklist

Crash Test:
Frontal. . . . . −
Side. . . . . −
Airbags:
Torso. . . . . . . Std. Fr. Pelvis/Torso from Seat
Roll Sensing . . . . .Yes
Knee Bolster . . . . Standard Front
Crash Avoidance:
Collision Avoidance. . . . . .None
Blind Spot Detection . . . . .None
Lane Keeping Assist . . . . .None
Pedestrian Crash Avoidance . . . . .None
General:
Auto. Crash Notification . . . .Op. Assist.-Fee
Day Running Lamps . . . . .Standard
Safety Belt/Restraint:
Dynamic Head Restraints . . . . .None
Adjustable Belt . . . . .None

^Warning feature does not meet suggested government specifications.

Toyota 86

Specifications

Drive. . . . . .RWD
Engine 2.0-liter I4
Transmission . . . . .6-sp. Automatic
Tow Rating (lbs.) . . . . −
Head/Leg Room (in.) . . . . .Very Cramped-37.1/41.9
Interior Space (cu. ft.). . . . . . . .Very Cramped-76.5
Cargo Space (cu. ft.) . . . . .Very Cramped-6.9
Wheelbase/Length (in.) 101.2/166.7

Toyota 4Runner — Medium SUV

Ratings—10 Best, 1 Worst

Combo Crash Tests	1
Safety Features	4
Rollover	1
Preventive Maintenance	9
Repair Costs	4
Warranty	2
Fuel Economy	2
Complaints	9
Insurance Costs	10
OVERALL RATING	**2**

Toyota 4Runner

Toyota 4Runner

At-a-Glance

Status/Year Series Started Unchanged/2006
Twins . . . . . Lexus GX, Lexus RX, Toyota Highlander
Body Styles . . . . SUV
Seating 5/7
Anti-Theft Device . . . . . . Std. Pass. Immobil. & Alarm
Parking Index Rating . . . . Average
Where Made. Tahara, Japan
Fuel Factor
  MPG Rating (city/hwy) . . . . Very Poor-17/21
  Driving Range (mi.) Long-428
  Fuel Type. . . . . Regular
  Annual Fuel Cost . . . . Very High-$1976
  Gas Guzzler Tax . . . . No
  Greenhouse Gas Emissions (tons/yr.)Very High-10.0
  Barrels of Oil Used per year . . . . Very High-18.3

How the Competition Rates

Competitors	Rating	Pg.
Buick Enclave	4	82
Chevrolet Tahoe	4	104
Volvo XC90	8	240

Price Range

	Retail	Markup
SR5 2WD	$34,410	9%
SR5 Premium 4WD	$38,115	9%
TRD Pro	$42,675	9%
Limited 4WD	$44,760	9%

Safety Checklist

Crash Test:
  Frontal. . . . . Very Poor
  Side. . . . . Poor
Airbags:
  Torso. . . . . . Std. Fr. Pelvis/Torso from Seat
  Roll Sensing . . . . Yes
  Knee Bolster . . . . Standard Front
Crash Avoidance:
  Collision Avoidance. . . . . None
  Blind Spot Detection . . . . None
  Lane Keeping Assist . . . . None
  Pedestrian Crash Avoidance . . . . None
General:
  Auto. Crash Notification . . . . Op. Assist.-Fee
  Day Running Lamps . . . . Standard
Safety Belt/Restraint:
  Dynamic Head Restraints . . . Standard Front
  Adjustable Belt. . . . . Standard Front

^Warning feature does not meet suggested government specifications.

Toyota 4Runner

Specifications

Drive. 4WD
Engine 4.0-liter V6
Transmission . . . . .5-sp. Automatic
Tow Rating (lbs.) Low-4700
Head/Leg Room (in.) Average-39.3/41.7
Interior Space (cu. ft.). . . . . Very Roomy-128
Cargo Space (cu. ft.) . . . . Very Cramped-9
Wheelbase/Length (in.) 109.8/190.2

Toyota Avalon — Intermediate

Ratings—10 Best, 1 Worst

Combo Crash Tests	8
Safety Features	10
Rollover	7
Preventive Maintenance	6
Repair Costs	4
Warranty	2
Fuel Economy	5
Complaints	8
Insurance Costs	5
OVERALL RATING	**8**

Toyota Avalon

At-a-Glance

Status/Year Series Started........ Unchanged/2013
Twins .... Lexus ES
Body Styles .... Sedan
Seating 5
Anti-Theft Device ...... Std. Pass. Immobil. & Alarm
Parking Index Rating .... Average
Where Made.................... Georgetown, KY
Fuel Factor
  MPG Rating (city/hwy)........... Average-21/31
  Driving Range (mi.) Average-418
  Fuel Type.........................Regular
  Annual Fuel Cost ....Average-$1496
  Gas Guzzler Tax ....No
  Greenhouse Gas Emissions (tons/yr.)..... High-7.5
  Barrels of Oil Used per year High-13.7

How the Competition Rates

Competitors	Rating	Pg.
Cadillac XT5	3	90
Chevrolet Impala	4	98
Volvo S60		237

Price Range

Price Range	Retail	Markup
XLE	$33,500	11%
XLE Premium	$36,700	11%
Touring	$37,900	11%
Hybrid Limited	$42,800	11%

Toyota Avalon

Safety Checklist

Crash Test:
  Frontal....................... Average
  Side........................ Very Good
Airbags:
  Torso Std. Fr. & Rear Pelvis/Torso from Seat
  Roll Sensing ....Yes
  Knee Bolster .... Standard Front
Crash Avoidance:
  Collision Avoidance.....Optional CIB & DBS
  Blind Spot Detection .... Optional
  Lane Keeping Assist........... Optional
  Pedestrian Crash Avoidance ..... Optional
General:
  Auto. Crash Notification ....Op. Assist.-Fee
  Day Running Lamps ....Standard
Safety Belt/Restraint:
  Dynamic Head Restraints...........None
  Adjustable Belt............Standard Front

^Warning feature does not meet suggested government specifications.

Toyota Avalon

Specifications

Drive.................................. FWD
Engine 3.5-liter V6
Transmission .... 6-sp. Automatic
Tow Rating (lbs.) .... Very Low-1000
Head/Leg Room (in.) Cramped-37.6/42.1
Interior Space (cu. ft.)........... Average-103.63
Cargo Space (cu. ft.) Cramped-16
Wheelbase/Length (in.) 111/195.3

Toyota Camry — Intermediate

Ratings—10 Best, 1 Worst	
Combo Crash Tests	9
Safety Features	10
Rollover	8
Preventive Maintenance	6
Repair Costs	3
Warranty	2
Fuel Economy	8
Complaints	8
Insurance Costs	5
OVERALL RATING	**8**

Toyota Camry

Toyota Camry

At-a-Glance

Status/Year Series Started Unchanged/2018
Twins . . . . -
Body Styles . . . . .Sedan
Seating 5
Anti-Theft Device . . . . . . Std. Pass. Immobil. & Alarm
Parking Index Rating . . . . Average
Where Made. . . . . .Georgetown, KY
Fuel Factor
 MPG Rating (city/hwy). Good-28/39
 Driving Range (mi.) . . . . Very Long-513
 Fuel Type. . . . . .Regular
 Annual Fuel Cost . . . . .Very Low-$1146
 Gas Guzzler Tax . . . . .No
 Greenhouse Gas Emissions (tons/yr.). Very Low-4.6
 Barrels of Oil Used per year Low-10.3

How the Competition Rates

Competitors	Rating	Pg.
Ford Fusion	4	121
Nissan Altima		196
Subaru Legacy	7	219

Price Range	Retail	Markup
LE	$24,000	9%
XSE	$29,000	10%
XLE Hybrid	$32,250	9%
XSE V6	$34,950	10%

Safety Checklist

Crash Test:
 Frontal. . . . . Very Good
 Side. . . . . .Good
Airbags:
 Torso Std. Fr. & Rear Pelvis/Torso from Seat
 Roll Sensing . . . . .Yes
 Knee Bolster . . . . Standard Front
Crash Avoidance:
 Collision Avoidance. . . Optional CIB & DBS*
 Blind Spot Detection . . . . Optional
 Lane Keeping Assist . . . . Optional
 Pedestrian Crash Avoidance . . . . .Standard
General:
 Auto. Crash Notification . . . .Op. Assist.-Fee
 Day Running Lamps . . . . .Standard
Safety Belt/Restraint:
 Dynamic Head Restraints . . . . .None
 Adjustable Belt . . . . .Standard Front

^Warning feature does not meet suggested government specifications.

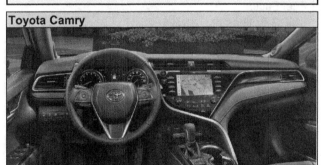
Toyota Camry

Specifications

Drive . . . . FWD
Engine 2.5-liter I4
Transmission . . . . .8-sp. Automatic
Tow Rating (lbs.) . . . . –
Head/Leg Room (in.) Cramped-38.3/42.1
Interior Space (cu. ft.). Average-100.4
Cargo Space (cu. ft.) Cramped-15.1
Wheelbase/Length (in.) 111.2/192.1

Toyota Corolla Compact

Ratings—10 Best, 1 Worst

Combo Crash Tests	4
Safety Features	7
Rollover	6
Preventive Maintenance	9
Repair Costs	7
Warranty	2
Fuel Economy	8
Complaints	10
Insurance Costs	3
OVERALL RATING	**7**

Toyota Corolla

At-a-Glance

```
Status/Year Series Started........ Unchanged/2014
Twins ......................................... -
Body Styles ............................ Sedan
Seating ....................................... 5
Anti-Theft Device ....... Std. Passive Immobil. Only
Parking Index Rating ...................... Easy
Where Made.................... Princeton, IN
Fuel Factor
  MPG Rating (city/hwy)............. Good-27/36
  Driving Range (mi.) ............... Average-402
  Fuel Type........................ Regular
  Annual Fuel Cost.................. Low-$1208
  Gas Guzzler Tax ...................... No
  Greenhouse Gas Emissions (tons/yr.)..... Low-5.8
  Barrels of Oil Used per year ....... Average-10.6
```

How the Competition Rates

Competitors	Rating	Pg.
Honda Civic	10	133
Nissan Sentra	5	204
Volkswagen Jetta		234

Price Range

Price Range	Retail	Markup
L	$18,500	6%
LE	$18,935	8%
SE AT	$20,445	8%
XSE	$22,680	8%

Toyota Corolla

Safety Checklist

```
Crash Test:
  Frontal........................... Poor
  Side.......................... Average
Airbags:
  Torso...... Std. Fr. Pelvis/Torso from Seat
  Roll Sensing ...................... Yes
  Knee Bolster ........... Standard Driver
Crash Avoidance:
  Collision Avoidance... Optional CIB & DBS*
  Blind Spot Detection ...............None
  Lane Keeping Assist ...........Standard
  Pedestrian Crash Avoidance ..... Optional
General:
  Auto. Crash Notification ...........None
  Day Running Lamps ...........Standard
Safety Belt/Restraint:
  Dynamic Head Restraints ...........None
  Adjustable Belt............ Standard Front
```
^Warning feature does not meet suggested government specifications.

Toyota Corolla

Specifications

```
Drive................................... FWD
Engine ........................... 1.8-liter I4
Transmission ................ 4-sp. Automatic
Tow Rating (lbs.) ................... Very Low-0
Head/Leg Room (in.) ........ Cramped-38.3/42.3
Interior Space (cu. ft.)............ Average-97.5
Cargo Space (cu. ft.) ......... Very Cramped-13
Wheelbase/Length (in.) ............ 106.3/182.6
```

Ratings—10 Best, 1 Worst

Combo Crash Tests	—
Safety Features	4
Rollover	6
Preventive Maintenance	10
Repair Costs	9
Warranty	2
Fuel Economy	8
Complaints	4
Insurance Costs	8
OVERALL RATING	—

Toyota Corolla Hatchback

Toyota Corolla Hatchback

Toyota Corolla Hatchback

At-a-Glance

Status/Year Series Started........ Unchanged/2019
Twins .... -
Body Styles .... Hatchback
Seating 5
Anti-Theft Device .... Std. Passive Immobil. Only
Parking Index Rating ....Very Easy
Where Made....................Tsutsumi, Japan
Fuel Factor
  MPG Rating (city/hwy)......... Very Good-32/42
  Driving Range (mi.) .... Very Long-475
  Fuel Type..........................Regular
  Annual Fuel Cost ....Very Low-$1181
  Gas Guzzler Tax ....No
  Greenhouse Gas Emissions (tons/yr.). Very Low-4.1
  Barrels of Oil Used per year Low-9.2

How the Competition Rates

Competitors	Rating	Pg.
Honda Civic	10	133
Mazda 3	6	182
Volkswagen Jetta		234

Price Range

	Retail	Markup
SE MT	$19,990	6%
SE AT	$21,090	8%
XSE MT	$23,385	8%
XSE AT	$24,090	8%

Safety Checklist

Crash Test:
  Frontal............................−
  Side...............................−
Airbags:
  Torso...... Std. Fr. Pelvis/Torso from Seat
  Roll Sensing ....Yes
  Knee Bolster .... Standard Driver
Crash Avoidance:
  Collision Avoidance... Standard CIB & DBS
  Blind Spot Detection ....None
  Lane Keeping Assist...............None
  Pedestrian Crash Avoidance ....None
General:
  Auto. Crash Notification ....None
  Day Running Lamps ....Standard
Safety Belt/Restraint:
  Dynamic Head Restraints...........None
  Adjustable Belt............Standard Front

^Warning feature does not meet suggested government specifications.

Toyota Corolla Hatchback

Specifications

Drive.................................FWD
Engine 2.0-liter I4
Transmission ....CVT
Tow Rating (lbs.) ....−
Head/Leg Room (in.) ....−
Interior Space (cu. ft.).......... Very Cramped-85
Cargo Space (cu. ft.) Average-18
Wheelbase/Length (in.) 103.9/169.9

Toyota Highlander   Medium SUV

Ratings—10 Best, 1 Worst

Combo Crash Tests	—
Safety Features	9
Rollover	3
Preventive Maintenance	7
Repair Costs	6
Warranty	2
Fuel Economy	2
Complaints	—
Insurance Costs	8
OVERALL RATING	—

Toyota Highlander

At-a-Glance

Status/Year Series Started. All-New/2020
Twins . . . . . . Lexus GX, Lexus RX, Toyota 4Runner
Body Styles . . . . SUV
Seating 7/8
Anti-Theft Device . . . . . . Std. Pass. Immobil. & Alarm
Parking Index Rating . . . . Hard
Where Made. . . . . Princeton, IN
Fuel Factor
  MPG Rating (city/hwy) Poor-20/27
  Driving Range (mi.) Long-411
  Fuel Type. . . . . Regular
  Annual Fuel Cost . . . . .Average-$1623
  Gas Guzzler Tax . . . . .No
  Greenhouse Gas Emissions (tons/yr.). High-8.2
  Barrels of Oil Used per year High-15.0

How the Competition Rates

Competitors	Rating	Pg.
Dodge Durango	2	113
Ford Explorer	3	118
Volkswagen Atlas	6	233

Price Range

	Retail	Markup
LE I4 FWD	$30,630	10%
LE Plus AWD	$36,520	10%
Limited AWD	$43,140	10%
Hybrid LTD Platinum	$47,880	10%

Toyota Highlander

Safety Checklist

Crash Test:
  Frontal . . . . –
  Side . . . . –
Airbags:
  Torso. . . . . . Std. Fr. Pelvis/Torso from Seat
  Roll Sensing . . . . Yes
  Knee Bolster . . . . Standard Driver
Crash Avoidance:
  Collision Avoidance. . . Standard CIB & DBS
  Blind Spot Detection . . . . Optional
  Lane Keeping Assist. . . . . .Standard
  Pedestrian Crash Avoidance . . . . .Standard
General:
  Auto. Crash Notification . . . .Op. Assist.-Fee
  Day Running Lamps . . . . .Standard
Safety Belt/Restraint:
  Dynamic Head Restraints . . . . .None
  Adjustable Belt . . . . .Standard Front

^W-arning feature does not meet suggested government specifications.

Toyota Highlander

Specifications

Drive. . . . . AWD
Engine 3.5-liter V6
Transmission . . . . .8-sp. Automatic
Tow Rating (lbs.) . . . . Very Low-2000
Head/Leg Room (in.) Roomy-39.9/40.4
Interior Space (cu. ft.). . . . . Very Roomy-141.3
Cargo Space (cu. ft.) Cramped-16.0
Wheelbase/Length (in.) 112.2/194.9

Toyota Prius | Compact

Toyota Prius

Ratings—10 Best, 1 Worst

Combo Crash Tests	5
Safety Features	7
Rollover	7
Preventive Maintenance	9
Repair Costs	5
Warranty	2
Fuel Economy	10
Complaints	4
Insurance Costs	5
OVERALL RATING	**7**

Toyota Prius

At-a-Glance

Status/Year Series Started	Unchanged/2016
Twins	-
Body Styles	Hatchback
Seating	5
Anti-Theft Device	Std. Passive Immobil. Only
Parking Index Rating	Very Easy
Where Made	Tsutsumi, Japan
Fuel Factor	
MPG Rating (city/hwy)	Very Good-54/50
Driving Range (mi.)	Very Long-589
Fuel Type	Regular
Annual Fuel Cost	Very Low-$705
Gas Guzzler Tax	No
Greenhouse Gas Emissions (tons/yr.)	Very Low-2.8
Barrels of Oil Used per year	Very Low-6.3

How the Competition Rates

Competitors	Rating	Pg.
Honda Civic	10	133
Nissan Leaf		199
Volkswagen Jetta		234

Price Range

	Retail	Markup
One	$23,475	6%
Three	$26,735	7%
Four	$29,135	7%
Four Touring	$30,015	7%

Safety Checklist

Crash Test:
Frontal . . . . . Average
Side . . . . . Average
Airbags:
Torso . . . . . Std. Fr. Pelvis/Torso from Seat
Roll Sensing . . . . . Yes
Knee Bolster . . . . . Standard Driver
Crash Avoidance:
Collision Avoidance . . . . Optional CIB & DBS
Blind Spot Detection . . . . . Optional
Lane Keeping Assist . . . . . Optional
Pedestrian Crash Avoidance . . . . . Optional
General:
Auto. Crash Notification . . . . Op. Assist.-Fee
Day Running Lamps . . . . . Optional
Safety Belt/Restraint:
Dynamic Head Restraints . . . . . None
Adjustable Belt . . . . . Standard Front

^Warning feature does not meet suggested government specifications.

Toyota Prius

Specifications

Drive	FWD
Engine	1.8-liter I4
Transmission	CVT
Tow Rating (lbs.)	–
Head/Leg Room (in.)	Very Cramped-34.4/42.3
Interior Space (cu. ft.)	Cramped-93.1
Cargo Space (cu. ft.)	Roomy-24.6
Wheelbase/Length (in.)	106.3/178.7

Toyota Prius Prime   Compact

Ratings—10 Best, 1 Worst

Combo Crash Tests	—
Safety Features	9
Rollover	6
Preventive Maintenance	9
Repair Costs	7
Warranty	2
Fuel Economy	10
Complaints	5
Insurance Costs	5
OVERALL RATING	**—**

Toyota Prius Prime

At-a-Glance

Status/Year Series Started	Unchanged/2017
Twins	-
Body Styles	Sedan
Seating	4
Anti-Theft Device	Std. Passive Immobil. Only
Parking Index Rating	Very Easy
Where Made	Tsutsumi, Japan
Fuel Factor	
MPG Rating (city/hwy)	Very Good-55/53
Driving Range (mi.)	Very Long-611
Fuel Type	Regular
Annual Fuel Cost	Very Low-$680
Gas Guzzler Tax	No
Greenhouse Gas Emissions (tons/yr.)	Very Low-1.3
Barrels of Oil Used per year	Very Low-3.0

How the Competition Rates

Competitors	Rating	Pg.
Chevrolet Bolt		93
Nissan Leaf		199
Volkswagen Jetta		234

Price Range

	Retail	Markup
Plus	$27,100	4%
Premium	$28,800	4%
Advanced	$33,100	4%

Toyota Prius Prime

Safety Checklist

Crash Test:
  Frontal . . . . −
  Side . . . . −
Airbags:
  Torso . . . . . . Std. Fr. Pelvis/Torso from Seat
  Roll Sensing . . . . Yes
  Knee Bolster . . . . Standard Front
Crash Avoidance:
  Collision Avoidance. . . . Optional CIB & DBS
  Blind Spot Detection . . . . Optional
  Lane Keeping Assist . . . . Optional
  Pedestrian Crash Avoidance . . . . . Standard
General:
  Auto. Crash Notification . . . . None
  Day Running Lamps . . . . Standard
Safety Belt/Restraint:
  Dynamic Head Restraints . . . . None
  Adjustable Belt . . . . Standard Front

^Warning feature does not meet suggested government specifications.

Toyota Prius Prime

Specifications

Drive	FWD
Engine	1.8-liter I4
Transmission	CVT
Tow Rating (lbs.)	−
Head/Leg Room (in.)	Roomy-39.4/43.2
Interior Space (cu. ft.)	Cramped-91.5
Cargo Space (cu. ft.)	Average-19.8
Wheelbase/Length (in.)	106.3/182.9

Ratings—10 Best, 1 Worst

Combo Crash Tests	—
Safety Features	7
Rollover	3
Preventive Maintenance	4
Repair Costs	7
Warranty	2
Fuel Economy	5
Complaints	10
Insurance Costs	10
OVERALL RATING	—

Toyota RAV4

Toyota RAV4

At-a-Glance

Status/Year Series Started. Unchanged/2019
Twins . . . . -
Body Styles . . . . SUV
Seating 5
Anti-Theft Device . . . . Std. Passive Immobil. Only
Parking Index Rating . . . . Easy
Where Made. . . . Woodstock, Ontario / Tahara, Japan
Fuel Factor
 MPG Rating (city/hwy). Good-27/34
 Driving Range (mi.) Long-435
 Fuel Type. . . . . .Regular
 Annual Fuel Cost . . . . Low-$1235
 Gas Guzzler Tax . . . . .No
 Greenhouse Gas Emissions (tons/yr.). Low-4.9
 Barrels of Oil Used per year Average-11.0

How the Competition Rates

Competitors	Rating	Pg.
Ford Escape	5	116
Honda HR-V	5	136
Hyundai Tucson	8	145

Price Range

	Retail	Markup
LE FWD	$25,895	7%
XLE FWD	$27,695	7%
Adventure AWD	$32,900	7%
Limited AWD	$34,900	7%

Safety Checklist

Crash Test:
 Frontal. . . . . Average
 Side. . . . . Very Good
Airbags:
 Torso. . . . . . . Std. Fr. Pelvis/Torso from Seat
 Roll Sensing . . . . .Yes
 Knee Bolster . . . . Standard Driver
Crash Avoidance:
 Collision Avoidance. . . Standard CIB & DBS
 Blind Spot Detection . . . . Optional
 Lane Keeping Assist . . . . .Standard
 Pedestrian Crash Avoidance . . . . . Optional
General:
 Auto. Crash Notification . . . .Op. Assist.-Fee
 Day Running Lamps . . . . .Standard
Safety Belt/Restraint:
 Dynamic Head Restraints . . . . .None
 Adjustable Belt . . . . .Standard Front

^Warning feature does not meet suggested government specifications.

Toyota RAV4

Specifications

Drive. . . . . AWD
Engine 2.5-liter I4
Transmission . . . . .8-sp. Automatic
Tow Rating (lbs.) . . . . Very Low-1500
Head/Leg Room (in.) Cramped-39.5/41.0
Interior Space (cu. ft.). Average-98.9
Cargo Space (cu. ft.) . . . . Very Roomy-37.0
Wheelbase/Length (in.) 105.9/180.9

Ratings—10 Best, 1 Worst

Combo Crash Tests	—
Safety Features	4
Rollover	2
Preventive Maintenance	6
Repair Costs	4
Warranty	2
Fuel Economy	1
Complaints	9
Insurance Costs	10
OVERALL RATING	**—**

Toyota Sequoia

At-a-Glance

Status/Year Series Started	Unchanged/2008
Twins	-
Body Styles	SUV
Seating	8
Anti-Theft Device	Std. Pass. Immobil. & Alarm
Parking Index Rating	Very Hard
Where Made	Princeton, IN
Fuel Factor	
MPG Rating (city/hwy)	Very Poor-13/17
Driving Range (mi.)	Short-384
Fuel Type	Regular
Annual Fuel Cost	Very High-$2528
Gas Guzzler Tax	No
Greenhouse Gas Emissions (tons/yr.)	Very High-12.8
Barrels of Oil Used per year	Very High-23.5

How the Competition Rates

Competitors	Rating	Pg.
Buick Enclave	4	82
Chevrolet Suburban	2	103
Volvo XC90	8	240

Price Range

	Retail	Markup
SR5 2WD	$48,300	10%
Sport 2WD	$51,015	10%
Limited 4WD	$60,020	10%
Platinum 4WD	$67,235	10%

Toyota Sequoia

Safety Checklist

Crash Test:
Frontal .... –
Side .... –
Airbags:
Torso ...... Std. Fr. Pelvis/Torso from Seat
Roll Sensing .... Yes
Knee Bolster .... Standard Front
Crash Avoidance:
Collision Avoidance .... None
Blind Spot Detection .... Optional
Lane Keeping Assist .... None
Pedestrian Crash Avoidance .... None
General:
Auto. Crash Notification .... None
Day Running Lamps .... Optional
Safety Belt/Restraint:
Dynamic Head Restraints .... None
Adjustable Belt ...... Standard Front & Rear

^Warning feature does not meet suggested government specifications.

Toyota Sequoia

Specifications

Drive	4WD
Engine	5.7-liter V8
Transmission	6-sp. Automatic
Tow Rating (lbs.)	Average-7100
Head/Leg Room (in.)	Very Cramped-34.8/42.5
Interior Space (cu. ft.)	–
Cargo Space (cu. ft.)	Average-18.9
Wheelbase/Length (in.)	122/205.1

Toyota Sienna   Minivan

Ratings—10 Best, 1 Worst

Combo Crash Tests	6
Safety Features	7
Rollover	5
Preventive Maintenance	2
Repair Costs	4
Warranty	2
Fuel Economy	3
Complaints	3
Insurance Costs	5
OVERALL RATING	**2**

Toyota Sienna

At-a-Glance

Status/Year Series Started. Unchanged/2004
Twins . . . . -
Body Styles . . . . .Minivan
Seating 7/8
Anti-Theft Device . . . . . . Std. Pass. Immobil. & Alarm
Parking Index Rating . . . . Hard
Where Made. . . . . Princeton, IN
Fuel Factor
　MPG Rating (city/hwy) Poor-18/25
　Driving Range (mi.) Average-412
　Fuel Type. . . . . .Regular
　Annual Fuel Cost . . . . .High-$1784
　Gas Guzzler Tax . . . . .No
　Greenhouse Gas Emissions (tons/yr.). High-8.6
　Barrels of Oil Used per year High-15.7

How the Competition Rates

Competitors	Rating	Pg.
Chrysler Pacifica	8	110
Honda Odyssey	9	137
Kia Sedona		159

Price Range

	Retail	Markup
L FWD	$29,750	8%
SE FWD	$36,110	8%
XLE Premium FWD	$39,505	9%
LTD Premium AWD	$47,310	9%

Safety Checklist

Crash Test:
　Frontal. . . . . Average
　Side. . . . . Average
Airbags:
　Torso. . . . . . . Std. Fr. Pelvis/Torso from Seat
　Roll Sensing . . . . .Yes
　Knee Bolster . . . . Standard Driver
Crash Avoidance:
　Collision Avoidance. . . . .Optional CIB & DBS
　Blind Spot Detection . . . . Optional
　Lane Keeping Assist . . . . .None
　Pedestrian Crash Avoidance . . . . .None
General:
　Auto. Crash Notification . . . .Op. Assist.-Fee
　Day Running Lamps . . . . Optional
Safety Belt/Restraint:
　Dynamic Head Restraints . . . Standard Front
　Adjustable Belt . . . . . .Standard Front & Rear

^Warning feature does not meet suggested government specifications.

Toyota Sienna

Specifications

Drive. . . . . FWD
Engine 3.5-liter V6
Transmission . . . . .6-sp. Automatic
Tow Rating (lbs.) Low-3500
Head/Leg Room (in.) Average-41/40.5
Interior Space (cu. ft.). . . . . Very Roomy-164.4
Cargo Space (cu. ft.) . . . . Very Roomy-39.1
Wheelbase/Length (in.) 119.3/200.2

Toyota Tacoma   Compact Pickup

Ratings—10 Best, 1 Worst

Combo Crash Tests	1
Safety Features	4
Rollover	2
Preventive Maintenance	9
Repair Costs	4
Warranty	2
Fuel Economy	3
Complaints	4
Insurance Costs	8
OVERALL RATING	**1**

Toyota Tacoma

Toyota Tacoma

Safety Checklist

Crash Test:
  Frontal . . . . Very Poor
  Side . . . . Very Poor
Airbags:
  Torso . . . . . . Std. Fr. Pelvis/Torso from Seat
  Roll Sensing . . . . Yes
  Knee Bolster . . . . Standard Front
Crash Avoidance:
  Collision Avoidance . . . . None
  Blind Spot Detection . . . . Optional
  Lane Keeping Assist . . . . None
  Pedestrian Crash Avoidance . . . . None
General:
  Auto. Crash Notification . . . . None
  Day Running Lamps . . . . Standard
Safety Belt/Restraint:
  Dynamic Head Restraints . . . . None
  Adjustable Belt . . . . Standard Front

^Warning feature does not meet suggested government specifications.

At-a-Glance

Status/Year Series Started Unchanged/2016
Twins . . . . -
Body Styles . . . . Pickup
Seating 4
Anti-Theft Device . . . . . . Std. Pass. Immobil. & Alarm
Parking Index Rating . . . . Very Hard
Where Made . . . . . San Antonio, TX / Tijuana, Mexico
Fuel Factor
  MPG Rating (city/hwy) Poor-19/23
  Driving Range (mi.) Long-435
  Fuel Type . . . . Regular
  Annual Fuel Cost . . . . High-$1783
  Gas Guzzler Tax . . . . No
  Greenhouse Gas Emissions (tons/yr.) High-7.3
  Barrels of Oil Used per year High-16.5

How the Competition Rates

Competitors	Rating	Pg.
Chevrolet Colorado	2	95
Ford Ranger		124
Nissan Frontier	1	204

Price Range

Price Range	Retail	Markup
SR Access Cab 2WD	$24,575	7%
SR5 Access Cab 2WD	$26,660	7%
SR5 Dbl Cab 4WD V6	$33,220	8%
Ltd. Spt. Dbl. Cab 4WD V6	$39,250	8%

Toyota Tacoma

Specifications

Drive 4WD
Engine 2.7-liter I4
Transmission . . . . .6-sp. Automatic
Tow Rating (lbs.) Low-3500
Head/Leg Room (in.) Roomy-39.7/42.9
Interior Space (cu. ft.) . . . . .Very Cramped-57.5
Cargo Space (cu. ft.) . . . . Very Roomy-33.5
Wheelbase/Length (in.) 127.4/212.3

Ratings—10 Best, 1 Worst

Combo Crash Tests	—
Safety Features	6
Rollover	2
Preventive Maintenance	6
Repair Costs	5
Warranty	2
Fuel Economy	1
Complaints	9
Insurance Costs	10
OVERALL RATING	**—**

Toyota Tundra

Toyota Tundra

Toyota Tundra

At-a-Glance

Status/Year Series Started	Unchanged/2007
Twins	-
Body Styles	Pickup
Seating	5/6
Anti-Theft Device	Std. Pass. Immobil. & Alarm
Parking Index Rating	Very Hard
Where Made	San Antonio, TX
Fuel Factor	
MPG Rating (city/hwy)	Very Poor-13/18
Driving Range (mi.)	Short-392
Fuel Type	Regular
Annual Fuel Cost	Very High-$2474
Gas Guzzler Tax	No
Greenhouse Gas Emissions (tons/yr.)	Very High-8.9
Barrels of Oil Used per year	Very High-20.6

How the Competition Rates

Competitors	Rating	Pg.
Chevrolet Silverado	101	Ford
F-150	9	119
Nissan Titan	1	205

Price Range

	Retail	Markup
SR Reg. Cab 2WD 5.7 V8	$32,390	8%
SR5 Dbl. Cab 4WD 5.7 V8	$37,150	8%
Ltd. Crew Max 4WD 5.7 V8	$45,300	8%
1794 Ed, Crew Max 5.7 V8	$50,130	8%

Safety Checklist

Crash Test:
  Frontal . . . . Very Poor
  Side . . . . –
Airbags:
  Torso . . . . . . Std. Fr. Pelvis/Torso from Seat
  Roll Sensing . . . . Yes
  Knee Bolster . . . . Standard Front
Crash Avoidance:
  Collision Avoidance. . . . . .None
  Blind Spot Detection . . . . Optional
  Lane Keeping Assist . . . . .None
  Pedestrian Crash Avoidance . . . . .None
General:
  Auto. Crash Notification . . . . .None
  Day Running Lamps . . . . .Standard
Safety Belt/Restraint:
  Dynamic Head Restraints . . . Standard Front
  Adjustable Belt . . . . . . Standard Front & Rear

^Warning feature does not meet suggested government specifications.

Specifications

Drive	4WD
Engine	5.7-liter V8
Transmission	6-sp. Automatic
Tow Rating (lbs.)	Very High-10000
Head/Leg Room (in.)	Average-39.7/42.5
Interior Space (cu. ft.)	–
Cargo Space (cu. ft.)	Very Roomy-67.1
Wheelbase/Length (in.)	145.7/228.9

Ratings—10 Best, 1 Worst

Combo Crash Tests	5
Safety Features	2
Rollover	5
Preventive Maintenance	9
Repair Costs	10
Warranty	2
Fuel Economy	9
Complaints	3
Insurance Costs	5
OVERALL RATING	**6**

Toyota Yaris

At-a-Glance

Status/Year Series Started Unchanged/2017
Twins . . . . -
Body Styles . . . . .Sedan
Seating 5
Anti-Theft Device . . . . Std. Passive Immobil. Only
Parking Index Rating . . . . .Very Easy
Where Made . . . . Salamanca, Mexico
Fuel Factor
  MPG Rating (city/hwy) . . . . Very Good-32/40
  Driving Range (mi.) Average-408
  Fuel Type . . . . .Regular
  Annual Fuel Cost . . . . Very Low-$1045
  Gas Guzzler Tax . . . . .No
  Greenhouse Gas Emissions (tons/yr.). Very Low-4.1
  Barrels of Oil Used per year Low-9.4

How the Competition Rates

Competitors	Rating	Pg.
Chevrolet Sonic	9	101
Honda Fit	9	135
Nissan Versa	1	206

Price Range

Price Range	Retail	Markup
Sedan MT	$15,950	4%
Sedan AT	$17,050	4%

Toyota Yaris

Safety Checklist

Crash Test:
  Frontal . . . . Poor
  Side . . . . Average
Airbags:
  Torso . . . . . . Std. Fr. Pelvis/Torso from Seat
  Roll Sensing . . . . .Yes
  Knee Bolster .None
Crash Avoidance:
  Collision Avoidance . . . . .None
  Blind Spot Detection . . . . .None
  Lane Keeping Assist . . . . .None
  Pedestrian Crash Avoidance . . . . .None
General:
  Auto. Crash Notification . . . .Op. Assist.-Fee
  Day Running Lamps . . . . .Standard
Safety Belt/Restraint:
  Dynamic Head Restraints . . . . .None
  Adjustable Belt . . . . Standard Front

^Warning feature does not meet suggested government specifications.

Toyota Yaris

Specifications

Drive . . . . FWD
Engine 1.5-liter I4
Transmission . . . . .6-sp. Automatic
Tow Rating (lbs.) . . . . –
Head/Leg Room (in.) Cramped-38.2/41.9
Interior Space (cu. ft.) . . . . .Very Cramped-85.9
Cargo Space (cu. ft.) . . . . .Very Cramped-13.5
Wheelbase/Length (in.) 101.2/171.7

Ratings—10 Best, 1 Worst

Combo Crash Tests	9
Safety Features	7
Rollover	4
Preventive Maintenance	3
Repair Costs	1
Warranty	10
Fuel Economy	3
Complaints	3
Insurance Costs	5
OVERALL RATING	**6**

Volkswagen Atlas

Volkswagen Atlas

Volkswagen Atlas

At-a-Glance

Status/Year Series Started........ Unchanged/2018
Twins .... -
Body Styles .... SUV
Seating 7
Anti-Theft Device ...... Std. Pass. Immobil. & Alarm
Parking Index Rating .... Hard
Where Made.............. Chattanooga, Tennessee
Fuel Factor
  MPG Rating (city/hwy)............... Poor-18/25
  Driving Range (mi.) Short-383
  Fuel Type................................ Regular
  Annual Fuel Cost .... High-$1784
  Gas Guzzler Tax .... No
  Greenhouse Gas Emissions (tons/yr.).. Average-7.2
  Barrels of Oil Used per year High-16.5

How the Competition Rates

Competitors	Rating	Pg.
Acura MDX	7	62
GMC Acadia	2	126
Toyota Highlander	8	224

Price Range	Retail	Markup
S FWD	$30,500	4%
SE FWD V6	$34,990	4%
SEL 4Motion V6	$42,690	4%
SEL Prem. 4Motion V6	$48,490	4%

Safety Checklist

Crash Test:
  Frontal........................... Good
  Side......................... Very Good
Airbags:
  Torso........... Std. Fr. Torso from Seat
  Roll Sensing .... Yes
  Knee Bolster .... None
Crash Avoidance:
  Collision Avoidance.... Optional CIB & DBS
  Blind Spot Detection .... Optional
  Lane Keeping Assist .... Optional
  Pedestrian Crash Avoidance ..... Optional
General:
  Auto. Crash Notification .... Op. Assist.-Fee
  Day Running Lamps .... Standard
Safety Belt/Restraint:
  Dynamic Head Restraints .... None
  Adjustable Belt .... Standard Front

^Warning feature does not meet suggested government specifications.

Volkswagen Atlas

Specifications

Drive.................................. FWD
Engine 3.6-liter V6
Transmission .... 8-sp. Automatic
Tow Rating (lbs.) Low-5000
Head/Leg Room (in.) Roomy-41.3/41.5
Interior Space (cu. ft.)......... Very Roomy-153.7
Cargo Space (cu. ft.) Average-20.6
Wheelbase/Length (in.) 117.3/198.3

Volkswagen Jetta   Compact

Ratings—10 Best, 1 Worst

Combo Crash Tests	—
Safety Features	2
Rollover	7
Preventive Maintenance	5
Repair Costs	4
Warranty	10
Fuel Economy	8
Complaints	1
Insurance Costs	3
OVERALL RATING	**—**

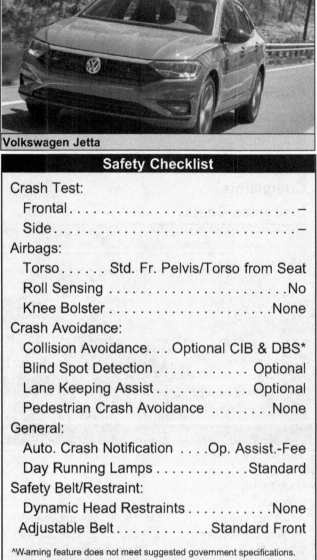
Volkswagen Jetta

Volkswagen Jetta

At-a-Glance

Status/Year Series Started........ Unchanged/2019
Twins .... -
Body Styles ....Sedan
Seating....................................5
Anti-Theft Device ...... Std. Pass. Immobil. & Alarm
Parking Index Rating ....Easy
Where Made....................Puebla, Mexico
Fuel Factor
  MPG Rating (city/hwy)............ Good-30/39
  Driving Range (mi.) Long-435
  Fuel Type............................Regular
  Annual Fuel Cost ....Very Low-$1098
  Gas Guzzler Tax ....No
  Greenhouse Gas Emissions (tons/yr.). Very Low-4.3
  Barrels of Oil Used per year Low-9.7

How the Competition Rates

Competitors	Rating	Pg.
Kia Forte		156
Nissan Sentra	5	204
Toyota Corolla	7	222

Price Range

Price Range	Retail	Markup
S MT	$18,545	4%
SE AT	$22,155	4%
SEL AT	$24,415	4%
SEL Premium AT	$26,945	4%

Safety Checklist

Crash Test:
  Frontal.............................. –
  Side................................ –
Airbags:
  Torso...... Std. Fr. Pelvis/Torso from Seat
  Roll Sensing ....No
  Knee Bolster ....None
Crash Avoidance:
  Collision Avoidance. . . Optional CIB & DBS*
  Blind Spot Detection .... Optional
  Lane Keeping Assist .... Optional
  Pedestrian Crash Avoidance ....None
General:
  Auto. Crash Notification ....Op. Assist.-Fee
  Day Running Lamps ....Standard
Safety Belt/Restraint:
  Dynamic Head Restraints...........None
  Adjustable Belt ....Standard Front

^Warning feature does not meet suggested government specifications.

Volkswagen Jetta

Specifications

Drive.................................. FWD
Engine 1.4-liter I4
Transmission ....8-sp. Automatic
Tow Rating (lbs.) .... –
Head/Leg Room (in.) .....Very Cramped-38.5/41.1
Interior Space (cu. ft.)............Cramped-94.7
Cargo Space (cu. ft.) Cramped-14.1
Wheelbase/Length (in.) 105.7/185.1

Ratings—10 Best, 1 Worst

Combo Crash Tests	5
Safety Features	2
Rollover	7
Preventive Maintenance	5
Repair Costs	5
Warranty	10
Fuel Economy	7
Complaints	3
Insurance Costs	1
OVERALL RATING	**4**

Volkswagen Passat

At-a-Glance

Status/Year Series Started	Apperance Change/2012
Twins	-
Body Styles	Sedan
Seating	5
Anti-Theft Device	Std. Pass. Immobil. & Alarm
Parking Index Rating	Average
Where Made	Chattanooga, TN

Fuel Factor
MPG Rating (city/hwy)	Good-25/36
Driving Range (mi.)	Very Long-536
Fuel Type	Regular
Annual Fuel Cost	Low-$1268
Gas Guzzler Tax	No
Greenhouse Gas Emissions (tons/yr.)	Low-5.0
Barrels of Oil Used per year	Average-11.4

How the Competition Rates

Competitors	Rating	Pg.
Acura TLX	9	64
Ford Fusion	4	121
Volvo S60		237

Price Range

	Retail	Markup
S 1.8T	$22,440	4%
R-Line 1.8T	$23,975	4%
SE 1.8T	$25,495	4%
SEL Premium V6	$33,995	4%

Volkswagen Passat

Safety Checklist

Crash Test:
  Frontal . . . . Very Poor
  Side . . . . Very Good
Airbags:
  Torso . . . . . . Std. Fr. Pelvis/Torso from Seat
  Roll Sensing . . . . Yes
  Knee Bolster . . . . None
Crash Avoidance:
  Collision Avoidance . . . . None
  Blind Spot Detection . . . . Optional
  Lane Keeping Assist . . . . None
  Pedestrian Crash Avoidance . . . . None
General:
  Auto. Crash Notification . . . . Op. Assist.-Fee
  Day Running Lamps . . . . Standard
Safety Belt/Restraint:
  Dynamic Head Restraints . . . . None
  Adjustable Belt . . . . Standard Front

^W-arning feature does not meet suggested government specifications.

Volkswagen Passat

Specifications

Drive	FWD
Engine	2.0-liter I4
Transmission	6-sp. Automatic
Tow Rating (lbs.)	–
Head/Leg Room (in.)	Cramped-38.3/42.4
Interior Space (cu. ft.)	Average-102
Cargo Space (cu. ft.)	Cramped-15.9
Wheelbase/Length (in.)	110.4/193.6

Ratings—10 Best, 1 Worst

Combo Crash Tests	—
Safety Features	3
Rollover	3
Preventive Maintenance	3
Repair Costs	4
Warranty	10
Fuel Economy	4
Complaints	4
Insurance Costs	10
OVERALL RATING	—

Volkswagen Tiguan

Volkswagen Tiguan

At-a-Glance

Status/Year Series Started........ Unchanged/2018
Twins . . . . -
Body Styles . . . . SUV
Seating 7
Anti-Theft Device . . . . . . Std. Pass. Immobil. & Alarm
Parking Index Rating . . . . Average
Where Made. .Puebla, Mexico
Fuel Factor
  MPG Rating (city/hwy) Poor-22/27
  Driving Range (mi.) . . . . Very Short-367
  Fuel Type. . . . . .Regular
  Annual Fuel Cost . . . . .Average-$1531
  Gas Guzzler Tax . . . . .No
  Greenhouse Gas Emissions (tons/yr.). . Average-6.1
  Barrels of Oil Used per year High-13.7

How the Competition Rates

Competitors	Rating	Pg.
Ford Escape	5	116
Lexus NX	5	171
Toyota RAV4		227

Price Range

	Retail	Markup
S FWD	$25,195	4%
SE FWD	$28,930	4%
SEL 4Motion	$33,850	4%
SEL Premium 4Motion	$37,550	4%

Safety Checklist

Crash Test:
  Frontal. . . . . –
  Side. . . . . –
Airbags:
  Torso. . . . . . Std. Fr. Pelvis/Torso from Seat
  Roll Sensing . . . . .Yes
  Knee Bolster . . . . .None
Crash Avoidance:
  Collision Avoidance. . . Optional CIB & DBS*
  Blind Spot Detection . . . . .None
  Lane Keeping Assist . . . . .Optional*
  Pedestrian Crash Avoidance . . . . .None
General:
  Auto. Crash Notification . . . .Op. Assist.-Fee
  Day Running Lamps . . . . .Standard
Safety Belt/Restraint:
  Dynamic Head Restraints . . . . .None
  Adjustable Belt . . . . Standard Front

^Warning feature does not meet suggested government specifications.

Volkswagen Tiguan

Specifications

Drive. . . . . FWD
Engine 2.0-liter I4
Transmission . . . . .8-sp. Automatic
Tow Rating (lbs.) . . . . Very Low-1500
Head/Leg Room (in.) Cramped-39.6/40.2
Interior Space (cu. ft.). Roomy-123.9
Cargo Space (cu. ft.) . . . . Very Cramped-12
Wheelbase/Length (in.) 109.8/185.1

Ratings—10 Best, 1 Worst

Combo Crash Tests	—
Safety Features	6
Rollover	8
Preventive Maintenance	5
Repair Costs	6
Warranty	8
Fuel Economy	7
Complaints	10
Insurance Costs	5
OVERALL RATING	**—**

Volvo S60

At-a-Glance

Status/Year Series Started	Unchanged/2019
Twins	-
Body Styles	Sedan
Seating	5
Anti-Theft Device	Std. Pass. Immobil. & Active Alarm
Parking Index Rating	Average
Where Made	Torslanda, Sweden
Fuel Factor	
MPG Rating (city/hwy)	Good-24/36
Driving Range (mi.)	Average-406
Fuel Type	Premium
Annual Fuel Cost	Average-$1628
Gas Guzzler Tax	No
Greenhouse Gas Emissions (tons/yr.)	Low-5.2
Barrels of Oil Used per year	Average-11.8

How the Competition Rates

Competitors	Rating	Pg.
Acura TLX	9	64
Audi A6		68
Subaru Legacy	7	219

Price Range

	Retail	Markup
T5 Momentum FWD	$35,800	6%
T5 Inscription FWD	$42,900	6%
T6 Inscription AWD	$47,400	6%
T8 Inscription Plug-in Hyb	$55,400	6%

Volvo S60

Safety Checklist

Crash Test:
  Frontal . . . .–
  Side . . . .–
Airbags:
  Torso . . . . . . Std. Fr. Pelvis/Torso from Seat
  Roll Sensing .Yes
  Knee Bolster .None
Crash Avoidance:
  Collision Avoidance. . . Std. CIB & Opt. DBS
  Blind Spot Detection . . . . Optional
  Lane Keeping Assist . . . . Optional
  Pedestrian Crash Avoidance . . . . .Standard
General:
  Auto. Crash Notification . . . .Op. Assist.-Fee
  Day Running Lamps . . . . .Standard
Safety Belt/Restraint:
  Dynamic Head Restraints . . . . .None
  Adjustable Belt . . . . .Standard Front

^Warning feature does not meet suggested government specifications.

Volvo S60

Specifications

Drive	FWD
Engine	2.0-liter I4
Transmission	8-sp. Automatic
Tow Rating (lbs.)	–
Head/Leg Room (in.)	Cramped-37.4/42.3
Interior Space (cu. ft.)	Cramped-96
Cargo Space (cu. ft.)	Very Cramped-12
Wheelbase/Length (in.)	113.1/187.4

Ratings—10 Best, 1 Worst

Combo Crash Tests	—
Safety Features	6
Rollover	6
Preventive Maintenance	2
Repair Costs	6
Warranty	8
Fuel Economy	7
Complaints	10
Insurance Costs	10
OVERALL RATING	**—**

Volvo V60

Volvo V60

At-a-Glance

Status/Year Series Started. Unchanged/2019
Twins . . . . -
Body Styles . . . . Wagon
Seating 5
Anti-Theft Device . Std. Pass. Immobil. & Active Alarm
Parking Index Rating . . . . Average
Where Made. . . . . Torslanda, Sweden
Fuel Factor
  MPG Rating (city/hwy) Good-24/36
  Driving Range (mi.) Average-406
  Fuel Type. . . . . .Premium
  Annual Fuel Cost . . . . .Average-$1628
  Gas Guzzler Tax . . . . .No
  Greenhouse Gas Emissions (tons/yr.). Low-5.2
  Barrels of Oil Used per year Average-11.8

How the Competition Rates

Competitors	Rating	Pg.
Lincoln MKZ	4	176
Toyota Camry	8	221
Volkswagen Jetta		234

Price Range

Price Range	Retail	Markup
T5 Momentum FWD	$38,900	6%
T5 R-Design FWD	$43,900	6%
T6 R-Design AWD	$48,400	6%
T6 Inscription AWD	$49,400	6%

Safety Checklist

Crash Test:
  Frontal . . . . –
  Side . . . . –
Airbags:
  Torso . . . . . . Std. Fr. Pelvis/Torso from Seat
  Roll Sensing . . . . Yes
  Knee Bolster .None
Crash Avoidance:
  Collision Avoidance. . . Std. CIB & Opt. DBS
  Blind Spot Detection . . . . Optional
  Lane Keeping Assist . . . . Optional
  Pedestrian Crash Avoidance . . . . .Standard
General:
  Auto. Crash Notification . . . .Op. Assist.-Fee
  Day Running Lamps . . . . .Standard
Safety Belt/Restraint:
  Dynamic Head Restraints . . . . .None
  Adjustable Belt . . . . Standard Front

^Warning feature does not meet suggested government specifications.

Volvo V60

Specifications

Drive. . . . . FWD
Engine 2.0-liter I4
Transmission . . . . .8-sp. Automatic
Tow Rating (lbs.) Low-3500
Head/Leg Room (in.) Cramped-38.6/42.3
Interior Space (cu. ft.). Cramped-94
Cargo Space (cu. ft.) Roomy-29.0
Wheelbase/Length (in.) 113.1/182.5

Ratings—10 Best, 1 Worst

Combo Crash Tests	—
Safety Features	10
Rollover	4
Preventive Maintenance	5
Repair Costs	6
Warranty	8
Fuel Economy	5
Complaints	9
Insurance Costs	10
OVERALL RATING	**—**

Volvo XC60

Volvo XC60

At-a-Glance

Status/Year Series Started........ Unchanged/2017
Twins . . . . -
Body Styles . . . . SUV
Seating 5
Anti-Theft Device . Std. Pass. Immobil. & Active Alarm
Parking Index Rating . . . . Average
Where Made. Ghent, Belgium
Fuel Factor
  MPG Rating (city/hwy). Average-22/28
  Driving Range (mi.) . . . . Very Long-458
  Fuel Type. . . . . .Premium
  Annual Fuel Cost . . . . .High-$1830
  Gas Guzzler Tax . . . . .No
  Greenhouse Gas Emissions (tons/yr.). . Average-6.1
  Barrels of Oil Used per year High-13.7

How the Competition Rates

Competitors	Rating	Pg.
Audi Q7	3	71
BMW X5		79
Lexus RX	4	173

Price Range

	Retail	Markup
T5 Dynamic FWD	$40,950	6%
T5 Inscription AWD	$42,950	6%
T6 Dynamic AWD	$46,950	8%
T6 R-Design AWD	$51,000	6%

Safety Checklist

Crash Test:
  Frontal . . . . –
  Side . . . . –
Airbags:
  Torso . . . . . . Std. Fr. Pelvis/Torso from Seat
  Roll Sensing . . . . .Yes
  Knee Bolster . . . . Standard Driver
Crash Avoidance:
  Collision Avoidance. . . Std. CIB & Opt. DBS
  Blind Spot Detection . . . . .Standard
  Lane Keeping Assist . . . . .Standard
  Pedestrian Crash Avoidance . . . . .Standard
General:
  Auto. Crash Notification . . . .Op. Assist.-Fee
  Day Running Lamps . . . . .Standard
Safety Belt/Restraint:
  Dynamic Head Restraints . . . . .None
  Adjustable Belt . . . . Standard Front

^Warning feature does not meet suggested government specifications.

Volvo XC60

Specifications

Drive. . . . . .AWD
Engine 2.0-liter I4
Transmission . . . . .8-sp. Automatic
Tow Rating (lbs.) Low-3500
Head/Leg Room (in.) . . . . . . Very Cramped-38/41.5
Interior Space (cu. ft.). . . . . Very Roomy-132.6
Cargo Space (cu. ft.) Roomy-29.7
Wheelbase/Length (in.) 112.8/184.6

Ratings—10 Best, 1 Worst

Combo Crash Tests	9
Safety Features	10
Rollover	3
Preventive Maintenance	3
Repair Costs	2
Warranty	8
Fuel Economy	5
Complaints	2
Insurance Costs	10
OVERALL RATING	**8**

Volvo XC90

At-a-Glance

Status/Year Series Started. Unchanged/2015
Twins . . . . -
Body Styles . . . . Wagon
Seating 7
Anti-Theft Device . Std. Pass. Immobil. & Active Alarm
Parking Index Rating . . . . Hard
Where Made. . . . . Torslanda, Sweden
Fuel Factor
  MPG Rating (city/hwy). Average-22/28
  Driving Range (mi.) . . . . Very Long-458
  Fuel Type. . . . . .Premium
  Annual Fuel Cost . . . . .High-$1830
  Gas Guzzler Tax . . . . .No
  Greenhouse Gas Emissions (tons/yr.). . Average-6.0
  Barrels of Oil Used per year High-13.7

How the Competition Rates

Competitors	Rating	Pg.
Buick Enclave	4	82
Chevrolet Tahoe	4	104
Infiniti QX80		150

Price Range

	Retail	Markup
T5 Momentum FWD	$45,750	6%
T5 R-Design FWD	$51,150	6%
T6 Inscription AWD	$57,050	6%
T8 Excellence AWD	$104,900	6%

Volvo XC90

Safety Checklist

Crash Test:
  Frontal. . . . . Very Good
  Side. . . . . .Good
Airbags:
  Torso. . . . . . . Std. Fr. Pelvis/Torso from Seat
  Roll Sensing . . . . .Yes
  Knee Bolster . . . . Standard Driver
Crash Avoidance:
  Collision Avoidance. . Standard CIB & DBS*
  Blind Spot Detection . . . . .Standard
  Lane Keeping Assist . . . . Standard*
  Pedestrian Crash Avoidance . . . . .Standard
General:
  Auto. Crash Notification . . . .Op. Assist.-Fee
  Day Running Lamps . . . . .Standard
Safety Belt/Restraint:
  Dynamic Head Restraints . . . . .None
  Adjustable Belt . . . . Standard Front and Rear

^Warning feature does not meet suggested government specifications.

Volvo XC90

Specifications

Drive. . . . . .AWD
Engine 2.0-liter I4
Transmission . . . . .8-sp. Automatic
Tow Rating (lbs.) Low-5000
Head/Leg Room (in.) Cramped-38.9/40.9
Interior Space (cu. ft.). Roomy-119.6
Cargo Space (cu. ft.) Cramped-15.8
Wheelbase/Length (in.) 117.5/194.8

So you're considering an electric vehicle? You're not alone! A recent survey by the Consumer Federation of America found that about one-third of potential car buyers would consider an EV. So it's no surprise that 16 major auto manufacturers have 46 new electric vehicles on the market with choices ranging from subcompacts to the luxury laden Tesla. While they're still more expensive than the corresponding gas powered vehicles, EV prices are on the way down and their benefits may warrant the added expense.

Energy from electricity is something we are all familiar with and, in fact, take for granted. We live in a plug-in world where most electrically powered products are extraordinarily convenient and highly functional. Imagine every night doing the same thing with your car as you do with your cell phone—simply plugging it in for the power it needs the next day. And then getting into a nearly silent, clean running car that glides effortlessly out of your driveway and likely has faster pickup than your gas powered car.

While there are a number of environmental reasons for buying an electric vehicle, the simplicity of operation, quiet ride, high tech feel and responsive performance are also major benefits. When you consider the complexity of a gasoline powered engine (most of us can't even identify the items under the hood!) and associated maintenance costs, the simplicity of electric power is refreshing, understandable, and very reliable. Owners of EVs report very low maintenance costs as there's very little to maintain.

SHOULD I EVEN CONSIDER AN ELECTRIC?

The big question most consumers have about EVs is: will I run out of power at the worst time possible—or anytime! Who hasn't needed a flashlight or tried to make a cell phone call only to find the battery is dead. In addition, many of us find it hard to imagine that the same type of engine that runs our blender, sewing machine or drill could possibly power a car! Finally, will I easily be able to plug this thing in at home? These concerns often dissuade people from looking further into the purchase of an electric vehicle.

The fact is, according to a recent analysis of consumer readiness for electric vehicles, 42% of car buyers meet the typical driving patterns, charging needs, and model preferences of the electric vehicles already on the market. Of households, 56% have access to charging, 95% transport 4 or fewer passengers, 79% don't require hauling, and 69% drive less than 60 miles on weekdays, well within the range of most battery-electric vehicles. Bottom-line, there's an excellent chance that an EV will meet your driving needs.

WHAT ARE MY CHOICES?

EVs come in various sizes, styles and price ranges. In addition, there are various types of EVs. The industry is trying to settle on acronyms to describe the different types, but here's a simple overview:

All Electric:

BEVs (Battery Powered Electric Vehicles) simply have a battery and an electric motor which powers the car. They are the simplest and "purest" form of electric vehicle. Because they depend solely on battery power, the battery systems have to be large which increases the cost of these vehicles. In addition to charging up at home, there are a growing number of publically available charging stations (almost 28,000 to date) in shopping centers, employee parking lots, and along the highway. The range of these vehicles is from 68-315 miles per charge.

Electric with Built-In Charging Systems:

EREVs (Extended Range Electric Vehicles) have a gas powered auxiliary power source, that can recharge the battery if you run low on power before getting home or to a charging station. They tend to have smaller batteries and depend on the auxiliary gas powered recharger in place of a larger battery. The battery range on these vehicles is from 47-81 miles. There are only two vehicles in this category and they are a bit different from each other. The BMW i3 has an auxiliary gas engine that simply recharges the battery; it does not power the vehicle. The Chevy Volt has a gas engine that can both recharge the battery and run the vehicle. At various times both the electric motor and gas motor will power the Volt. With the auxiliary recharging engines, the range is 200 miles for the BMW i3 and 420 miles for the Chevy Volt. When the Volt reaches about 37 mph, the gas engine kicks in regardless of the state of the battery.

Dual Electric and Gasoline Vehicles:

PHEVs (Plug in Hybrid Electric Vehicles) have both an electric and gasoline motor which power the wheels at separate times. They are different from the now common hybrid vehicles, because you can plug them in to recharge. If your daily mileage is low, then these can be used like exclusively electric vehicles. Because the gasoline engine will kick in when the battery depletes, the range of these vehicle is similar to gasoline powered vehicles. The electric range is 11-48 miles per charge and the gasoline engine range is 330-600 miles.

WHAT ABOUT CHARGING?

There are three basic types of charging systems, two of which will work in your home.

Level 1: This is the simplest and least expensive system to set up in your home. All you need is a dedicated circuit (nothing else being used on the circuit) and a common household outlet. Level 1 charging is the slowest method because it uses standard 120 volt household current. Your electric vehicle will come with a Level 1 charging cord that you plug into a regular household outlet. The cord comes with a control box

which monitors charging. Typically, it will take about an hour to get 4.5 miles of range. Complete charging times range from 3 to 57 hours.

Level 2: This requires a dedicated 240 volt circuit, the same one you would need for an electric dryer or other large appliance. First, your home has to have 240 electrical service (all newer homes will) and second, if there is not a readily available line, it will have to be run to where it is needed from the circuit breaker box. Not only will this require an electrician, but if walls or ceilings are disturbed, carpentry, drywall and painting may also be necessary. In addition, once the circuit is available, you will need a special device to plug into the circuit which monitors the electrical charge to the car. Depending on features, these devices can range from $500-$2500. Before these costs scare you off, it is worth investigating the actual cost (you may be lucky enough to have a circuit box in your garage or very close) and determine if your utility company will offer any financial assistance (many do as they want to sell you more electricity). In addition, you need to consider the fact that this installation will save you hundreds of dollars in gasoline costs as well as being much more convenient than going to a gas station to refuel. Typically an hour's charging will provide 24 miles of driving. Complete charging times range from 1.5 to 13 hours.

Level 3 or DC Fast Charge: This feature enables the car to be connected to a public charging station, many of which have very fast charging systems. This is great if you have an EV and your office provides charging

stations or you're on the road and find one on the highway or in a shopping center. You can get up to 40 miles of range with just 10 minutes of charging. Overall charging times can be as low as 20 minutes.

One of the issues the industry is struggling with is a universal plug. There are three types of fast charge plugs, one of which is proprietary to the Tesla. Tesla does offer adaptors that can be used in the various types of outlets. If you are planning to charge your vehicle at work, be sure to check out the DC fast charge plug before you buy. Final Note: Because EVs are so quiet, pedestrians may not hear them coming so the government is considering requiring some type of added noise making capacity. When driving an EV use care when around pedestrians.

FOLLOWING IS *THE CAR BOOK'S* SNAPSHOT GUIDE TO THE 2020 EVs:

This is a very basic guide to many of the key features on today's EVs. It's important to take a good, long test drive in order to make a selection that best meets your needs and to get the details behind the features that are really important to you.

You'll find the following items in the EV snapshot:

Range: The first number is how far you can go on a single charge on just battery power. The second number shows the range with auxiliary power. In some cases that auxiliary power just recharges the battery, in other cases it powers the wheels just like a gas engine. In addition to the estimated range, we have provided two comparative ratings. The first rating is the total electric range which includes the range added with an auxiliary recharging engine. The second includes the range with the auxiliary engine that directly powers the wheels. This range is compared to the range of standard gasoline engines. The ratings for electric and electric + auxiliary vehicles range compares just these vehicles. Beware, driving with a "lead foot" and using heat and air conditioning will reduce your range.

Charging Time: This is the total time for a complete charge using Level 1 and Level 2 systems. We did not include the DC fast charging time because there is significant variation in the power of public stations.

MPGe: This is the equivalent of the traditional gasoline miles per gallon converted to electricity (thus the small 'e' at the end). While it is not actually miles per gallon, it gives you a way to compare the efficiency of EVs with gas powered vehicles. We've presented the 'combined' mileage rating which combines highway and city driving. The rating following the estimate compares the mileage with all other electric vehicles running on just battery power.

Introduction: This is the year the vehicle was first introduced. The longer the production time, the more likely the manufacturer is to have worked out any bugs. On the other hand, more recent introductions will contain more sophisticated technology and safety features.

Price: This is the manufacturer's suggested retail price which gives you a general idea of EV pricing. It's important to check for federal and local rebate programs and to comparison shop. Car pricing is notoriously variable and that's no different for EVs. To get the best price consider using the services of the non-profit CarBargains program (page 50).

Size Class/Seating: This provides a general idea of the size of the car. Most consumers compare vehicles within the same size class.

On Board Charger: The greater the kW (kilowatt) rating, the faster the charger. In addition we indicate which vehicles have DC Fast Charging (Level 3) built-in which enables you to take advantage of speedy (and sometimes free) public charging facilities.

Auxiliary Power/MPG: This indicates whether or not (and what kind) of auxiliary power the vehicle may have. There are two types—engines that recharge the battery and engines that drive the wheels. For electric vehicles with auxiliary engines that power the car, we've included the EPA combined MPG estimate. The rating following the estimate compares the mileage with all other gasoline powered vehicles in *The Car Book*. See the descriptions on pages 241-242.

Crash Test Rating: Not all EVs have been crash tested. This tells you which one's were crash tested and how they performed using *The Car Book's* rating system based on government's tests. (See page 16.)

Safety Features: Safety has become critically important to today's car buyer, so we've identified 3 key safety features and indicated if the EV has those features. AEB stands for *Automatic Emergency Braking* – this system automatically applies the brakes if a collision is imminent. We do not indicate, here, if the vehicle has other forms of automatic braking technologies such as brake assist or forward crash warning. *Blind Spot Detection* is a blind spot monitor that uses radar or other technologies to detect objects in the driver's blind spot. *Lane Assist* moves you back into your lane if you're drifting. We do not indicate if the car simply provides a warning.

Warranty: Warranties vary so here's how the car's overall warranty stacks up in comparison with all other warranties.

Battery Warranty: Electric vehicle batteries are relatively new products and critical to the car's operation. As such, you want to be sure that your *battery* comes with a good, long warranty.

Interior Space/Cargo Space: This is another indication of the car's size. The ratings are relative compared to all of the vehicles in the *The Car Book*.

Parking Index: This rating takes into consideration the vehicle's key dimensions and determines an estimate for 'ease of parking' compared to other models. This is a general guide and no substitute for a good long test drive.

Sales: This indicates January 2020 year to date total sales for the 2020 version of the vehicle indicating the general popularity of the EV.

For more complete information on many of these vehicles, please see the corresponding vehicle on the car ratings pages.

Audi A3 Plug-in Hybrid

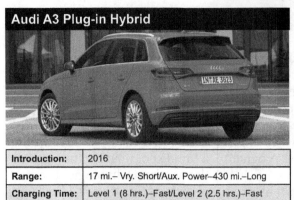

Introduction:	2016
Range:	17 mi.– Vry. Short/Aux. Power–430 mi.–Long
Charging Time:	Level 1 (8 hrs.)–Fast/Level 2 (2.5 hrs.)–Fast
MPGe:	Electric–86–Low

On Board Charger:	3.3 kW
Auxiliary Power/MPG:	Yes (PHEV)/MPG–39–Very High
Crash Test Rating:	—
Safety Features	AEB–Yes*; Blind Spot Detect-Yes*; Lane Asst–Yes*
Warranty:	4 years/50,000 mi.
Battery Warranty:	8 years/100,000 mi.
Size Class/ Seating:	Compact/5
Interior/Cargo Space:	89 cf–Vry. Cramped/13.6 cf–Cramped
Parking Index:	Easy
Sales:	2,597
Price	$37,900 (MSRP)
Notes:	*Indicates optional feature

BMW 330e

Introduction:	2016
Range:	14 mi.–Vry. Short/Aux. Power - 350 - Vry. Short
Charging Time:	Level 1 (10 hrs.) - Avg/Level 2 (2.2 hrs.) - Vry. Fast
MPGe:	71 - Very Low

On Board Charger:	3.5 kW
Auxiliary Power/MPG:	Yes (PHEV)/MPG–30–High
Crash Test Rating:	-
Safety Features	AEB-Yes*; Blind Spot Detect-Yes*; Lane Asst-No
Warranty:	4 years/50,000 mi.
Battery Warranty:	8 years/100,000 mi.
Size Class/ Seating:	Compact/5
Interior/Cargo Space:	96 cf-Cramped/13 cf-Cramped
Parking Index:	Average
Sales:	2,615
Price	$44,100
Notes:	*Indicates optional feature

BMW 530e

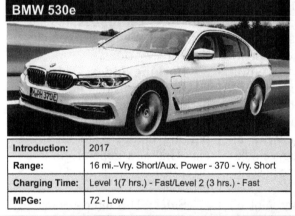

Introduction:	2017
Range:	16 mi.–Vry. Short/Aux. Power - 370 - Vry. Short
Charging Time:	Level 1(7 hrs.) - Fast/Level 2 (3 hrs.) - Fast
MPGe:	72 - Low

On Board Charger:	3.5 kW
Auxiliary Power/MPG:	Yes (PHEV)/MPG–29–High
Crash Test Rating:	-
Safety Features	AEB-Yes; Blind Spot Detect-Yes*; Lane Asst-Yes
Warranty:	4 years/50,000 mi.
Battery Warranty:	8 years/100,000 mi.
Size Class/ Seating:	Mid-Size/5
Interior/Cargo Space:	99 cf-Average/10 cf-Very Cramped
Parking Index:	Average
Sales:	9,889
Price	$51,200
Notes:	*Indicates optional feature

BMW 740e

Introduction:	2017
Range:	14 mi.–Vry. Short/Aux. Power - 340 - Vry. Short
Charging Time:	Level 1(12 hrs.) - Avg/Level 2 (3 hrs.) -Fast
MPGe:	64 - Very Low

On Board Charger:	3.7kW
Auxiliary Power/MPG:	Yes (PHEV)/MPG–27–High
Crash Test Rating:	-
Safety Features	AEB-Yes*; Blind Spot Detect-Yes*; Lane Asst-Yes*
Warranty:	4 years/50,000 mi.
Battery Warranty:	8 years/100,000 mi.
Size Class/ Seating:	Large/5
Interior/Cargo Space:	114 cf-Roomy/14.8 cf-Cramped
Parking Index:	Very Hard
Sales:	350
Price	$89,100
Notes:	*Indicates optional feature

BMW i3

Introduction:	2014
Range:	153 mi.–Very Long/Aux. Power–200 mi.–Vry. Short
Charging Time:	Level 1 (10 hrs.)–Average/Level 2 (3 hrs.)–Fast
MPGe:	Electric-124–Very High

On Board Charger:	7.4 kW; DC fast charge optional
Auxiliary Power/MPG:	Optional (EREV)/MPG–39–Very High
Crash Test Rating:	—
Safety Features	AEB–Yes*; Blind Spot Detect-No; Lane Asst–No
Warranty:	4 years/50,000 mi.
Battery Warranty:	8 years/100,000 mi.
Size Class/ Seating:	Subcompact/4
Interior/Cargo Space:	83.1 cf–Vry. Cramped/2.8 cf–Vry. Cramped
Parking Index:	Very Easy
Sales:	7,608
Price:	$44,450 (MSRP)/$48,300 w/battery ext.
Notes:	*Indicates optional feature

BMW i8

Introduction:	2014
Range:	15 mi.–Vry. Short/Aux. Power–330 mi.–Vry. Short
Charging Time:	Level 1 (3.5 hrs.)–Vry. Fast/Level 2 (1.5 hrs.)–Vry. Fast
MPGe:	Electric-76–Low

On Board Charger:	5 kW; DC fast charge standard
Auxiliary Power/MPG:	Yes (PHEV) /MPG–28–High
Crash Test Rating:	—
Safety Features	AEB–Yes*; Blind Spot Detect-No; Lane Asst–No
Warranty:	4 years/50,000 mi.
Battery Warranty:	8 years/100,000 mi.
Size Class/ Seating:	Compact/4
Interior/Cargo Space:	80.9 cf.–Vry. Cramped/4.7 cf–Vry. Cramped
Parking Index:	Hard
Sales:	942
Price:	$136,500 (MSRP)
Notes:	*Indicates optional feature

BMW x5 xDrive Plug-in Hybrid

Introduction:	2016
Range:	14 mi.–Vry. Short/Aux. Power–540 mi.–Vry. Long
Charging Time:	Level 1 (3.7 hrs.)–Vry. Fast/Level 2 (2.7 hrs.)–Fast
MPGe:	Electric-56–Very Low

On Board Charger:	3.5 kW
Auxiliary Power/MPG:	Yes (PHEV)/MPG–24–Average
Crash Test Rating:	—
Safety Features	AEB–Yes*; Blind Spot Detect-No; Lane Asst–No
Warranty:	4 years/50,000 mi.
Battery Warranty:	8 years/100,000 mi.
Size Class/ Seating:	Medium SUV/5
Interior/Cargo Space:	cf– /34.2 cf–Very Roomy
Parking Index:	Very Hard
Sales:	4,438
Price:	$63,045 (MSRP)
Notes:	*Indicates optional feature

Cadillac CT6 Plug-in

Introduction:	2017
Range:	31 mi- Avg./Aux. Power - 440 - Long
Charging Time:	Level 1 (12.5 hrs.) - Avg./Level 2 (4.5 hrs.) - Avg.
MPGe:	62 - Very Low

On Board Charger:	3.6kW
Auxiliary Power/MPG:	Yes (PHEV)/MPG–26-Average
Crash Test Rating:	-
Safety Features	AEB–Yes*; Blind Spot Detect-Yes*; Lane Asst-Yes*
Warranty:	4 years/50,000 mi.
Battery Warranty:	8 years/100,000 mi.
Size Class/ Seating:	Mid-Size/5
Interior/Cargo Space:	106 cf-Roomy/10.6 cf-Vry. Cramped
Parking Index:	Hard
Sales:	232
Price:	$75,095
Notes:	*Indicates optional feature

Chevrolet Bolt

Introduction:	2017
Range:	238 mi.–Vry. Long
Charging Time:	Lvl. 1 (51 hrs.) - Vry. Slow/Lvl. 2 (9 hrs.) - Vry. Slow
MPGe:	119-Very High

On Board Charger:	7.2 kW; DC fast charge optional
Auxiliary Power/MPG:	No
Crash Test Rating:	–
Safety Features	AEB-Yes*; Blind Spot Detect-Yes*; Lane Asst-Yes*
Warranty:	3 years/36,000 mi.
Battery Warranty:	8 years/100,000 mi.
Size Class/ Seating:	Subompact/5
Interior/Cargo Space:	95 cf.–Cramped/16.9 cf–Average
Parking Index:	Very Easy
Sales:	21,909
Price	$37,495
Notes:	*Indicates optional feature

Chrysler Pacifica

Introduction:	2017
Range:	33 mi.–Short/Aux. Power - 570 - Vry. Long
Charging Time:	Level 1(12 hrs.) - Average/Level 2 (2 hrs.) - Vry. Fast
MPGe:	84-Low

On Board Charger:	6.6kW
Auxiliary Power/MPG:	Yes (PHEV)/MPG-32-High
Crash Test Rating:	5 stars
Safety Features	AEB-Yes*; Blind Spot Detect-Yes*; Lane Asst-Yes*
Warranty:	3 years/36,000 mi.
Battery Warranty:	10 years/100,000 mi.
Size Class/ Seating:	Minivan/7
Interior/Cargo Space:	165 cf-Vry. Roomy/32.3 cf-Vry. Roomy
Parking Index:	Very Hard
Sales:	9,054
Price	$41,995
Notes:	*Indicates optional feature

Fiat 500e

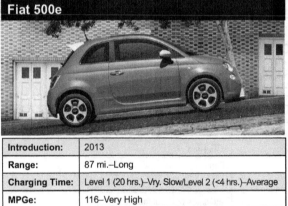

Introduction:	2013
Range:	87 mi.–Long
Charging Time:	Level 1 (20 hrs.)–Vry. Slow/Level 2 (<4 hrs.)–Average
MPGe:	116–Very High

On Board Charger:	6.6 kW
Auxiliary Power/MPG:	None
Crash Test Rating:	–
Safety Features	AEB–No; Blind Spot Detect-No; Lane Asst–No
Warranty:	4 years/50,000 mi.
Battery Warranty:	8 years/100,000 mi.
Size Class/ Seating:	Subcompact/2
Interior/Cargo Space:	71.6 cf–Vry. Cramped/7 cf–Vry. Cramped
Parking Index:	Very Easy
Sales:	2,443
Price	$31,800 (MSRP)
Notes:	*Indicates optional feature

Ford Fusion Energi

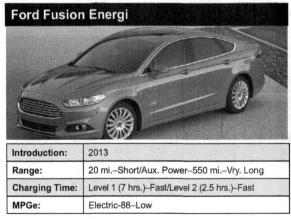

Introduction:	2013
Range:	20 mi.–Short/Aux. Power–550 mi.–Vry. Long
Charging Time:	Level 1 (7 hrs.)–Fast/Level 2 (2.5 hrs.)–Fast
MPGe:	Electric-88–Low

On Board Charger:	3.3 kW
Auxiliary Power/MPG:	Yes (PHEV)/MPG-38–Very High
Crash Test Rating:	5 stars
Safety Features	AEB–Yes*; Blind Spot Detect-Yes*; Lane Asst–No
Warranty:	3 years/36,000 mi.
Battery Warranty:	8 years/100,000 mi.
Size Class/ Seating:	Midsize/5
Interior/Cargo Space:	102.8 cf–Roomy/8.2 cf–Vry. Cramped
Parking Index:	Average
Sales:	9,952
Price	$33,900 (MSRP)
Notes:	*Indicates optional feature

Honda Clarity PHEV

Introduction:	2018
Range:	48 mi.–Average/Aux. Power–340 mi.–Vry. Short
Charging Time:	Level 1 (12 hrs.) - Average/Level 2 (2.2 hrs.) - Vry. Fast
MPGe:	Electric-110-High

On Board Charger:	6.6 kW; DC fast charge optional
Auxiliary Power/MPG:	Yes (PHEV)/MPG-42–Very High
Crash Test Rating:	—
Safety Features	AEB-Yes; Blind Spot Detect-Yes; Lane Asst-Yes
Warranty:	3 years/36,000 mi.
Battery Warranty:	10 years/100,000 mi.
Size Class/ Seating:	Midsize/5
Interior/Cargo Space:	102 cf-Average/16 cf-Cramped
Parking Index:	Easy
Sales:	2,145
Price	$33,400
Notes:	

Hyundai IONIQ Electric

Introduction:	2017
Range:	124 mi- Very Long
Charging Time:	Level 1 (9 hrs.) - Fast/Level 2 (4 hrs.) - Average
MPGe:	136 - Very High

On Board Charger:	6.6kW
Auxiliary Power/MPG:	No
Crash Test Rating:	—
Safety Features	AEB-Yes*; Blind Spot Detect-Yes*; Lane Asst-Yes*
Warranty:	5 years/60,000 mi.
Battery Warranty:	10 years/100,000 mi.
Size Class/ Seating:	Compact/5
Interior/Cargo Space:	96.2 cf-Cramped/23.8 cf-Roomy
Parking Index:	Very Easy
Sales:	2,252
Price	$29,500
Notes:	*Lifetime battery warranty for original owner

Hyundai Sonata Plug-in Hybrid

Introduction:	2016
Range:	27 mi.–Short/Aux. Power–600 mi.–Vry. Long
Charging Time:	Level 1 (8.7 hrs.)–Fast/Level 2 (2.7 hrs.)–Fast
MPGe:	Electric-99–Average

On Board Charger:	3.3 kW
Auxiliary Power/MPG:	Yes (PHEV)/MPG-40–Very High
Crash Test Rating:	—
Safety Features	AEB–No; Blind Spot Detect-Yes*; Lane Asst–No
Warranty:	5 years/60,000 mi.
Battery Warranty:	10 years/100,000 mi.
Size Class/ Seating:	Midsize/5
Interior/Cargo Space:	106.1 cf–Roomy/9.9 cf–Vry. Cramped
Parking Index:	Easy
Sales:	605
Price	$34,600 (MSRP)
Notes:	*Lifetime battery warranty for original owner

Jaguar I-Pace

Introduction:	2019
Range:	234 mi, –Very Long
Charging Time:	Level 1 (60 hrs.)–Vry. Slow/Level 2 (13 hrs.)–Vry. Slow
MPGe:	Electric-76–Very Low

On Board Charger:	7 kW
Auxiliary Power/MPG:	No
Crash Test Rating:	—
Safety Features	AEB–Yes; Blind Spot Detect-Yes; Lane Asst–Yes
Warranty:	5 years/60,000 mi.
Battery Warranty:	10 years/100,000 mi.
Size Class/ Seating:	Compact/5
Interior/Cargo Space:	—
Parking Index:	Average
Sales:	752
Price	$80,500
Notes:	

Kia Niro PHEV

Introduction:	2018
Range:	26 mi.–Short/Aux. Power–560 mi.–Vry. Long
Charging Time:	Level 1 (6 hrs.)–Fast/Level 2 (2.5 hrs.)–Fast
MPGe:	Electric–105–High

On Board Charger:	3.3 kW
Auxiliary Power/MPG:	Yes (PHEV)/MPG–46–Very High
Crash Test Rating:	27 mi.–Short/Aux. Power–600 mi.–Vry. Long
Safety Features	AEB–Yes*; Blind Spot Detect–Yes*; Lane Asst–Yes*
Warranty:	5 years/60,000 mi.
Battery Warranty:	7 years/150,000 mi.
Size Class/ Seating:	Subcompact/5
Interior/Cargo Space:	101 cf–Average/19 cf–Average
Parking Index:	Very Easy
Sales:	4,431
Price:	$28,840
Notes:	

Kia Optima PHEV

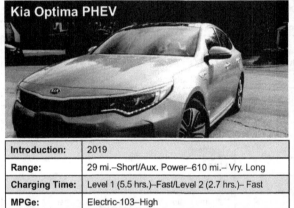

Introduction:	2019
Range:	29 mi.–Short/Aux. Power–610 mi.– Vry. Long
Charging Time:	Level 1 (5.5 hrs.)–Fast/Level 2 (2.7 hrs.)– Fast
MPGe:	Electric–103–High

On Board Charger:	3.3 kW
Auxiliary Power/MPG:	Yes (PHEV)/MPG 40–Very High
Crash Test Rating:	—
Safety Features	AEB–Yes; Blind Spot Detect–Yes; Lane Asst–Yes
Warranty:	5 years/60,000 mi.
Battery Warranty:	7 years/150,000 mi.
Size Class/ Seating:	Midsize/5
Interior/Cargo Space:	104.8 cf–Roomy/15.9 cf–Cramped
Parking Index:	Easy
Sales:	1,075
Price:	$35,390
Notes:	

Kia Soul EV

Introduction:	2015
Range:	93 mi.–Long
Charging Time:	Level 1 (24 hrs.)–Vry. Slow/Level 2 (4.5 hrs.)–Average
MPGe:	105–High

On Board Charger:	6.6 kW; DC fast charge optional
Auxiliary Power/MPG:	None
Crash Test Rating:	—
Safety Features	AEB–No; Blind Spot Detect-Yes*; Lane Asst–Yes
Warranty:	5 years/60,000 mi.
Battery Warranty:	7 years/150,000 mi.
Size Class/ Seating:	Compact/5
Interior/Cargo Space:	97.1 cf–Average/18.8 cf–Average
Parking Index:	Very Easy
Sales:	1,143
Price:	$33,950 (MSRP)
Notes:	Only available in CA, GA, HI, MD, NJ, NY, OR, TX, and WA.

Mercedes-Benz S550e Plug-in Hybrid

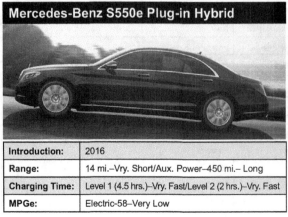

Introduction:	2016
Range:	14 mi.–Vry. Short/Aux. Power–450 mi.– Long
Charging Time:	Level 1 (4.5 hrs.)–Vry. Fast/Level 2 (2 hrs.)–Vry. Fast
MPGe:	Electric–58–Very Low

On Board Charger:	3.3 kW
Auxiliary Power/MPG:	Yes (PHEV)/MPG-26–Average
Crash Test Rating:	—
Safety Features	AEB–Yes; Blind Spot Detect–Yes*; Lane Asst–Yes*
Warranty:	4 years/50,000 mi.
Battery Warranty:	8 years/100,000 mi.
Size Class/ Seating:	Large/5
Interior/Cargo Space:	112 cf–Roomy/13.9 cf–Cramped
Parking Index:	Very Hard
Sales:	191
Price:	$95,650 (MSRP)
Notes:	*Indicates optional feature

Mini Countryman SE PHEV

Introduction:	2018
Range:	12 mi.–Vry. Short/Aux. Power–270 mi.– Vry. Short
Charging Time:	Level 1 (6 hrs.)–Fast/Level 2 (3 hrs.)–Fast
MPGe:	Electric-51–Very Low

On Board Charger:	3.7 kW
Auxiliary Power/MPG:	Yes (PHEV)/MPG–27–Average
Crash Test Rating:	—
Safety Features	AEB–Yes*; Blind Spot Detect–No; Lane Asst–No
Warranty:	4 years/50,000 mi.
Battery Warranty:	8 years/100,000 mi.
Size Class/ Seating:	Compact/5
Interior/Cargo Space:	97 cf–Average/17.4 cf–Average
Parking Index:	Very Easy
Sales:	1,644
Price	$37,000
Notes:	

Mitsubishi Outlander PHEV

Introduction:	2018
Range:	22 mi.– Short/Aux. Power–310 mi.–Vry. Short
Charging Time:	Level 1 (8 hrs.)-Fast/Level 2 (3.5 hrs.)-Average
MPGe:	Electric-74–Low

On Board Charger:	3.7 kW; DC fast charge optional
Auxiliary Power/MPG:	Yes (PHEV)/MPG 25–Low
Crash Test Rating:	–
Safety Features	SEB–Yes*; Blind Spot Detect-Yes*; Lane Asst–No
Warranty:	5 years/60,000 mi.
Battery Warranty:	8 years/100,000 mi.
Size Class/ Seating:	Midsize SUV/7
Interior/Cargo Space:	112 cf–Roomy/13.9 cf–Cramped
Parking Index:	Easy
Sales:	5,062
Price	$35,795
Notes:	*Indicates optional feature

Nissan Leaf

Introduction:	2018
Range:	150 mi.–Vry. Long
Charging Time:	Level 1 (22 hrs.)-Slow/Level 2 (7.5 hrs.)-Slow
MPGe:	114–Very High

On Board Charger:	6.6 kW; DC fast charge optional
Auxiliary Power/MPG:	None
Crash Test Rating:	–
Safety Features	AEB–Yes; Blind Spot Detect-Yes; Lane Asst–Yes
Warranty:	3 years/36,000 mi.
Battery Warranty:	8 years/100,000 mi.
Size Class/ Seating:	Compact/5
Interior/Cargo Space:	128.2 cf–Vry. Roomy/10.3 cf–Vry. Cramped
Parking Index:	Very Easy
Sales:	17,969
Price	$29,990 (MSRP)
Notes:	

Porsche Cayenne S E-Hybrid

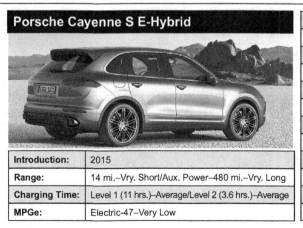

Introduction:	2015
Range:	14 mi.–Vry. Short/Aux. Power–480 mi.–Vry. Long
Charging Time:	Level 1 (11 hrs.)–Average/Level 2 (3.6 hrs.)–Average
MPGe:	Electric-47–Very Low

On Board Charger:	3.6 kW
Auxiliary Power/MPG:	Yes (PHEV)/MPG 22–Low
Crash Test Rating:	–
Safety Features	AEB–Yes; Blind Spot Detect-Yes; Lane Asst–Yes
Warranty:	4 years/50,000 mi.
Battery Warranty:	7 years/70,000 mi.
Size Class/ Seating:	Midsize SUV/5
Interior/Cargo Space:	—/20.5 cf–Average
Parking Index:	Hard
Sales:	1,337
Price	$77,200 (MSRP)
Notes:	

Porsche Panamera S E-Hybrid

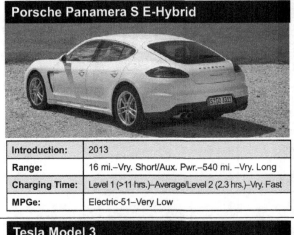

Introduction:	2013
Range:	16 mi.–Vry. Short/Aux. Pwr.–540 mi. –Vry. Long
Charging Time:	Level 1 (>11 hrs.)–Average/Level 2 (2.3 hrs.)–Vry. Fast
MPGe:	Electric–51–Very Low

On Board Charger:	3.6 kW
Auxiliary Power/MPG:	Yes (PHEV)/MPG-25–Average
Crash Test Rating:	—
Safety Features	AEB–Yes*; Blind Spot Detect-Yes*; Lane Asst–Yes*
Warranty:	4 years/50,000 mi.
Battery Warranty:	7 years/70,000 mi.
Size Class/ Seating:	Large/5
Interior/Cargo Space:	—/11.8 cf–Vry. Cramped
Parking Index:	Very Hard
Sales:	2,566
Price	$96,100 (MSRP)
Notes:	*Indicates optional feature

Tesla Model 3

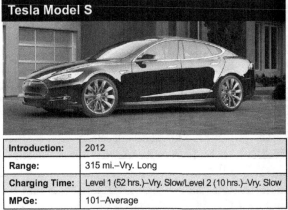

Introduction:	2017
Range:	310 mi.–Vry. Long
Charging Time:	Level 1 (57 hrs.)–Vry. Slow/Level 2 (12 hrs.)–Vry. Slow
MPGe:	126–Very High

On Board Charger:	7.7 kW
Auxiliary Power/MPG:	None
Crash Test Rating:	–
Safety Features	AEB–Yes; Blind Spot Detect-Yes; Lane Asst–Yes
Warranty:	4 years/50,000 mi.
Battery Warranty:	8 years/unlimited mi.
Size Class/ Seating:	Intermediate/5
Interior/Cargo Space:	–/15.0 cf–Cramped
Parking Index:	Average
Sales:	187,057
Price	$35,000 (MSRP)
Notes:	

Tesla Model S

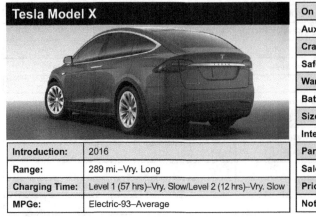

Introduction:	2012
Range:	315 mi.–Vry. Long
Charging Time:	Level 1 (52 hrs.)–Vry. Slow/Level 2 (10 hrs.)–Vry. Slow
MPGe:	101–Average

On Board Charger:	11 kW; DC fast charge optional
Auxiliary Power/MPG:	None
Crash Test Rating:	5 stars
Safety Features	AEB–Yes; Blind Spot Detect-Yes; Lane Asst–Yes
Warranty:	4 years/50,000 mi.
Battery Warranty:	8 years/unlimited mi.
Size Class/ Seating:	Large/5
Interior/Cargo Space:	94 cf–Cramped/31.6 cf–Vry. Roomy
Parking Index:	Hard
Sales:	29,495
Price	$71,070 (MSRP)
Notes:	

Tesla Model X

Introduction:	2016
Range:	289 mi.–Vry. Long
Charging Time:	Level 1 (57 hrs)–Vry. Slow/Level 2 (12 hrs)–Vry. Slow
MPGe:	Electric–93–Average

On Board Charger:	10 kW; DC fast charge optional
Auxiliary Power/MPG:	None
Crash Test Rating:	5 stars
Safety Features	AEB–Yes; Blind Spot Detect-Yes; Lane Asst–Yes
Warranty:	4 years/50,000 mi.
Battery Warranty:	8 years/unlimited
Size Class/ Seating:	Mid-Size/7
Interior/Cargo Space:	120 cf–Roomy/26 cf–Roomy
Parking Index:	Very Hard
Sales:	31,600
Price	$80,000 (MSRP)
Notes:	

Toyota Prius Prime

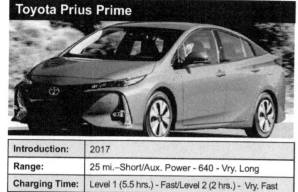

Introduction:	2017
Range:	25 mi.–Short/Aux. Power - 640 - Vry. Long
Charging Time:	Level 1 (5.5 hrs.) - Fast/Level 2 (2 hrs.) - Vry. Fast
MPGe:	133 - Very High

On Board Charger:	3.3kW
Auxiliary Power/MPG:	Yes (PHEV)/MPG-54-Very High
Crash Test Rating:	-
Safety Features	AEB-Yes*; Blind Spot Detect-Yes*; Lane Asst-Yes*
Warranty:	3 years/36,000 mi.
Battery Warranty:	8 years/100,000 mi.
Size Class/ Seating:	Mid-Size/5
Interior/Cargo Space:	91.5 cf-Cramped/19.8 cf-Average
Parking Index:	Very Easy
Sales:	35,520
Price:	$27,100
Notes:	*Indicates optional feature

VW e-Golf

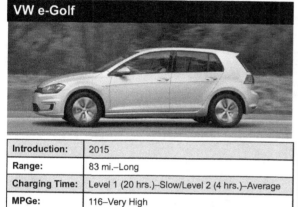

Introduction:	2015
Range:	83 mi.–Long
Charging Time:	Level 1 (20 hrs.)–Slow/Level 2 (4 hrs.)–Average
MPGe:	116–Very High

On Board Charger:	7.2 kW; DC fast charge standard
Auxiliary Power/MPG:	None
Crash Test Rating:	—
Safety Features	AEB–Yes*; Blind Spot Detect-Yes*; Lane Asst–Yes*
Warranty:	4 years/50,000 mi.
Battery Warranty:	8 years/100,000 mi.
Size Class/ Seating:	Compact/5
Interior/Cargo Space:	93.5 cf–Cramped/22.8 cf–Average
Parking Index:	Easy
Sales:	2,621
Price	$28,995 (MSRP)
Notes:	*Indicates optional feature

Volvo XC60 PHEV

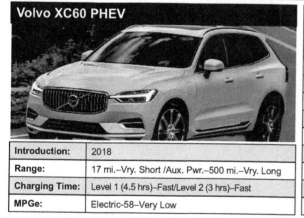

Introduction:	2018
Range:	17 mi.–Vry. Short /Aux. Pwr.–500 mi.–Vry. Long
Charging Time:	Level 1 (4.5 hrs)–Fast/Level 2 (3 hrs)–Fast
MPGe:	Electric-58–Very Low

On Board Charger:	3.5 kW
Auxiliary Power/MPG:	Yes (PHEV)/MPG-26– Average
Crash Test Rating:	–
Safety Features	AEB–Yes; Blind Spot Detect-Yes; Lane Asst–Yes
Warranty:	4 years/50,000 mi.
Battery Warranty:	4 years/50,000 mi.
Size Class/ Seating:	Medsize SUV/5
Interior/Cargo Space:	132.6 cf–Roomy/29.7 cf–Roomy
Parking Index:	Average
Sales:	2,775
Price	$53,700
Notes:	

Volvo XC90 Plug-in Hybrid

Introduction:	2016
Range:	17 mi.–Vry. Short /Aux. Pwr.–490 mi.–Vry. Long
Charging Time:	Level 1 (4 hrs.)–Fast/Level 2 (2.5 hrs.)–Fast
MPGe:	Electric-53–Very Low

On Board Charger:	3.5 kW
Auxiliary Power/MPG:	Yes (PHEV)/MPG-25– Average
Crash Test Rating:	5 stars
Safety Features	AEB–Yes; Blind Spot Detect-Yes; Lane Asst–Yes
Warranty:	4 years/50,000 mi.
Battery Warranty:	4 years/50,000 mi.
Size Class/ Seating:	Large SUV/7
Interior/Cargo Space:	119.6 cf–Roomy/15.8 cf–Cramped
Parking Index:	Hard
Sales:	1,904
Price	$68,100 (MSRP)
Notes:	